MW01628456

WHISTLER'S LEGACY

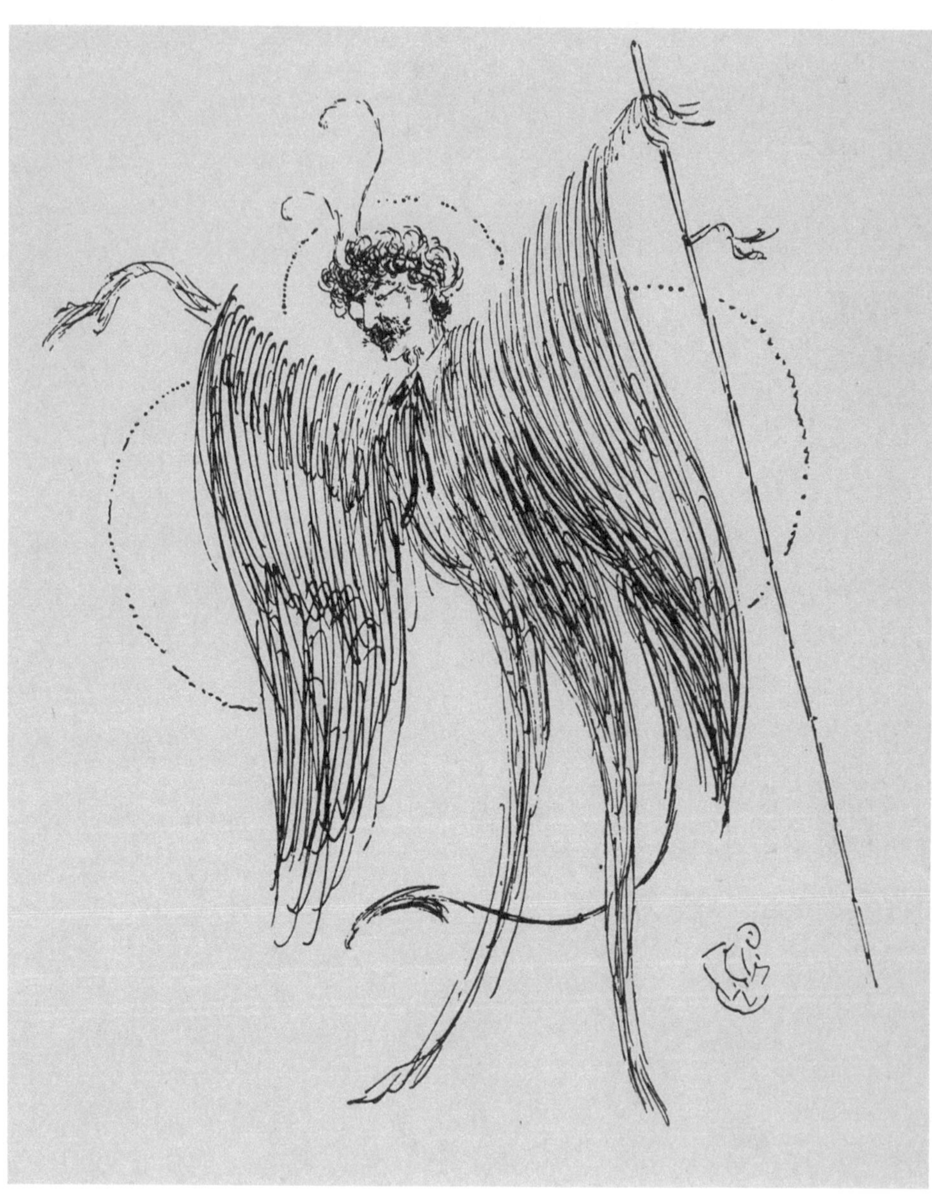

Whistler's *Legacy*

Daniel E. Sutherland

THE PENNSYLVANIA STATE UNIVERSITY PRESS
University Park, Pennsylvania

Frontispiece: *Whistler as a Butterfly* (fig. 19).

Library of Congress Cataloging-in-Publication Data

Names: Sutherland, Daniel E., author.
Title: Whistler's legacy / Daniel E. Sutherland.
Description: University Park, Pennsylvania : The Pennsylvania State University Press, [2026] | Includes bibliographical references and index. | Summary: "Traces the posthumous reputation of James Abbott McNeill Whistler, examining how perceptions of his art and character have shifted since 1903. Challenges popular and scholarly assumptions by reassessing the factors behind his controversial legacy and offering new insights into his critical reception"— Provided by publisher.
Identifiers: LCCN 2025049406 | ISBN 9780271101286 (hardback)
Subjects: LCSH: Whistler, James McNeill, 1834-1903—Criticism and interpretation. | Whistler, James McNeill, 1834-1903—Appreciation.
Classification: LCC ND237.W6 S815 2026
LC record available at https://lccn.loc.gov/2025049406

Printed in the United States of America
Published by The Pennsylvania State University Press,
University Park, PA 16802–1003

The Pennsylvania State University Press is a member of the Association of University Presses.

It is the policy of The Pennsylvania State University Press to use acid-free paper. Publications on uncoated stock satisfy the minimum requirements of American National Standard for Information Sciences—Permanence of Paper for Printed Library Material, ANSI Z39.48–1992.

GPSR Authorized Representative: Logos Europe, 9 rue Nicolas Poussin, 17000 La Rochelle, France, contact@logoseurope.eu.

CONTENTS

ILLUSTRATIONS

ACKNOWLEDGMENTS

This is my third book about James McNeill Whistler, including a biography of his mother coauthored with Georgia Toutziari. It is probably my last. Each book has built on the preceding one, as do my debts of gratitude. I began to study and write about Whistler a quarter century ago, but many of the people who tutored and nurtured me throughout those years continue to influence my thinking about him.

I have two lasting impressions of my beginnings. First, I remember how welcoming the scholars were who had already been studying Whistler, some of them for many years. I was an experienced historian, but my expertise had been outside the realm of art history. These accomplished authorities might well have pooh-poohed me, even totally ignored me. Who was I to infringe on their turf, to think I could simply step into their world? But I experienced none of that. Instead, my new friends told me what to read, pointed me in the most fruitful directions for understanding Whistler, warned of what hurdles to expect and what pitfalls to avoid. This included a crash course in art history, which enhanced my ability to interpret and appreciate Whistler's art in the context of his times.

Second, sliding in the back door, as it were, as a biographer, I experienced another revelation. I quickly learned that in order to understand and truthfully depict Whistler's life, I had to know the biographies of the many, many people around him, whether family, friends, acquaintances, or enemies. What did his interactions with all those people tell me about him? What were their opinions of him, whether expressed privately or publicly? So, for instance, while it was mandatory that I read Whistler's own correspondence and publications, I had equally to read the private and public writings of his circle.

Foremost among my tutors were Margaret F. MacDonald and Nigel Thorp. Margaret was already well on her way to becoming the *grande dame* of Whistler studies; Nigel was directing the not-yet-completed Whistler correspondence project. Together they oversaw the Centre for Whistler Studies at the University of Glasgow. I would have been in a sorry state without their guidance and, dare I say, friendship.

Many other people followed—always encouraging, accepting my deficiencies, and improving my work exponentially. I here thank them (in alphabetical order): David Park Curry, Jane Dini, Lee Glazer, Catherine Carter Goebel, Martin Hopkinson, Norman MacDonald, Justin McCann, Linda Merrill, Patricia de Montfort, Kenneth John Myers, Ayako Ono, Grischka Petri, Julieta Ogaz Sotomayor, Robin Spencer, Martha Tedeschi, Arabella Teniswood-Harvey, and Simon Wartnaby. My sincerest apologies to anyone I may have missed.

Archivists and librarians in scores of institutions have guided and assisted me over the years. They are far too many to credit by name, but those who deserve praise for their help with the present book include the hard-working and efficient staffs at Special Collections, University of Glasgow; Manuscript and Archives Division, New York Public Library; Billy Rose Theatre Division for the Performing Arts, New York Public Library; British Library; BBC Written Archives Centre (especially Tom Hercock); Kensington and Chelsea Register Office; Clapham Library; Kensington Central Library; Wandsworth Town Library; and Chelsea Arts Club Archives (which means Stephen Bartley). Also, thanks to Darcy Sullivan for his consistently valuable tips about Whistler in popular culture, and to Sam Smiles and Greg Brookes for advice and encouragement.

I must also mention several people personally involved in maintaining Whistler's legacy. Sara M. Bogosian, as President and Executive Director of Whistler House Museum of Art, not only maintains the artist's two-hundred-year-old birthplace in Lowell, Massachusetts, but also works tirelessly to promote and exhibit the work of contemporary artists. Similarly, William Colburn, Director of the Freer House in Detroit, and Diana Greenwald, Lunder Curator of American Art at the Freer Gallery, are important agents in maintaining Whistler's story. I am also personally grateful to members of the Whistler Society for more than a decade of friendship and collaboration.

At Penn State University Press, I very much appreciate the guidance and efficiency of Ellie Goodman, Alex Ramos, Jennifer S. Norton, Brian Beer, Regina Starace, and Maddie Caso, and the patience and editorial skills of Catherine Osborne.

Finally, a special word of gratitude for Georgia Toutziari, not only my coauthor in our biography of Anna Whistler but also an unfailing friend since those long-ago days at the Centre for Whistler Studies.

ABBREVIATIONS

INSTITUTIONS AND COLLECTIONS

AAA Archives of American Art, Washington, DC

APC American Play Company Records, Billy Rose Theatre Division, New York Public Library for the Performing Arts

AWD Anna M. Whistler Diary, 1842–48, Manuscripts Department, New York Public Library

BBC Programme Scripts, BBC Written Archives Centre, Reading, UK

BC A. L. Baldry Correspondence, National Art Library, Victoria and Albert Museum, London

BCW Walter S. Brewster Collection of Whistleriana, Art Institute of Chicago

CL Clapham Library, Lambeth, London

FC GLASC-Mss:5078 [Maud Franklin Correspondence], Special Collections, University of Glasgow Library. FC preceded by document letter and number

FP Charles Lang Freer Papers, Freer Gallery of Art, Washington, DC

GUW *Correspondence of James McNeill Whistler, 1855–1903*, ed. Margaret F. MacDonald, Patricia de Montfort, and Nigel Thorp, including the *Correspondence of Anna McNeill Whistler*, 1855–1889, ed. Georgia Toutziari. University of Glasgow, 2003, online edition at http://www.whistler.arts.gla.uk/correspondence. *GUW* followed by record number

HL Autograph File P, 1554–2005, Houghton Library, Harvard University, Cambridge, MA

LP James Laver Papers, Special Collections, University of Glasgow Library

MD Benjamin Moran Diaries, Manuscripts Division, Library of Congress, Washington, DC

NAL National Art Library, Victoria and Albert Museum, London

PP Joseph and Elizabeth R. Pennell Papers, 1832–1951, Harry Ransom Humanities Research Center, University of Texas at Austin

PS Playscripts Collection, PS 1938, British Library, London

PWC Pennell-Whistler Collection, Library of Congress, Washington, DC

RC Joseph Whistler Revillon Collection, Special Collections, University of Glasgow Library

RSP Rowland Stebbens Papers, Manuscripts Division, New York Public Library

SP Denys Sutton Papers, Special Collections, University of Glasgow Library

WC Whistler Collection, Special Collections, University of Glasgow Library. WC preceded by document letter and number

WPA Works Progress Administration Radio Scripts, Billy Rose Theatre Division, New York Public Library for the Performing Arts

YMSM Margaret F. MacDonald and Grischka Petri, *James McNeill Whistler: The Paintings, a Catalogue Raisonné*, University of Glasgow, 2014, online edition at http://whistlerpaintings.gla.ac.uk. YMSM followed by catalogue number

PEOPLE

AW	Anna M. Whistler
CLF	Charles Lang Freer
DS	Denys Sutton
ERP	Elizabeth Robins Pennell
FC	Frederick W. Coburn
JL	James Laver
JP	Joseph Pennell
JR	Joseph W. Revillon
JW	James McNeill Whistler
RBP	Rosalind Birnie Philip
WH	William Heinemann

PUBLICATIONS

AD	*Art Digest*
CAM	*Reh's Galleries Comments on the Art Market*
CT	*Chicago Tribune*
GAME	James McNeill Whistler. *The Gentle Art of Making Enemies.* 2nd ed. London: William Heinemann, 1892.
LW	Elizabeth R. Pennell and Joseph Pennell. *Life of Whistler.* 2 vols. London: William Heinemann, 1908.
NYT	*New York Times*
TLS	*Times Literary Supplement*
WJ	Elizabeth R. Pennell and Joseph Pennell. *The Whistler Journal.* Philadelphia: J. B. Lippincott, 1921.
WS	*Whistler Society Newsletter*
WSJ	*Wall Street Journal*

Introduction

His death took everyone by surprise. There had been reports of ill health, and one rumor had him dying in Holland a year earlier. Yet friends thought him so youthful, even at age sixty-nine, that death seemed impossible. Enemies thought him too contrary to die. As people came to grips with the fact that there would be no more paintings, no new etchings, no more pamphlets, no verbal jousts with critics, no new chapter in the saga of James Abbott McNeill Whistler, they took stock. What had it all meant, all those turbulent decades? One thing was certain. He had been one of those rare artists who compelled people to ponder the very meaning, purpose, and definition of art.

He had always been a maverick, rambunctious as a child and stubbornly independent as a young man. As an artist, he was attracted initially to a sober type of "realism," a clearly subversive style at odds with the establishment's preference for classicism. Then, just as realism seemed to gain an equal footing with classical forms, Whistler decided that the older style suited his needs after all. He wished to be more like Ingres and less like Courbet. When that style, too, failed to satisfy his artistic vision, and having been further influenced by Asian art, he developed his own "Whistlerian" forms, not only in painting but also in etching, pastels, and lithography. He depicted the world as he saw it, not as others observed it. Critics were confused. Some dubbed him an Impressionist. Others placed him in the Symbolist camp. In fact, he had simply created his own brand.

People were still trying to decipher him when he died. "Whether he was quite the master that some think him, or had quite the range and that grasp which they believe to be his, time will perhaps open the eyes of succeeding generations and show," decided the *Manchester Guardian*. "The influence of his work has been very marked on the younger generations of painters in France, England, and the United States," observed the *Boston Transcript*. "Whether it will continue long after his death it is impossible to say."

The same could be said of most artists, but naturally, inevitably, things were more complicated with Whistler. The art had become nearly inseparable from his public image, and many who praised the artist could not embrace the man. It was his own fault. He had consciously created the combative persona that came to define him. He stood against the critics, the art establishment, and anyone else unwilling or unable to accept his artistic theories and purpose. Evidence of his determination came in 1890, with the publication of the book that cemented his image: *The Gentle Art of Making Enemies*. Some people called it his "bible"; Whistler thought of it as his autobiography. For anyone who missed the point, a second edition, published in 1892, included an additional section titled "Auto-biographical."

He pounced on upstarts who dared write anything resembling his biography. They were not to be trusted, any more than the ill-informed art critics who had failed to appreciate his work. He instructed his executor to guard his private correspondence, allowing no one to publish it lest his own words be distorted and misinterpreted. Realistically, though, he knew that the "biografiends," as James Joyce dubbed them, would eventually run him to ground. Even friends, Whistler assumed, would produce their versions of his life and work. He tried to limit the damage by cautiously and selectively revealing parts of his life to Elizabeth and Joseph Pennell, to be used in a catalogue of his work that he agreed they should publish.

He made a halfhearted stab at telling his own story in the early 1890s, after publication of *The Gentle Art*. "Determined that no mendacious scamp shall tell foolish truths about me when centuries have gone by," he began in a self-styled "memoir," "I now proceed to take the wind out of such speculation by immediately furnishing myself the fiction of my own biography." He got no further than three scant pages, in which he told at least as many lies. Of course, Whistler had been selling a fictional version of himself most of his adult life. That was the problem. He revealed only glimpses of James Whistler, with few people ever understanding the whole man. It would make for a very mixed legacy, but it was the one he created.

In the end, Whistler hoped his work would define him. He destroyed paintings and etchings he feared would injure his reputation. "To destroy is to survive" became his mantra. He had also been careful, especially toward the end of his life, to place paintings in the hands only of people who appreciated them. The art was an extension of him, and in that sense, it was part of the autobiography. People entrusted with his work were merely caretakers. One wonders if the more than sixty museums and galleries and the many individuals now possessing Whistler's work appreciate his point of view.

My own biography of Whistler, published in 2014, proposed that the best way to understand this intense, introspective, and contradictory man is to appreciate the self-doubt and relentless pursuit of perfection that motivated him, shaped his character, defined his art, and determined his estimation of others. A biography of his mother, Anna McNeill Whistler, coauthored with Georgia Toutziari in 2018, added to that interpretation by expanding indirectly on other factors that shaped the son's life, most obviously his relationship with his parents and siblings.

This book picks up where those accounts ended by exploring how Whistler's life and art have been judged since his passing in 1903. His reputation has endured highs and lows, ups and downs, during that time, but overall he has fared well, especially in the twenty-first century. Some people still allow the image—or perhaps better phrased, the legend—of the man to affect their appreciation of the art, but so it goes.

I have divided this exploration into three parts. Part 1, titled "Witnesses," evaluates the roles of the people responsible for laying the foundation of Whistler's legacy. Most influential were the Pennells, whose 1908 book about Whistler is often described as *the* biography of the artist. I contend it is better termed a *chronicle*, and that we should be wary of it. Next come the friends, associates, and acquaintances whose "foolish truths" Whistler had so dreaded. Once the most influential sources of information about his life and work, these personal perspectives, of which scores were published, can be both useful and problematic. I discuss their strengths and weaknesses. Finally, I look at three people who might have contributed significantly to that early foundation: Whistler's mistress-muse Maud Franklin, his son Charles James Whistler Hanson, and his sister-in-law Rosalind Birnie

Philip. Maud and Charlie remained mute; Rosalind created her own mixed legacy.

Part 2, "Explanations," challenges three components of Whistler's life and work that have done the most to either distort or confuse his legacy. They include the exaggerated image of Whistler as a "dandy"; his misconstrued reputation as quarrelsome, ill-tempered, and petulant; and the inspiration for his signature group of paintings, the nocturnes. Readers may find this the most revealing part. I certainly hope so.

Part 3, "Image," offers a broad view of the forces shaping Whistler's reputation between 1903 and the 2020s. First, I explore how his image was created and perpetuated in popular culture through cartoons, advertisements, fictional literature, poetry, song, radio, film, television, theatrical performances, and such kitsch items as coffee mugs, men's ties, trading cards, and bobbleheads. Whistler is one of only a handful of artists whose legacy has been defined in this way. Next comes a longer exploration, divided by World War II into two chronological parts, which untangles assessments of Whistler's legacy by other artists, art critics, collectors, historians, biographers, and museum directors. It also asks about the cultural and financial forces that influenced those judgments.

Taken together, I believe these varied yet connected perspectives provide a fuller portrait of one of the most consequential artists of the nineteenth century.

PART 1
Witnesses

CHAPTER 1

The Petulant Pennells

Any consideration of James McNeill Whistler's legacy must begin with Elizabeth R. and Joseph Pennell. They published their two-volume *The Life of James McNeill Whistler* in 1908, followed over the next twenty-two years by six more English editions, a French edition, and three more books about Whistler, most notably *The Whistler Journal*. By the time they donated their mountain of research materials to the Library of Congress, the Pennells had entrenched themselves as the leading authorities on the artist. Many commentators still refer to them as "Whistler's biographers," rather than as his first or earliest biographers. In fact, the Pennells might better be described as "chroniclers." This is not to suggest that they were mere compilers or storytellers, or that they offered no analysis or interpretation of Whistler's life and art. Yet these latter features were not their strong suit, and so their book should be used with caution, both for what it says and for what it fails to say.

It is not as though modern scholars have been blind to the *Life*'s defects. Some people go as far as to call it "fundamentally flawed," and nearly everyone recognizes its hagiographic nature. Joe, as he was universally known, is most often singled out as a "slavish admirer" of Whistler, but Elizabeth's devotion to the artist's legacy, concedes her biographer, was also "limitless." At the very least, say others, the Pennells were "touchingly naïve" and "somewhat gullible" in their determination to preserve the Whistler "legend."[1]

Yet many of these same people, and more besides, have called the *Life* "indispensable" and relied absolutely on it for their own work. They praise the couple's book, despite its flaws, as the "factual basis for all Whistler studies." Linda Merrill, a scholar of the highest order and the first to downgrade the Pennells from biographers to chroniclers, said something similar when, in 1998, she deemed it the "fundamental source for Whistler scholarship," even as she went on to dismantle the *Life*'s handling of the Peacock Room.[2]

So, where did the Pennells go wrong, and who were they? Both were born in Philadelphia: Elizabeth in 1855, Joe in 1857. Both were middle class. Elizabeth's family was the more affluent, but her father, a financier, suffered economically during the American Civil War. Consequently, though afforded an excellent convent education, Elizabeth had to make her own way in the world. Luckily, her uncle Charles Godfrey Leland, a well-known author and philologist, nudged her toward writing, and she soon found a comfortable niche penning articles for several Philadelphia newspapers. Her gracious manner contrasted sharply with Joe's belligerent personality. Reared and educated as a Quaker, he was an irascible and contentious loner but also a gifted graphic artist who proved himself as a student at the Pennsylvania Academy of Fine Arts.

The two met in 1882, when they were fortuitously paired to produce an article for *Century Magazine*. Married two years later, they traveled almost at once to London, where Joe had received another magazine assignment, and settled there for the next thirty-three years. Immersing themselves in the city's cultural and literary worlds, they were drawn initially to the socialist political circle of George Bernard Shaw before drifting toward more artistic groups in the 1890s. Elizabeth blossomed in the new environment, becoming a prolific author and art critic who published in both American and British newspapers and periodicals. She also wrote thirteen books, six of them with Joe, besides their work on Whistler. Joe, too, proved himself as a writer but was better known as an excellent etcher, illustrator, and lithographer. By the time the couple returned to America in 1917, Joe, observed a friend, "remained as saltily American as pie for breakfast," while Elizabeth had "come to look like a well bred distinguished Englishwoman and spoke with just a suggestion of British accent."[3]

Joe claimed not to have cared much for Whistler when first meeting him, but, as things turned out, they were much alike. Both men were energetic and hardworking. Both could be opinionated, truculent, and quarrelsome, although as one Whistler scholar has put it, Pennell lacked

"Whistler's polish." A friend called Pennell "his own worst enemy" and believed that without Elizabeth's "good sense and quiet but ceaseless support" he "would probably have worn himself out fighting shadows, mostly friends and spectres raised by himself." The same could be said of Whistler, and where Pennell was concerned, the two men shared some of the same "enemies."[4]

Then came *The Life of Whistler*. Most contemporary reviewers accepted it as definitive. The publisher, William Heinemann, who had also been Whistler's publisher and a friend of long standing, rejoiced over its "splendid reception," with "hardly . . . a discordant voice in the press." Minor errors of fact, generally attributed to "a slip of the pen," were noted here and there. The *Nation*, to which Elizabeth had once been a regular contributor, was wary of the Pennells' "extreme admiration" for their subject, but the consensus declared the Pennells' efforts "delightful" and "authoritative."[5]

Many friends of Whistler were not so enthusiastic. Even before reading the book, they questioned the couple's credentials for such an important undertaking. Artist George H. Boughton, who disapproved of both the Pennells and Heinemann, thought it an evil day when that trio had set upon Whistler. Always wary of "Joe and his schemes," he scoffed at their "tumbling over each other" to write about Whistler's life. "Great Scott!!" he exclaimed to art critic and painter Alfred L. Baldry. "The grim irony of it all!!" The ordinarily genial Boughton did not expect to find even "a few grains of truth" in their book.[6]

Other people pointed to the book's many errors. Alan S. Cole, of the South Kensington Museum, was particularly dismayed because he had contributed to the Pennells' research, going as far as to provide extracts from his personal diaries. Artist Louise Jopling was "much amused . . . by some of the inaccuracies." Though she graciously conceded that some errors "might not have been the writer's fault," parts of the book, including behavior attributed to people that Jopling knew to be impossible, simply rang false to her.[7]

Marie Spartali Stillman, whose sister Christina had been the model for Whistler's *La Princesse du Pays de la Porcelaine* in the early 1860s, had reluctantly and guardedly shared her recollections with the Pennells, whom she regarded as mere "collectors of anecdotes." Afterward, she regretted cooperating. "Of course, all those who had known Whistler knew that the Pennells had not known him during the interesting part of his career," she complained in 1911, "& it is evident that they very much amplify their data. I think they have overdone their job—they are not subtle. . . . I think we get far too much silly chit chat ab[ou]t interesting people—it . . . is so wearisome."[8]

Richard Canfield, an avid collector of Whistler's work and one of the last people to sit for him, feared the Pennells had buried "the real man" with their "abject sycophancy." The book displayed a "lamentable ignorance . . . particularly in the second volume," Canfield complained, and he could not fathom why Joe Pennell, whom he scarcely knew, had gone out of his way to insult him in its pages. Charles Lang Freer, Whistler's foremost patron, endorsed Canfield's concerns. "I glanced over my copy of two volumes last evening," he confided to his fellow collector, "and of course quickly discovered the silliness of the undertaking. . . . Instead of writing in a dignified manner of matters of importance in connection to Whistler's life and art, he has contented himself by repeating a lot of trivial items long since worn thread-bare by other incompetent story-tellers." The book lacked "dignity" and "justice," Freer concluded, besides including "numerous errors."[9]

Walter Sickert, who spoke for most skeptics, had refused a request by Heinemann to "collaborate" with the Pennells. "We will let them scold their way solidly through 300 pages," he told the hopeful publisher. "And when their portrait of my fascinating and impish master in the character of the American Ecce Homo is complete, you and I might do a readable little monograph on the subject." Subsequently, given a chance to review the Pennells' book for the *Fortnightly Review*, Sickert found it full of false assumptions, inaccurate critiques, and questionable stories. "When the truth is improbable," he declared, "it had perhaps better not be recorded."[10]

However, the Pennells' severest critic, not to say nemesis, was Whistler's sister-in-law and executor, Rosalind Birnie Philip. Firmly believing that Whistler never would have permitted anyone to write his biography, she did everything possible to thwart the Pennells. She refused, as holder of the copyright to his correspondence, to let them quote from any of Whistler's letters they had collected, and in 1907 she took them to court to halt publication of the book. She lost on that score, but the judge did prohibit the Pennells from quoting from the correspondence.[11]

Freer hoped the legal rebuff might dissuade the Pennells from ever publishing their book. Instead, they acted as quickly as possible to capitalize on their partial court victory. There was already a rush by Whistler's friends to publish their recollections of him. William Webb, Whistler's longtime attorney and now Rosalind's legal adviser, raged against them as "money suckers." The Pennells saw them as competitors. Determined to have their book out in time for Christmas, they published in late October.[12]

The speed with which the Pennells acted is extraordinary. They had been scrupulous in collecting every scrap of evidence they could find about Whistler's life, a task left primarily to the tireless Joe. He solicited piles of reminiscences, personal diaries, and correspondence from people in Whistler's past. Joe, insisted one friend, "made it [the book] a success by sheer energy and will-power." Elizabeth worked just as hard but with less focus. She was already writing a biography of her uncle, Charles Leland, and penned reviews of over one hundred art exhibitions between 1904 and 1908, a bit more than half of them in 1904. She published another forty-nine reviews in the last half of 1903, after Whistler's death.[13]

Their speed also says something about the furtive way in which the Pennells undertook the *Life*. They insisted repeatedly that a letter written to them by Heinemann in May 1900 bestowed Whistler's blessing on the project. They stuck to this story throughout their lives. In 1928, two years after Joe had died and barely six years before her own passing, Elizabeth assured the public in her final book, *The Art of Whistler*, that Whistler himself had appointed them "his biographers." However, the couple failed to produce this letter at the trial, largely because they, Heinemann, and their attorney thought it might be "misconstrued" and do their case "a great deal of harm." The letter subsequently disappeared. In 1921, when the Pennells published portions of Elizabeth's diaries as *The Whistler Journal*, they altered or deleted entries concerning their commission and the missing letter.[14]

For people who preserved thousands of documents about Whistler's life, this gap in the record seems passing strange, and in the opinion of Dugald Sutherland MacColl, art critic and keeper, in turn, of the Tate Gallery and the Wallace Collection, it did "not promise well for scruple." After reviewing the court documents of Birnie Philip's suit against the Pennells, he confided to Whistler's sister-in-law, "I think the conclusion could not be avoided that Whistler [did] <u>not</u> let himself in for a Life." It seemed to MacColl, who had experienced his own disputes with Joe, that the "defendants did not feel very sure of their ground, or they would not have attempted to chaff, as they did at more than one point."[15]

Several of Whistler's other old friends, including former protégés Inez Bate Addams and Harper Pennington, expressed surprise when told of the Pennells' supposed commission. Freer, Rosalind's staunchest ally and never a friend of the Pennells, pointed to the most obvious flaw in the couple's claim. "The facts are, that Mr. Whistler's original intention undoubtedly was, to permit the Pennells to prepare an illustrated catalogue of his paintings," he explained to a friend, "similar to the way in which he allowed other writers to prepare catalogues of his etchings and lithographs." Then, touching on what had been the gist of the court case, Freer emphasized, "During Mr. Whistler's late years, he cooperated with the Pennells along these lines, furnishing them with photographs of many of his pictures, and certain data pertaining thereto, but he gave them no letters, nor other Mss. Material, out of which to write 'A Life.'" More than that, Freer continued, "If Mr. Whistler had intended the Pennells to write 'A Life' he surely would have mentioned this to his heir and executrix Miss Birnie Philip, in whom he had unlimited confidence."[16]

Freer's interpretation mirrored that of the judge in *Philip v. Pennell*, who proposed that Whistler had only licensed the couple to compile a catalogue of his work, albeit one that contained biographical information. That was good enough for the Pennells, who celebrated their triumph at the Café Royal, one of Whistler's favorite restaurants. Yet they did not adhere even to that limited assignment. Ignoring their own claim that they had been asked to write an illustrated "book on him," they now said that Whistler had envisioned a two-volume work, one devoted to "his life, the other his work." Instead the biography itself became two volumes, a format apparently agreed on by the Pennells and Heinemann after the trial. The Pennells did assemble some portion of a catalogue, and in fairness, they may have been stymied by the unwillingness of Freer to allow access to his extensive collection of Whistler paintings. Even so, a catalogue would have taken far more care and time than the Pennells were willing to invest in it.[17]

Heinemann, though, was not pleased with the results. In reviewing what he hoped would be the final draft of their book, he objected to its repetitious nature, which again pointed to the haste of composition, but also to much of what he regarded as superfluous detail concerning the "technical considerations" of Whistler's art. These, he thought, would be better suited to a separate book. The Pennells would have none of it, with Elizabeth replying in a sharply worded letter that she and Joe were the experts on Whistler and the best arbiters of what should and should not be included. "We alone are in a position to record them" (that is, the "technical considerations"), she scolded, which the Pennells believed would "constitute the greatest value of the book."

Heinemann, who was notorious for "improving" the work of his authors, held his ground and repeated his belief that it would be "absolutely fatal" to introduce "any extraneous matter in the simple telling of Whistler's life." Such material belonged in footnotes or an appendix, he insisted, and was, in any event, best "relegated to the Catalogue." Even after the book had been published, with a second printing required within weeks, Heinemann continued to speak of the yet-to-be-written "catalogue." The Pennells ignored him. The *Life*, by any definition, remained their book.[18]

They tried to resolve the catalogue issue by employing what had become a standard practice for artist biographies and books on art history. Rapid advances in photographic technology, mostly out of France, had made it possible to reproduce quality images of works of art. Théophile Silvestre's *Histoire des artistes vivants*, published in the mid-1850s, became the model, not only because of Silvestre's innovative use of photography but also because he was the first artists' biographer to consult the notebooks, diaries, personal correspondence, and recollections of his subjects. By combining direct quotations from the artists with images of their work, he reinforced the "veracity" of his account, even to the extent of blurring the line between biography and autobiography. The Pennells never mentioned Silvestre as an inspiration, but they certainly followed his methods. The two volumes of their first edition boasted 160 photographs, including 130 of Whistler's art.[19]

The Pennells defended their credentials as authorities on Whistler by exaggerating the importance of their friendship with him, but dozens of other people enjoyed a greater acquaintance, even intimacy, with the artist. The Pennells admitted to relying on reminiscences and other testimony for their knowledge of Whistler before the mid-1880s. In writing about an event in 1890, they confessed, "We hardly knew Whistler personally" at the time. They "saw him oftener" from that year forward., but not until around 1896, only seven years before Whistler's death, did they claim—rather improbably—to enjoy an "almost daily" acquaintanceship with him.[20]

Joe Pennell tried to undermine the authority of anyone who presumed to know more than he did about Whistler. Artist and author John Rothenstein thought it sheer jealousy. "He was an uncritical worshipper of Whistler," Rothenstein explained, "resentful of sharing Whistler's friendship with people who showed independence." In 1912, Pennell wrote a scathing review of the many other books that had been published about

Whistler by then. His dismissive comments expose Pennell as boorish and ungrateful, for nearly all those authors had shared their own reminiscences with him and were purported in his private correspondence to be friends. One target of his disdain, Haldane MacFall, told the Pennells in 1905 that he would do "anything" to help them and even dedicated his own book on Whistler to the couple. Pennell described the honor ungraciously as "amusing." Perhaps guilt, or at least insecurity, plagued both Pennells. They referred incessantly to their book as the "authorized" biography. Within a year, they identified it by the faux title of the *Authorized Life*.[21]

Having complained bitterly and quite publicly for decades about how Birnie Philip had interfered with their ability to tell Whistler's story, the Pennells became obstructionists in their own right. When one of Anna Whistler's descendants, hoping to write a biography of Whistler's mother, asked Elizabeth if she had any letters written by Anna, Pennell replied untruthfully that she had none. While more honest than his wife in such instances, the prickly Joe was also blunter. He responded to similar requests by refusing permission to copy letters and documents or use photographs and drawings the couple had collected. "If we did not," he insisted, "the whole collection would become the sport of American historians[,] young ladies boarding schools[,] and old hens underwear shops."[22]

So, what is wrong with the *Life*, beyond its obvious partisanship? The first notable problems are the organization, structure, and style of the book. Those issues may sound unimportant, but they say a lot about the Pennells as researchers and authors. The original two-volume format, with a total length (not counting appendixes and index) of 619 pages, is badly out of balance. The first volume covers the first fifty years of Whistler's life in only 316 pages; the second volume devotes 303 pages to the remaining nineteen years. The Pennells implied that this lopsided arrangement was caused by a lack of information about Whistler's life in the decades before they knew him, but the quality and types of sources used in the second volume are not markedly different from the first one. The Pennells simply appear to have been more invested in the later years.[23]

Elizabeth was primarily responsible for this arrangement. As a journalist and essayist by trade, she was the better stylist of the two, and while some people assumed that Joe had written the book, she was the principal author (fig. 1). She has been rightly praised as one of several female art critics and historians who, with a variety of periodicals open to them in the 1880s and 1890s, began to cross the "boundaries between journalism and

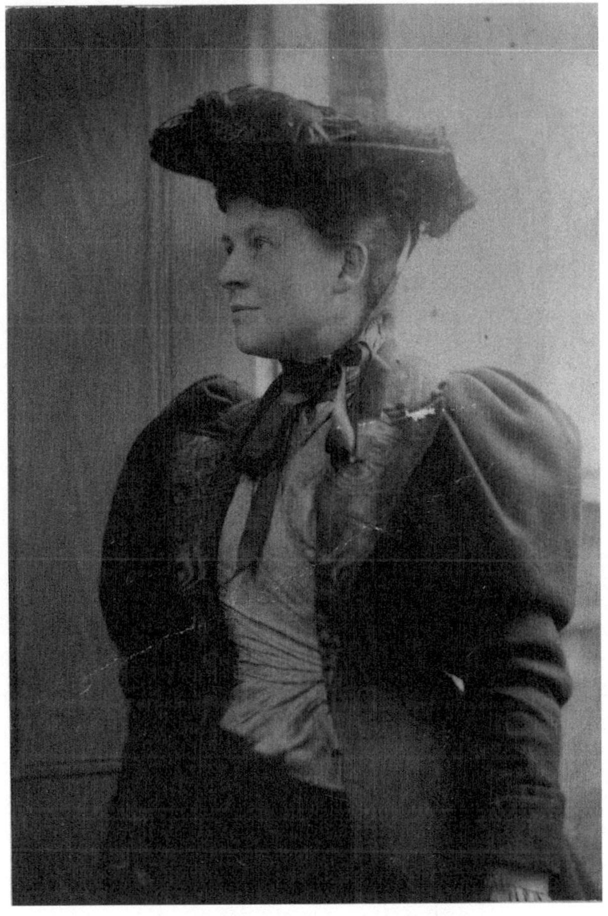

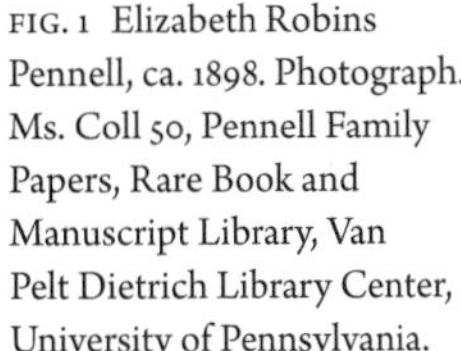

FIG. 1 Elizabeth Robins Pennell, ca. 1898. Photograph. Ms. Coll 50, Pennell Family Papers, Rare Book and Manuscript Library, Van Pelt Dietrich Library Center, University of Pennsylvania.

literature." Unfortunately, her experience as a journalist was ill-suited to the construction of a forceful six-hundred-page narrative. She wrote large sections merely to introduce documents, either letters or diary entries, which were then quoted at length, often for several pages. Scholars who praise the Pennells' work as "indispensable" usually have these admittedly valuable documents in mind, but in some instances, the quotations constitute the majority, even the entirety, of chapters. Pennell had written her two-volume (846 pages) biography of Charles Leland in the same fashion. As she confessed in that book, "I have been content to give this bare outline of his life . . . for the simple reason that the details are so well filled in by . . . his letters." While forbidden by the court from using the same "life-and-letters" formula for Whistler, the Pennells made do with excerpts from their conversations with the artist and reminiscences of his friends. It is very much a cut-and-paste affair.[24]

These features typified Victorian biography as it had evolved by the end of the nineteenth century, but the Pennells' handling of the Victorian template is curiously awkward, as when extended quotations come not from Whistler or his friends but from Joe Pennell. In chapter 25 of the second volume, six of the eight and a half pages consist of a statement by Joe, placed in quotation marks. The remaining pages are an extended quotation from a 1904 article by American art dealer Frederick Keppel. Similarly, fifteen of the sixteen pages of chapter 37 in that same volume are Joe's account, again placed in quotation marks, of Whistler's return to London from a residence in Paris in 1892. The Pennells apparently hoped the quotation marks would bolster the appearance of authenticity.[25]

Even more unfortunately, their narrative is episodic, with little effort made to convey the flow of Whistler's life. Despite the outwardly chronological development of the book, with each chapter addressing inclusive and sequentially assigned years, there is much movement back and forth in time. The technique, a device used by many biographers, is certainly legitimate, but in this instance it dilutes an already weak sense of cause and effect in Whistler's life. The result is a mere collection of stories tied together by brief transitions. Perhaps this is why the "eccentric but formidable" Pennells have been cited more often for their "dogged" and "relentless" research, undertaken with "Boswellian fervor," than for their prose. It all makes for a reasonable chronicle but hardly a thoughtful biography.[26]

Most serious is the unreliability of the biography, which may be attributed to several types of dissembling. First, as Whistler's friends made clear, the Pennells get many facts wrong, including some quite basic ones. For instance, they state that Whistler added his middle name of McNeill while at West Point. This simply is not true, as the Academy's records clearly demonstrate. Providing accurate dates is also a frequent problem. They even misstate the day of Whistler's funeral, which they attended, and the very first sentence of the *Life* says he was born on July 10, rather than July 11. One might quibble about the significance of such errors. After all, it is a rare book that may be called flawless. The Pennells' missteps may only betray a careless and rushed handling of the evidence. Yet their inaccuracies went uncorrected in subsequent editions, and coming as they do from the "authorized" biographers, they have been repeated by generations of subsequent writers.

And some errors betray a second, more fatal failing: the altering of facts that did not suit them. For example, Whistler's growing contempt for British (primarily English) critics and the artistic tastes of the "B.P.," or British People, as he dubbed them, is well known. It was the principal reason he moved to Paris in 1892. Yet the Pennells would have us believe that this anti-English bias began as early as 1874, apparently as a means of stressing a main theme in their book: Whistler as a lone artistic visionary—an *American* visionary—standing against the prejudiced and small-minded philistines. Along these same lines, they exaggerate the number of times that Whistler's work was rejected for exhibition by the Royal Academy. The truth is that none of the paintings he submitted was rejected in the instances they cite. The portrait of his mother was nearly turned down in 1872, which would be the last time he did exhibit at Burlington House, but you would never know that from the way the Pennells tell the story.[27]

Third, the Pennells misquote or mischaracterize some sources by altering the wording of documents to strengthen or verify their version of events. For instance, Edgar Degas once famously scolded Whistler for behaving as though he had no "talent." In the hands of the Pennells, talent becomes "genius." More egregious are the excerpts quoted from Anna Whistler's Russian diary. They give no clue as to how they acquired the eleven pages of excerpts used, but not a single entry is completely accurate. Compare any entry in their book to the original diary: words have been changed, sentences deleted, and phrases added. The alterations do not always alter Anna's intent, but they are nonetheless spurious embellishments. And again, they have been repeated by successive generations of writers relying on the Pennells rather than consulting the diary itself.[28]

A fourth reason to be wary of the Pennells is their willingness to believe everything Whistler told them, even in the face of contrary evidence. Whistler was never very careful with the truth, but he assumed that everyone knew it. For him, that was part of the fun. It was all done with a wink and a nod. The Pennells never seem to have caught on to his game—either that, or they were smug enough to think he would always be forthright with them. They certainly failed to take account of Whistler's prejudices against certain people, and how those prejudices became engrained over the course of decades.

This weakness is often disguised by one of the apparent strengths of the *Life*, which is to employ long quotations by Whistler himself. As it turns out, this exposes a fifth reason to be wary of the Pennells. They insist that these supposedly definitive statements about his experiences, artistic methods, and aesthetic purposes were a result of his desire to assist them in every way possible. There is no denying that Whistler provided the Pennells with much useful information, often related to them at dinners and soirees in their Adelphi Terrace apartments, but he told many of the same stories to multiple friends, as may be seen by their published reminiscences.

More to the point, to believe that Whistler said everything attributed to him precisely as he said it beggars the imagination. Some quotations used by the Pennells go on for more than a page. They are not statements but soliloquies. Elizabeth Pennell recorded most of them hours or days later, and while she quite likely caught the gist of the conversations, probably even recalling some especially memorable turns of phrase or *bons mots*, she could not possibly have recorded them verbatim or in detail. She admitted as much to another person who once visited their home on the same evening as Whistler and made her own notes about the occasion. Her friend's account, Elizabeth acknowledged, was "much more full than mine."[29]

In fact, virtually all the lengthy quotations attributed to him are as much Pennell as Whistler, which must stand as the most suspect part of both the *Life* and the subsequent *Whistler Journal*. A likely explanation for the deception is the Pennells' determination to record Whistler's own voice as a means of authenticating their work. Denied the legal right to quote from his correspondence, it was the ideal tactic to skirt the court's prohibition and get the better of Birnie Philip. Their methods become amusing when one considers how the Pennells treated an 1890 interview with Whistler in the *Pall Mall Gazette*. While quoting it in the *Life*, they pointedly dismiss its reliability by saying, "Though we hesitate to accept the words as his [Whistler's], this is still an interesting statement inspired by him."[30]

The subterfuge, which goes beyond mere literary license, is shown by comparing passages in the *Life* with Elizabeth's diary, the supposed source of the quotations, and the edited manuscript for the published *Journal*. A notable example is the account of Whistler's trip to Chile in 1866. Pennell recorded a summary of Whistler's version of the adventure, based on a conversation from the previous day, but then embellished her lengthy summation and published it as a direct quotation. The original diary says, of his escape on horseback during the bombardment of Valparaiso, "He had a sense of himself, all the time, that the riding was splendid, but the one idea was to get away." Both the *Life* and the *Journal* state, "The riding was splendid and I, as a West Point man, was head of the procession." The description continues for an entire page, not only turning a third-person summary into a first-person account but also, as in the case of Anna Whistler's diary, deleting and adding whole phrases.[31]

Perhaps most fanciful is the story that Whistler was dismissed from West Point because he misidentified silicon as a gas on a chemistry examination. That examination had involved complex principles of chemistry, not a simple identification of elements, and Whistler had failed it utterly. Col. Charles W. Larned, one of the people on whom the Pennells depended for information about Whistler's time at the Academy, told them as much. He pointed to "prototypes of other noted graduates" for the "silicon story," which he called a "joke connected with celebrities." Yet nearly every Whistler biography since then has endorsed the Pennells' account, as told to them by Whistler.[32]

The Pennells were determined to make Whistler fit his own self-image, whatever the facts. Another of his best-known yet demonstrably false public claims was that he had been born a "Southerner." At one time or another, he insisted that the place of his nativity had been Baltimore, South Carolina, or Virginia—even adding St. Petersburg, Russia, to the list during a court trial. The Pennells knew full well that Whistler was a New Englander, born in Lowell, Massachusetts, but they did their best to twist the Whistler family genealogy to endorse his Southern lineage. While acknowledging that Anna Whistler had been born in North Carolina, they announced that Whistler's strongest link to the Southern heritage he craved was that the McNeills were "related by marriage to the Fairfaxes and other well-known Virginia families." It is true that one of Anna's sisters married a Fairfax, but that hardly constitutes the generational link suggested by the Pennells.[33]

Much else, to define a sixth category of deception, is either pure fabrication or fancy. Whistler's two-year-old brother Charles Donald Whistler did not die of "sea-sickness" on the voyage from Travemünde to St. Petersburg in 1843, as the Pennells would have it. He succumbed to inflammation of the bowels. Henri Fantin-Latour was not older than Whistler but almost two years younger. Anna Whistler was neither a Puritan nor (like Joe) a Quaker but an Episcopalian. Nor was she "always with" her son between 1864 and 1875. Indeed, they were sometimes separated for months at a time. When she died in January 1881, it was during the opening of Whistler's

Venice pastels exhibition, not its closing. Whistler stayed in Rotherhithe, not Wapping, when making his Thames etchings of 1859. He did not begin his famous Sunday breakfasts immediately upon moving to Lindsey Row but only after ill health had forced his mother to leave their home to reside in Hastings. Although carefully noting it may be a "legend," the Pennells describe a meeting (the "first," they call it) between Whistler and Mark Twain. In fact, there is no evidence that the two men ever met, although that has not stopped other writers, perhaps inspired by the Pennells, from telling similar stories.[34]

Other events are asserted without proof. For instance, it is untrue that Whistler attended West Point "against his will." While it is fair to say that his three uncles, two of them Academy graduates, urged him in that direction (though not his mother, as the Pennells also contend), Whistler relished the idea of being a cadet, having once visited there. Following his inglorious career at West Point, the Pennells say he "resigned" from his job with the US Coast and Geodetic Survey, but in fact it remains unclear whether he resigned or was fired. When he then returned to Baltimore, no effort was made, as the Pennells insist, to have him work at the Winans locomotive works. On the contrary, Thomas Winans, who would be a patron for many years, fed Whistler's desire to be an artist by providing him with a studio and seeking commissions for him. As far as we know, no ex-Confederates ever visited Whistler's home in Lindsey Row, as the Pennells contend, nor did (as they also tell us) the many French artist refugees who flocked to London during the early 1870s.[35]

Then there are the slight or insufficient explanations the Pennells offer for some significant events and decisions in Whistler's life. In their telling, the circumstances for his move to Paris from America in 1855 are obscure. They imply that Whistler had been inspired by reading Henri Murger's *Scènes de la vie bohème*, a claim most subsequent biographers have accepted without question. In fact, there is no evidence that Whistler ever read Murger's book, or if so, when. Whistler's reason for moving from Paris to London in 1859 is equally dark.[36]

No explanation is offered for Whistler's close friendship with Edwin and Elizabeth Edwards, important members of Whistler's social-artistic circle, other than to say that the Edwards house "was always a pleasant one to visit." The Pennells do not even tell us Elizabeth's first name, despite the fact that she wrote a long letter to them in 1906. They quote only a small portion of that letter and certainly did not include Elizabeth's opinion that

Whistler's "great conceit was his ruin." And as usual, the Pennells could not resist changing the wording of even the portion of the letter they did quote. Thus, instead of Whistler being "always very economic," he became "always very eccentric."[37]

Such gaps in the story are numerous. Elsewhere, they give no hint as to why Whistler suddenly visited the coast of Brittany in the summer of 1861. They tell us Anna Whistler was "persuaded to leave America and come to England" in 1863, but persuaded by whom? Other than to suggest that she endured "arduous times" in the American Civil War, her circumstances are a mystery. The tale of Whistler's momentous rupture with his brother-in-law Francis Seymour Haden, which began around this same time, depends wholly on Whistler's version of events and does not tell the complete story.[38]

Neither were the Pennells inclined to pursue Whistler's acrimonious split with close friend Alphonse Legros, which they describe merely as his "difference" with the Frenchman. They blame that gap in their narrative on Whistler's failure to give "his own" account of the altercation. Yet they had been told at least something of the breakup by both William Rossetti and Thomas Armstrong. They later justified their failure to discuss the Legros affair by saying Rossetti had cautioned, in their words, that "the details . . . were unfit for publication." In fact, Rossetti said no such thing, although Armstrong had told them, "I can't think you need say anything about it in the book—at least about the assault."[39]

And it is not simply that their narrative is full of errors, omissions, and fabrications. At least two vital parts of Whistler's character are ignored: his frequent bouts of self-doubt, loneliness, and self-pity, and the single-minded devotion to art that too often exposed a disturbing selfishness. The Pennells give us all of Whistler's positive qualities—his artistic genius, his wit, his gaiety, his generosity—but that reveals only part of the man. The closest they come to the stark reality of his self-doubt, for instance, is to acknowledge that following his return from Chile in late 1866, he passed "through a moment of experiments, difficulties and discouragements." They go on to dismiss even this period as a "transition" that lasted but a single year. They were right to see it as a period of transition, but it was only one of several, nearly all of them inspired by similar feelings of failure and self-doubt, and each one marking a significant detour in Whistler's life.[40]

In at least one instance, the Pennells distort events in which they had participated. Whistler was convinced by some younger artists in the late 1890s to join them in creating and promoting a new artistic "congress," soon to be known as the International Society of Sculptors, Painters and Gravers. However, the Pennells make it seem as though the International was "Whistler's idea." In fact, the English journalist, critic, and painter Francis Howard initiated the project, aided almost immediately by several young Scots artists, including John Lavery, Edward A. Walton, and James Guthrie, the so-called Glasgow Boys. Whistler, who was living in Paris at the time, pledged support but did not become closely involved until his friend Alfred Gilbert resigned as chair of the organization. Whistler replaced him shortly thereafter, with the title of president.

The Pennells also mention the fractious nature of the International, which saw "personal jealousies, and personal preferences," divide its leadership. That was true enough, but they fail to mention that Joe, whom Whistler insisted become a member of the governing council, caused much of the discord. Ultimately Whistler's leadership, described by the Pennells as that of an "intelligent autocrat," kept the International going, but he also produced his unique brand of friction, as he had done when he was president of the Royal Society of British Artists a decade earlier.[41]

Curiously, given that Whistler had clearly expected the Pennells to produce a catalogue of his paintings, the seventh and weakest part of their book is the shallow, sometimes inaccurate, treatment they often give the work. In discussing his first exhibited painting, *At the Piano*, they note the influence of Rembrandt, the "uncompromising realism of Courbet," the "arrangement of the lines," and the "harmonious balance of spaces black and white." Yet they say nothing about the dramatic cropping of the picture, perhaps its most innovative element, and clearly inspired by Whistler's familiarity with seventeenth-century Dutch painting generally, not to mention Jean-Baptiste-Siméon Chardin. Instead, seeking always to promote Whistler's instinctive, untutored genius, they emphasize how the painting showed him to be far ahead of other painters of his generation.[42]

The extraordinarily important *White Girl*, later titled *Symphony in White, No. 1*, receives even less analysis. After stating the obvious point that its subject matter does not conform to "Victorian standards" and noting but not explaining Whistler's "bewildering decision" to paint "white upon white," the Pennells are more interested in quoting remarks about the painting's mixed reception at the Salon des Refusés. Their commentary on *The Little White Girl* is no more satisfying. Other than pointing to the "details" of Japanese culture on display, the reflection of "Joe's" face (their consistent misspelling of Jo Hiffernan's name) in the mirror, and Whistler's experiment with thinner paint, their final analysis of the picture merely states, "Method and design alike give the repose of the perfect work."[43]

Whistler's inspiration for other works receives the same short shrift. The Pennells dismiss his *japonisme* paintings of the mid-1860s as "so many excuses for him to render a beauty foreign to Western life and English atmosphere." They never consider that Whistler was also taking advantage of the enormous burst of popularity in Asian art and culture that had recently seized London. He saw an opportunity to cash in, quite literally, on the craze by creating his own version of Asian art. This was likewise the case with a series of drawings Whistler made for two English magazines in 1862. The Pennells say it was "natural" for Whistler to join the other "brilliant" young artists who had turned their hand to working for the illustrated magazines, without noting his desperate need of "tin" at the time.[44]

The Pennells have no idea how to treat the nocturnes. They begin by saying, "Whistler was the first to paint the night." Evidently realizing that judgment was unsupportable, they modify it a few pages later by admitting, "He painted the effect that the world at night produced on him." That was better, and then, toward the end of their analysis, they state the obvious: these were "not invariably pictures of night, but at times of dawn or of twilight." Yet in none of this do the Pennells seem interested in identifying the inspiration for this magnificent series, one of the defining elements of Whistler's legacy. The continuing influence of *japonisme* is their best guess, so that in the end, Whistler, in creating his nocturnes, merely "translated" Asian techniques to his own purpose.[45]

The Pennells also muddle the sequence in which some work was either begun or completed. They describe Whistler's portrait of his mother as the "first" of his large portraits, although they subsequently admit that they could not say when he started the painting. In any event, they seem to have forgotten that he was already working on a portrait of Frederick R. Leyland and would begin a portrait of Frances Leyland before completing Anna's picture. They also misstate the portrait's early exhibition history. They err as well in saying that Whistler's "first experiments in lithography" came in 1878. In fact, he *returned* to lithography that year, though admittedly in far more serious fashion. His first genuine "experiments" in the medium had come nearly a quarter century earlier, before he left the United States. Small wonder that James Laver, the next Whistler biographer to come along (in 1930), concluded that some dates given by the Pennells, as well as their conclusions about some paintings, were "excessively unlikely."[46]

Not wishing to confront the Pennells personally, Harper Pennington informed William Heinemann that his authors had "misapprehended certain things . . . in Whistler's aims, and in his method of working," besides leaving unexplored, if not rejecting outright, important artistic influences on Whistler. They scoff at his admiration of Jean-Auguste-Dominique Ingres. They dismiss his well-known expression of regret over having not studied with the French master as "an absurd piece of modesty." They totally miss the profound influence of Albert Moore on Whistler's painting, maintaining that "if it existed at all," it "was as ephemeral and superficial as Rossetti's." They also fail to notice the rather obvious influence of Moore's cartouche on the earliest version of Whistler's butterfly signature, which, they mistakenly claim, did not appear on Whistler's canvases until the nocturnes and portraits of the 1870s. That Moore was also one of Whistler's closest and truest friends for nearly three decades seems to escape them, although, since Moore had died in 1893, this would have been before the Pennells' "intimacy" with Whistler.[47]

The work of Whistler's later years, done when the Pennells claimed their closest association with him, is almost totally ignored. This is especially peculiar given Elizabeth's well-earned reputation as a perceptive art critic. A possible explanation, and indeed one that applies to the Pennells' general mishandling of both the content of Whistler's paintings and the people and circumstances that inspired or defined his work, is Elizabeth's affinity for the "New Art Criticism." Others of this persuasion included many of Whistler's strongest advocates, including D. S. MacColl, Frederick Wedmore, Alfred L. Baldry, Charles Whibley, George Moore, and Robert A. M. Stevenson. In modern terms, these critics prized "formalism" in painting—that is, the structure, line, color, composition, and other technical details of a picture. That Whistler also valued these elements above content or other didactic qualities is clearly one reason Elizabeth was drawn to him. She was one of a group of female critics, including Cecila Waern, Alice Meynell, and Vernon Lee, who helped define Britain's late nineteenth-century contemporary art scene. For Pennell, Whistler represented all the best in that art. This was certainly so by the 1930s, as she tried to ward off the onslaught of "Matisse and Picasso and the rest" of their generation. Yet her narrowly defined critical approach did not serve Whistler well when it came to placing his work in the larger context of a biography.[48]

As for Joe Pennell, he was not quite the expert on Whistler's art that he fancied himself (fig. 2). Frequently asked to authenticate Whistler paintings

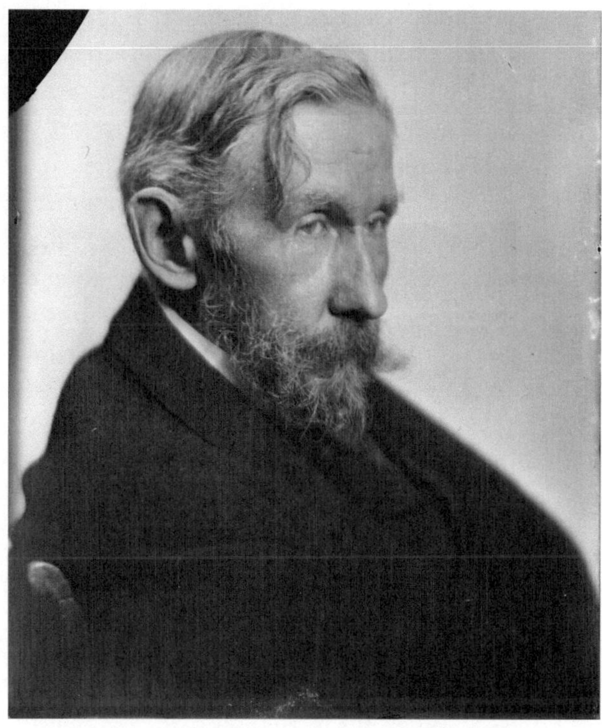

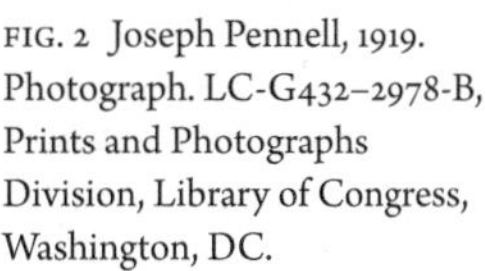
FIG. 2 Joseph Pennell, 1919. Photograph. LC-G432–2978-B, Prints and Photographs Division, Library of Congress, Washington, DC.

and prints, in the mid-1920s he was shown some pastels that Whistler had supposedly done in Chile. He initially declared them genuine, only to reverse himself sometime later. It would not be the only occasion when he did so, but in this instance the owner of the pastels pressed him on the issue. Consequently, Pennell invented additional reasons to question their authenticity and "got a bit wild in his arguments," clearly perturbed at being challenged as "the arch-priest at the Whistler shrine." The owner of the pastels publicized their impasse in the New York press, upon which Pennell, according to his antagonist, "lapsed into profound silence; would see no reporter; would make no further comment." As it happened, Pennell was right to doubt the authenticity of the pastels. Whistler made none in Chile. He rarely used that medium for finished works until his 1879–80 sojourn in Venice, something that Pennell should have known.[49]

A decade earlier, in a more celebrated instance, Pennell had challenged the authenticity of several paintings by Walter Greaves. Indeed, he went so far as to accuse Greaves of either plagiarizing Whistler's work or stealing some pieces and presenting them as his own. He became obsessed with Greaves, to the extent that Walter Sickert accused him of having "Greaves-on-the-brain." Charles Freer thought the unseemly witch hunt "very amusing."[50]

Perhaps the most disturbing thing about the Pennells' embrace of Whistler, and surely a factor that would have made the artist regret whatever license he had granted them, was the way they turned him into a cottage industry. Marie Stillman did not mince words on this subject. The Pennells, she observed in 1922, had been "exploiting their recollections ever since" publishing the *Life*. Even had Whistler asked them to write his biography, he certainly would not have anticipated their *re*writing and issuing subsequent editions of the book, especially not the truncated and "cheap one-volume [fifth] edition," as Elizabeth described it. Whistler would have understood the danger of overexposure, just as he knew that unlimited prints of his etchings and lithographs lessened their value. In preparing the French edition in 1913, the Pennells, to their credit, tried to correct several errors and misinterpretations in the translation. However, they appear to have accepted William Heinemann's reminder that this edition was intended not as a literal translation but rather as a condensed "adaptation" of their work. When one recalls how particular Whistler had been with his friend Stéphane Mallarmé's translation of the "Ten O'Clock," the contrast is stark.[51]

Some scholars believe *The Whistler Journal* more valuable than the *Life*, primarily because of its documentary nature; it is filled with raw information taken from correspondence and interviews with the artist's relatives, friends, and acquaintances. On balance, this is probably a valid assessment, even though the *Journal* suffers from many of the same weaknesses as the *Life*. Its most serious flaw, as shown, is to embroider and present Elizabeth's summaries of conversations with Whistler as direct quotations. Similarly, the organization and text of the published version are greatly altered from those of the original diaries. There are deletions, additions, and alterations galore, as well as entries for one date that combine multiple entries. The *Journal* was structured to reflect Elizabeth's original manuscript diaries, kept between 1898 and 1903, but those entries were interspersed in the published version with gossip and conversations from as late as 1913. Elizabeth then kept another series of diaries from 1915 through 1922, upon the Pennells' return to the United States, although none of that material appears in the *Journal*.

It is also notable that J. B. Lippincott, the American publisher, who wished to publish Elizabeth's diaries as a way to "supplement" the sixth edition of the *Life*, insisted that the Pennells expunge some passages from the *Journal* for fear of offending people. So resistant were they that J. Bertram Lippincott, president of the firm, told Joe in a personal letter that it was "unfair" to "let off steam on benighted individuals. . . . [C]ut out that stuff." The authors themselves voluntarily excised unflattering descriptions or references to people they did not wish to offend or antagonize, including Heinemann, Inez and Clifford Addams, and Maud Franklin. That said, they let stand enough offensive and possibility actionable references to such people as Charles Lang Freer, Frederick Wedmore, Walter Greaves, George Moore, and John Singer Sargent for Heinemann's company to decline issuing a British edition. William Webb called the book "vile" and believed Joe had "forced" Elizabeth to publish it. Birnie Philip, after spending an "unprofitable day" inspecting it, did not think the *Journal* would injure Whistler's memory, even if it caused her to suffer further "from the vulgarity of the Pennells." To longtime Whistler admirer D. S. MacColl she complained, "Nothing is sacred from their desire to advertise themselves."[52]

One should also consider the Pennells' rationale for publishing their *Journal*, which they said was intended to reveal "much that was left unsaid, or half-said, in the *Life*." This, they insisted, would "spare" Whistler "the dissection, the misrepresentation of busy-bodies, from which too many great men have suffered." A noble goal, perhaps, had they not spoiled this explanation by adding, "Nothing in Whistler's life needs to be concealed." For people who claimed to know him so intimately, they should have realized that Whistler would have been astonished by that proposition. Birnie Philips knew it, and MacColl, in referring to both the *Life* and the *Journal*, concluded, "Enough at present to say that the chief sufferer from their methods is Whistler himself." Of the *Journal*, he cautioned, "There is a good deal in it that calls for checking."[53]

There is no denying that we have reason to thank the Pennells. Flawed as it is, the *Life* made thousands of people aware of Whistler's achievements. Their later writings also contributed to his legacy at a time, during the 1910s and 1920s, when his style of painting and artistic philosophy were being challenged by artists and critics enthralled by Post-Impressionism, Expressionism, and any number of other new avant-garde schools. Even the public controversies in which they became embroiled kept his name alive. Most importantly, they contributed their massive collection of Whistler's correspondence, which they had scrupulously assembled, and the reminiscences of dozens of the artist's family, colleagues, and friends to the Library of Congress in 1917. When also considering the collection's numerous photographs, newspaper clippings, and other bits of Whistleriana, it amounts to some 96,000 items. For this, all people interested in the life and work of Whistler must be grateful.[54]

But as for the Pennells' published work on Whistler, especially the *Life*, the public beware. Granted, they were sometimes hampered by the lack of information available to them. Their research and writing met the standards of the day, as may be seen in the *Life*'s several editions, but that is no reason to ignore its obvious imperfections. Copies of all their books, including three different editions of the *Life*, sit on my bookshelves, and I have found them useful. But my pursuit of Whistler, like that of many others, has differed markedly from theirs. We study and write about Whistler to better understand him. We constantly prod and dissect his life and work. We are eager to learn what others think and write about him. Our view of him is still evolving. The Pennells, for their part, believed they had nothing new to learn. They showed no curiosity. There was no growth. Everything they published after 1908 was intended to bolster and justify their initial work. One may share their admiration of Whistler, but the Pennells undermined their status as "authorized" biographers by making their advocacy of the artist more about themselves than him.

CHAPTER 2

Voices from the Past

By the time the Pennells issued *The Life of Whistler*, a score of people had already published their reminiscences or "memories" of the artist. Several others had written biographical sketches or books about his art. In the decades that followed, dozens more friends and acquaintances felt compelled to have their say about him. Whistler made as good copy in death as in life.

Some people were appalled by the flood, either because they did not think Whistler deserved such recognition or because they thought it overdone. "I am scandalized at the vulgarity of the multitude who are advertised as writing about the man with whom they had so little in common & who misjudged him in every way," declared English artist Francis E. James in September 1903. He, for one, refused to take advantage of his friendship with Whistler in such a crass way. It would have been "an insult to the memory [of] that refined nature as I knew him," James insisted. American art critic and professor John C. Van Dyke thought differently. "Everybody is having a fling at poor Whistler," he admitted to the Pennells. He feared the artist would soon be "'explained' out of existence," but that did not deter Van Dyke from writing his own article for the *Ladies' Home Journal*.[1]

The result is a treasure trove of information about Whistler's life. For many years, biographers and historians depended almost entirely on these reminiscences to flesh out Whistler and evaluate his work. Today, with virtually all his correspondence available in a magnificently transcribed and annotated online edition, it is easy to neglect these dusty ruminations. That is a shame. These voices from the past—of people who knew Whistler, collaborated with him, and lived alongside him—offer insights missing from correspondence and diaries. They provide an expanded view of Whistler's world and remind us through their frequently conflicting perspectives of what an extraordinarily complex fellow Whistler could be and of the importance of his art to his contemporaries.

But which are the most reliable accounts? That depends, partly, on what one seeks. Some writers, drawing on their personal relationships with Whistler, emphasize his character, personality, eccentricities, domestic life, quarrels, and public image. Others are more interested in his art. They discuss his painting techniques, studio habits, methods of printing etchings, and the significance of his portraiture. Still others touch on both man and artist, as they seek to explain each through the other.

The writings take different forms, too. A few devoted friends wrote entire books about Whistler. More often, people included him in memoirs of their own lives, in which he appears as one of many characters. What this second type of book lacks in breadth or depth, it sometimes makes up for in penetrating truths and significant details about Whistler's life and work. The same may be said of the personal reminiscences or assessments of his art that appeared in a staggering variety of magazines and journals, from the *Art Journal* and *Magazine of Art* to *Century Magazine* and *Scribner's*.

As for their value, several factors come into play. For instance, the length of time a person knew Whistler must be considered, as should the time in his life when they were acquainted. Did the author's personal experiences with him extend over many years, even decades, or were they limited to particular circumstances and occasions? Did the more limited encounters come early, late, or in the middle of Whistler's life? *How* had they known Whistler—that is, in what capacity? A student or follower would have had a very different perspective than a fellow artist. Patrons and models would know a different Whistler from his society friends, members of his clubs, art critics, and journalists. We might trust the judgment of an art critic on the historical value of Whistler's art but be more persuaded by a student or friend on questions of personal habits.

How long after knowing Whistler did people record their impressions? How fresh were their memories? Were they writing immediately after

Whistler's death or decades later? Sooner is obviously better than later, and not just because age may dim or alter memories. Were their recollections tainted by what others had told them or by what they may have read in the interim? Then again, if rushing into print too soon, perhaps they did not allow sufficient time for reflection or check their facts as carefully as they might have done.

Did the authors confine themselves to their own experiences with Whistler, or did they inflate their narratives with secondhand anecdotes or comment on events they could not possibly have observed? When recounting events outside of their personal knowledge, what were their sources of information, and how reliable were those sources? If discussing a lengthy span of time, how did they verify the chronology, the sequence of events? It is not enough to say that Whistler told them this or that. He never tired of talking about himself, but we also know that he often exaggerated, fabricated, or omitted details, and he told different versions of the same story to different people.

Writers often repeated secondhand anecdotes about Whistler, usually to illustrate his "wit and originality." "The papers teem with Whistler stories," one journalist noted within days of the artist's death. An August 1903 magazine article titled "Whistler, the Man" consisted entirely of anecdotes, with the author unable to confirm any of them from personal experience. They had become true through mere repetition. As another journalist recalled, reflecting on the art world of the late nineteenth century, "The extraordinary prevalence of these personal stories was characteristic of the times. They were repeated and repeated."[2]

The lesson is to proceed with caution. So varied, even contradictory, are these writings that it is dangerous to rely on any single account as definitive. Whistler's life must be pieced together from multiple perspectives. Were his eyes brown, blue, or "black?" Did he have an American, English, or French accent? Did he paint with a hand palette or use a palette table? Did he scrape or rub out unwanted portions of a painting? All these assertions could be true (except for the eyes, which were definitely blue) but at different times, in different places, and under varying circumstances.

Finally, it is important to consider why people wrote. Did they wish to praise or bury Caesar? Some people wrote at the request of editors or publishers, while several journal editors chose to share their own thoughts, opinions, and experiences. A few people doubtless wrote for money, an opportunity to cash in, literally, on Whistler's name. Others likely believed that being known as an associate of the artist would enhance their own reputation or image. A select group wanted to settle old scores without fear of a withering response from Whistler.

To take each of the three types of writings in turn—the book-length reminiscences devoted to Whistler, the general memoirs, and the periodical literature—the first category clearly holds the most potential for shaping our perceptions of the artist. Seven of these books were published within a decade of Whistler's death. That could suggest a desire to exploit his name had the authors not sincerely admired either Whistler or his work, usually both.

Top of the group goes to a pair of books by Thomas R. Way, son of Thomas Way. The senior Way had rekindled Whistler's interest in lithography in the late 1870s, and thereafter father and son served as his principal printer and helped to publicize his work. Way's first volume, written in collaboration with George R. Dennis, an established writer and editor, appeared only weeks after Whistler's passing. The authors had begun writing it nearly two years earlier in hopes of demonstrating "their admiration for his genius" during Whistler's lifetime. Having missed their deadline, they dedicated the book to Whistler's sister Deborah, Lady Seymour Haden.[3]

Effusive in its praise, the book remains useful for tracing the arc of Whistler's career. Following a brief sketch of his life, Way renders judgments of Whistler's work that hold true today. He identifies "an indefinable suggestion of mystery" as the defining element of his art, whether on canvas or paper. As for the paintings, Way acknowledges the nocturnes, those "exquisite poems in color," as the most innovative work but believes the portraits to be Whistler's "highest achievement."[4]

Way then published his personal reminiscences of Whistler in 1912. The strength of this volume is its analysis of the lithography. His observations about such events as the Ruskin trial, the bankruptcy, the quarrels, and personal relationships are decidedly thinner and often based on secondhand knowledge. Way had also been drawn into the Pennells' inner circle by then because of his own disagreement with Rosalind Birnie Philip over publication of Whistler's correspondence, which the Ways had in abundance. He dedicated this book to another partner in that battle: Helen Whistler, widow of Whistler's brother William.[5]

While regretting the "lamentable dissensions" that had divided "friends who should have sunk every difference to do full honour to the artist," Way does not shy away from discussing his father's fatal falling out with Whistler. His first book maintained that public hostility toward Whistler had been overblown and unwarranted but also acknowledged that the artist could be his own worst enemy. Way echoes that ambiguous note in his reminiscences. While emphatic about Whistler's greatness as an artist, he praises the "craftsman" more often than the man.[6]

Second in importance is Otto Henry Bacher, another author who had to deal with Birnie Philip. She had objected to his reproduction of several Whistler letters when his book was published in 1908. Given the recent court verdict against the Pennells, Bacher's publisher agreed to remove them. Regardless, the book provides the best description, outside of Whistler's own correspondence, of the artist's life in Venice. "He could always adapt himself to any situation," the American-born Bacher insists, "and, at the same time, retain his dignity and personality." A few errors creep into his account, as when mistakenly saying that Whistler wielded a Japanese bamboo "wand" in Venice and misrepresenting the origins of Whistler's stinging butterfly.[7]

However, the most valuable part of Bacher's book is its description of Whistler's working habits and methods. The twenty-four-year-old Bacher hung on Whistler's every word, be it stories about his past, his estimation of other artists, or advice on etching. That Venice marked a crucial moment in the evolution of Whistler's etchings and pastels makes Bacher's recollections particularly useful. Above all, he recalls the "delicacy" of Whistler's work, especially in etching. "Delicacy seemed to him the keynote of everything," Bacher insists, "carrying more fully than anything else his use of the suggestions of tenderness, neatness, and nicety." Bacher also discusses his time with Whistler in England between 1881 and 1886. Here, unfortunately, he falls into the trap of (frequently inaccurately) describing events that he did not witness. Still, his relationship with Whistler was a close one, and the master's playful way of teasing Bacher reveals his affectionate side.[8]

Five years earlier, in 1904, Theodore Duret had produced the third-best volume of reminiscences. The French art critic and connoisseur had known Whistler since 1880, about as long as had Way and Bacher, but his relationship with the artist went unbroken by either emotional or geographical distance. Besides sitting for his portrait in 1883–84, Duret also owned several Whistler paintings and had written sympathetically and knowingly about his work for the *Gazette des Beaux Arts* and other publications. More notably, he helped persuade the French government to purchase Whistler's portrait of his mother and to bestow the Légion d'honneur on his friend. He writes in broad strokes about Whistler, and his facts are often wrong, especially for the years before he knew the artist. For instance, he describes the artist's trip to Chile as a voyage for his health and completely misses the links between Whistler's break with Frederick R. Leyland, the John Ruskin trial, and his bankruptcy. Charles Lang Freer was not impressed with the results. "So far as I have been able to learn," he told Richard Canfield, "Duret has fallen into the error of nearly all hackney art writers, and has treated his subject in an altogether too conventional way."[9]

Nonetheless, Duret steers clear of anecdotes to give us a Whistler based on personal observation. French poet and novelist Camille Mauclair, who knew Whistler in the 1890s and would also write about him, praised Duret's "careful respect for documents and disdain for gossip." His understanding of Whistler's etching and printing techniques, the effect of Venice on his etching style (though less precise on the pastels), and purposes in painting are impressive. He also fights against the image of Whistler as sinister jester. To again quote Mauclair, "Monsieur Duret restores to us the thoughtful man, whose irony was but the veil of his sensibility, whose bitter revolts sprang only from his horror of false art."[10]

Duret is at his best when describing the rise of Whistler's artistic reputation from the mid-1880s, when a new generation of younger artists "savoured his originality." Understandably, he also emphasizes the French influence on Whistler's art. He calls Whistler "an American en-Frenchised," meaning American by birth but French in his artistic and personal sympathies. This was why, Duret insists, Whistler's work was so belatedly appreciated in England and the United States. Duret felt his death deeply and begged to be a pallbearer at Whistler's funeral.[11]

Though very different in kind, Duret's book is also superior to the better-known reminiscences of Mortimer Menpes, published in the same year but only worthy of a fourth-place ranking. Australian by birth, Menpes, like Duret, first met Whistler in 1880. He was a twenty-year-old art student, and Whistler, seeing promise in the lad, agreed to teach him etching. Thereafter, despite several fallings out with the master, Menpes became a devoted follower, even asking Whistler to be godfather to his second daughter. Given this long and close relationship, his reminiscences are disappointingly uneven, and he makes many odd and clearly wrong or doubtful assertions about Whistler's private life. Consistency and chronology are not strong suits either.[12]

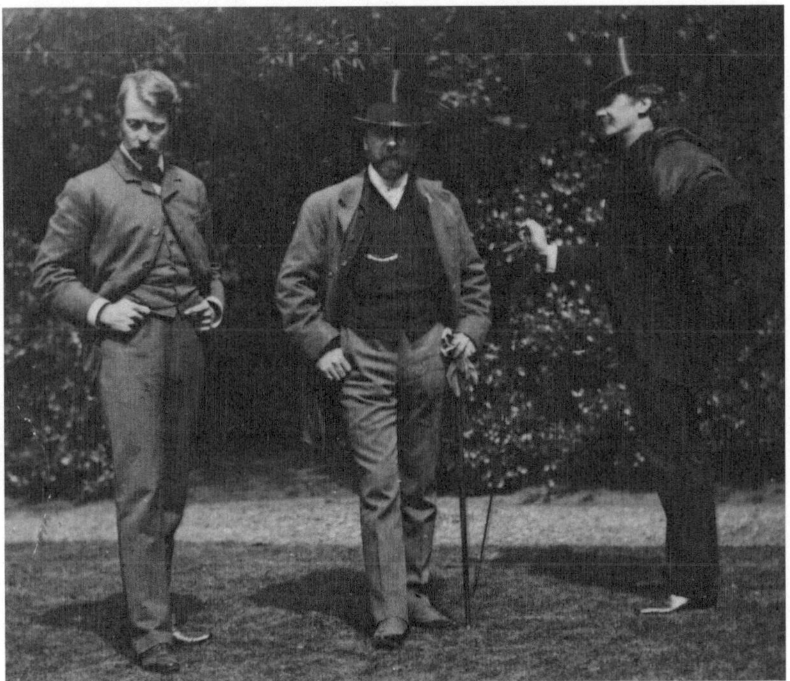

FIG. 3 Mortimer Menpes, William Merritt Chase, and James McNeill Whistler standing together outdoors, ca. 1880–1900. Photograph. LC-DIG-ds-04745, Prints and Photographs Division, Library of Congress, Washington, DC.

Menpes says quite a bit about Whistler's personal habits and conveys the artist's inscrutable nature, but some of his best examples come from anecdotes, rather than from Menpes's personal knowledge. He is better, even valuable, when sticking to such personal experiences as his sojourn with Whistler at St. Ives in 1883–84, a trip with Whistler and William Merritt Chase to Brussels in 1886, and Whistler's reign as president of the Royal Society of British Artists (fig. 3). His comments about Whistler's methods of etching, painting, and mounting of exhibitions are also strong, though he tends to exaggerate his own influence on the master. Menpes's surviving correspondence with Whistler should be used to balance and correct the reminiscences.

Arthur Jerome Eddy ranks fifth in this category of book-length reminiscences. Like Way, he published within months of Whistler's death, but whereas Way had known Whistler for a quarter century, Eddy, a Chicago-based lawyer, collector, and writer, had not met him until 1894, when

Whistler painted his portrait. The severely critical Freer deemed the book a "failure." Indeed, he dismissed both the Eddy and Way books as "utterly foolish and inadequate" and predicted that Menpes's book, which had not yet been published, would be "equally impossible." He was largely correct about Eddy.[13]

The most useful—and accurate—part of Eddy's *Recollections and Impressions* remains the description of Whistler's studio and methods of paintings in the mid-1890s. Much of the rest is either ill-conceived or based on the observations of other people. Even then, Lady Archibald Campbell, who had sat for Whistler in the 1880s, complained that Eddy had quoted her in a conversation with Whistler that "never took place at all." He also mistakenly adopted a biographical approach, which dilutes and mars what might have succeeded as a purely personal estimation of Whistler's work. He does offer an interesting chapter on Whistler as portrait painter and a discussion of what makes a "portrait," but there remain too many questionable explanations and theories about the art. Like the Pennells, Eddy offers impossibly long verbatim quotations, the result, he assures us (again as do the Pennells) of many conversations with Whistler. Unlike Way, he plays up the hostility and prejudice against Whistler in England and the United States. As though taking up the cudgels for his hero, he sprinkles the narrative with caustic, very Whistlerian, remarks about art critics.[14]

That leaves Bernhard Sickert, whose sharp commentary probably deserves a higher ranking, but he is more interested in analyzing Whistler's work and marking his place in history than in commenting on his personal life, about which he knew little in any event. Nonetheless, his perceptive comments on Whistler's personality and character have value, and he is superior even to Way in explaining the technical and stylistic dimensions of Whistler's work, other than the lithography. He had been asked by a publisher a year before Whistler's passing to write a "small book" about him, but when Whistler failed to give his blessing, Sickert thought it wise to decline the offer. By 1908, there were no barriers. As a younger brother of Walter, Sickert thought Whistler quarrelsome and given to "mountebank airs" but concedes the universal and timeless nature of his work. Sickert ranks him below Velásquez and Thomas Gainsborough as a portrait painter but judges the etchings to be masterful and believes the nocturnes capture the "awe and majesty" of night. Yet as a man, Whistler remained an enigma to Sickert, an "arrangement in black."[15]

These six witnesses are essential for any understanding of Whistler as man and artist, but numerous other people wrote about their association with him in more general memoirs. These vary widely in quality. Some people said little about him, but their brief observations have value. Others devote entire chapters to him, while many more include him only as a bit player in their lives, expressing neither affection nor resentment. Still, the best of these memoirs provide interesting and sometimes unique perspectives.

While lacking the quality of some other memoirs, those of Thomas Armstrong and Lucas (Luke) Ionides come first because they knew Whistler longest. Most other people writing about him encountered Whistler at best twenty years later. It was a matter of attrition. Few people Whistler's own age were still alive or took time to record their recollections after 1903, and those few generally provided the barest of carefully selected details. As artist Frank Short, more than twenty years Whistler's junior, admitted in 1906, "I am very bad at remembering." Other friends simply did not have much to say, were not natural writers, wished to remain discreet, or had not known Whistler well enough to share their impressions of him.[16]

Not even Armstrong and Ionides wrote until late in life, and both of their books were published posthumously. Armstrong came first, in 1912. The first half of his book is a biography of him by Lucy M. Lamont, widow of Thomas Lamont, who had been an artist friend of both Armstrong and Whistler during their student days in Paris. The second half is divided equally between Armstrong's own recollections of Whistler and George du Maurier, with additional references to Whistler in the du Maurier section. Armstrong remained close to Whistler until the mid-1880s, where his reminiscences quite correctly close, although he conveys little sense of chronology in any event.

The richest part tells of their joint struggles and pleasures as students in the 1850s and of Whistler's early years in London. Armstrong declines to say anything about Whistler's methods of painting but does comment on how he mixed his paints and prepared his canvases. While clearly fond of Whistler, Armstrong is not uncritical. He identifies the 1860s as the "highest point" of Whistler's career and regrets that his friend "never again made the same sustained efforts." He thinks Whistler's war against the Royal Academy misplaced, but that judgment may reflect Armstrong's own official position as a Companion of the Bath, an honor bestowed on him for his tenure as art director at the South Kensington Museum. He did believe Whistler never sought the early quarrels that came to define him. Observations about the 1870s come mostly secondhand, including his accounts of the Peacock Room, the Ruskin trial, and Whistler's bankruptcy.[17]

Luke Ionides first published his "memories" of Whistler in the *Transatlantic Review* only weeks before he died, in 1924. That article then became the first chapter of a book-length memoir, published the following year. Like Armstrong, Ionides was part of the "Paris gang" of the 1850s, but he grew even closer to Whistler once removed to London. His father, Greek shipping magnate Alexander Constantine Ionides, became an early patron of Whistler, and his cousin Helen married Whistler's brother William. Given this access to Whistler's life, Ionides's memoirs are disappointing. Fewer than three pages of the twelve-page chapter on Whistler deal with Paris, and while the London years are richer, including comments about Whistler's fondness for amateur theatricals and spirit-rapping and his quarrels with Alphonse Legros and Frederick R. Leyland, there are many errors of fact. The chapter ends in 1880, although Ionides provides insights concerning Whistler's interaction with other people in later sections devoted to such people as du Maurier, Dante Gabriel Rossetti, W. S. Gilbert, Richard Burton, and Charles Augustus Howell.[18]

It could be argued that George du Maurier, mentioned prominently by both Armstrong and Ionides, recorded his reminiscences of Whistler in his sensational 1894 novel *Trilby*. All the "Paris gang" is included, with Whistler famously caricatured as Joe Sibley, the "Idle Apprentice." Some Whistler biographers have even relied on the novel to flesh out their accounts of his student days. Yet Armstrong, one of du Maurier's dearest friends, judged his portrait of the old Latin Quarter overblown and "something of a fraud." Whistler certainly moved aggressively enough to have his name disassociated from the book. Far more valuable for understanding Whistler are du Maurier's published letters from the 1860s.[19]

Looking to Whistler's later years, the best general memoir is by English artist and writer William Rothenstein. Wonderfully chatty, wide-ranging, and largely accurate, Rothenstein's depiction of London's cultural scene from the 1890s through the 1930s reveals how Whistler interacted with other leading artists and literary figures of the period, including Oscar Wilde, Henri Fantin-Latour, John Singer Sargent, Algernon Swinburne, George Moore, Aubrey Beardsley, Auguste Rodin, Legros (with whom Rothenstein studied at the Slade School of Art), and Edgar Degas (the single most important artistic influence on him). Having drawn Whistler's wrath for associating with known "enemies," he was not blind to his friend's faults, but Rothenstein was also perceptive enough to appreciate his vulnerabilities and insecurities. "No one adored Whistler more than myself," he insists. "He, and his art, had counted for much in my life; and he drew from me from the first, loyalty and devotion."[20]

Yet Rothenstein knew Whistler for little more than a decade. Four other sets of memoirs, two by fellow artists and two by an art critic, offer a longer view. Albert Ludovici, the son of an artist, studied art in London and Paris before establishing himself in London during the 1870s. He knew Whistler for two decades, encountering him first through the Society of British Artists, and his detailed description of Whistler's controversial role in that society, provided in both his memoirs and a pair of articles, is the best first-person account of those tumultuous years. The memoirs also provide an insider's view of Whistler's leadership of the International Society of Sculptors, Painters and Gravers and offer insights into Whistler's paintings of the 1880s and 1890s, including his use of shadows, the importance of his varnishing, and what prices he fetched. There is a good description of Whistler's studio in Fitzroy Street and the surrounding neighborhood and an informed appraisal of the International's 1905 memorial exhibition for Whistler. Ludovici makes a few factual errors, wanders off script from time to time, and comments on some events he did not witness, but his access to Whistler makes this one of the best memoirs by the artist's associates.[21]

George Percy Jacomb-Hood, another English artist who had studied at the Slade, comments on many of the same events over the same years as Ludovici, but he is chattier, less precise, and offers fewer personal observations. He does describe Whistler in his studio, at home in the Vale (with Maud Franklin), his Paris home and garden at 110 rue du Bac, and the Royal Society of British Artists. Rather than Fitzrovia, he gives us the flavor of artist life in Chelsea when describing Whistler's interaction with his followers and such people as Edward W. Godwin, the Hadens, and Lillie Langtry.[22]

Unlike Ludovici and Jacomb-Hood, Joseph W. C. Carr, better known as J. Comyns Carr, had observed the London art scene as critic, editor, poet, and playwright beginning in 1869, a world he brought to life in a pair of engaging memoirs. The first, published in 1908, includes Whistler among the "eminent Victorians" he had known. He recounts Whistler's wit, quick mind, battles against the critics, struggle to gain recognition, Sunday breakfasts, and relationship with Charles Howell. Surprisingly, he says little about

Whistler's art, although he does defend him against accusations that his paintings betrayed a "willful neglect." "Nothing really could have been more unjust or more untrue," Carr insists. "I have often sat in his studio while he was at work, and found ample reason to be convinced that not a touch was ever set upon canvas that was not finely considered and fastidiously chosen."[23]

Neither in 1908 nor in his second book, published in 1914, did Carr say much about his personal relationship with Whistler, but he summarizes the artist's character and artistic goals succinctly and sympathetically. Childish in many ways, with a genuine belief in his own genius and originality, Carr says, Whistler was nonetheless a deeply learned and fascinating conversationalist, even if relentless in his raillery and sarcasm. Carr does not agree with Whistler's theories about the "science" of art or his quest to "challenge the supremacy of nature," but Whistler, he concludes, was better than his theories. "His instinct was sure," Carr maintains, "and within the limits he assigned to himself he moved with faultless security of taste."[24]

Finally, among the memoirs worth mentioning in detail, W. Graham Robertson wrote along the same lines and at the same time, if at lesser length and with fewer insights, as Rothenstein. This English painter and collector was another friend from the 1890s. He had his own portrait painted by Sargent but bought several of Whistler's pictures, including the portrait of Rosa Corder, which he insists was "by far the best" of the celebrated "black portraits." While scattering references to Whistler throughout the memoirs, he also devotes a substantial chapter to him. Unafraid to voice his opinions, Robertson judges much of Whistler's late work to have been poorly executed and overly praised, including the portrait of their mutual friend Robert de Montesquiou. He attributes this failure, as do some other people, to age and physical weakness, even though he calls Whistler and Sarah Bernhardt "the two most vital people" he had ever known. "Life was to them an art and a cult," Robertson declares; "they lived each moment consciously, passionately." His memoirs are diminished by attempts to reconstruct entire conversations, but he does stick largely to his own experiences and conveys something of Whistler's working methods, private life, and character, which he respected.[25]

Other book-length memoirs, while not featuring Whistler as prominently, still provide valuable information or observations. Novelist, critic, and sometimes foe George Moore, for instance, had written about Whistler and his art during the artist's life in both critical reviews and an 1886 memoir,

Confessions of a Young Man. The latter praises Whistler's work, if not the man, but insists that his art was more "classical" than "modern." "No Greek dramatist ever sought the synthesis of things more uncompromisingly than Whistler," Moore concludes. However, in a second memoir, the three-volume *Hail and Farewell*, published first between 1911 and 1914 (to be revised in 1933), Moore is more subdued. He mocks Whistler's sometimes childish behavior, and while still admiring the art and the "Ten O'Clock" lecture, he challenges one of Whistler's most unshakable beliefs: that Nature seldom sings in tune. Moore's most startling (and doubtful) assertion came in a 1916 interview, when he claimed Beatrice Whistler told him that her husband always wore square-toed shoes because of a "deformed foot."[26]

Author, poet, and diplomat James Rennell Rodd became part of London's Bohemian/Aesthetic circles in the early 1880s, when he was in his mid-twenties. His memoirs, published forty years later, detail his friendships with several people besides Whistler, most notably Wilde and Edward Burne-Jones, and Whistler's interactions with those same people. Unfortunately, his observations about Whistler are either commonplace or questionable, and confined to the artist's conception of art and methods of printing etchings, with which Rodd occasionally assisted. He also believes, unlike most observers, that Whistler showed signs of "bitterness" while residing in Paris during the early 1890s, when he was already "growing old."[27]

Edward Simmons studied in Paris after graduating from Harvard in 1874 and did not meet Whistler until moving to London. His references are scattered and few but surprisingly valuable. He remembers, for example, Whistler's reaction to the first Impressionist exhibition, to which he had declined to contribute: "Oh, I know those fellows; they are a bunch of Johnnies who have seen my earlier work." Simmons's memoir, though not published until 1922, also provides the first English translation of Whistler's important 1867 letter to Fantin-Latour, in which he regrets the influence of Gustave Courbet on his painting. Equally revealing is Simmons's experience as a member of the American jury for the 1889 Paris World's Fair. Stunned when a majority of his colleagues rejected most of the etchings submitted by Whistler, he pressed for an explanation. An influential member of the jury matter-of-factly replied that he simply "did not like Whistler, and would not vote for anything by him, anyway!"[28]

Journalist and editor Frank Harris admired Whistler as an artistic "genius" and entertaining companion beginning in the mid-1880s, but Harris's reputation for bluster and florid exaggeration cause one to distrust him.

His writings, submitted one critic of his methods, "teem with inaccuracies, guesses, contradictions." He does, indeed, exaggerate public hostility to Whistler's work and contradicts himself on several issues. Having admitted Whistler's courage as a "fighter," he goes on to accuse him of wasting his "time and talent in unworthy and absurd quarrellings. He neglected his art and allowed his gift to humanity to be diminished in order to gratify his vanity and temper."[29]

A less sensationalist journalist, Arthur Warren, knew Whistler more intimately and wrote more perceptively. While serving as a correspondent for the *Boston Herald* in the late 1880s and early 1890s, Warren became a neighbor of Whistler on both Tite Street and Cheyne Walk. His account of domestic life in Tower House—Whistler's third Tite Street home—reveals a dainty and impulsive man who freely advised him on the decoration of his flat. "My dear boy," the artist patiently explained, as he gestured here and there with his bamboo wand, "this is the whole secret—tone and line. The good colour—the right one—and the good line—the right one—cost no more than the wrong." Of their several late evening conversations, Warren relates most fully those about the sale of Whistler's portraits of Thomas Carlyle and Anna Whistler and of Whistler's attitude toward "public taste" in America and England.[30]

American journalist George W. Smalley knew Whistler for some twenty years, from the late 1870s. His memoirs, published in 1912, stress Whistler's courage and devotion to art and relate several incidents involving such people as Lillie Langtry and Benjamin Disraeli. However, Smalley, for all his claims of knowing Whistler "for many years, in many places, in many ways," failed to understand his vulnerable side. In both the memoirs and a 1903 tribute to Whistler in the *Times Literary Supplement*, Smalley falsely claims to have been at the Ruskin trial on the day Judge John Walter Huddleston rendered his verdict.[31]

Other people might have said more in their memoirs. John James Cowan, an Edinburgh businessman who bought dozens of the artist's paintings and drawings, primarily recalled the grueling experience of sitting for his portrait in the 1890s. Edward F. Benson, the English novelist and writer, speaks frequently of Whistler in his gregarious memoirs but offers nothing substantial. Especially disappointing are the reminiscences of journalist and critic Dugald Sutherland MacColl. He says little of his friendship with Whistler, even though he knew him well in the 1890s, when he wrote knowingly about his art. Art critics Sidney Colvin and Charles J. Holmes also commented on Whistler's art during his lifetime but almost ignore him in their memoirs. Likewise illustrator Harry Furniss, and Leslie Ward's cheerfully rambling account of London club life is notable only for its comments about Whistler as a subject for caricature. Print dealer Algernon Graves, who with his father aided Whistler financially from the mid-1870s into the 1890s, is scarcely better.[32]

Herbert Vivian knew Whistler principally as the founder and editor of the *Whirlwind,* to which Whistler contributed several lithographs in the 1890s. Most of his observations, published anonymously as "X" in 1923, are anecdotal or a retelling of stories (not always reliable) told him by Whistler and others. He spends several pages satirizing the bailiffs who haunted Whistler's home prior to his bankruptcy, but he took one of those stories directly, and nearly verbatim, from a 1903 magazine article. He also has Whistler living, when in Venice, with a "peasant model." A more reliable episode concerns the artist's unsuccessful efforts to have Disraeli sit for a portrait. He also offers vivid examples of Whistler's mannerisms and animated way of telling stories.[33]

Most of Whistler's fellow artists are equally disappointing. First to publish was Charles Edward Hallé, in 1909. "I do not pretend to share the excessive admiration it is now the fashion to lavish upon Whistler," he begins; "but it is impossible to deny that Whistler had great gifts which should have been recognized at the time." Unfortunately, Hallé does not follow through to suggest why Whistler had to struggle, although as the original manager of the Grosvenor Gallery, he does provide a useful sketch of its founding and operation and of the exhibition world of the 1860–70s.[34]

Chiming in many years later, John Lavery, who served as a pallbearer at Whistler's funeral, stressed the considerate and sympathetic side of his nature but dwells primarily on their connection through the International Society. Even so, far more on that subject may be learned from their correspondence. American painter Walter Gay briefly describes a "touching visit" to see Whistler shortly before the artist's death, but his principal conclusion is that it was always "a privilege to hear Whistler talk about art."[35]

Edwin A. Ward, in addition to a useful chapter about Chelsea, devotes one to Whistler, but it is a rather jumbled collection of incidents, mostly designed to illustrate Whistler's pugnacity and "merciless nature." The lengthiest account concerns Whistler's famous confrontation with William Stott of Oldham at the Hogarth Club. Ward's final judgment is that Whistler possessed "a keen knowledge of his own limitations (a very rare quality) . . .

and a profound belief that effrontery would foozle all the silly people he might meet in the shallow waters of artistic London."[36]

Some people were even more reticent. Algernon Bertram Freeman-Mitford, Lord Redesdale, a neighbor and confidant during those same years, mainly offers some admiring anecdotes about Whistler's generosity and "spirit of wit and devilry" when writing in 1916. Lillie Langtry is similarly reserved. Beyond a physical description of Whistler and the so-called White House—his first home in Tite Street—the larger part of her "memories" of him come in a long quotation from an article (as much about her as Whistler) by George Smalley. Louise Jopling became "great friends" with Whistler in the mid-1870s and, having urged him to marry the widowed Beatrice Godwin, was among the select group to attend their wedding, but her recollections, which end with 1887, are frustratingly disjointed. She mentions her relationship with Whistler in mere snippets, often in the form of brief quotations from his letters to her. Jopling does, however, correctly state that Whistler had blue eyes.[37]

Harrison S. Morris and Archibald S. Hartrick did not publish their memoirs until the 1930s. Morris, as the managing director of the Pennsylvania Academy of Fine Art, wrote chiefly of his efforts to acquire Whistler's paintings for the museum or exhibitions. He recounts a variety of stories told him by Whistler, whom he first met in the early 1890s, but is more interesting when relating conversations he had with other people, especially William Merritt Chase, about the artist. Hartrick, an accomplished illustrator and painter who studied with Legros at the Slade and in Paris at the Académie Julian, said of Whistler, "He had the quickest brain of anyone I have ever known, and he used it like an artist to be perfectly charming or perfectly impossible." Most of the anecdotes he tells are secondhand, with the most reliable part of his memoir being the operations of the International, to which he belonged. He describes Whistler's funeral in some detail, including the "disturbance" caused by the arrival of Maud Franklin, though it is unlikely she attended.[38]

Among nonartists, the memoirs of two American women are disappointingly thin. Novelist and critic Gertrude Franklin Horn Atherton knew Whistler socially in the late 1880s, and her comments about him, published in the 1930s, are restricted to those occasions. He was constantly "buzzing," she says, "like a mosquito ready to pounce." Her most useful observations are about his relationship with Mrs. Whistler, and of how skillfully Beatrice managed him at difficult moments. It is hard to say when Louisine Waldron

Havemeyer wrote her memoirs (despite the title, *Sixteen to Sixty*), but they were not published until 1961, more than thirty years after her death. In any event, her memory clearly failed her on several issues. She claims to have first met Whistler in her teens, when she bought five Venice pastels from him, but the year was 1882, when she was in her mid-twenties. She was also a friend of Charles Freer and recounts some of her conversations with him about Whistler. Havemeyer only criticizes Whistler for abandoning Maud to marry Beatrice.[39]

Far more interesting and detailed is the novelist Julian Hawthorne, son of Nathaniel Hawthorne. Julian and his wife May ("Minnie") cultivated a wide circle of friends when resident at Twickenham from 1874 to 1882. Minnie even published an excellent article describing her visit to Whistler's studio in 1881. Julian, whom Whistler came to know through the Arts Club, published an article ten years later that recounted their friendship and praised Whistler's latest publication, *The Baronet and the Butterfly*. At that time, he described Whistler as a "champion of art" for his legal stand against William Eden, a compliment that did not go unnoticed by Whistler. He gushed over the article in a letter to William Heinemann, calling it "really delightful!—beautifully done!—So crisp and bright, and in such perfect taste! The prettiest piece of work you have seen for a long time."[40]

In his memoirs, published in 1928, Hawthorne suggests that Whistler never painted "so whole-heartedly" after publishing the *Gentle Art*. That said, he also calls him "sweet at the core, and free from personal jealousies, though jealous of art." He gives a good account of Whistler as he painted a portrait of Valerie Meux and relates several anecdotes, though only a few come firsthand. In 1934, shortly before his own death, Hawthorne wrote an article that contained much of the same material but added that he always thought Whistler a lonely person. Like many a solitary genius, he suggests, "Whistler never lacked both friends and foes, but he had no intimates." However, his most telling observation, based on what he had read or heard, was how very much changed Whistler was in his later years. Instead of the "charming and vivid and, withal, gentle-hearted companion of long ago," the artist seemed "to have lost his mental equilibrium" and "protected himself with superciliousness which, from a pose, became a habit."[41]

Several targets of Whistler's superciliousness might well have endorsed Hawthorne's assessment, for not everyone recalled Whistler fondly. Irish-born painter Henry Jones Thaddeus first met Whistler in 1886 at a supper party given by Menpes, but unlike his host, he never "worshipped at the shrine of the 'White Lock.'" He recalls Whistler as a spiteful little man full of "venom and hatred." American writer and critic Logan Pearsall Smith was somewhat more generous. He had known Whistler in Paris, where he sometimes stood in for Robert de Montesquiou when Whistler was painting the count's portrait in 1891. Smith's account of that experience has value, and he does acknowledge that Whistler's "taste in matters of art was infallible and exquisite." He even finds his "mockery of the official side of English institutions . . . extremely amusing." However, Smith deplores the "loud bar-frequenting American" side of Whistler, who was overly fond of "publicity and self-advertisement" and ultimately not "deserving of much estimation."[42]

Frederick Wedmore also had doubts about Whistler but cloaked them in the manner of Tom Way. A prolific art critic for a variety of publications, he had perhaps reviewed Whistler's work more than any single critic from the 1870s through the 1890s. His first meeting with the artist had been an uncomfortable, even "nasty," experience, for Whistler, knowing Wedmore to be a critic, made himself purposely disagreeable. He grew less waspish in time, but Wedmore would remain a "Podsnap" to Whistler and was one of the critics he purposely misquoted in his celebrated 1883 catalogue of Venice etchings. Wedmore says little about this in his memoirs or in an excellent 1904 essay about Whistler's place in history, for despite the friction, he continued to think highly of the work. Whistler, he concludes, rivaled the best of his contemporaries in his "complete acceptance of Modern Life, of the modern world."[43]

Besides these volumes of memoirs and reminiscences, some Whistler associates wrote more directly about him in periodicals. The earliest articles, coming in 1903–4, were hastily written memorials or extended obituaries, but a few are quite thoughtful, and they continued to appear until the last of Whistler's contemporaries had passed away. Indeed, it was a rare magazine that failed to publish something about Whistler during those decades. *Century Magazine* led the way with seven pieces between 1906 and 1923, but nearly thirty other periodicals carried at least one article.

One of the people who knew Whistler longest was among the first to share his recollections in this briefer format. Valentine Prinsep had known Whistler since his earliest days in London, when they both enjoyed breezy bohemian gatherings at Little Holland House, the home of Val's mother, in Melbury Road. Their paths diverged about 1870, and in 1884, Prinsep became the son-in-law of Frederick R. Leyland. There is no telling how that influenced his estimation of Whistler as a person, but Prinsep recounted none of the happy days when writing in 1903. He chose, instead, to dwell on Whistler's art, and he was not uncritical. A half-dozen or so "first-rate" pictures, he proposes, hardly qualified Whistler as a master. Whistler was either too impatient or too disdainful of concentrated study to master the art of painting, Prinsep insists. His was a shallow sort of art, despite Whistler's "true feeling" for color and tone. His needless quarrels, used to keep his name before the public, only marred a genuinely "warm heart and the truest artistic temperament." Prinsep could but hope Whistler would be forgiven by future generations.[44]

Marion H. A. Spielmann offered one of the most incisive early accounts of Whistler's career. Beginning as an art critic for the *Graphic, Pall Mall Gazette,* and other newspapers in the early 1880s, he eventually served as editor of the *Magazine of Art* from 1887 to 1904. Spielmann was a powerful voice in Victorian art criticism and understood Whistler as well as any of his contemporaries. His two-part article, published in the autumn of 1903, shows a good feel for Whistler's body of work and his place in history. Equally, he refuses to become bogged down in retelling old anecdotes. In fact, Spielmann takes pains to show that some of the stories about Whistler either originated as tales about other people or had been badly misinterpreted.

Spielmann shared Whistler's respect for the Old Masters but praises him for pursing "a path . . . which they had never explored." It was this respect for Western tradition and his adoption of "Japanese impressionism" that lent Whistler's pictures their charm. He created "renderings that *translated* but never merely *imitated,* and appreciated the sentiment and poetry of colour and effect for their own sake." As an example, Spielmann offers the entirely plausible possibility that Whistler's notorious *Nocturne in Black and Gold: The Falling Rocket* owed as much to Claude Lorrain's etchings of fireworks as to Utagawa Hiroshige's *A Night Festival at Yeddo* (better known as *Fireworks over Ryōgoku Bridge*). The two defining traits of Whistler as an artist were his "versatility" and the fact that "whatever the style, subject, or medium," he operated as a "decorator," with composition and pattern uppermost in mind.[45]

Spielmann expresses himself equally well on personal matters. He found Whistler's humor, of which he had sometimes been the target, "somewhat Mephistophelian," meant to "sting" rather than "tickle." The quarrels his "wit" sometimes provoked remained an unnecessary blemish on his image as an artist, but Spielmann has a more cynical view of this issue than someone like Rothenstein. "Though he was perhaps a little spoilt by the unctuous worship of his blind devotees," Spielmann submits, "he was . . . endowed with too much common sense to accept their adoration otherwise than as the homage of persons who were instruments convenient enough for the spread of his artistic tenets and dogmas." Spielmann fails to mention that he was the only journalist to witness and report firsthand on Whistler's wedding but does provide a lengthy and revealing discussion of Whistler's contentious relationship with the Royal Academy.[46]

Nearly as good at presenting both man and artist was Robert Goodloe Harper Pennington. His friendship with Whistler, like Bacher's, began in Venice and continued in London until his return to the United States in the mid-1880s. However, unlike Bacher, Pennington stayed in touch with Whistler until just a few months before the master's death. He was also the only one of Whistler's followers to write about him during his lifetime. That article, which described Pennington's time in Venice, sat on the publisher's desk for nearly two years before appearing in *Century Magazine*, reportedly because it included a caricature of Whistler, drawn by Pennington, that the editor feared would incite the artist's wrath. "Harrpurrr," as Whistler delighted in calling him, knew better, and when it was finally published in 1902 Pennington sent him a copy of the article. "You cannot realize, of course," he assured Whistler in an accompanying letter, "how much you did for me, or how grateful I shall always be. The printed words are part of my effort to express myself with gratitude."[47]

Pennington continued to pay homage in two more articles, one each in 1904 and 1910. The 1904 piece is mainly a critique of Menpes's book, too much of which, Pennington says, was based on "trivial gossip," filled with "dubious stories," and containing little of "what Whistler really taught him." Going beyond the year in Venice, Pennington stresses Whistler's "radical" approach to painting, pointing especially to the portraits. He dwells on the "chemistry" of the paintings and Whistler's "exactitude of tone." He regrets that those tones were often so dark that in time some pictures might become "almost indistinguishable." Yet as someone who savored the "gaiety and sparkle of modern life," Whistler could not have painted otherwise: "If he chose low tones it was from a conviction that they more truly represented what we really see than do color schemes which exhaust the resources of the palette." For that reason, Pennington concludes, as well as for the "decorative" quality of his work, Whistler's paintings were superior to those of both Turner and the Impressionists.[48]

Pennington repeats much of this in his fuller and more personal reflections of 1910, which include more information about Whistler's diet, health, and the furnishings and decoration of his homes. However, his main theme, as it would be for many of Whistler's friends, is how nobly the master battled the artistic establishment. The adversity he faced fully justified Whistler's "quick, stinging tongue, and his uncompromising attitude," which, Pennington points out, may have left his own generation in "mortal terror" of him but endeared him to younger artists.[49]

While Pennington was only a follower, no one did more to promote Whistler's career after 1880 than David Croal Thomson. First as art dealer for the London branch of Boussod, Valadon & Cie, then as editor of London's *Art Journal,* Thomson praised and explained Whistler's work. His brief tribute in 1903 attempts the same. Rather than adding to the anecdotes about Whistler's "wit and ready power of repartee," Thomson emphasizes his "extraordinary powers of concentration when painting" and "most wonderful perseverance when in pursuit of some effect of tone or colour either in flesh or landscape." He also describes his own roles in bringing public attention to the Carlyle portrait, convincing the French government to purchase "The Mother," and, perhaps most importantly, organizing the 1892 retrospective of Whistler's work, which more than any single event in his lifetime solidified the artist's reputation as a modern master.[50]

Then there is Professor Van Dyke's *Ladies' Home Journal* article, which proved to be surprisingly revealing. Whistler "objected to the obvious and the grandiose," he says, which in itself suggests "the truer and nobler side of the man." He was a man of "taste," as proved by the selection, design, and composition of all his work. Writing later in a pair of books about art, Van Dyke stressed the "subtility" of Whistler's work, a quality made even more impressive and valuable by the "extreme simplicity of his compositions."[51]

Among Whistler's fellow artists, the tribute of English-born but American-reared George H. Boughton provides a cogent account of his nearly forty-year association with Whistler. They first met in the early 1860s, after both had moved from Paris to London. Like other people who appreciated Whistler's complex personality, Boughton describes the "various Whistlers" he had known. He vividly recalls the excitement inspired by *At the Piano,* the first Whistler painting to be exhibited at the Royal Academy, and the "succès d'exécration" of *The White Girl.* He was struck as well by the early Japanese-inspired paintings, especially *The Balcony,* although Whistler confessed to him that, over time, he had come to think of it as "too much elaborated; not *nearly simple* enough." He claims to have been the person who urged Whistler to sue John Ruskin for libel and remarks in jest that Whistler might have been president of the Royal Academy had he only behaved himself and at least pretended to be "serious and dignified enough" for the role. One thing was certain, Boughton assures us: "I can't remember a time when his affairs and his doings and sayings did not fill the artistic air."[52]

Alfred A. Baldry, a close friend of Boughton, had like Robertson studied with Albert Moore and so had always appreciated Whistler's art. He also became a prolific writer on art, with books about Joshua Reynolds and Velásquez and such contemporaries as Marcus Stone, Hubert von Herkomer, and John Everett Millais. In 1908, he published *Three Great Modern Painters: Leighton, Burne-Jones and Whistler,* but his most personal and useful assessment of Whistler came in the autumn of 1903, as part of a collection of articles on the artist in *Studio* magazine. Like all who knew Whistler well, Baldry discounts the significance of his self-advertising. A man of lesser ability might have been trying to conceal his lack of talent and ability, but Whistler's genius was never in question. His "rare decorative instinct" allowed him to recognize the "artistic possibilities of . . . the common places of the modern world" and embrace the "beauty of everyday life." The scope of his work was narrow, Baldry concedes, but in an echo of Comyns Carr he insists that within the self-imposed limitations of his art, Whistler could never be duplicated.[53]

In the mid-1880s, Whistler had used the Royal Society of British Artists (made "royal" under his leadership) to challenge the authority of the RA. One of his staunchest supporters in that crusade was Sidney Starr, a painter whose own work showed marked "Whistlerian" elements. "No artist of our time, leaving us, has been the subject of so much writing, so many recollections," Starr points out. "Never has unliterary painting caused so much literature." It was a clever remark, which is the very word Starr uses to describe his friend's paintings. Whistler's critics had also called him "clever," Starr concedes, though not (as in the case of Prinsep) as a compliment. Writing in 1908, Starr fondly recalls numerous anecdotes and incidents, most of them either from personal experience or told him by Whistler, that illustrate Whistler's artistic convictions. Starr is especially good on Whistler's presidency of the RSBA and his own role in helping to sell *Nocturne in Black and Gold* in 1892. Like Hawthorne, Starr portrays Whistler as a sensitive and often lonely man.[54]

Another artist friend, this one an American, Edmund H. Wuerpel, published three article-length reminiscences of Whistler. The first one, part of the rush of 1904, dwells on his "friend"; the next two, published in 1934, the centenary of Whistler's birth, consider "the man." Himself brilliant and multitalented, Wuerpel came late to art, having first studied engineering in his native St. Louis. He also became known for his work with dental orthodontics. However, he devoted the larger part of his life to art, as both painter and longtime lecturer on art at Washington University, where he had himself studied in his early twenties. While in Paris to continue his studies at the Académie Julian and the École des Beaux-Arts in 1892–94, Wuerpel grew close to Whistler and Beatrice before returning to the United States. Thereafter, he corresponded with Whistler into the spring of 1903. As a painter, Wuerpel's limited "tonalist" palette and atmospheric landscapes show Whistler's influence.

Wuerpel's two late essays emphasize Whistler's kindness, generosity, and "sensitive nature." Whether in his studio or at 110 rue du Bac, at private dinners or Sunday breakfasts, reminiscing about the past or discussing the Old Masters, prowling the Louvre or inspecting a private collection of paintings, Wuerpel always felt at ease in his company. He dwells on Whistler's childlike qualities and the delight he took in his own work but also offers many details about Whistler's studio methods and painting techniques. Like Atherton, he also describes Beatrice's calming influence on this highly energetic, "worried, and irresponsible little man" and how much he depended on her.[55]

Although Léonce Bénédite, director of the Musée du Luxembourg between 1892 and 1916, only corresponded with Whistler during the last two years of the artist's life, his series of four articles on Whistler's art, published in 1905, are worth mentioning. He and Duret had been trying to arrange an exhibition of Whistler's work at the Luxembourg when Whistler died. An art historian and prolific writer in addition to being a curator, Bénédite does an excellent job, in the manner of Way, Duret, and Bernhard Sickert, of placing Whistler's work (primarily his paintings) in context and tracing the early stages of his developing style. He refers often to Duret's book, but his perspective is most fully shaped by Whistler's correspondence with Fantin-Latour. Bénédite was the first person to quote extensively from that correspondence, later to be purchased by the Pennells, and it is the most rewarding part of his study. Regrettably, when the correspondence ends, so does the value of his articles, as he glosses over the last two decades of Whistler's life in a mere three pages. Still, Bénédite stands with Duret as a staunch early French advocate and interpreter of Whistler's art.[56]

Another early assessment of the art came from Royal Cortissoz. He did not meet the artist until the 1890s, but as art editor of the *New York Tribune* for more than half a century, beginning in 1891, Cortissoz would help shape the artistic legacy of Whistler. He was not impressed with the man, whom he considered unnecessarily rude, and he had grave concerns about his ability as a painter. Like Prinsep, he believed Whistler lacked the necessary training to be a great painter. He was much better as an etcher, but even there only when considered within "his own sphere." A master of delicate patterns and arrangements, Whistler's lack of "anatomical knowledge" meant that he could never surpass Rembrandt or even Seymour Haden in that field. Only his "unique" style salvaged his reputation as an etcher, although that did not deter Cortissoz from being a lifelong advocate of Whistler's work.[57]

Naturally, some people aired old grudges. Henry Quilter, as both artist and art critic, had praised much of Whistler's work, especially the etchings and pastels. However, Quilter had also snatched up Whistler's beloved White House during the bankruptcy sale, subsequently altering its exterior. Whistler never forgave "Arry," whom he repeatedly ridiculed in the press. Quilter never forgave Whistler, either, despite claims to the contrary. His "Memory and a Criticism" of 1903 reviews their personal history from his perspective and portrays Whistler as the loser in a senseless quarrel. He then explains why Whistler could "not be ranked with the greatest painters" and enumerates "the chief defects and excellencies of his art." Ultimately, Quilter, who incidentally admired John Ruskin, proposes that Whistler failed because he valued "social ambitions" more than art. "He had grown impatient, possibly incapable of prolonged effort, of quietly considered work," Quilter concludes; "he was intoxicated with the sense of power."[58]

Frederick Keppel, a New York publisher and print dealer who became an important collector and agent of Whistler prints, could sympathize with Quilter. He first described his falling out with Whistler in a 1904 article, but when, he says, the magazine's editor "suppressed" important parts of the story, Keppel followed up with a pamphlet, published at his own expense. Calling it *The Gentle Art of Resenting Injuries,* and decorating the cover with Whistler's stinging butterflies, Keppel clearly intended to mock the artist. The pamphlet concludes with a bitingly satiric poem.[59]

Yet Keppel continued to collect and sell Whistler prints. In 1905, he even commissioned a student of Augustus Saint-Gaudens to sculpt a relief bust of Whistler for the facade of his New York gallery, to be paired with one of Rembrandt. Two years later, apparently satisfied that he had finally bested the dead artist, Keppel published a more balanced article about him. This time, he offered an excellent summary of Whistler's development as an etcher, in which he submits that Whistler's "refractory bent" in fact aided his growth as an artist by causing him to rebel against "rules and methods which were not of his own making." Not that Keppel had entirely relinquished his self-righteous anger. Whistler's love of quarrels, he maintains, even with so "peaceable a person" as himself, explained why it took so many years for him to receive due recognition as a great artist.[60]

A friend from the 1890s, Welsh-born Symbolist poet, writer, and critic Arthur Symons, did not remember Whistler that way, but then he wrote largely of Whistler's art. He became one of many poets, including Swinburne, Wilde, and Stéphane Mallarmé, captivated by Whistler, and his several essays and articles about him were nothing short of brilliant. He attempted no summary of the life and did not say much about his own interactions with the man but captured Whistler's character and personality sublimely, and no one has stated his purposes and philosophy more directly or succinctly. "His whole life was a devotion to art," Symons declares. He "talked of art, certainly for art's sake, with the passionate reverence of the lover." Symons knew Whistler only when the artist's age had begun to show. Even so, he insists, "I never saw any one so feverishly alive as this little, old man." He was enthralled by how exquisitely Whistler explained himself in the "Ten O'Clock" and *Gentle Art*, but then Whistler's art was also poetry, "never . . . a statement, always an evocation."[61]

Several people who knew Whistler only briefly or under very particular circumstances help flesh out smaller, usually personal, parts of his life. The best-known and one of the most valuable of these accounts comes from William Merritt Chase. The American artist spent several weeks during the summer and autumn of 1885 with Whistler and made numerous shrewd observations during his sometimes tumultuous visit. At one moment all attention and courtesy, Whistler would suddenly unleash his "biting tongue." "It was impossible," Chase complains of the Jekyll and Hyde atmosphere, "for any man to live long in harmony with him." At the same time, Chase recognizes the posturing behind many of Whistler's antics. Like all close observers of the artist, Chase credits him with having "two distinct

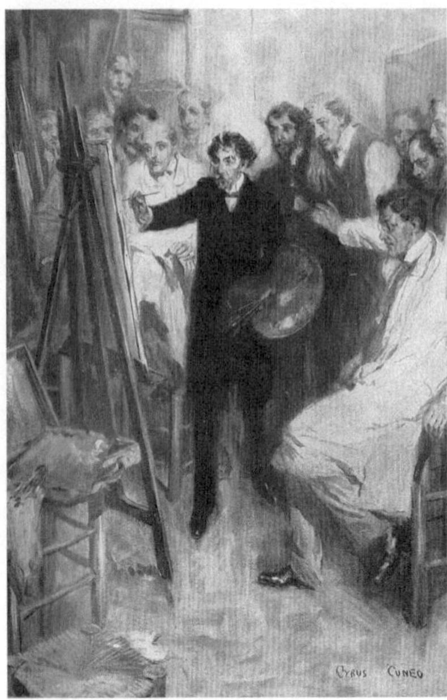

FIG. 4 Cyrus Cuneo (1879–1916), Whistler with students at the Académie Carmen, ca. 1898. *Century Magazine* (November 1906). Photo: University of Arkansas Libraries, Fayetteville, AR.

and striking personalities." One of them, the fop and vain cynic, he offered for public display. The other, the serious and tireless artist, he reserved for the studio. "He took no one and nothing seriously," Chase insists; "he was sublimely egotistical, and seemed to delight in parading his conceit," all "to amuse himself at the expense of others."[62]

Yet Chase's understanding of Whistler was nearly as schizophrenic as the artist's behavior. At times, he seems sympathetic and ready to accept the biting Whistler, even as he exposes that less pleasant side. He also underappreciated Whistler as a painter. Much like Prinsep and Quilter, he believed Whistler had not taken the study of painting seriously and had never absorbed creditable academic training. Whistler was brilliant at conveying "the rare interpretations that his wonderful imagination pictured for him," but of "detail and construction he knew little and cared less." Chase could only trust that his "*real self*," the Whistler of the studio, would be remembered when all the "eccentricities" had been forgotten.[63]

Several people who had known Whistler only in the United States shared their recollections. Two West Point classmates, Thomas Wilson and Henry M. Lazelle, wrote extremely short (three and one pages, respectively) accounts of those formative years, with Wilson's article being published toward the end of Whistler's life.[64] More usefully, John Ross Key recalled working with Whistler at the US Coast and Geodetic Survey. His description of Whistler's initiation in etching is valuable, as are his comments about the artist's early bohemian life, even though his insistence that Whistler "had no bad habits, and did not smoke" is demonstrably false. Key is closer to the mark when he tells us, "He was the most indolent young man I have ever known." The recollections of Adolphus Lindenkohl, Whistler's only other coworker at the survey to speak about him, came secondhand, in interviews with the authors of two articles published in 1898 and 1904, respectively.[65]

Another narrow, though more important, perspective comes from several students—two men and two women—who attended the Académie Carmen, the Paris atelier Whistler conducted in the 1890s. All of these artists recognized the uniqueness of their training under Whistler, although all, too, mention how seldom he visited the school and the vagueness, save for the memorable "Propositions," of his personal instruction. One student, Cyrus Cuneo, illustrated his article with four nice drawings of the atelier's interior and of Whistler in action as teacher (fig. 4). One of the women, Isa Glenn, reproduced copies of her correspondence with Whistler, to whom she was distantly related.[66]

Edith Shaw did not write about her visits to Whistler's studio at 8 Fitzroy Street until 1968, but she claimed to recall vividly the years between 1898 and 1902 when, starting at age twelve, she haunted the place as studio rat and model. Her mother owned the studio, which allowed Edith to observe Whistler's routines, habits, and interactions with people, especially children, during a time when he used several prepubescent and adolescent girls as models. Edith posed for *Little Lady Edith of Eden* and was to have been the model for *Little Lady Sophie of Soho* until she fell ill and her younger sister—Sophie—became the subject. She also describes how Whistler discovered another young model for *Brown and Gold: Lillie 'In Our Alley!'* when looking for subjects, as was his habit, in the side streets near the studio.[67]

While not herself a model, Maria Victoria Torrilhon Buel, wife of Clarence Clough Buel, longtime editor of *Century Magazine*, spent a day in 1899 visiting Whistler's Paris studio in rue Notre Dame des Champs and his home in rue du Bac. She gives yet another account of his studio methods and the undisguised delight he took in his own work. Buel was not impressed with the house but left believing that the "real Whistler" was a "kind, genial, courteous, humanly sorrowful and sorrowing man of genius."[68]

Another brief encounter with the artist produced a different reaction. In 1915, American artist and journalist Henry Russell Wray described how he first met Whistler, like Buel, in his Paris studio in 1899, but he left seeing "more than one side of the many-sided" artist. Initially disillusioned and a bit disgusted with Whistler's exaggerated English accent and "ladylike appearance," he went away vowing never again to see the "affected little creature." However, when chance brought them together a few days later over cocktails, Wray acknowledged that he admired Whistler's portrait of his mother. Whistler's eyes grew moist, and as the cocktails began to take effect he became downright chummy. Wray, as he recounts the story, then began to tease the artist in ways that allowed him to boast of getting the better of an inebriated Whistler.[69]

In the end, the most truthful of these voices are the ones that appreciate Whistler's complexity. No one of them captured him completely, which is how he would have wanted it. His sister-in-law Rosalind Birnie Philip decided as early as 1908 that "the real Whistler in time I suppose will entirely be lost in the multitude of books produced by his intimate friends and apprentices!" She took satisfaction, though, in knowing how Whistler wished to be remembered. "The work," she understood, "will remain which is a great consolation."[70]

CHAPTER 3

Family Ties

The voices of friends are not enough to secure a person's legacy. Surviving family and loved ones also influence reputations, for good or ill. At the very least, they testify to a person's virtues and accomplishments, to what was achieved or left undone. They possess knowledge and can recount experiences buried deep in the past, things that might be revelatory if they choose to speak of them. To echo Whistler's own words, written in 1887, "It is almost hopeless to 'begin back' and say all the things that are to be said! . . . Only there are lots to be told—and I have been so much in it all!!"[1]

Most of the people closest to Whistler, including his mother, wife, and last surviving brother, died before him. His sister followed five years later. Some people thought they saw Joanna Hiffernan, Whistler's mistress/muse of the 1860s, at his funeral, but the "White Girl" had died of bronchitis in 1886, aged forty-four. That left only three Whistler intimates to nurture his legacy: Maud Franklin, who replaced Jo in his affections; his son Charles James Whistler Hanson; and his sister-in-law Rosalind Birnie Philip. Their lives took very different paths after 1903, as did their roles as keepers of the flame. Regardless, beyond satisfying a natural curiosity about their fates, those separate paths tell us something about Whistler's legacy.

Maud Franklin lived with Whistler longer than any other woman, save his mother and sister (fig. 5). She first posed for him around 1871, at age

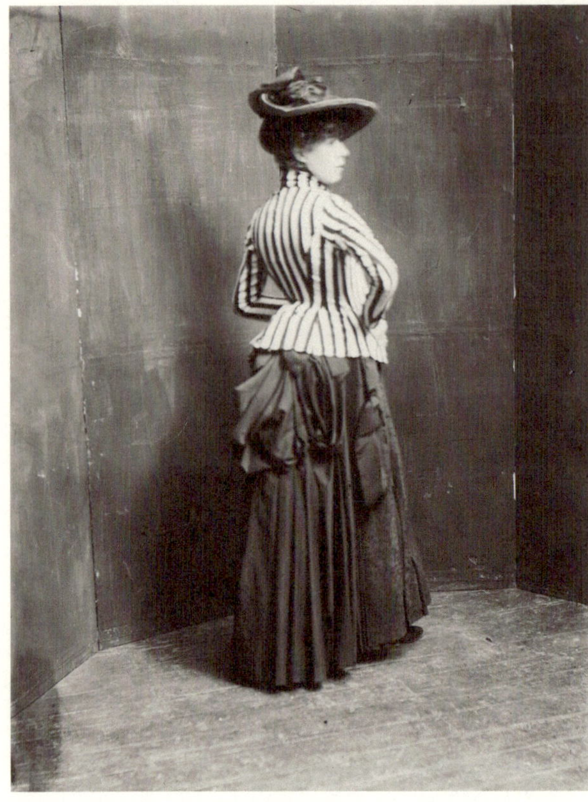

FIG. 5 Maud Franklin, ca. 1880–1900. Photograph. LC-DIG-ds-14209, Prints and Photographs Division, Library of Congress, Washington, DC.

fourteen. She had the same Titian-red hair as Jo and, like Jo, cooked for him, presided over his Sunday breakfasts, kept track of his neglected correspondence, and paid overdue bills. She also bore him two children. The first, named Ione, was born around 1876; a sister, Maud, came in 1879. Both girls were put out to foster parents, though who made that decision is unknown. Their mother became known as Maud Whistler to tradespeople in Chelsea and often signed her correspondence in that way, despite no evidence of a legal marriage. Maud also showed artistic talent, even exhibiting small oils at the Grosvenor Gallery and with the Royal Society of British Artists under the name Clifton Lin in the mid-1880s.[2]

It all ended in August 1888, when Whistler suddenly married Beatrice Godwin. Maud probably saw it coming. She had been visiting in and around Paris since at least June, possibly January, and felt the distance, both physical and emotional, that had grown between her and Whistler. Months before the wedding, she spoke of "separation griefs" to friends. Whistler had treated her shabbily on occasion, going as far as to deposit her in a London hotel during her second pregnancy so that he could concentrate on his battle against John Ruskin. Few people knew about that episode, but even some close friends, recognizing her years of "self-sacrifice" with Whistler, condemned his "unpardonable" conduct in dispensing with her altogether.[3]

At sixes and sevens, Maud found sanctuary with Whistler's longtime Paris dealer George A. Lucas. He had always been fond of Maud. She had dined at his Paris house in the rue de l'Arc de Triomphe during the early summer of 1888 and was at his summer home in Boissise when Whistler married. Lucas visited her on successive days following their return from Boissise, and she dined at his home three times the following week. When she decided to remain in France, he treated her like a daughter and thought of her as such until his death in 1909.[4]

The warmth and companionship shown by Lucas and his family soon put Maud right. Where she first lived is uncertain. She had stayed at 12 rue Jacob in the spring of 1888, on a street where Whistler had once lived during his student days. That was a good distance from Lucas, but she remained in close contact with her benefactor. She and Lucas dined together (including breakfasts and luncheons) or visited each other at least eighty times in 1889–90, and she spent the summer of 1890 in Boissise. To ease her further into a new life, Lucas introduced Maud to numerous artists, dealers, and critics. She already knew some of them, such as the American critic and journalist Theodore Child and the American artist William Turner Dannot, through Whistler, but Lucas expanded this circle to include American artists William Baptiste Baird and Ogden P. Wood.[5]

As their friendship acquired a comfortable informality, Lucas met at least one of Maud's sisters and a niece. He occasionally loaned her money and presented her with gifts, including three pieces of Chapelet flambé and a drawing by Adolf-Karl Sandoz. They stood together as godparents to the granddaughter of Lucas's longtime mistress Octave-Josephine Marchand. Appreciating all that Lucas did for her, Maud entrusted him with Whistler etchings in her possession. He sold many of them on Maud's behalf while keeping others for his own extensive collection of Whistler prints. Maud also helped organize his art collection, suggested potential clients, delivered messages, collected payments, arranged sales, and even recommended a gentle dentist. One new client was Mary Cassatt. Cassatt's regular dealer was Paul Durand-Ruel, and while she considered Lucas "a dear old man, &

so upright," she knew Maud through Whistler and wished to help her. She may even have paid Maud to model.[6]

Maud's association with so many of Whistler's friends and acquaintances raised the prickly question of how they should now treat the pair, but Maud was too sympathetic a figure to have suffered their displeasure. Some, like Cassatt, admired Whistler as an artist but thought him sometimes childish. Theodore Child, a close friend of Lucas for over a decade, had been friendly with Whistler, too, and they appear to have remained on good terms until Child's death in 1892. Lucas, who had known Whistler since the 1850s and had been a friend of his brother George, continued to collect his etchings, but he met the artist only twice after the break with Maud. Some evidence suggests that Whistler had angered him two years earlier by refusing to sign an etching, but it is just as likely that their friendship grew muted once Lucas became Maud's chief benefactor.[7]

Maud's feelings toward Whistler were similarly complex. She felt initially as though Whistler had "burned all the joy and brightness out of her life." It was not at all like his break with Jo Hiffernan, with whom he remained on good terms. In that sense, Maud's sale of his etchings could be seen as retribution. The Pennells, though somewhat sympathetic, noted that Maud had both a "high temper" and "the jealousy that goes with it." One report says that when Whistler and Beatrice moved to Paris in 1892, she took an apartment near their home in the rue du Bac, supposedly to annoy them, but there is no evidence of such spite.[8]

Regardless, Maud's attitude toward Whistler softened over time. When his health began to fail in 1903, Theodore Duret, another mutual friend, kept Maud and Lucas advised of his condition. She was on the French coast when Whistler died but there is no record of her reaction. It is unlikely that she joined the mourners in London, despite reported sightings of her. Still, whatever residue of resentment Maud may have felt gradually dissolved. She shared information about Whistler with Duret and Mortimer Menpes, who were writing their reminiscences of the artist, but would say nothing about her life with him. She avoided the Pennells when they approached her and would not communicate directly even with Duret. Using Lucas as a go-between, she told the art dealer, "I should be glad if you will fill in the answers to the questions so that I should not appear in any way in the matter, you understand what I mean, I hope & believe."[9]

Indeed, Maud had an entirely new life by 1903. She married a wealthy American, John A. Little of New Jersey, seemingly in the mid-1890s. The date is hard to determine, but she and Little had a son—John Franklin Little, called Jack—who would be old enough to serve in World War I. Her husband, who made his fortune in banking and railroads, could afford both a home in Paris and a château, "La Picholiere," complete with stables, at Yport on the Normandy coast. It was there that Maud learned of Whistler's death. The Paris home was at 43 rue de Chazelles, less than a half mile northeast of the Arc de Triomphe and very near Lucas's apartment.

It is unclear if Ione, her one surviving daughter, ever joined Maud, either before or after her marriage, but the girl would have been about twelve in 1888, and it is difficult to imagine Maud abandoning her. When Ione married her cousin Warwick A. Tyler in 1899 and moved to Salt Lake City, Maud agonized over her future. Not only did the miles between them seem incomprehensible, but Ione had also been pregnant at the time. Maud understood that their relocation offered Warwick a financial opportunity the couple could not ignore, but she still hoped the separation would be temporary. "You must leave that outlandish place as soon as possible," she advised her daughter. "It is absurd that you two should be there away from all who love you in order to earn so little."[10]

Maud compensated for her loss by keeping busy. She took up photography, which would have intrigued Whistler. The new pastime allowed her to send Ione "snapshots" of herself, Little, and their dog Paddy. She apologized for a batch of photographs that had been "very badly printed" in April 1902. She was "only beginning to learn anything," she explained to her daughter, and promised that "the artist" would do better in future. Maud also relished, as she had always done, the shops and cultural attractions of Paris, especially the theater and concerts. Louisine Havemeyer, a patron of Whistler, claimed to have seen Maud at one concert. "I looked and saw a beautiful woman, exquisitely dressed, elegant and dignified," she recalled. Maud saw her, too, as well as Mary Cassatt, who was seated beside her friend Havemeyer. Visibly "uneasy" at having been spotted, Maud looked in another direction and abruptly left before the end of the performance.[11]

She led a quieter life at Yport. Once a mere fishing village, the town had more recently earned a reputation as a seaside resort, complete with casino. However, situated as it was midway between Etretat and Fecamp, Maud and Little found Yport's pebble beach, surrounded by high chalk cliffs, an idyllic place to escape the noise and congestion of Paris. The beautiful scenery offered marvelous photographic subjects, and as Little came to share Maud's enthusiasm, the couple relished long walks through the countryside.[12]

Sadly, Little did not enjoy robust health. In search of a cure, the couple spent one summer in Nauheim, a German spa known for its effervescent brine baths and hydrotherapy. "I feel sure a few weeks cure there will do him no end of good even if it is not an absolute cure," Maud told her daughter. "For myself I am perfectly strong & well." Whatever improvement Little enjoyed proved temporary. He died in March 1904.[13]

Widowed, in a sense, for a second time, Maud at least suffered no financial woes. She gave up the Paris apartment, which she had come to "hate" even before Little's death. "It is so full of memories," she explained. She kept the château and soon found another house in Paris, but she also traveled more than had been possible with her husband. England remained an occasional diversion, where she still had family, and she spent at least one Christmas with friends in the Swiss Alps. She ate and slept "wonderfully well" in the fresh mountain air. She also enjoyed the "sleighing" but declined invitations to ski. By 1910, in her mid-fifties, she was beginning to feel her age. Thinking herself "wrinkled" and an absolute "fright," she told Ione, "It is lucky that with a thick veil on I don't look so bad."[14]

Ione was now her principal concern. She sent money regularly, usually $100 to $200 at a time, and advised her daughter on all manner of household issues, including the handling of servants. When Ione fretted about a second pregnancy in 1907, Maud reminded her that childbirth was "the most natural thing in the world." "If it is Gods will you should have a child you ought to be very happy. Just find a good doctor," she advised, and ignore "old womans stories." Ione eventually had three children. In more lighthearted moments, Maud shared her thoughts about the latest fashions in dress, most of which she deplored. The new clothes made women look like "Caricatures," she ventured, particularly the "harem skirt," introduced in 1910 by Parisian designer Paul Poiret, which was nothing more than a pair of baggy pants fitted at the ankle.[15]

Then, around 1911, Maud married another wealthy American, Richard H. S. Abbott, eighteen years her junior. Originally from New York, Abbott had been selling American automobiles in France for the Locomobile Company. Described as "dashing" and "athletic," he also raced automobiles and once held the record for the fastest time between New York and Philadelphia. Ironically, in becoming Mrs. Abbott, Maud gained a title Jo Hiffernan had claimed when living with Whistler. She and Richard took a house at 6 rue Commandant Marchand, a short, private street less than half a mile northwest of the Arc de Triomphe. They kept the château at Yport and added a villa near Cannes.[16]

However, what looked to be a happy third chapter in Maud's life was soon disrupted by the Great War. She and Richard fled Paris to live at Yport. They felt safer there but also isolated and "bottled up." Learning that their house in Paris was near army fortifications in the city, Maud feared it must soon be "blown to smithereens." "But what is that," she reasoned, "compared to the awful loss of life." All the young men she knew, in both France and England, had rushed to join the army. The young men she worried most about were a pair of nephews and her son Jack, who carried messages to the front as a motorcyclist. He had been made a lieutenant because of his fluency in three languages, but his duties placed him constantly in harm's way. "It is very dangerous work," Maud informed Ione, "but he is doing his duty & I am proud of him." The war also injured Abbott's business interests when his company was suddenly sold. "You must not look for the usual cheques," Maud lamented to her daughter.[17]

The uncertainty of events took an emotional toll on Maud. She suffered from "delirium" early in the war, which weakened her for at least a year. She sought treatment at Bournemouth in England for several months in 1914–15 but remained fragile. An English doctor prescribed complete rest, advising her, for the sake of her "nerves," not even to write letters. She felt strong enough to return to Yport by June, besides having "tired of hotel life" and its "enormous expenses," but being back in a "war zone" restricted her movements. She and Richard were unable even to use their new automobile, a lightweight, two-seater "Smith Flyer," except for short trips to nearby Fecamp. "The strain on both of us is hard," she confessed to Ione, "& the fact that we are far from every body else."[18]

Richard spoke of getting away for a time, perhaps to California, but both he and Maud were reluctant to leave Europe. They wanted to be in France for "the end," though God only knew when that might be. Finally, in late November 1915, having secured special passports, they visited the capital for "a little change." A week's stay at the Majestic Hotel, which offered special wartime rates, refreshed Maud. "It is an awful strain on one being away from a big city with a scarcity of news into the bargain," she told Ione. That said, Maud was equally glad to return to her "sea side home."[19]

Two years later, the ever-changeable Maud had come to "hate" Yport. "Just think of it," she told Ione, "the place that I loved & where I passed so many happy summers is distasteful to me & I hate seas." After spending another week in Paris that December, this time at the Prince Edward VII Hotel, she and Richard rented a villa, "Ande-Bébelle," at Le Cannet, near Cannes. It was "not as pretty" as La Picholiere but had a more luxurious garden, "with long palm & shade trees." It was warmer, too, close to the Mediterranean rather than on the English Channel. Coal for heating had become scarce, as had petrol for the car, but they had plenty of wood for their "American wood stove."[20]

Maud was by now in a precarious mental state following another nervous breakdown the previous year. She would never completely recover. "Once I had the idea that I had killed people—that I had assisted at the battle of Verdun & was wanted by police as a witness etc," she revealed to Ione. She thanked God that the darkest of those shadows had passed, but she still found it an "effort to get through a hopeless day alone . . . & a hideous night with[out] narcotics." Until her recent illness, she had "never tasted Chloral," but the drug now became her "curse." What was worse, she felt herself rapidly aging. Her longtime servant Clara insisted that she only imagined the decline, "but I only have to look in the glass," Maud replied.[21]

She fretted, as well, about the people dearest to her. Most poignantly, her favorite niece Maud Sheen, now in her mid-thirties, had suffered much in the war. First, her husband had been killed at the front. She tried to cope with that loss by volunteering to work as a Red Cross nurse, which did help. Maud thought she looked lovely in her white uniform and visited her several times, first in England and later when she was working near Paris and Rouen. Now, though, with the United States entering the war, the army hospitals were "filled with American nurses," and she was sent back to London to work in a government office. Maud thought it a blessing, for her niece looked worn out when she stopped at Yport on the return to England. The visit helped restore her, but she remained "very delicate."[22]

The end of the war found Maud and Richard still at Le Cannet. Having escaped the deadly influenza outbreak that ravaged much of France and the world, her biggest complaints in the winter of 1918–19 were the cold weather and shortages of food. She yearned most for some chocolate, which cost "an enormous price for a very little." She rejoiced that her son Jack had survived the war, but then came the Depression, which hit everyone financially. The Abbotts managed to keep their homes at both Le Cannet and Yport, which Maud, in the end, would not abandon, but they never again lived in Paris. Maud continued to send money to Ione and Warwick, though less frequently and in smaller amounts. "My income is not what it used to be," she apologized in 1931.[23]

Then came a dreadful, hardly credible moment. Ione visited Maud in 1935–36, shortly after Warwick had passed away, but what should have been a joyful reunion went horribly wrong. First, Maud told Ione she was a year younger than she had thought, born in 1877, when Maud would have been only twenty. More importantly, she revealed that Ione was the daughter of James McNeill Whistler. How Ione reacted is unknown, but Maud apparently delivered the news in such an abrupt and insensitive way that Richard later apologized for his wife's behavior. What Ione might have said had she known Maud had all but eliminated her from her will can only be imagined. Ione's only bequest was to be a third of the value of Maud's jewelry, the remainder to be evenly divided between Richard and Maud Sheen.[24]

Richard remained unaware of the full extent of Maud's actions until she died in November 1939, aged eighty-two, a result of "senile decay following partial paralytic stroke." He then drew the unpleasant task of revealing all to Ione. First came a detailed account of the will, which besides the inexcusable division of the jewelry granted Clara Theiler, Maud's "faithful servant" since at least 1900, a bequest of £1,500. Even more shocking, Maud Sheen, besides her share of the jewelry, received an additional £3,000, the single largest monetary bequest. Apologizing for both himself and Maud Sheen, Richard said they had agreed with "heart-felt pity and sympathy" to give Ione the entire value of the jewelry. Maud Sheen asked only to keep one of her aunt's ruby rings as a remembrance.[25]

Richard also tried to explain how his wife's long, painful mental decline, marked by "years of camouflage and deceit," had sadly culminated in Ione's visit. "Never have I known of a nature so complex, with so much that was noble and so much, alas, that was despicable," he admitted to Ione. "Let us be charitable and offer the suggestion that the years of a gnawing disease, lasting over a quarter century, made chemical changes that were responsible for the paradox." He did not mention a further paradox. Richard listed Maud as "an American citizen" on her death certificate, even though there is no evidence that the English-born Maud (unlike her daughter and son-in-law) ever relinquished British citizenship. Yet the three men with whom she had been most intimately bound were all Americans. Maud had also lived up to the Old German meaning of her name, "powerful battler."[26]

Richard quickly sold their two homes and left France for the United States. He eventually settled in Sausalito, California, probably for his health, although it so happened that Ione had been living there since the death of Warwick. Four years later, in 1948, as his health worsened, Richard committed suicide by hanging at his home in the Casa Madrona hotel. He left the bulk of his estate, including some £8,000 of Maud's money, to his sisters. Ione received nothing.[27]

His passing also revealed a final tie to the past. When Maud Sheen learned of his death, she informed Ione that Richard had left England with several works by Whistler, including an "Etching Portrait" of her mother. "If you found them among his personal effects," Maud urged, "for goodness sake keep them for yourself, as they must be of value." The purported portrait of her mother turned out to be a self-portrait, which Ione did retrieve, along with several etchings, a drawing, and a watercolor by her father. All the works are now preserved at the Terra Museum of American Art, Evanston, Illinois. Ione herself died in 1951, aged seventy-three. She asked, as had her mother, to be cremated.[28]

Whatever his relationships with women, Whistler's most poignant personal legacy is tied to his son. Charles James Whistler Hanson was born in 1870, the result of an apparently singular encounter with a twenty-one-year-old parlor maid, Louise Fanny Hanson. Whistler referred to the liaison as his "infidelity to Jo." The boy may have been named Charles after Whistler's uncle, who had died a year earlier. Initially cared for by a wet nurse like Ione and little Maud, by age five he was being reared by Jo, whom he called "auntie." Charlie, as he became known, did not see much of his father until his late teens, when Whistler employed him for three years as a private secretary. It was a very formal relationship. Whistler addressed his son as Mr. Hanson; Charlie called him Mr. Whistler or "Boss." They were busy years for Whistler, when he had his hands full directing the Royal Society of British Artists, compiling selections for *The Gentle Art of Making Enemies* (a task performed largely by Charlie and Sheridan Ford), and swapping Maud for Beatrice.[29]

Charlie struck out on his own when he turned twenty-one, in 1891. In search of an occupation, he took a pair of chemistry courses at King's College London, paid for by Whistler, but that ended his formal education. Charlie showed no flair for art, as seen in his few surviving drawings and sketches, but he did have the Whistler gene for technical drawing. Accordingly, his father arranged an apprenticeship as an electrical engineer with an old friend, Charles Ambrose McEvoy.[30]

Charlie was already leading an active social life. His diaries for 1887–89 record numerous friendships and activities, though, frustratingly, many entries are too obscure (a few are even written in code) to appreciate fully all he did during those years. Like his father, he became interested in the supernatural, as evidenced by the séances he attended. He mentions many young ladies, but most intriguing, beginning in 1889, he frequently visited the home of his mother, or at least the home of someone he calls "Mom." He went at least once a month, often on a Sunday, and was sometimes joined by friends. They included the sculptor Joseph Edgar Boehm and the painter George Percy Jacomb-Hood. Both were good friends of Whistler, and Charlie had visited Boehm's studio as a child.[31]

However, the identity of "Mom" remains something of a mystery. It is hard to imagine why so many artists would have congregated at the home of his birth mother, Fanny Hanson. A better bet, for two reasons, is that the journals' "Mom" was Jo's sister Agnes Hiffernan. First, Charlie once referred to Agnes as "my aunt—Mom." While both Whistler and Charlie had called Jo "auntie," she had really been his surrogate mother. With Jo's passing in 1886, it is likely that Agnes assumed that role. Second, on two occasions in 1889, Charlie mentioned having dinner with Mom and Charles J. Singleton, who would eventually marry Agnes. Thereafter, Charlie also spent much more time with Singleton, with whom Whistler had always been friendly. He also saw Mom at "Gilbert's." This may well have been the sculptor Alfred Gilbert, who had studied under Boehm and would later train Edward Francis "Teddy" Godwin, Charlie's stepbrother.[32]

Whistler is not much help in clarifying this issue, even though he was well aware of the woman known as Mom. In October 1888, while on his wedding tour in France, he berated Charlie, then serving as his secretary, for not keeping him advised of events in London. "I have begun to wonder if you are ill—which I should be sorry for," he told his son, "but in such case you should have written—or your Mommie who has found no difficulty in writing herself might have been done so for you." However, none of Whistler's surviving correspondence suggests the identity of the mysterious mother-figure.[33]

Charlie lived in at least five different areas of London between 1888 and 1895, including Chelsea, Marylebone, Bloomsbury, and Clerkenwell. He finally landed at 11 Great Ormond Street, Queen Square, where his life became more settled. In June 1896 he married Sarah Ann Murray, daughter of a deceased bootmaker. She was twenty-one, he twenty-six. How they met is unknown, but they lived near each other, she at 10 Frederick Street, Gray's Inn Road. The wedding was held at a Catholic chapel in Sardinia Street. Whistler did not attend, being somewhat miffed that Charlie had sought "neither advice nor counsel" from him about the wisdom of marriage. That said, it is also true that Beatrice had died only a month earlier, which plunged Whistler into despair. Agnes Hiffernan attended and signed the marriage register as a witness, adding credence to her identity as Mom. When she and Singleton finally wed, in 1901, Charlie reciprocated by serving as a witness.[34]

Charlie and Sarah attended Whistler's funeral, even though they had been shamelessly excluded from his will in favor of Beatrice's son Teddy Godwin and Rosalind Birnie Philip. Whistler is last known to have communicated with his son two years earlier. He still sometimes addressed him as Mr. Hanson, but they were kindly contacts, in letters signed "Always affectionately." Charlie and Sarah had moved by then to Camden Town, at 24 Harrington Square. A son, Adrian Charles Whistler Hanson, was born to them there in September 1902, though whether the grandfather was aware of it is unclear.[35]

Then, about 1905, Charlie made a most interesting move. Having lived all his life north of the Thames, he settled in Clapham, where he had been born. He may have done so for business reasons. He had established himself as an inventive and successful electrical engineer under McEvoy's tutelage. Whether he continued working with McEvoy after his apprenticeship or struck out on his own is unclear, but it so happened that McEvoy died in 1905. Clapham was a rapidly growing community, as was the entire borough of Wandsworth. It had only one advertised electrical engineering firm, while several such businesses were located in nearby Brixton and Camberwell. Again, whether or not Charlie worked independently in Clapham is unknown, but he did file at least eight patents between 1896 and 1909, which suggests he knew something about the business. He and Sarah lived initially in a flat at 39 Gauden Road, where their second child, Joan Eleanor Whistler Hanson, was born the day after Christmas in 1905. Sadly, she died in 1908, the same year her parents moved into the upper half of a semidetached house at 2 Gauden Road. It was a pleasant, settled neighborhood. Most of the houses on Gauden dated from the mid-1870s, with exteriors that boasted columned porches, balustraded balconies, and elaborate stucco decoration.[36]

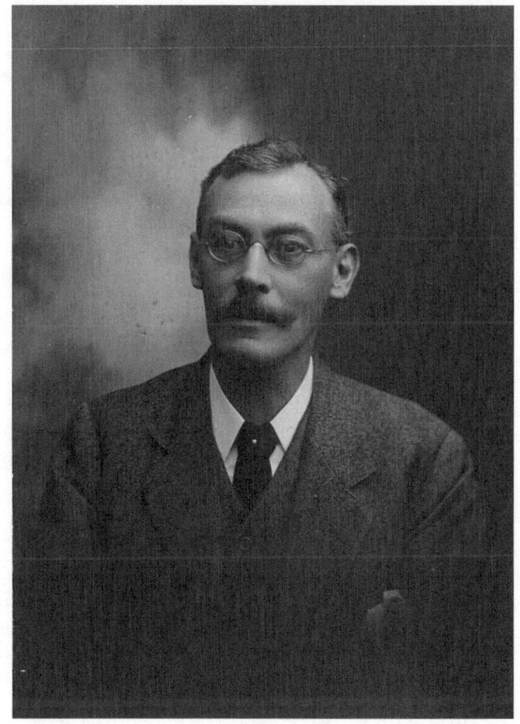

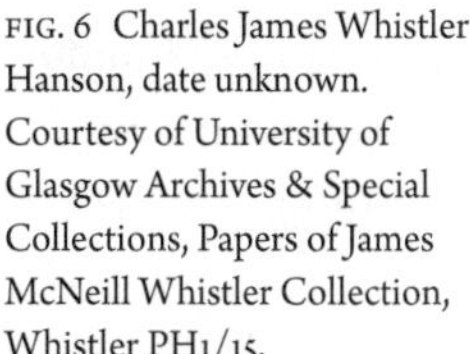

FIG. 6 Charles James Whistler Hanson, date unknown. Courtesy of University of Glasgow Archives & Special Collections, Papers of James McNeill Whistler Collection, Whistler PH1/15.

Even more intriguing than the move to Clapham was a 1917 move from Gauden to 48 Larkhill Rise, on the corner of Killyon Road. It was the very street where his real mother lived at the time of his birth, in 4 Grantley Villas. Was it all by chance, or a sentimental return to his roots, perhaps even because he had learned that his true mother still resided there? Regardless, the move does show Charlie to be prospering. His new home was a detached, single-family house, built, like the ones on Gauden, in the mid-1870s. Tax records show that his share of the Gauden house had a gross value of £27, a ratable value of £22, and an annual tax rate of £4.0.8. The Larkhill property had a gross value of £48, a ratable value of £40, and an annual tax rate of £8.8.0.

Charlie spent the remainder of what appears to have been a happy and largely secure life on Larkhill Rise. He was too old for military service in the Great War. The Depression years did not affect his business or the value of his home. The success of the women's suffrage movement allowed Sarah to add her name to the voting rolls for both local and parliamentary elections in 1918. We know nothing of the Hansons' politics, although Charlie belonged to a Conservative club in his youth. In due course, Adrian followed his father in an engineering career. He and two partners, describing themselves as "Electrical and Mechanical Engineers and Manufacturers," operated their own firm, the Precision Engineering Company, in London for a time. However, the partnership was dissolved "by mutual consent" in 1947, with all outstanding debts received and paid by Adrian. He died in Stoke Newington, northeast London, in 1967.[37]

Charlie appears to have been ambivalent about the name Whistler, even though he passed it down to each of his children. He did not resemble his father in facial features. An undated photograph shows him in middle age, perhaps taken around the time he left London, the picture's setting (fig. 6). He wears a nicely tailored three-piece suit and is fitted with wire-rimmed spectacles. He has the same firm jaw as his father and sports a mustache, but his graying hair is closely cropped and betrays none of his father's famous curls. More than that, he appears to be a very modest person. There is no posturing, no dramatic pose, no mischievous smile. It is the portrait of an undemonstrative man content with his place in life.

Charlie sold much of his considerable correspondence with Whistler through Sotheby's in late 1923. That might suggest financial difficulties, but the timing may also be tied to the fact that Joseph Pennell had been trying to contact him around then. It is unclear who bought the letters, although the Pennells eventually obtained some of them. The interesting thing is that they were offered at auction as correspondence between "Whistler and his Secretary." No mention was made of a blood relationship. It was widely known that Whistler had a son, but not even the Pennells knew his name until 1921. Charlie was not publicly identified as Whistler's son until Sotheby's sold a second batch of letters in 1965, probably offered by Adrian. Charlie owned only a few of his father's sketches. He sold a pair of them in 1917 and another in 1924, again suggesting the need for cash. Surviving family members, probably Adrian, sold the rest in the 1950s.[38]

Charlie passed away on September 10, 1935, from a combination of myocardial degeneration, arterial sclerosis, and chronic gastritis. He was only sixty-five years old, four years younger than his father at death. The father died after a lifetime of wandering. The son, who seems never to have left the environs of Greater London, departed this world on the street where he had entered it.[39]

If Charlie's story is the most poignant among Whistler's family, the road traveled by Rosalind Birnie Philip is the most intriguing. The youngest of

Trixie's nine siblings, Rosalind was only twenty-two when, with her sister's passing, she assumed the role of secretary, housekeeper, and confidant to Whistler. As the "Major," she became aide-de-camp to the "General." Her mother and three sisters, especially Ethel, who had married Whistler's friend Charles Whibley, would also attend assiduously to his health and well-being, but Whistler showed his fondness and respect for Rosalind by making her his legal ward. He trusted her judgment and enjoyed her outspoken nature.[40]

Yet no one could have foreseen the central role Rosalind would play in preserving—even shaping—Whistler's legacy. Having been made executor in his will, she assumed control, with Whistler's passing, of the copyrights to his art, publications, and private correspondence. She also claimed to know how he wished to be remembered. The result would be a series of titanic clashes with people who thought they knew better than she. Certain of Whistler's friends, most importantly Charles Lang Freer, sided with Rosalind. Other people, most persistently the Pennells, became implacable foes.[41]

At just twenty-nine, Rosalind found herself nearly overwhelmed by calls for memorial exhibitions of Whistler's work, claims on unfinished pictures, the valuation of his work, distributions of royalties, printing of etchings and lithographs, financial claims on the estate, and suspected thefts and forgeries of paintings. Friends feared for her health, and a mere three weeks after Whistler's funeral she admitted to Freer, "Everything is so vexing and sad." Slender and slight, Rosalind lacked the vivaciousness of her older sisters, especially Beatrice and Ethel. Photographs show her to be not unattractive, but with a serious, purposeful look (fig. 7). Harper Pennington, who was not an enemy, described her as "a drab looking woman whose skirt always trailed in the mud behind & who always dressed in dreary grey garments which didn't suit her." However, she shared with all the Philip clan a formidable stubbornness and resolve. She patiently and methodically handled every issue thrown at her and confronted anyone she suspected of subverting Whistler's wishes or profiting from his name. That much, Rosalind regarded "as a sacred trust."[42]

Her initial challenge came when Whistler's friends sought to honor him with several memorial exhibitions, the most ambitious to be staged in London by the International Society of Sculptors, Painters and Gravers. Rosalind refused to donate any work to that effort and asked friends, including Freer, Arthur Studd, Jerome Eddy, and Edward Canfield, to boycott any "British" exhibition. Whistler, she reminded them, wanted "no

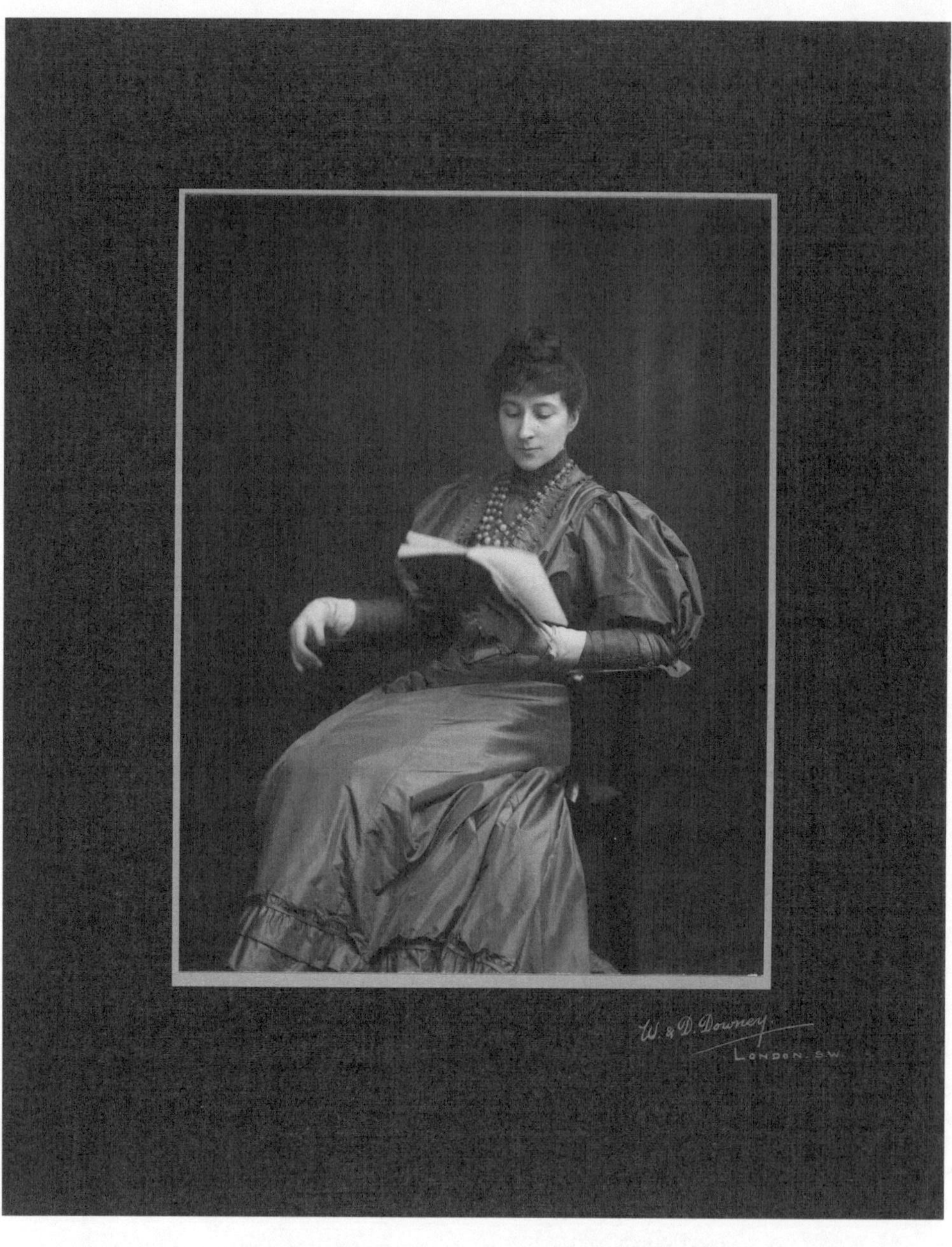

FIG. 7 Rosalind Birnie Philip, ca. 1890. Charles Lang Freer / National Museum of Asian Art Archives, Smithsonian Institution, Washington, DC. Charles Lang Freer Papers, FSA A.01 12.03.19.

demonstration of any kind in London." Rosalind did attend the exhibition when it opened in February 1905. She thought the pictures well hung but deplored the colors and decor of the galleries. Elizabeth Pennell was also there, but after spotting Rosalind "immediately hurried on!" Rosalind did cooperate with exhibitions in Glasgow, Paris, Venice, and, most importantly, Boston. She also gave her blessing to an exhibition of Whistler's etchings in Chicago, sponsored by the Caxton Club.[43]

Only twice did Rosalind allow pictures under her control to be used in London exhibitions, and that was not until several years later. In 1912, she loaned a few pictures to the Tate for a brief showing, but when the director hinted at the possibility of keeping them longer—perhaps to hold them permanently—Rosalind informed him that "Mr. Whistler had expressly desired that none of the work . . . should be given to English Institutions." Three years later, she anonymously loaned fifty-one paintings and drawings to the New Bond Street gallery of Colnaghi & Obach for an exhibition benefiting the Professional Classes War Relief Council. Rumors circulated as to the owner of this "private collection," but given the works on display, people in the know had no problem identifying Rosalind. Elizabeth Pennell, who attended the private view, had no doubts, and lambasted Rosalind for hypocrisy.[44]

Exposing forgeries became a problem almost from the start. They had already been an annoyance during Whistler's lifetime. As his old friend Tom Armstrong observed, "It is not so very difficult to do a second- or third-rate Whistler, which would deceive the unwary." No wonder that without Whistler around to authenticate his work forgeries popped up everywhere. Several London shops were selling fake lithographs only a year after Whistler's death, and for nearly as much as originals. Rosalind learned of nearly a dozen forged etchings in Paris as early as 1905. Freer came across a dodgy *Nocturne* in New York City the following year.[45]

Similar issues arose concerning the copyrights for Whistler's publications. Rosalind's immediate concern was *The Gentle Art*, which was being reissued in separate editions in London and New York. Acting at first to ensure she received the royalties, Rosalind became equally determined to halt bootleg editions. This threat first emerged in 1907, when a pirated copy of *The Ten O'Clock* surfaced in Chicago. Freer, taking swift legal action as her "agent," forced the publisher to cease production, surrender all unsold copies, and send a letter of apology to Rosalind. "The wrong done was wholly unintended," the frightened man pleaded. When Freer suggested that a new authorized edition might prevent future problems, Rosalind selected a small New York publisher to do the job, although she dictated every detail of the printing process, just as Whistler would have done. Freer then saw to distribution and renewal of the copyright.[46]

The more enduring difficulty concerned the copyright to Whistler's correspondence. Several potential biographers, including, besides the Pennells, Duret, Menpes, and Tom Way, wished to reproduce or quote from his letters. Rosalind could be lenient with the reproduction of paintings and lithographs, less so with etchings, but she was adamant that Whistler wanted none of his private correspondence made public. William Webb, who had served as Whistler's attorney for many years, assured Rosalind of her legal rights but urged her to handle even the most persistent petitioners with "politeness not hostility." Then came the Pennells and their "authorized" biography. Elizabeth Pennell tried twice on personal visits to persuade Rosalind that Whistler's "family"—meaning the Hadens and Willie's widow Helen—approved of the project and that "many witnesses" could verify that Whistler had asked them to write the book. When Webb published a notice in several London newspapers to insist that no biography had been sanctioned, Joseph Pennell's solicitor issued a statement to contradict it. By the time American newspapers reprinted both letters, the lines were drawn.[47]

William Heinemann, who was committed to publishing the book, tried to soften Rosalind on a personal visit, but things did not go well. As she saw it, he had come to "bully" her and place her "in the wrong." Heinemann insisted that he came as a "peace maker" who wanted to avoid the "scandal" that would result if she and the Pennells went "to law." But Webb and Freer had already urged Rosalind to resist any effort by Heinemann or the Pennells to "project themselves into Mr. Whistler's private affairs and upon an unoffending world." Freer dramatically cautioned, "Under their thin veil of boasted friendship lie quivering coils of self interest, ready to spring. Don't let it strike you!" When none of Heinemann's cajoling moved her, the publisher turned sentimental. "He tried to make his eyes look tearful when he thought of all the talk in the newspapers & how bad it would appear in the eyes of the world," Rosalind marveled, but she remained unmoved and undeceived. She would honor Whistler's memory in every respect, declaring, as the "General" himself would have done, that "West Point principles were not being put lightly aside."[48]

So, they did end up in court. Rosalind conceded privately that Whistler may have spoken to Joe Pennell about doing "a catalogue of his complete works, . . . a kind of book of reference," to which she had no objection. However, she was determined to shield the correspondence and was in "fighting trim" for the two-day court battle in July 1907. It proved to be a draining experience for both her and the ever-supportive Ethel. Rosalind performed well under cross examination and thought the defense witnesses "terribly untruthful." Joe Pennell was so "rude" that the judge asked him "to behave and answer his questions more politely," and his attorney produced no written evidence of the Pennells' supposed commission. In retrospect, Rosalind's attorney might have asked the Pennells why, in all the time she had known them and been in their company, almost always with Whistler, they had never mentioned their intended biography. Rosalind had also engaged Elizabeth Pennell more than once in private discussions with no reference made to the book and no attempt to tap her insights.[49]

In the end, Rosalind did secure legal copyright to Whistler's correspondence, but when the Pennells' book finally reached the public in October 1908, she reacted with despair. It was "so full of errors and lying statements, that one hardly knows how to act for the best," she told Freer. She almost regretted that her sister ever married Whistler. "It is terrible to think how we have been watched and every detail noted in the Pennells' note books!" she exclaimed. "We never ought to have known such people."[50]

Rosalind nearly took legal action against the Pennells a second time in 1911, claiming to have suffered greatly from their "vulgarity" and continued slanders by the "contemptible" Joe. She went so far as to round up witnesses for the prosecution before being persuaded that it would not be worth the "worry and annoyance" to pursue the case. As the Pennells continued to churn out books and articles about Whistler, she lamented to D. S. MacColl in 1922, "Nothing is sacred from their desire to advertise themselves." That was the year the Pennells published *The Whistler Journal*. After spending an "unprofitable day" reading it, Rosalind pronounced the book "a very badly written load of lying rubbish," although she also found some parts "so outrageous as to be almost amusing."[51]

She had scant time to be amused, for protecting Whistler's legacy was not her only responsibility. She and her mother, Frances Black Philip, had been forced to abandon 74 Cheyne Walk, where they and Whistler had spent his final years, when the lease expired in early 1904. She spotted a "beautiful" eighteenth-century house near Chiswick, where Whistler and Beatrice had been buried in a quiet churchyard, but found it "damp," and with a "huge garden which would have required much money expended on it." She settled, instead, for a house in Battersea, at 103 Albert Bridge Road. It was an emotional location, less than one hundred yards from the Thames. Standing on the bridge and looking upriver, she could see her former home and Chelsea Old Church. The new house depressed her at first. "Why I cannot tell," she confessed to Freer. Yet she would live there for nearly forty years, to be dismissed henceforth by the Pennells as that "Lady at Battersea."[52]

Meantime, Rosalind took personal charge of a matter Whistler had always supervised himself: the printing of his etchings and lithographs. She began within weeks of his death by tracking down surviving etching plates and lithographic stones. Learning that Marcus Huish, of the Fine Art Society, still had plates for two Venice etchings, from which Whistler had wanted to make a total of thirty-eight impressions, Rosalind commissioned the well-established printers Frederick and Charles Goulding to make them. Delighted when the etchings brought in £19, she realized this could be a means of securing a reliable stipend as well as keeping Whistler's work in circulation.[53]

Concerning the lithographs, she asked Robert Dunthorne, a London dealer with whom Whistler had dealt, to help her compile a list of existing proofs. Tom Way and a French printer had already surrendered over one hundred stones plus eighteen transfer drawings to her. Way thought his stones were exhausted, but Freer advised Rosalind to get the opinion of another printer. If the stones turned out to be in good condition, she should consider large print runs of at least thirty-five or forty, to be issued according to the demands of the market. "In the coming years," Freer reminded her, "there will be many museums and collectors extremely anxious to get copies."[54]

Rosalind again put her faith in the Gouldings, with whom she got on famously. The brothers had first printed Whistler etchings in 1861 but clashed with him over their methods for printing lithographs. Nonetheless, Rosalind found them entirely reliable, and "very funny" in their eccentricities. Frederick, the elder brother, wore "mouse-colored clothes and a skull cap, a pale blue tie and blue blouse." Charles, who supervised the actual printing, looked like Father Christmas, "only with a hard blue eye instead of a kind one." He always wore slippers. "The two brothers never agree together," she laughed to Freer, "but each one, when alone, approves of what the other says."[55]

They printed the lithographs secretly between October 1903 and May 1904 in their workshop on Shepherd's Bush Road, with Rosalind personally observing their progress most afternoons. They used only ninety-two of the available stones and ten of the transfer papers, and the number of impressions varied widely, but they provided Rosalind with a substantial inventory for only £200. Even Tom Way acknowledged that the brothers had succeeded as well as could be expected "with so difficult a task." Dunthorne promoted their achievement by exhibiting fifty-five of the prints at his gallery in Vigo Street. Whistler had sometimes criticized how Dunthorne marketed his etchings and was skeptical of his close association with Francis Seymour Haden, but the dealer had provided Whistler with one of his last sales, worth £341, a month before he died.[56]

Turning to pricing and marketing, Rosalind insisted that the object should not be profit, but to make Whistler's work available to enthusiasts. She even made a gift of eighty-seven lithographs to the Bibliotheque Nationale in Paris because of Whistler's admiration of the French and their artistic influence on him. At the same time, she did not want to sell him cheap but to establish future prices at the levels Whistler "meant them to be." Ethel told her to charge whatever dealers demanded, and prices did, in fact, rise for all his work in the year after Whistler's death. Still, Rosalind wondered aloud, "Is this the point?"[57]

Her experience in assisting Whistler in these matters also guided Rosalind. She understood the importance of the number of impressions made. To ensure the value of the lithographs then on hand, she ordered all but eight of the stones destroyed. She also knew that in pricing his prints, Whistler had always considered "their artistic value as well as their money value" and had eventually foregone the mass market to sell to "the few" who could appreciate their artistry. Rosalind made no single dealer her agent, a decision applauded by Freer. She did, though, come to rely heavily on Colnaghi & Obach, with whom she had consulted early on about the wisdom of printing the lithographs.[58]

Whatever Rosalind's hesitancy to exploit Whistler's work for profit, she came to earn a comfortable if uneven income from the etchings and lithographs. The market fluctuated but based on her account with Colnaghi & Obach—the most extensive surviving one—Rosalind made several thousand pounds between 1916 and 1935. That was far more than she realized from her 15 percent royalties on sales of *The Gentle Art*. Between 1909 and 1925, those payments amounted to less than £500.[59]

Freer contributed to Rosalind's financial security by investing her inheritance from Whistler in railroad bonds. The estate had been valued at £9,900, on which Rosalind had paid "death dues" of £1,300. That left a tidy sum. Freer also purchased more of Whistler's paintings and other work from her. The Pennells accused him of exploiting Rosalind, and she of cashing in on Whistler, but she was happy to oblige her friend, especially as he developed plans to establish what would become the Freer Gallery of Art in Washington, DC. His most spectacular purchase was the Peacock Room. The asking price of £11,000 gave him pause. He thought at first to buy only the three shutters and the wall panel of fighting peacocks for £5,000, but at Rosalind's urging—nearly pleading—he rescued the entire room, which might otherwise have been demolished. Instead, it was dismantled and installed in Freer's Detroit home.[60]

Freer also joined Rosalind's campaign to acquire as many as possible of Whistler's letters. Her immediate goal was to keep them from the Pennells, but she knew other biographers would follow them. Even before the Pennell trial, she had successfully forced the withdrawal or revision of two books that had reproduced some of the letters. She did not want to appear petty, she told Freer, but it was difficult to assist authors who "could never work from the same inspiration" as herself.[61]

Understanding her feelings, Freer provided the cash to purchase letters that came on the market. In 1911, he paid $200 for four letters written by Whistler to Sidney Starr. They missed a valuable cache held by Helen Whistler shortly after the Pennell trial. Helen had asked Rosalind for permission to publish about fifty letters from Whistler to Willie. Rosalind declined, thinking what a boon that would be for the Pennells, with whom Helen was friendly. Six years later, in 1913, Helen sold some of her letters through a dealer, but Rosalind succeeded that same year in buying, with Freer's money, Whistler's correspondence with Lady Colin Campbell and Thomas Way. Told the letters might cost as much as £2,000, she was thrilled to acquire both lots, plus an etching and inscribed copy of the published *Ten O'Clock*, for only £350.[62]

After Freer's death in 1919, Rosalind relied on her own resources to buy what she could afford or persuaded people who still held the artist's letters not to publish them. In 1922, she purchased at auction forty-eight letters exchanged between Whistler and Marcus Huish, a former editor of the *Art Journal* and director of the Fine Art Society, for £320. When Sotheby's offered eight letters in 1923 and she had only £100 to spare, the auction house helped her acquire the entire lot for £94.2.0.[63]

Rosalind also borrowed and copied correspondence held by friends and advertised for the loan of letters. Alan Cole allowed her to copy entries from his diaries, although he had done the same for the Pennells. She considered for a time publishing a selection of what she had accumulated but then thought better of it. "Evidently they are longing for the letters, and, of course, the sooner I publish them, the sooner the Pennells will be able to quote from them," she explained to Freer. "I think we must guard the treasures until the demise of these two worthy people."[64]

Rosalind remained cautious even after both Pennells had passed on. When a distant relation of Anna Whistler asked to see Whistler's correspondence with his mother in 1929, she volunteered only to answer any questions the woman cared to pose. As for publishing any portion of the correspondence, Rosalind explained, "I do not think that my brother-in-law would have wished it." She continued asking Whistler's friends to refrain as well. In 1939, she reached an agreement with Stéphane Mallarmé's daughter, of whom Whistler had been extremely fond, that neither of them would release any correspondence between those two friends.[65]

By now, Rosalind had gained a fearsome reputation among potential biographers who sought her cooperation. Neither James Laver nor Denys Sutton, the next biographers after the Pennells, could win her over. Laver, a poet, novelist, and popular writer on art and costume, published his book in 1930 without consulting Rosalind, but as he considered making changes to a second edition toward the end of World War II, he contacted her. She went to meet him at the Victoria and Albert Museum, where Laver was Keeper of the Theatre Collection, but spent most of the time pointing out mistakes in the Pennells' and his own books. In the end, she declined to give Laver "even a glimpse" of the letters.[66]

More than twenty years later, Sutton only wished to inspect some of her many paintings. Besides writing his own book, he was helping Joseph Whistler Revillon, a grandnephew of the artist, compile a catalogue of Whistler's paintings. He finally arranged what turned out to be a fairly successful "interview" with Rosalind. She declined to assist with his "scheme of a biography" but agreed to share some of the pictures at a subsequent meeting. It never took place. After procrastinating for nearly two years, Rosalind decided against helping Sutton at all—"uncooperative as anticipated," a weary Sutton informed Revillon.[67]

Revillon made his own bid in the mid-1940s. "She is a very well preserved woman of seventy or thereabouts," he reported to his collaborator, Frederick W. Coburn, a writer and art critic based in Lowell, "large and looks rather like a female policeman." He might have laughed to know that Whistler had once referred to Rosalind as the "Chelsea constable" because of her sometimes stern disposition. When Revillon finally "plucked up" the courage to write to her, he received "a short & sweet reply" but also the definitive answer that "the only person who should have supervised such a work was Whistler himself."[68]

In October 1903, Rosalind had told Freer, "It is too bad to feel all these things must come to an end. When everything is in order, I shall become no doubt a worthy woman, and take to cross stitch, or some such worthy occupation." It never happened. Rosalind became consumed by her trust—some would say obsessed by it. As years and decades passed, more people questioned her tight hold on Whistler's legacy, especially with regards to his correspondence. By the mid-1930s, the letters of such artists as Vincent Van Gogh and Paul Gauguin had been published, making them, in a very real sense, better known and more highly appreciated than Whistler.[69]

Utterly sincere in her belief that she knew Whistler's wishes, Rosalind became something of a hoarder, even a miser, in the way she kept people at arm's length. Freer had unintentionally reenforced her attitude. "You are perfectly justified in letting yourself grow miserly," he once assured her. "I feel pretty much as you do about certain things in my own care, for I cling to them most tightly and jealously hide them from the sight of the curious." Whistler thought the same way in his insistence that when selling a painting, he was merely placing it in the buyer's care; the picture still belonged to him.[70]

Rosalind showed no sign of loosening her grip until 1934, when officials from the University of Glasgow convinced her to entrust some portion of Whistler's correspondence and artwork to them. She thought Glasgow an appropriate and safe depository for her treasures. Glasgow had been the first city to purchase one of Whistler's paintings, the portrait of Thomas Carlyle. Some of his most enthusiastic and supportive followers—the so-called Glasgow Boys—had been young Scottish artists. Most notably, the university had conferred an honorary degree on Whistler in the final year of his life. Rosalind believed he would have approved her decision, and it seemed a good way to secure his legacy.

She had no telephone, so Robert S. Rait, Principal and Vice Chancellor of the university, had to discuss "legal provisions" for Rosalind's "noble gift" mostly by post. Having also visited her in London, and seeing how attached she was to her collection, Rait labored to create a personal bond. He inquired about her health, expressed concern about an injured knee, and sympathized with her "domestic trouble and anxiety." He described the specially constructed display cases, made of polished Austrian oak and secured by stout Yale locks, that would exhibit parts of her gift. Everything would be done to her satisfaction, he told her, all her wishes observed "in both letter and spirit."[71]

The new Whistler Collection of nearly three hundred items included smaller artworks—etchings, lithographs, and pastels—and "personal relics," such as Whistler's china, silver, etching and engraving tools, medals and decorations, canceled etching plates, and Beatrice's garnet jewelry. Rosalind parted with very little of the correspondence, and the only painting she relinquished was William Boxall's portrait of a fifteen-year-old Whistler. When the first installment reached Glasgow in May 1935, an ecstatic Rait immediately asked permission to mount an exhibition, which Rosalind granted. Rait solicited her advice about its details, including recommendations for some "distinguished authority" to open the show. He suggested Sir John Lavery, who had known Whistler. Rosalind doubted that any "authority" was needed, inasmuch as "Whistler was a law unto himself in his individual artistic outlook." However, she thought the Duchess of Atholl might preside. "Most of the work in connection with the gift has been done by women," Rosalind reasoned, "and the Duchess is a good worker and I am told has strong artistic and musical leanings." She had not known Whistler personally, Rosalind acknowledged, but that was just as well: "Old friends are apt to be indiscreet after the object of their regard has gone."[72]

Poor health prevented Rosalind from attending the October 1935 opening, but she was pleased to learn that the exhibition had been extremely popular, with people attending "from all parts of the country." Encouraged by the reaction, she sent a selection of paintings to the university in April 1936, this time also visiting to inspect arrangements for exhibiting and protecting the collection. She was doubly pleased to learn that John Walton, a Professor of Biology, had been named honorary curator of all the university's paintings. He was the son of Edward A. Walton, an artist friend of Whistler who had lived next door to them in Cheyne Walk during her brother-in-law's final year. Professor Walton, who still remembered that as a boy he had seen Whistler, told Rosalind of his hopes for a new art gallery at the university, where Whistler's paintings would make "a magnificent show."[73]

With the death of Rait soon after the 1935 exhibition, Walton and his wife Dorothy became Rosalind's main links to the university. Like Rait, they stayed in close contact through the post and visits to London (Rosalind never installed a telephone). Not to attribute ulterior motives to the couple, but she did still have all those letters. However, while their relationship remained cordial, Rosalind showed no sign of relinquishing her cache. "It appears they are all frightened to death of her," observed Joseph Revillon in 1945 of the people in Glasgow, "& dare do nothing which might prejudice their hopes of being left a large collection of Whistler's letters which she still has."[74]

The Second World War left everyone in limbo. Rosalind witnessed the war firsthand when Nazi bombs pummeled her neighborhood on September 20, 1940. "That night was a terrifying experience," she reported to Walton, "for six mines fell in the district, & hardly any one escaped damage in one way or another. None of us look improved by the nocturnal visits." Hardest hit was Anhalt Road, one street west of the Albert Bridge Road, with buildings almost directly behind her obliterated. Seven months later, on the night of April 16–17, 1941, her old home at 74 Cheyne Walk was demolished, along with every other house on that block and much of Chelsea Old Church. Rosalind became one of the tens of thousands to flee Chelsea and Battersea. By 1942, no one lived on her stretch of the Albert Bridge Road.[75]

Rosalind stayed in Chelsea but moved farther east, on Tite Street, to live with her only surviving sibling, Frances Septima Philip. Frances had resided at Dhu House, 48 Tite Street, before and after Whistler's death, but moved to No. 54 in the 1930s. The house stood almost directly opposite No. 33, where Whistler had lived for several years following his return from Venice and later shared a studio with John Singer Sargent. Several artists, including Augustus John, who had admired Whistler and whose sister had studied with him in Paris, still lived there. The White House, No. 35, stood next door.[76]

Besides the destruction of such an important physical part of Whistler's life, the war brought other worries. First came word that the elderly man who had faithfully tended the grounds around Whistler's gravesite was retiring. Rosalind had always cared for the tomb itself, even having it professionally bronzed every year. It had been designed by Teddy Godwin, who kept in touch with "Aunt Lin" for several years. Now she would have to find someone new to keep nature in check. About the same time, Rosalind had to fend off another pair of eager authors. One of them wanted to write a book about Whistler's watercolors and pastels. The other was an American writer and journalist named Forrest Wilson. He had recently won a Pulitzer Prize for his biography of Harriet Beecher Stowe and now wanted to write a new biography of Whistler. He considered the Pennells' book "prejudiced," but not even that clear-eyed assessment could sway Rosalind from her role as guardian. "My position is that Whistler did not wish a Life to be written," she explained to Walton, "& that I am bound by his wish." As it turned out, Wilson passed away only days after seeking Rosalind's assistance.[77]

However, in the wake of war and with advancing age—she was now over seventy—Rosalind once more considered the fate of Whistler's letters. By 1951, she had already been forced to sacrifice some of the remaining smaller paintings. Apparently facing financial troubles, she sold a study for Whistler's 1898 painting *Brown and Gold: Lillie in our Alley!* to Colnaghi in December 1945. She then paid some medical bills by giving her physician a small oil on wood, *The Shop*. In 1950, she gave the Boston Public Library studies for the decorative panels Whistler was to have done for them but never completed. That was the year after her sister Frances died, leaving Rosalind alone in the world.[78]

Not coincidentally, she invited John Walton to visit her in 1951 to discuss the letters. Rosalind's copyright would end in July 1953. The biographical vultures would then descend. It was best to place the correspondence in safe hands. Misunderstanding how the publishing business worked, she told Walton, "I feel that if the materials should ever be used, that the proceeds should be shared by the University & the author of the book, for I suppose the author would be a member of the University." That said, Rosalind would only surrender the correspondence after compiling an "explatory" catalogue to put it in context. "Someone will write a biography of Whistler in future years," she conceded, "and the catalogue might protect the letters from any wild constructions being put on harmless statements."[79]

The Waltons burst into action. Rosalind had recently recovered from both a "sudden chest attack" and pneumonia, so legal arrangements required alacrity. Her "method" of sorting the letters also raised concerns.

"I am destroying what could be of no interest," she informed John Walton, the same thing she had told an anxious James Laver. She also believed that copies of Whistler's replies to correspondents should "not be read except by those who own the original letters," but decided to grant the university "the power to make the final decision as to the keeping or throwing out of the materials."[80]

That was in March 1952; Rosalind spent the next two years sorting, listing, and organizing nearly five thousand pieces of correspondence, besides ledgers, books, catalogues, and press cuttings. The Waltons and Sir Hector Hetherington, who had replaced Rait as Principal of the university, occasionally inspected her progress on visits to Tite Street, where she always served them freshly baked cakes. She asked a widowed neighbor, Kathleen Gay, who had a flat next door in Shelley Court, to help her sort and prepare the materials for shipment to Glasgow. Rosalind refused to let "any stranger" assist her, but she had known Gay since moving to Tite Street, and Gay's mother had known Charles Whibley, Ethel's husband. She later acknowledged that she never could have managed without her neighbor. "She has good judgment & artistic appreciation," Rosalind assured the Waltons of Gay, and did "not let the grass grow under her feet," which Rosalind confessed to be her own failing. "I am a fearful trial to her sometimes I fear," she admitted.[81]

Appreciating the historical importance of their task, Gay, whose husband had been a decorated army officer, agreed to help because of Rosalind's "failing health" and the knowledge that she was "often very lonely and grateful for the company." However, the task was daunting. They began with "immense piles of letters" that had been stored in a variety of boxes, drawers, and baskets in Rosalind's attic. They were slowed, too, by Rosalind's tendency to reminiscence about each letter and regale Gay "with enthralling stories of the past." Gay soon realized how very painful Rosalind found the process of sorting all those old letters. "The whole of her life is centered in them and once they are in order and she has decided which are to be kept she will have nothing left to live for," Gay informed Dorothy Walton. "After a while I began to feel that she does not really want to finish them!" Worse still, Rosalind continued to destroy letters, especially those between Whistler and Beatrice.[82]

Somehow, by April 1954, they had finished and loaded their precious cargo into a "dreary-looking chest" that reminded Gay of a coffin. They sealed the knot of the securing cord with wax and stamped it with a butterfly.

Having been ill since Christmas and suffering from a tumble on the stairs thanks to an arthritic knee, Rosalind's depression over relinquishing the letters resurfaced when asked to sign the requisite legal documents. She nearly balked and said, according to Gay, that "she really ought to have burned the lot." To Dorothy Walton she confessed, "I only hope I haven't done foolishly."[83]

As Rosalind's health continued to fail, she saw, like many elderly people, an entire world in decline. One Christmas she complained, "The shops are a depressing experience & things are really scandalous." She had trouble finding reliable "domestic help," though she did make and share a Christmas dinner with her laundress. A trip to the dentist left her nerves feeling "rather unbalanced," and her arthritis worsened. She walked whenever she went out because she believed getting on and off buses "too dangerous for the aged." She refused to participate in a campaign to have a plaque placed on Oscar Wilde's old Tite Street house because she thought Whistler would have disapproved. She suddenly feared that if his correspondence with Wilde fell into the wrong hands, it would never be seen again. Only her three cats, two of whom she had rescued from the streets, were a comfort. She declared, "We all hang together for good or ill."[84]

She enjoyed visiting an Art Council exhibition of Whistler's etchings at the Tate shortly after shipping the letters to Glasgow. The best part for Rosalind, thought Kathleen Gay, who remained a reliable friend, was when she could point out errors in the catalogue to the director of the gallery. However, Gay worried about Rosalind living alone in her "large & artic house," warmed in winter only by a "miserable little electric stove." She succumbed to influenza in January 1955 but refused to remain in bed. When rushed unconscious to the Belgravia Nursing Home after suffering a slight stroke, she awoke in a fury and insisted on going home. She attributed the stroke to medicine given her for the flu. She also blamed the harsh winter weather on the testing of hydrogen bombs. Before leaving the nursing home, she instructed the young nurses, whom she identified as mostly Irish, on "how to conduct their affairs (or rather <u>not</u> to), which greatly amused them."[85]

She remained in contact with Colnaghi & Company, as the firm was now known, which still sold the Goulding lithographs. She also sold the gallery three small Whistler oils on wood panels: *The Sea, Pourville*; *The Shore, Pourville*; and *Howeth Head, Near Dublin*, all done between 1899 and 1900. "I am trying to find out where Whistler is supposed to rank in the dealers world," she informed Dorothy Walton shortly before her stroke.

"I have no doubt myself but I am much amused secretly." She had not forgotten Glasgow, and despite the magnificent gifts already presented to the university she arranged for a final bequest upon her death. It would consist mostly of her own correspondence but also include more paintings, works on paper, books, and a large collection of prints.[86]

Rosalind carried on for another three years, until February 6, 1958. She died at home, aged eighty-four, from a combination of bronchopneumonia, influenza, and arteriosclerosis. She was interred at the sprawling Brompton Cemetery, where many of her family, including her parents, lay. So, too, such luminaries from Whistler's life as Valentine Prinsep, Sir Henry Cole, and Frederick R. Leyland. Rosalind's grave is distant from those gentlemen and more modest. She shares the narrow plot (5½ × 4½ feet) with her sister Frances, who rests below her. They were given no headstone, only a stone marker, but I found the general location, in a grove of trees, through the cemetery's register. It is a pleasant spot, even on a raw, wet day in March, but it was a sad visit. All trace of Rosalind's grave, including the stone marker, have disappeared. I assume she is still there, somewhere below ground.[87]

PART 2

Explanations

CHAPTER 4

Whistler a Dandy?

"Before meeting Whistler, I had been led to expect a diabolical sort of being," confessed art critic, poet, and novelist Camille Mauclair, "a magnetizer strange and ferocious, an alchemist and dandy whose laugh, like that of the German fairy, was inexorable and deadly." Mauclair's apprehension proved groundless, as he was immediately disarmed by Whistler's "lively cordiality" and "fine courtesy." His experience did not keep Mauclair, four years later in 1898, from casting Whistler as the witty but acerbic Norwegian painter Niels Elstiern in his roman à clef *Les Soleil des morts*, but he did not present Whistler/Elstiern as a dandy.[1]

Mauclair did not count dandyism as a positive attribute. Nor did most of Whistler's contemporaries, who regarded dandies as shallow people: mere fops, coxcombs, and popinjays. Something of that suspicion lingers even today. Yet it has become part of the historical image of Whistler. Mention his name, and many people immediately think of him as a conceited toff, dressed in form-fitting double-breasted frock coat, wearing patent-leather pumps, monocle firmly planted, and a long walking stick, or "wand," in hand. If not also sporting a silk French top hat, it is only because he wishes the world to admire his glistening white forelock.

But is this a completely accurate image? Most of Whistler's biographers have accepted it, describing him variously as an "eccentric," even "aggressive" and "provocative" dandy. Commentators on his art have followed suit with references to his "rebellious" or "flamboyant" dandyism. To their credit, not all writers have fallen into this trap, but neither have they confronted or tried to refute the characterization.[2]

Historians of visual culture and fashion have reinforced the image by using Whistler, along with Oscar Wilde, as a poster boy for Victorian dandyism. This perspective is often melded with investigations of nineteenth-century gender roles and definitions of "manliness," which further complicate matters by playing into an image of "precious femininity." The result is a Whistler with a "dandified sensibility" and "dandy fastidiousness." Even when he is not specifically accused of dandyism, the charge is implied by his association with Wilde, the ultimate "decadent dandy." That would have galled Whistler to no end, but he had only himself to blame after so carelessly, on one occasion, claiming that he had "invented" Oscar.[3]

Still others have suggested highly imaginative interpretations of Whistler's dandyism. One author, seeking to emphasize the artist's American roots and flair for showmanship, rescued him from being a "European dandy" by making him a "Yankee-Doodle dandy," akin to a "cowboy glorying in a silver-chased saddle and fancy boots." Another writer discovered a "dandified definition of value" in Whistler's art. Conceding that the artist was "too flashily dressed, too floridly pugnacious to count as a dandy of the most exquisitely inert kind," he maintained that Whistler's dandyism is most clearly evident in his paintings, which exude an "implacable refinement of taste."[4]

Granted, a precise definition of dandyism is elusive. Dress and appearance count for much, but so do manner and style, and the importance of particular qualities can seem paradoxical when examined in different places or eras. To speak of dandyism in the abstract can only result in useless generalizations. Twenty-first-century dandyism, for instance, is defined almost entirely by attire, as seen in a recent article about the "New Dandies" in *GQ*. Similarly, the British publication *Chap* emphasizes wardrobe and appearance as it celebrates the modern dandy and "dandizette," or female dandy. Yet the concept remains a broad one, with other important qualities, such as a contempt for societal norms and values, an "affinity for the perverse," and a "self-destructive" impulse often cited.[5]

Most attempts to brand Whistler a dandy rely on French poet and essayist Charles Baudelaire, with whom Whistler was acquainted, as their authority. In his 1863 essay "The Painter of Modern Life," Baudelaire declared, "It [dandyism] is first and foremost the burning need to create for oneself a personal originality. It is a kind of cult of the self. . . . It is a type of revolt, too, a means of combating and destroying triviality."

That much certainly sounds like Whistler, but he fails other, crucial parts of Baudelaire's nineteenth-century ideal. For example, the poet emphasized that dandyism is a way of life, not a cloak to be donned only occasionally or used as a pose when in public. His dandy is "rich and idle," a man who has "no other occupation than the perpetual pursuit of happiness," someone "whose solitary profession is elegance." Baudelaire's dandy must also be "blasé." There is "simplicity in his air of authority," his "distinguishing characteristic" being "an air of coldness which comes from an unshakeable determination not to be moved." When was the impulsive, irrepressible Whistler any of those things?[6]

Other writers have tried to conflate the dandy and the flaneur. No one can doubt Whistler's passion for strolling the streets, alleys, and byways of any place he inhabited or visited, be it Paris, London, Venice, Amsterdam, Brussels, or Valparaiso. However, the flaneur as dandy is supposedly listless, moving from one scene to the next with no definite destination or fixed purpose. Baudelaire dismissed such a man as a "mere flaneur." Whistler's rambles better fit Baudelaire's definition of an "artist poet" in search of "modernity." He seldom had any destination in mind, but his wandering rarely lacked intent. He sought, as Baudelaire would have it, "the ephemeral, the fugitive, the contingent, the half of art whose other half is eternal and immutable."[7]

People who knew Whistler conceded his vanity, self-promotion, individuality, and sense of style and fashion, but the most worldly-wise and astute of them rarely associated those traits with dandyism. Rather, they called him "dapper" or "fastidious," someone who exuded the same "old-world courtesy" that had disarmed Mauclair. Artist George H. Boughton, a loyal friend known to detest "vanity and pretence," regarded Whistler as "breezy, buoyant, and debonair." Lillie Langtry found his appearance "oddly arresting," designed to express a "studied eccentricity in keeping with . . . [his] whimsical personality." His hereditary tuft of white hair, which was mostly gray and barely noticeable until the 1870s, she regarded as "weird." Others thought it "a rallying point of humor."[8]

Whistler had a style all his own. "Whistler . . . was unlike anything or anybody else," confirmed Algernon Bertram Freeman-Mitford, Lord Redesdale, a London neighbor for several years. "He was delicate, playful, whimsical, a creature of fancy." While always "neatly dressed," observed author and journalist Frank Harris, Whistler retained "something particular in his attire—the artist's self-conscious protest which gave him a certain exotic flavor and individuality." He possessed, Harris said, "a certain perky distinction." Another friend thought him "always immaculately though eccentrically dressed."[9]

In this light, it is worth considering that Whistler's purported dandyism depends heavily on either a collapsing of time or a total disregard for it. Exactly when was he supposed to have been a dandy? An authoritative collection of Whistler images insists that his "appearance changed considerably over the . . . years." Arthur Jerome Eddy, whose portrait Whistler painted in 1894, reinforced this impression. "Nearly every sketch, drawing, or portrait of Whistler gives some phase of his many-sided personality," Eddy observed, "but not one—not even those by himself—gives anything like an adequate conception." Perhaps this is why Mortimer Menpes, one of Whistler's most devoted followers, found it impossible in three well-known multiple-image drypoints of the master to settle on a single pose or facial expression.[10]

Whistler's parents certainly did not rear him to be a dandy. Both George and Anna Whistler were aware of the latest fashions. George, occupying as he did important positions in the railroad business, always looked the part of a gentleman and was "fastidious in matters of dress, neatness and appropriateness." But both parents were suspicious of fashionable society, or the "snobs" as George called them. Surviving childhood photographs and other early images of his son show a neatly dressed young man who seemed destined to emulate the father.[11]

Not unnaturally, youthful rebellion temporarily eroded that early influence. Caricatures Whistler drew of fellow cadets at West Point reflect a disdain for the dignity sometimes associated with military uniforms and a martial bearing. Years later, being inordinately proud of having attended the Academy, he reminisced about looking "very dandy in grey" as a cadet, but that is a quite different use of the word. The many demerits Whistler received for his unkempt appearance testify to his rebellious streak. As one classmate recalled, "He was not soldierly in appearance, bearing or habit."[12]

This rejection of conformity became obvious after his dismissal from West Point in 1854. Whistler then turned bohemian and became known for a "leaning towards the style of the artist in the selection of his clothing." That remained his inclination for the next decade, as he embraced the bohemian life of a young artist in Paris and London. Some writers trace his dandyism to the Paris years, primarily because he sometimes wore a summer suit of "cool . . . linen duck and . . . jaunty straw-hat." Yet while that "lively attire," as George Boughton noted, may have seemed eccentric in European cities, the hat, at least, was "common enough in America." Englishman Thomas Armstrong, a fellow student in Paris, described the hat as a "Yankee hat" and the entire outfit as "American." When "well-groomed," Armstrong contended, Whistler "made a very good appearance," although his chief concern was to define himself as an anti-bourgeois artist, not a dandy.[13]

Some scholars contend that bohemianism is simply another type of dandyism. They point to a "garret assembly" style of dress prevalent from the 1860s to 1890s, when the principal sartorial goal of artistic rebels was to set themselves apart from academy-trained artists and the vulgar middle classes. The result of this "refined Bohemianism" was the "bohemian dandy." The larger point of these writers, which certainly has merit, is to suggest the ease with which artists could change identities. Yet to conflate bohemianism and dandyism obscures more than it reveals, especially because, as one scholar insists, even at the time the definition of bohemianism was "simply all over the place." It is especially confusing when one considers the variety of Whistler's early bohemian experiences, including student days in Paris and his association with what writer and novelist Vernon Lee called "the little clique of more mystical and Bohemian pre-Raphaelites."[14]

Another scholar has suggested that Whistler displayed a "dandified sensibility" by combining bohemian dress with "references to the dandy and the gentleman." While this attempt to make him a dandy and gentleman simultaneously is as confusing as turning bohemians (or cowboys) into dandies, the interpretation does explain why Whistler eventually shed his bohemian appearance in order to attract middle-class patrons and buyers. However, the writer's analogy falls flat when linking "dandyish fastidiousness" to the care Whistler lavished on his hair, which is described rather awkwardly as being "fashioned in a dandified and coiffured bohemianism." He ignores the fact that Whistler had always taken pride in his dark brown curly locks, an inheritance from his father. His reluctance to have his hair cut at West Point produced a slew of demerits. Vanity, yes, but not dandyism.[15]

Friends and fellow bohemians from the 1850s and 1860s were more struck by the "humorous vent" this "gallicized Yankee" gave his stories than by his manner or attire. Alan S. Cole, who first met Whistler when they were children, in the 1840s, became a lifelong friend during those later decades.

He mentioned the artist frequently in his diaries, which ran into the 1890s, but never described him as a dandy. Neither did Henri Fantin-Latour, Tom Armstrong, or George du Maurier. Upon first spotting Whistler in the Louvre, Fantin thought him "eccentric," a "strange character wearing a bizarre hat." Armstrong went no further than to describe his friend's appearance as "at all times remarkable," and du Maurier, despite his later spoof of Whistler as Joe Sibley in *Trilby*, saw more of the bohemian than the dandy in him. In 1860, du Maurier drew the first published images of Whistler in cartoons for *Punch*. One showed him in artistic attire that could pass, at worst, as bohemian. The other presented him as a middle-class gentleman, the only possible eccentric touch being a monocle, which he sported in both drawings.[16]

It is also worth noting that Anna Whistler lived with her son for the majority of the 1860s and well into the 1870s in London, and any attempt at dandyism under her watchful eye was not likely to succeed. Artist Valentine C. Prinsep, one of the "Bohemian pre-Raphaelites" mentioned by Vernon Lee, observed how the "irrepressible Jimmy" abandoned all pretense when with his mother, whom he indulged in every possible way.[17]

During those same years, Benjamin Moran, a member of the US diplomatic legation in London, had occasional encounters with members of the Whistler family as they entered and exited England. James Whistler, he decided in 1867, exhibited a "strong dash of the Bohemian" but nothing more. This, too, from a man who was horrified by the appearance and behavior of the "half formed dandies" he encountered at the notorious Cremorne Gardens.[18]

Several scholars have made a case for Whistler's dandyism in the 1860s by pointing to his appearance in Fantin-Latour's masterful painting *Homage à Delacroix*. It might almost be called *Homage à Whistler*, for Fantin placed his friend, whom he considered the leading painter of their generation, front and center in this group portrait. Whistler is nearly a mirror image of the recently deceased Delacroix, whose portrait hangs on the wall immediately behind him. In as much as Delacroix was considered a flaneur and dandy in his day, Fantin's Whistler does project something of that air. Yet while arguably more elegant looking than other men in the picture, he is not appreciably better dressed. One Whistler authority thinks he resembles a "military officer in mufti," which also suggests that it is a soldier's bearing, as much as his uniform, that gives the appearance of dandyism. Another scholar finds an "urban masculinity" in Whistler's appearance and posture.[19]

Considered from this perspective, the comments of artist Jacques-Émile Blanche about Fantin's painting are revealing. Blanche became a friend of Whistler in the 1880s, and while not uncritical of his behavior or his art, he made no reference to him as a dandy when recalling their friendship in 1927. He seems to have forgotten that nearly a decade earlier he had described Whistler's appearance in *Homage à Delacroix* as that of "a young dandy." His memory also failed him when he recalled Whistler wearing a monocle and sporting his white forelock in the painting, neither of which is true. Blanche had apparently read or heard of Whistler presented so often as a dandy over the intervening years that the fanciful image became fact for him.[20]

Thomas Carlyle did not have to depend on memory to know that Whistler was no dandy, at least not in the early 1870s. A year before Whistler was born, Carlyle published one of the first attacks on dandyism in his satirical *Sartor Resartus, or The Tailor Re-Tailored*. While the book is a complex, philosophical musing on social issues of his day, the dandy's decadent effect on society was chief among Carlyle's concerns. Being only slightly removed from the days of the Regency and the dandyism of Beau Brummel, he ridiculed the dandy as the last vestige of a failed aristocratic order.

In this respect, Carlyle's perspective is the opposite of Baudelaire, who, rather than denigrating the dandy, praised him as part of a new aristocracy, defined by intellectual or artistic achievements rather than economic or social position. Yet both men associated dandyism with a way of life and agreed on the dandy's desire to be noticed. "Every faculty of his soul, spirit, purse, and person," Carlyle said of the dandy, "is heroically consecrated to this one object, the wearing of clothes wisely and well: so as others dress to live, he lives to dress."[21]

Carlyle was not blind to Whistler's eccentricities, on one occasion describing him as "the most absurd creature on the face of the earth." Irish poet William Allingham insisted that Carlyle referred to Whistler simply as "The Creature." Maybe so, but after sitting many hours for his portrait in 1872–73, he also came to know the artist as "a very remarkable person." Almost amusingly, Carlyle, who was known for the very undandy-like "loose and careless" fit of his own clothes, complained midway through the sittings that Whistler seemed more interested in painting his attire than his face or person. It is fascinating to contemplate, as did Tom Armstrong, what two such "utterly different" men talked about during those sittings, or afterward, as Whistler escorted Carlyle home in walks along the Thames. More certain is that for all his suspicions of Whistler, the Sage of Chelsea, who "did not suffer fools gladly," never leveled a charge of dandyism against him.[22]

There would seem then to be only two relatively brief periods in his life when the word *dandy* might apply to Whistler: the late 1870s and the first half of the 1880s, though with a sharp break in between. The late 1870s were the years of the first Grosvenor exhibition and the budding Aesthetic movement. Whistler relished his association with the Grosvenor, even though it linked him to a new type of precious dandyism, personified by the Aesthetes, who were mercilessly parodied by du Maurier in the pages of *Punch*. This was the moment, in 1877, when John Ruskin maligned a Whistler painting as an example of "Cockney impudence," the work of a mere "coxcomb."

Not coincidentally, the earliest published image of Whistler as dandy—and the only one before the mid-1880s—is a caricature drawn by his friend Leslie Ward for a January 1878 issue of *Vanity Fair*. Whistler professed to be "very fond" of the drawing, and indeed, no one laughed more heartily than he over attempts, either in words or pictures, to depict him as a dandy. Yet friends did not think it "especially characteristic" of him. Ward, too, knew the caricature, even by definition, to be an exaggeration. Whistler made "an excellent subject," he said, but his outer appearance conveyed nothing more than a surface impression of the man. Whistler's "unlimited peculiarities lay more in his gesture and speech and habits," Ward submitted. It is equally important to appreciate that the drawing accompanied a flattering article that identified Whistler as one of the "Men of the Day," praised his work, and described him as "the most charming, simple, and witty of men."[23]

In any event, this spurt of superficial dandyism was neither consistent nor enduring. Two months later, in March, du Maurier portrayed Whistler in gentlemanly attire at a musical soiree in the home of their artist friend Louise Jopling. In May, a journalist who interviewed Whistler for the *World* emphasized the artist's "intense earnestness" and gentlemanly appearance. Dressed in a blue serge yachtsman's suit and "natty" square-toed shoes, Whistler acknowledged that people thought him "eccentric," but the journalist also recognized in him a "genuine enthusiast and persistent seeker for perfection." Whistler proudly reprinted the article in *The Gentle Art of Making Enemies* as "The Red Rag."[24]

Another six months brought Whistler's lawsuit against Ruskin for libel, his subsequent bankruptcy, and his voluntary exile to Venice. We see nothing of the dandy during the artist's impoverished year in that city. Otto

Bacher, who became one of his most ardent followers, described him upon their first meeting in Venice as "a curious, sailorlike" figure. His usual attire consisted of dark sack coat and wide-brimmed, soft, brown hat. A "narrow black ribbon" served as a tie. Harper Pennington, who also first met Whistler in Venice, insisted, "His clothes, generally black, were always simple in the extreme and spotless, even when, in . . . dreadful poverty, they were worn thread bare—actually in holes." Another young artist, having spotted Whistler in the Piazza San Marco, noted, "He wears a little straw hat and is 'ordinary' of looks and speech." Whistler himself, on one of the rare occasions when he mentioned dandyism, ridiculed a "dandy about town" he had seen in Venice.[25]

That leaves the first half of the 1880s, following his return to London, as the most compelling moment for a dandified Whistler. These were the years of his vigorous, almost bitter, rebellion against the philistines. Whatever his previous eccentricities, he now exaggerated them as a means of outraging bourgeois society and the artistic establishment. He was more combative, more quarrelsome, and absolutely determined to live by his own rules. This required a visible change in behavior and dress.

Artist and critic Robert A. M. Stevenson left a striking description of Whistler's most flamboyant attire during these years. His frock coat, which had a "magnificent but wholly unfashionable 'flare,'" was as black and glossy as his tall, flat-brimmed, French-style top hat. "His trousers were of an unheard-of lilac-grey, and 'peg-tops' at that; his waistcoat was pale lemon-coloured with black buttons; . . . the shoes were of patent leather, very long and elegant and pointed; and the finishing touch was an ebony cane adorned with a yellow-butterfly silk bow with streamers!" His handkerchief, like the vest, was lemon-colored.[26]

Whistler's most fantastic prop, his "wand," was largely a product of the 1880s. In the late 1870s, he sometimes used a very thin cane, "about the size of a darning needle." Or, as pictured by Leslie Ward, he might substitute a maulstick for a traditional walking stick, meant to suggest, perhaps, the small, useless cane associated with eighteenth-century dandies. Whistler fancied his wand because its length added a dramatic touch should he wish to point or gesture, one might even say perform, with it. It could also be a means of intimidation, the equivalent of a rapier. "I keep this for the critics," he once chuckled.[27]

The critics and popular press pounced. While acknowledging Whistler's "capricious talent," the *Pall Mall Gazette* declared in May 1882, "We protest against those foppish airs and affectations by which Mr. Whistler impresses on us his contempt of public opinion." Then came the "charming foppery" of the 1883 Fine Arts Society exhibition of his Venice etchings, shown as "An Arrangement in White and Yellow." Whistler wore yellow socks to the private view and encouraged people attending the carnival to adorn themselves with yellow flowers, kerchiefs, cravats, and boutonnieres. Firmly linked to Oscar Wilde's exaggerated brand of Aestheticism by this time, Whistler also suffered from the abuse heaped upon that entire movement. Aesthetes, declared the *Pall Mall Gazette,* had not acquired their "zeal for Art . . . out of a genuine love of beauty, but out of fashion and love of display." In France, the press spoke of Whistler's "supreme dandyism."[28]

They were suggesting, as had Ruskin, that Whistler, the fop, dandy, and coxcomb, was neither a gentleman nor a serious artist. Virtually every reference to him in these terms came from art critics who disapproved of both his behavior and his paintings, the implication being that he was neither as talented nor as respectable as such artists as John Everett Millais, Edward John Poynter, or, most especially, Frederic Leighton. All these men were friends of Whistler, and they admired his work, but in the public eye, they, unlike him, had managed to remain both creditable artists and gentlemen.[29]

Whistler, who bristled at any suggestion that his commitment to art was less than genuine and unconditional, realized that he had badly miscalculated in this new flirtation with dandyism. So, with charges of "foppish airs" threatening to taint his work, he pulled back. He first revealed his concern by distancing himself from Oscar Wilde. It is going too far to say, as has one scholar, that "Whistler's get-up, almost verging on fancy dress, was as outré as Wilde's," and the artist would eventually fall out with Wilde over far more serious matters than attire, but to be linked with the Irishman's excesses sobered Whistler. At the very least, being associated with Wilde—whose Aestheticism soon became associated with decadence—threatened Whistler's ability to control his public image.[30]

Consequently, William Merritt Chase's famous 1885 portrait of Whistler is not what it seems (fig. 8). Whistler's amusingly insolent stance, with hand on hip and both right foot and wand thrust aggressively forward, seems to mark him as a classic dandy, and in some ways the painting does summarize his popular image in the early 1880s. But two things undermine it. First, Chase knew the pose to be false. He later admitted, even emphasized, that the Whistler in the portrait was "merely Whistler at play." Chase, like many others, knew there were two Whistlers: the public one, with all his

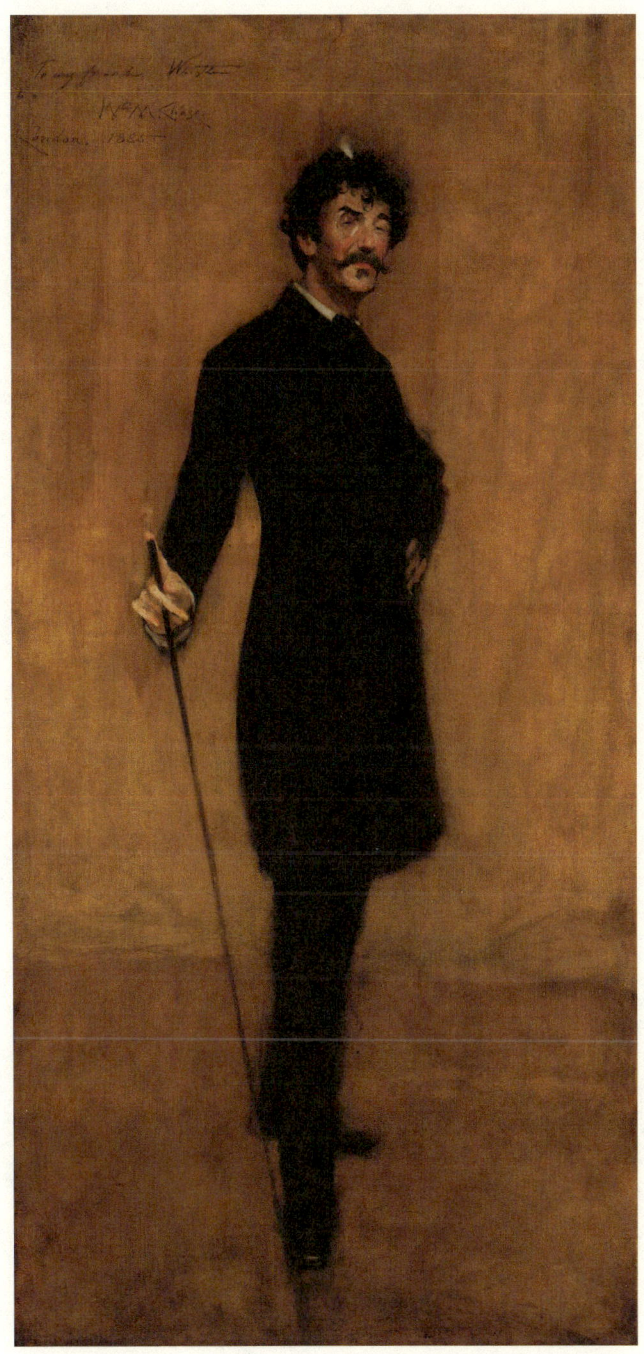

FIG. 8 William Merrit Chase (1849–1916), *James Abbott McNeill Whistler*, 1885. Oil on canvas, 188.3 × 92.1 cm. 18.22.2, Metropolitan Museum of Art, New York. Bequest of William H. Walker, 1918.

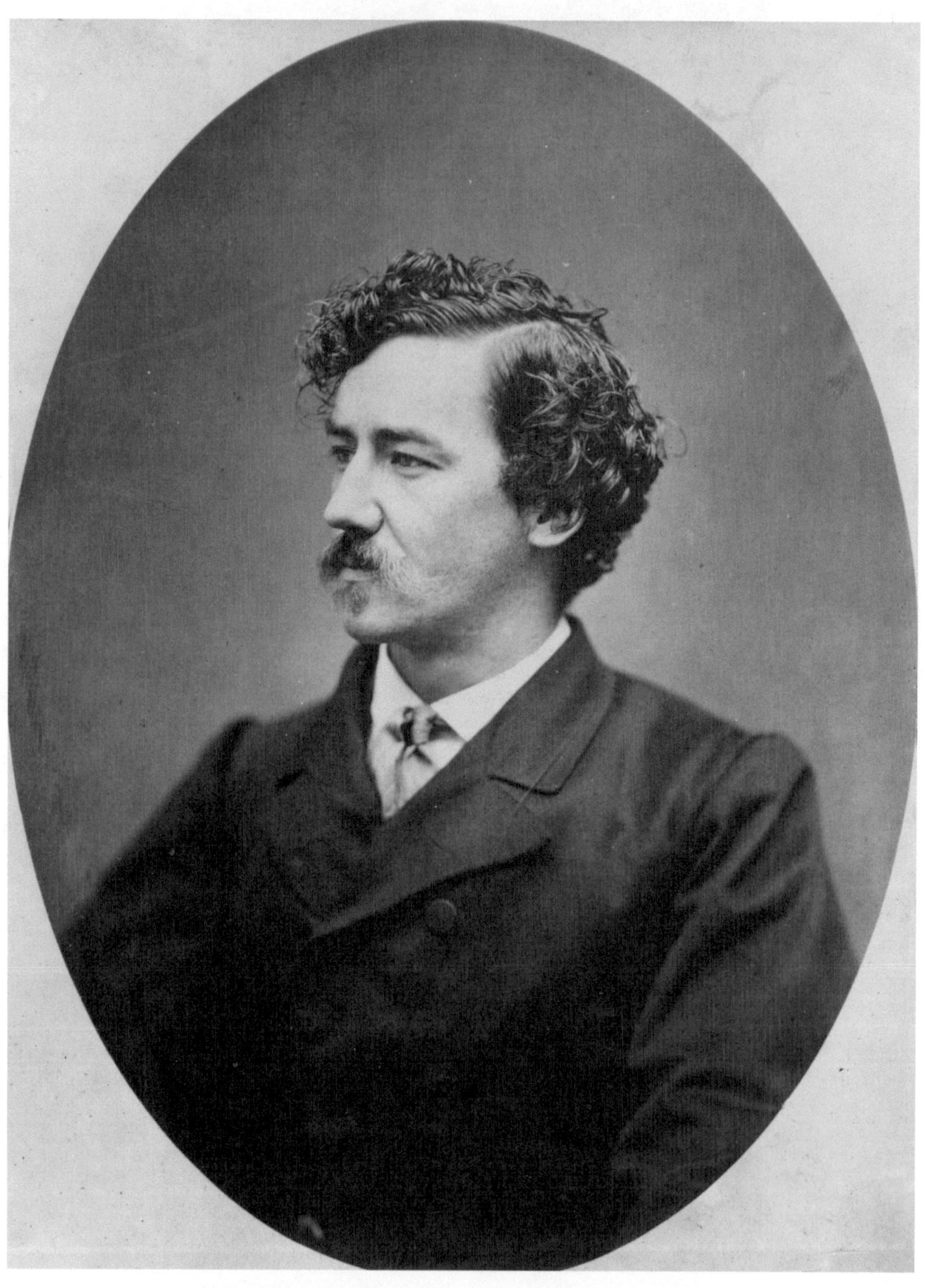

FIG. 9 James McNeill Whistler, 1885. Photograph. LC-DIG-ds-04747, Prints and Photographs Division, Library of Congress, Washington, DC.

playfulness and what Whistler called "gimcracks," and the private man, the "only one genuine" Whistler, the serious artist and "tireless, slavish worker."

Then there is Whistler's reaction to the portrait, which he came to hate. He thought the pose a bit of sport at the time, as though asking the world, as Chase interpreted it, "You've never taken me seriously, why should I be serious with you?" However, when Chase subsequently exhibited the painting in America, expressly against Whistler's wishes, only to have both it and his subject ridiculed by the critics, Whistler dismissed the work as a "monstrous lampoon."[31]

In that same year of 1885 Whistler further separated himself from the Aesthetes with his masterful "Ten O'Clock" lecture. You will find no hint of dandyism in the "Ten O'Clock." Quite the opposite. Whistler used the lecture to attack "vulgarity" in all its forms, and though he never mentioned him by name, the dandified image of Oscar Wilde, that "Gentle priest," had become the essence of vulgarity for Whistler, both sartorially and intellectually. "The Dilettante stalks abroad," he warned the audience, with Wilde sitting in the sixth row to his right. "The amateur is loosed. The voice of the aesthete is heard in the land, and catastrophe is upon us." Concerning foppish airs, Whistler insisted, "Costume is not dress. And the wearers of wardrobes may not be doctors of taste!"[32]

The next year, 1886, Whistler became the quite respectable, if controversial, president of the Society of British Artists (fig. 9). Under his stewardship, it became a *Royal* society, emblematic of his desire to project a dignified appearance, both personally and through the organization's public image. Albert Ludovici, one of his staunchest supporters in reshaping the society, described him as "always neatly dressed, in black in winter and white in summer." Whistler always changed for dinner during these years, and he donned evening dress when attending society meetings. As his friend Theodore Duret commented, Whistler took for granted that "gentlemen" wore evening dress "at dinner, in society, at the theatre, at a ball." Members either hostile to their leader's proposed reforms or unfamiliar with his ways regarded this as "snobbish," but not even his adversaries thought of him as a dandy.[33]

Alice Carr, wife of art critic J. Comyns Carr, knew Whistler particularly well in the 1880s and had a different take on the "two Whistlers." Considering herself a thorough bohemian, she always thought of Whistler as belonging to that world. Where he differed, she believed, was in his ability to navigate between what she called the "social and Bohemian worlds." Before

Whistler came along, those two worlds had "always revolved in . . . distinctly separate orbits." Yet the "irrepressible Jimmy" moved easily between them, not necessarily as two different people, but by making himself acceptable in the "social" realm through his charm, wit, and disarming if "despotic self-appreciation."[34]

Traces of dandyism may be seen in Giovanni Boldini's 1897 portrait of Whistler, but then Boldini painted most people—men and women—that way. Whistler's pose, if aristocratic, is more that of a gentleman, the same impression conveyed in every photograph of him from the 1890s, or indeed, throughout his life. Besides that, he is quite clearly an aging, if not elderly, gentleman, at sixty-three years old long past the time when he might be mistaken for a dandy. One of Whistler's biographers describes his appearance in the painting as a "combination of Satanic boulevardier and music-hall prestidigitator." Maybe that is why Whistler disliked this portrait, too.[35]

By the 1890s, only the gentleman remained. Some caricaturists, such as Max Beerbohm, continued to portray him as a dandy well into the twentieth century, but their work was neither informed nor very imaginative. Indeed, the irritatingly smug Beerbohm, who fancied himself an expert on the subject, asserted in 1896 that Whistler only "wished" to be a dandy. As one scholar of fashion has observed, while Whistler "had some dandy moments," he was always "less conventional in his clothes than a dandy." He had a "highly individual feeling for fashion as part of a decorative whole." Theodore Duret observed that "the gentleman and artist were curiously mixed" in Whistler's attire.[36]

A friend and neighbor of the 1890s, Edmund H. Wuerpel, said Whistler could be "as fastidious as a dandy" but only to emphasize his high standards. Some people even thought him occasionally ill-dressed or inclined toward "certain peculiarities of dress" during these years. Yet there remained the old "sprightly daintiness of manner." Harrison S. Morris, directing manager of the Pennsylvania Academy of Fine Arts in the 1890s, recalled a "mincing figure, dainty, indecisive, delicate of taste in dress and manner." Someone else thoughted him "indefinably one of the old-world *noblesse*"; the French recognized him as *un parfait gentilhomme* and *bel esprit*. A Paris neighbor from the early 1890s described Whistler as "always very neatly dressed," "very quiet in manner," and exuding "an air of distinction even in the way in which he asked the concierge for his letters." An acquaintance who had often met him socially in the 1890s saw nothing dandified about him. "He was slightly built, refined-looking, and carried himself well, even gracefully," this man insisted. "But Whistler looked a gentleman, not like a *boulevardier*." Gone was the wand, which Joseph Pennell could recall Whistler using only once in the twenty years he knew him. W. Graham Robertson, who knew Whistler nearly as long, recalled only a "little cane." Eddy insisted that he occasionally used a rolled-up umbrella as walking stick.[37]

An anecdote offered by Mortimer Menpes is often used to confirm the master's dandyism. It involves a visit to a Regent Street hairdresser's shop, where Whistler displayed an obsessive concern with his curly locks and white plume. What supporters of Whistler's dandyism leave out in retelling this story is that Menpes rejected the episode as evidence of dandyism, vanity, or any sort of artifice. "Whistler treated his hair," Menpes declared, "as he could not but treat everything about him, purely from the artistic standpoint, as a picture, a bit of decoration." So, too, his "mode of dress." With Whistler, it was "always the artist who talked, and not the vain man of fashion."[38]

More to the point, Whistler's personality simply did not lend itself to many popular notions about dandyism. For instance, its associations with a stereotypical limp-wrist effeminacy, which had begun to take hold by the 1890s, falls flat for the artist. J. Comyns Carr observed in Whistler's entire "character and personality something of the charm, something also of the weakness, that is commonly supposed to be exclusively feminine." One might also speculate that Whistler's well-documented knowledge of fashion, including women's fashions, suggests an effeminate nature. People, for instance, noted the care he took with his appearance, all that "fussing and primping like a woman." Yet Joseph and Elizabeth Pennell, who did think Whistler's dandyism "one very charming and characteristic side of him," insisted that he was "neither vain nor effeminate," merely "fastidious about his personal appearance." Carr's wife, Alice, made a similar point. Identifying "Jimmy's particular vanity" as his hair, she imagined it took him as long as any woman to arrange, but only because he was so "tremendously proud of his personal appearance."[39]

Possibly a more accurate word than dandy, and one often used by his contemporaries to describe Whistler, is *poseur*. Granted, we must be careful here. *Poseur* can imply a charlatan, an impostor, a mountebank, inauthenticity, and no one walked a finer line between respectability and buffoonery, between artist and huckster, than Whistler. That had been a crucial issue in the Ruskin trial. However, Whistler's friends and admirers understood the word differently when applying it to him. His poses, they understood, were lighthearted, intended to draw attention to himself, but in a playful way.

Eddy, recognizing the "two Whistlers" identified by Chase, insisted that the artist was "a poser in the sense [that] . . . he was one man before the public and another in work." Another observer maintained that "with his temperament it would indeed be extraordinary if he were not something of a *poseur*." American journalist William H. Rideing, upon being introduced to Whistler at London's Arts Club, tagged him at once as "an unmistakable poseur, long-limbed and nonchalant, with a drawl as sesquipedalian as that of Mark Twain." Theodore Duret denied that Whistler was "a mere man of fashion." Rather, Duret maintained, he combined the "manners of a gentleman with the pose and fantastic get-up of the artist." The monocle, the wand, the bows were all theatrical props: simply gimcracks, never universally employed, and to be put aside in real life, which for Whistler meant the studio.[40]

This is an important point, not a mere question of semantics. Whistler, who as an adult sought perfection in all things, wished always to be regarded as a gentleman. He never "posed" as one. That part of him was inbred, another inheritance from his father, and it became part of his fabric. The question is, can a gentleman be a dandy? It would seem not, at least according to Baudelaire, Carlyle, and other experts on the subject. Does eccentricity of dress or behavior disqualify one as a gentleman? Possibly, if the eccentricity is erratic, vulgar, or irrational. But what if eccentricity is itself a pose? That is where we stand with Whistler. Being a dandy is serious business, a way of life, and taken seriously by men who wish to be so known. Whistler's extravagances were staged.

By the 1870s, Whistler knew the promotional value of a pose for keeping himself in the public eye. He did this most often with his solo exhibitions, Sunday breakfasts, verbal jousts with his critics, and provocative remarks about art, but eccentricity in dress and behavior also helped. Consequently Whistler, as a modern self-publicist, helped to craft the role of artist as "provocateur," "performer," and "poseur." American journalist George W. Smalley, a friend of twenty years, put it this way in 1885: "He had the wit to see that genius must in these days wear the crown of eccentricity." For instance, while being genuinely far-sighted, and in need of spectacles, the still "keen-eyed Whistler" often relied on his monocle, as artist and author William Rothenstein put it, for "fixing" a person as he leaned into them during conversation. On other occasions, he waved it in circles, screwed it into his eye for emphasis, or let it drop to the floor while he fumbled in his waistcoat pocket for a replacement—his way of stalling for time when in debate. Rumor had it that he carried four or five eyepieces for that very purpose.[41]

One scholar has recently pointed to the cocked elbow Whistler displays in the Chase portrait and in some photographs as an overlooked part of his pose. With hand on hip, arm jutting upward, he assumes an attitude of power, authority, and confidence. In this mode, the elbow serves not as a mere affectation but as a signal of his desire to project his artistic ascendency. It could also mask his insecurities.[42]

Of course, it could be said that to present oneself as a dandy is itself a pose, a "theatrical stance," as one scholar puts it, the "blurring of life and theater." Harper Pennington acknowledged a certain "dandified attitude" in the master but also knew this to be an "assumed" identity, used "especially when chaffing someone who deserved it." As Joseph Pennell came to realize, Whistler's appearance "was to him merely a part of the 'joke of life.'" Comyns Carr insisted that, in addition to being "impishly militant," Whistler "took a childish delight in any little studied departure from the rules of ordinary costume." These "calculated eccentricities," Carr explained, might include the very undandylike combination of "spotless white ducks beneath his long black frock-coat," but there was far more than that to Whistler. While at times, Carr said, he exhibited a "strange blend of the man of genius and the showman," no one, as man or artist, was "more exacting and fastidious in the demands he made upon himself." There was, Carr emphasized, "nothing of the charlatan" in Whistler, a point endorsed by John C. Van Dyke when he denied that Whistler was some "cheap *poseur*."[43]

Numerous people agreed. "He had quite made up his mind as to the part he intended to play and the light in which he wished to be regarded," insisted T. Martin Wood in a brief 1908 biography of the artist. Whistler, always the poseur, "designed himself." Val Prinsep called him a poseur in the sense that he was "always acting a part. He even dressed the character." Yet, chimed in Charles Edward Hallé, who helped Sir Coutts Lindsay establish the Grosvenor Gallery, Whistler remained a man of taste, in stark contrast to Oscar Wilde, whose "repulsive appearance and tedious paradoxes" did the Aesthetic movement of the 1870s "great harm" and "made sensible people weary of the whole thing before they realized what it meant."[44]

A famous woodcut portrait of Whistler in evening dress done by William N. P. Nicholson in 1899 says a lot about his posing and the image

Whistler wished to project. Probably best remembered as illustrator of *The Velveteen Rabbit* and father of modernist painter Ben Nicholson, the senior Nicholson considered himself a disciple of Whistler. Admiring as he did Nicholson's woodcut portrait of Queen Victoria, done in 1897, Whistler asked the illustrator to make one of him. The result could be mistaken for the portrait of a dandy, with monocle firmly set, a casually held cigarette, and a confident, somewhat quizzical, tilt of the head, but Whistler intended it to be a caricature, not a likeness, and he instructed Nicholson in precisely how to present him.[45]

That Whistler showed different sides to different people is acknowledged by virtually all commentators on his life and work, even those who use the "dandy" label. Unfortunately, either for the sake of consistency or because of the ingrained habit of calling Whistler a dandy, they seldom grapple with the dichotomy. Consequently one scholar, who recognizes both the bohemian and the dandy in Whistler, acknowledges that his "dandified persona" was a "pose" but somewhat confusingly describes that pose as both a "mask" and a means to "proclaim his aestheticism." Like many other rebellious artists in the nineteenth century, he says, Whistler used "art as a refuge from a vulgar and materialist society." Another writer, in the tradition of Chase, Duret, Eddy, and Carr, correctly understands that the publicly flamboyant Whistler bore little resemblance to the "serious, indefatigable artist" but goes on to confirm his "dandified, prickly façade."[46]

In this context, Whistler better fits a crucial artistic quality in another Baudelaire essay, "On the Essence of Laughter." Writing in 1855, eight years before "The Painter of Modern Life" and the same year that Whistler first arrived in Paris, Baudelaire sought to explain the "absolute comic" he observed in all artists. The absolute comic's defining feature is a "permanent dualism," he wrote, "the power of being oneself and someone else at one and the same time." Baudelaire insisted, "An artist is only an artist on condition that he is a double man and that there is not one single phenomenon of his double nature of which he is ignorant." Equally, though, he must never appear to be aware of this dualism. That, Baudelaire insisted, would spoil the fun and ruin the effect.[47]

Bernhard Sickert, younger brother of Walter, agreed. In considering Whistler's life and legacy several years after the artist's death, Sickert found his "peculiarities" refreshing. He hesitated to call Whistler a poseur, for he saw neither pose nor affectation in his "antics." If he "outraged decorum," it was through a "natural inclination toward eccentricity," Sickert maintained.

"To many I suppose all this is simply puerile and obnoxious," he continued, "but I count myself among those who are grateful to anybody who has the courage to vivify our drab lives. . . . Laughter is a good thing, and whether we laugh with or at our rebels, what matters it?" Whistler may have been a "mysterious sprite, half Mephistopheles, half child," who "outraged decorum," Sickert proposed, but better that than be counted among the "pretentious dullards."[48]

So, beyond the posing, who or what was Whistler? He was both vain and modest, self-confidant and insecure, quarrelsome and repentant, loveable and mean-spirited, devious and honest, selfish and open-hearted, demanding and patient, thoughtful and reckless, a conformist and a rebel, an artist and . . . well, that is it, really. From the age of fourteen, an artist was all he ever wanted to be. None of the rest matters.

CHAPTER 5

Whistler the Magnanimous

Not long ago, I became unsettled while enjoying an exhibition of Whistler paintings at the Sackler Gallery in Washington, DC. There were some marvelous works, including a pair of nocturnes I had never seen in person. I also enjoyed watching the other visitors, looking for signs, either through facial expressions, body language, or comments to companions, that they appreciated the art. I fancied universal satisfaction until I happened upon a pair of elderly women. One of them was mostly silent, seemingly there to learn about Whistler and depending on her friend for enlightenment. That was well enough, as the summary judgments by the authority were by and large positive. However, as I was about to move on, one endorsement concluded with, "but you know, he really was a terrible man. He quarreled with everyone."

My heart sank. Of course, the woman, in a superficial way, was correct. Whistler did have his fair share of quarrels, verbal exchanges, legal battles, and violent confrontations, but for those instances, rather than the art, to have defined him for this woman reminded me of how Whistler so carelessly allowed his argumentative, pugnacious, cantankerous, and litigious side to help shape his legacy. No modern biographer has failed to recount the tales of "scalps" he collected, and caricatures of him as Mephistopheles rival those of the dandy.

Naturally, we need to keep things in perspective. Other artists have been known for their disagreeable personalities, aggressive tendencies, and worse. Titian was deceitful, Benvenuto Cellini an embezzler and bully, and J. M. W. Turner could be both vulgar and mean. Whistler's friend Edgar Degas entered into many a thoughtless quarrel without the spark of Whistler's wit to soften his contentious nature. Paul Gauguin qualifies by modern standards as a pedophile. Pablo Picasso has been described as "a foul maniac who revelled in sex and degradation." At least Whistler, unlike Caravaggio, never killed anyone, as one scholar has light-heartedly reminded us.[1]

Some of Whistler's contemporaries thought that too much had been made of the quarrels. Bernhard Sickert blamed the situation partly on his countrymen, who, unlike the French, seemed incapable of judging an artist solely by his work. The English, he said, could not countenance Whistler's "mountebank airs." English artist Francis E. James took a similar view. He attributed Whistler's "superficial combative side" to a philistine public. "The 'scalp' business was the result of common treatment at the hands of the common," James maintained. In any case, he scoffed, "his enemies fully deserved all they got." Neither did American art critic and writer John C. Van Dyke blame him. Only "when goaded by ignorant criticism or loaded with rank abuse," Van Dyke maintained, did Whistler attack.[2]

However, Van Dyke, who considered Whistler a "sensitive and sensible man with definite ideas about art," also saw a problem in Whistler's reactions. He sometimes went too far, and that became his failing. "He should have treated criticism with silence and allowed his art to speak for him," Van Dyke insisted in 1904. "Had he done so perhaps he might have held a higher niche in the temple than he at present holds."

That concerned Mortimer Menpes. Admittedly one of Whistler's most fervent followers, he worried that future generations would exaggerate the extent and seriousness of the quarrels. Whistler's legacy, he feared, would be defined by *The Gentle Art of Making Enemies*, a book Menpes wished could be "swept away." People who knew Whistler, even people with whom he had quarreled, understood "his foibles," he insisted. However, if read without that personal knowledge of the man, who in most respects was "loveable, delightful," the impression left by the *Gentle Art* could be damaging. People might unfairly mistake his "gentle ironies [for] venom, spite, and bourgeois ill-temper," Menpes predicted.[3]

Menpes had cause to worry, for there is no dodging the sheer number of altercations. Depending on how one measures or defines these things, and conceding that some quarrels were more consequential than others, Whistler had heated exchanges, either in person or in writing, with over thirty people between 1864 and 1903. Many of these instances were only verbal blasts against his critics, but not a few involved friends, not to forget his brother-in-law Francis Seymour Haden. Six cases wound up in court, and there were six instances of violence, with two of those being prosecuted.

What accounts for such an appalling record? One could argue that Whistler was predisposed to be a troublemaker, the victim of an irrepressible nature. In this sense, the adult provocateur was no different from the mischievous boy or defiant younger man. At West Point, he nearly shattered all existing records for laxness in his duties, and both fellow cadets and professors acknowledged his lively disposition. But they also knew him, just as importantly, to be honest and of good heart. There is only one known bout of fisticuffs (cause unknown) during his three years at the Academy. As one classmate recalled, Whistler was more often "addicted to pranks, not malicious, but harmless to every one except himself."[4]

Most of Whistler's friends and contemporaries recognized this proclivity for mischief, even if their explanations for it varied. Novelist and poet George Meredith explained, "He was a lively companion, never going out of his way to take offence, but with the springs in him prompt for the challenge." Herbert Vivian, the British journalist and political agitator, blamed the artist's notoriety on the people who failed to appreciate his essentially impish nature. Exchanges with his critics in the press were meant largely to attract attention and elicit laughter at their expense, Vivian maintained. He called Whistler a "champion tease."[5]

Reflecting on Whistler's life in 1903, one memorialist contended that he simply "delighted in controversy, in sallies with a malicious sting, in bitter wit, and more bitter sarcasm." He attributed this habit "not less to his earnestness than to his intense egotism." He went on to quote Whistler, who reputedly had said, "Yes, I have many friends and I am grateful to them; but those whom most I love are my enemies—not in a biblical sense; oh no! But because they keep one always busy, always up to the mark, either fighting them or proving them to be idiots."[6]

J. Comyns Carr, the critic and playwright, knew Whistler starting in the 1870s. "Combat was the delight of his life," Carr admitted. "I do not think he was ever quite happy unless one of those pretty little quarrels was on hand." Nonetheless, Carr insisted, "In spite of his undisguised desire to make enemies, the singular charm of his nature brought him many friends, and I think there is not one who knew him well who does not cherish his memory." Neither cruel nor mean-spirited, Whistler was merely "impishly militant" and "sometimes only half conscious of the wounds he inflicted." Philadelphia-born artist Thomas Alexander Harrison, nearly twenty years Whistler's junior, went further. "When off his guard," Harrison observed, "he was often a pathetic kid & [I] have spotted him in bashful moods altho' it would be hard to convince the 'bourgeois' of this. Wit, pathos, gentleness, affection, audacity, acidity, tenacity, were brought instantly to the sensitive surface like a flash."[7]

As a young artist, Walford Graham Robertson had been "brought up . . . in the knowledge and love of Whistler," but so fearsome was Whistler's reputation that Robertson quaked at the thought of meeting "the Great Man" in 1890. What a relief, then, when instead of the "Whistler legend," he encountered "a wholly delightful" man, "whose old-world courtesy smoothed away all awkwardness and who exercised an almost hypnotic fascination." As he came to know him over the next decade, Robertson realized that Whistler's delight in quarreling was "mischievous rather than malicious" and that "enemies, having served their turn, seemed if not forgiven, at least forgotten." In daily life, Whistler remained "courteous, kindly, and affectionate," with a "loveable side to his nature."[8]

Yet many people felt helpless in the face of what they saw as his often senseless and self-destructive behavior. Art critic Marion H. Spielmann lamented that Whistler was too often "affected by trifles, irritated by the unimportant, . . . and attacked where it would have been to his greater dignity to have ignored." A permanent split with the artist resulted from Spielmann's reporting on Whistler's raucous presidency of the Royal Society of British Artists, but the critic later accepted some blame for the breach. He had not, at the time, fully appreciated "the forbearance, the patience, and the humour with which he bore what he considered my youthful impatience and absurd squeamishness." Thomas R. Way, who, along with his father, had felt the heat of Whistler's displeasure, declared, "I do very much deplore the physical wear and tear and time which he devoted to press correspondence and fights with people of no importance whatever." Thomas Armstrong, a friend from the time of their student days in Paris, thought it "a pity . . . that the energy wasted in later years in 'making enemies' was not spent on his painting." He recalled that even though Whistler "did not avowedly go out of the way to make enemies" in the 1860s, "his gibes at some of the most popular and commercially successful members of the Academy were enough to embitter them."[9]

Whistler dismissed these reactions to his confrontational style with amusing, if vexing, quips. "I wrap myself in a species of misunderstanding," he explained, a ploy recognized by his friend Edgar Degas: "Whistler loves to wrap mystery around him as a cloak—and then go off in it and be photographed." Another person observed, "Again and again he took deliberate pleasure in befuddling people." Whistler as good as confessed his game to Spielmann. Upon asking the artist why he failed to correct a demonstrably false rumor about himself, Whistler replied with a chuckle, "No, no, to explain is to be found out." Some people, like William Merritt Chase, remained baffled. "You don't seem to understand," Whistler patiently told him. "It is commonplace, not to say vulgar, to quarrel with your enemies. Quarrel with your friends," he advised, "that's the thing to do."[10]

In other words, we again see Whistler the *poseur*, or so thought Valentine C. Prinsep. They had known each other since the early 1860s, and while Prinsep never had cause to argue with him personally, as the son-in-law of Frederick R. Leyland he was keenly aware of Whistler's stormy side. Yet Prinsep regarded most of his "wranglings" as pure showmanship, "to keep his name before the public." They were a "mere 'pose,'" the product, Prinsep submitted, of a "well-considered determination to exalt himself, which he found in the long run paid, even as all judicious publicity is said to bring in a sure percentage of profit." The quarrels were just another of Whistler's "eccentricities," though unfortunately they obscured a genuinely "warm heart and the truest artistic temperament."[11]

Still, a predisposition to mischief is not explanation enough. There must be a trigger, a root cause for such a variety of quarrels, so varied in their origins and conducted over so many years. I suggested in my biography of Whistler that the answer may be found in his compulsion for perfection, which he demonstrated in every aspect of his adult life, from the way he dressed to his insistence on proper standards, and most assuredly in his sense and understanding of personal honor. He demanded this of himself and expected it of others. Even his famous streak of egotism reflected a belief that perfection was both desirable and obtainable, and that, of course, his own judgments were always the correct ones. Consequently, and not surprisingly, all of Whistler's quarrels resulted from what he perceived as either unwarranted challenges to his art or untenable breaches of conduct.

Paradoxically, too, in this most conflicted and paradoxical of men, Whistler's demand for perfection also masked a deep insecurity, demonstrated by periodic bouts of self-doubt over the quality of his work that haunted him throughout his life.

In no other part of his adult life did Whistler seek perfection more persistently than in his art. Art was his life. Nothing and no one—with rare exceptions—was more important to him. Not surprisingly then, his devotion to art, and more particularly his insistence on the correctness of his own ideas about art, explain the majority of his quarrels and his reputation for confrontation. American journalist George W. Smalley, whom Whistler discarded after twenty years of cordial association, understood. "If he broke with you," Smalley admitted, "it was when he thought himself the champion of a cause in comparison with which human affections were of slight account." One observer even believed that where "the dignity of art and the independence of the artist" were concerned, Whistler was "thoroughly justified in at least half of his controversies." Someone else, while regretting that Whistler's "controversial style" too often caused him to be "insulting through an overweening sense of the justice of his cause," had to agree that "artistically he was nearly always in the right."[12]

People who saw only arrogance and egotism in Whistler's behavior badly misunderstood his motives. They said his famously dismissive remarks about Diego Velázquez and Frederic Leighton showed him unwilling to concede the merits of any other artist, living or dead. In fact, these were light-hearted quips, intended, in Whistler's perverse fashion, to acknowledge the gifts of Velázquez and Leighton. Luke Ionides, a friend since student days, admitted that Whistler showed "no patience with men whom he considered bad artists," but it was equally true that "he could appreciate art that differed from his own method, if it appealed to him as the result of genuine inspiration." This is evidenced by his willingness as president of the International Society of Sculptors, Painters, and Gravers to solicit the work of Henri Toulouse-Lautrec, Jean-Édouard Vuillard, Pierre Bonnard, and Paul Cézanne, with whom he had nothing in common, for the society's exhibitions. It was all about the art.[13]

Whistler's early artistic training and environment shaped his inclination to attack anyone who challenged his work. Until the early 1860s he was known for his nonchalance, not to say lethargy. Though tireless when it came to making art, and always keen to debate artistic issues, no one thought of Whistler as being physically aggressive, disagreeably confrontational, or purposefully insulting. Yet his natural passivity gradually waned, beginning with his student days in Paris. In that respect, Bernhard Sickert seems to have been on to something when he counted nationality as a factor in Whistler's reputation. Many people would eventually blame Whistler's lack of "repose" on his American roots, but that would have been apparent all along. Rather, it was the early French influence that disturbed any tendency toward tranquility, for as one commentator maintained, "Whistler was almost a Frenchman."[14]

Whistler's initiation as an artist exposed him to all the bluster that characterized the mid-nineteenth-century Parisian art world. One of his heroes was Gustave Courbet, a self-styled "savage" who reveled in notoriety and challenged fellow artists and art critics with boisterous manifestoes. Even so, while Courbet bore the title of "the most arrogant man in the world," he was only the most outrageous Frenchman. Verbal attacks on the Salon, rival schools, and the state of art generally were part of the clamor that Whistler joined nightly in Paris cafés. Henri Murger, who captured the essence of that world in *Scènes de la Vie de Bohème*, documented the "audacity" of the language. Soon after settling in London, in 1860, Whistler fell in with several equally audacious and nonconforming Pre-Raphaelites, who confirmed the lessons learned in France. Not surprisingly then, his first public quarrel came in 1862, when he responded to a critic who had mischaracterized one of his paintings.[15]

The word "enemy" did not appear in his private correspondence until 1864, and then only to be used in a humorous vein. His target was his brother-in-law, Francis Seymour Haden. The two men had been extremely close for many years, but Whistler became irritated by Haden's mounting reputation as an etcher. He regarded Haden, a physician by profession, as a mere amateur and undeserving of the public adulation he received. The relationship gradually deteriorated, as much because of Haden's arrogance as Whistler's pique, until Whistler received an "insolent letter" from him concerning Joanna Hiffernan. Suddenly reverting to his military training at West Point, Whistler identified Haden as the "enemy" as he joyfully laid out his "campaign" for the coming "war."[16]

Whistler repeatedly employed military metaphors in future quarrels, but even so, he rarely invoked the word "enemy" over the next dozen years. Only during his battles with the Burlington Fine Arts Club in 1867, which had also been instigated by Haden, and his clash with Frederick R. Leyland over payment for the Peacock Room in the mid-1870s, did that word resurface. He did not speak of multiple enemies until 1876, when he was over forty years old. "My enemies all around I shall rout and ruin and in short slay all over the place!" he confided to Frances Leyland, his patron's wife. Significantly, he then added, "All this of course concerns my pictures." Enemies then became the norm as he battled John Ruskin and suffered the indignity and dishonor of bankruptcy.[17]

Perceptive observers accepted this impulse and sympathized with Whistler's perspective. Alice Carr believed that Whistler's "love of quarrelling" surfaced most often when "the subject of painting was under discussion." Spielmann, while regretting that Whistler was consumed by "trifles," also believed that "the reputation of the artist . . . was [for him] a thing apart from the reputation of the man," in which case, there was no such thing as trifles. David Croal Thomson, a stout supporter for over two decades as an art dealer and editor of the *Art Journal,* said that Whistler "never quarreled with people who showed a desire to understand and to like his work." More to the point, Thomson insisted that Whistler's "true character was that of a man supremely devoted to his art, who was an artist to his finger-tips." Louisine Havemeyer, recalling him from the early 1880s, observed that Whistler defended "his muse" as "Loge the fire god, restless, excitable, with a burning intelligence . . . [and] a power that enjoyed the shock it produced, and a gay spontaneous irrelevance. . . . He loved to be Loge to his critics and to see them sizzle and squirm as he showered the sparks of his witticisms about them."[18]

So what should we make of so many quarrels? How serious were they, what circumstances sparked them, and what forms did they take? As one observer conceded, Whistler was "always a little more serious than he seemed when he joked in print, and always a little less serious than he seemed when he quarreled." Certainly, there were different types of quarrels, and we must always distinguish between the genuinely bitter confrontations and mere mischief-making, which Whistler dearly loved.[19]

Most numerous were Whistler's literary jousts with people who criticized, misunderstood, or misrepresented his work. These were the mildest of his confrontations, generally full of wit and inventive turns of phrase. They show Whistler at his most juvenile, wanting to be the cleverest lad in the room. He slipped clippings of his latest antics into his coat pockets for the express purpose of reading them aloud to friends, laughing and winking at his own brilliance as he did so. The larger part of the *Gentle Art* consists of these barbed thrusts of the Butterfly's tail at the likes of Philip Hamerton,

Harry Quilter, Frederick Wedmore, Wyke Bayless, Sidney Colvin, Tom Taylor, and Oscar Wilde. He aimed similar pokes at Max Beerbohm, Aubrey Beardsley, John Calcott Horsley, and Hubert von Herkomer.

The majority of these men were art critics, whom he recognized as potential threats to his reputation as an artist. He had attacked them collectively in his pamphlet *Whistler v. Ruskin: Art and Art Critics* following the Ruskin trial. He delivered additional and more personal jabs in the press and famously used the catalogue for the first exhibition of his Venice etchings to embarrass several past critics. The public appreciated the humor of these taunts, which, while often tinged with "an irritating touch of rudeness," were only occasionally delivered in a "malicious and vituperative manner."[20]

Not a few artists lauded Whistler for standing up to an artistic establishment that often thwarted their own ambitions. As artist and journalist Wynford Dewhurst put it, "Whistler was a man after my own heart. An artist & a fighting man. He deserved well of the world & particularly of all artists of independent character." George Percy Jacomb-Hood, who stood should-to-shoulder with Whistler in attempts to reform the Society of British Artists and nurture the International, insisted in his memoirs, "Artists owe a debt of gratitude to Whistler for the example he set them in defying the critics."[21]

In all this, Whistler was concerned not simply with his immediate reputation but also with his ultimate legacy. His clash with Frederick Keppel illustrates this awareness of the long game. Though cordial, Whistler never warmed to the Irish-born New York print dealer and writer on art, partly because he believed Keppel overcharged for his prints while failing to compensate him accordingly. So, when Keppel promoted an ill-conceived biography and analysis of Whistler's work, the artist upbraided him in an angry letter. London dealer Edward G. Kennedy, one of Whistler's closest confidants, told him he was overreacting to both the publication and Keppel's actions. Whistler replied, "No, this stuff is official and I must protest." A stunned Keppel described the letter as a "brilliant specimen of characteristic abusive Whistlerism." Recounting the episode after Whistler's death, he called his antagonist a "supposedly tamed wild animal" that would "suddenly and unprovokedly turn and bite."[22]

Unfortunately, Whistler's aggressive impulses were encouraged, if not actually endorsed, by friends who failed to rein him in. Unlike the more cautious Kennedy, they regularly praised, congratulated, or otherwise expressed delight in his bravado. Both Ernest G. Brown, assistant manager of the Fine Art Society, and William Heinemann, Whistler's publisher, laughed with him for a "splendid" public slap at Frederick Wedmore as a "Podsnap." Heinemann raved, "The letter is a beauty! And you can be as cocky as you like about it." Edmund Yates, in search of controversy, allowed Whistler to pummel his enemies freely in the pages of the *World*, which he edited. In the case of Harry Quilter, Yates instigated an incident by inviting Whistler to respond to the critic's application as the Slade Professor at Cambridge. More darkly, Will Rothenstein explained, "Whistler was not really so quarrelsome as people thought, or as Whistler himself would have them believe. It was people like Pennell who played on Whistler's vanity and prejudiced him against certain people."[23]

In the face of unwarranted—which is to say dishonorable—attacks by his critics, Whistler expected genuine friends to defend him and his theories against all comers. Those who failed him incurred his displeasure. Fellow artist Edwin A. Ward maintained that, in the case of younger artists such as Menpes, Whistler "could not brook the slightest appearance or suggestion of independence or insubordination." Otherwise, he became "ruthless in the pursuit of friend or foe who fell under the ban of his displeasure." Writer and political activist Laurence Housman, whose "spiritual father" was John Ruskin, recalled first meeting Whistler at the home of a mutual friend. Having "sprawled into the room with a slow defiant swagger," the artist started grousing about his latest grievance by reminding loyalists that his injuries, antagonisms, and quarrels were their own. Housman was not impressed by this display of "querulous pugnacity."[24]

Then there were the people he cut socially or personally. These quarrels, all with friends rather than art critics, came when Whistler believed he had been betrayed in some way. His reaction was usually swift and merciless. He caught George Moore, Sickert, and Rothenstein associating, unwittingly or no, with people Whistler regarded as enemies. Chase, as suggested, exhibited his portrait against Whistler's wishes (fig. 10). Wilde and Menpes, he insisted, had passed off his artistic ideas as their own, and Menpes had the audacity to travel to Japan, the spiritual home of much of Whistler's thinking about art. Swinburne had mocked the "Ten O'Clock" lecture, and Kennedy, in a reversal of roles, had dared to warn Whistler against associating with Richard A. Canfield, a notorious gambler whom Kennedy regarded as unsuitable company.

Not all these cases proved fatal or were regarded by Whistler as irreparable. The impeccably loyal Albert Moore and the Greaves boys, Walter

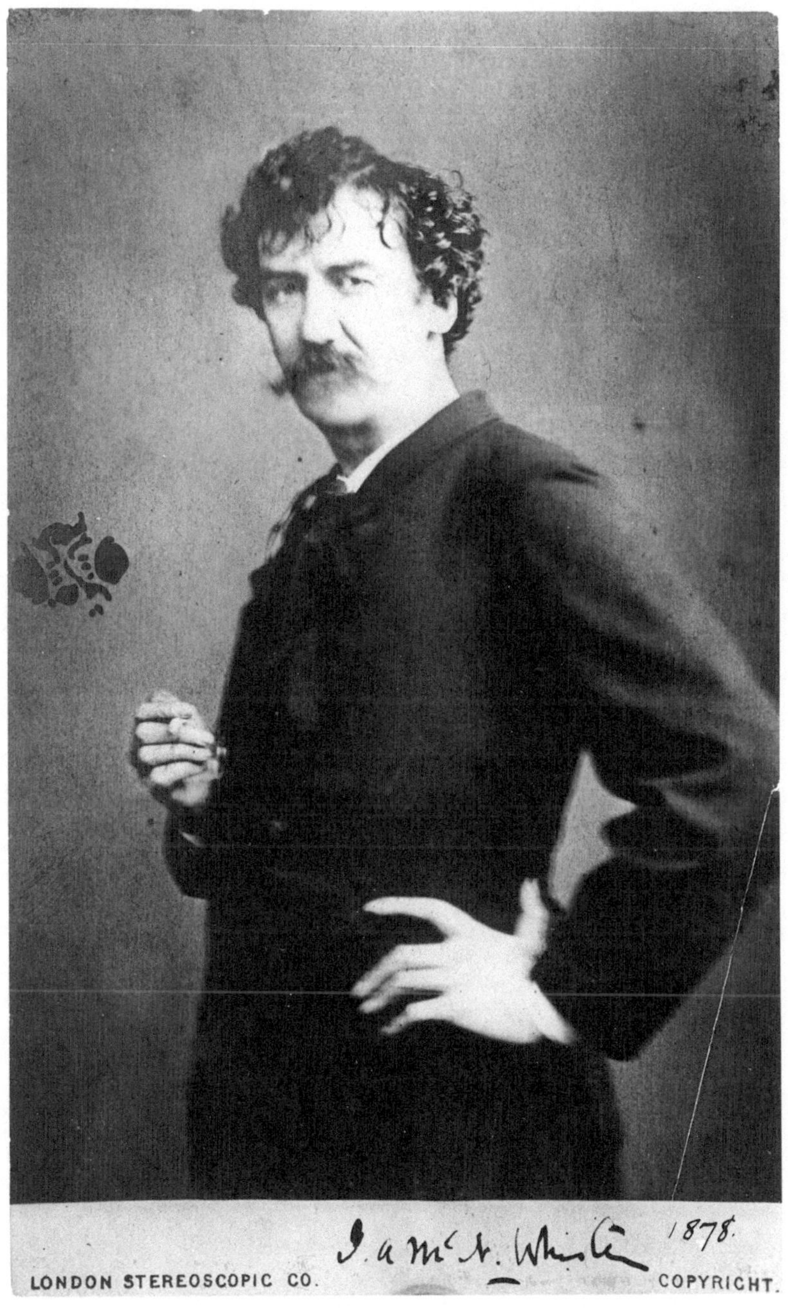

FIG. 10 James McNeill Whistler, 1878. Photograph. LC-DIG-ds-04750, Prints and Photographs Division, Library of Congress, Washington, DC.

and Henry, received only gentle reproofs for trespassing on his artistic turf. In other instances, he delivered an indirect warning—sometimes seriously, often not—by facetiously denying that he knew the offending party. It was his way of saying the person had disappointed, aggrieved, or insulted him in some way. "Eh, what? Meneps—who's Meneps?" he would ask after breaking with Mortimer, purposefully mispronouncing his name. With other people, such as Joseph Pennell, the loss of memory was an open joke. "Oh! *that* man," he suddenly recalled of Pennell. "I once knew him but I don't know him now. He had the audacity to appropriate the title of Little Venice to one of his etchings; now that title belongs to me. No, I don't know him at all."[25]

People disagreed about the depth of Whistler's indignation. Menpes, whatever his discomfort, wrote fondly of Whistler in his reminiscences, although an English actor and writer who once heard Whistler rail against some of his followers believed his "indignation was absolutely genuine and unfeigned." Henry Tonks agreed and believed Whistler's anger often came from a genuine sense of betrayal. Without mentioning names, Whistler had once told him, "with some bitterness," of his disappointment with "younger friends who had learnt so much from him." Tonks concluded that the normally "delightful" Whistler, if "roused by abuse, or by what he considered an insult," could be "a tiger for revenge." Yet a self-styled "psychographer" of the artist, who thought Whistler a "snarled soul" and condemned his many quarrels as "disgusting and disgraceful," perceived "no real hatred at the bottom of his attacks," with some of them even being "a good deal of fun—of a kind."[26]

Or he might simply be disappointed, according to his standards, in the behavior of a fellow artist. When Whistler was slow to present Frederick Leyland with a commissioned portrait of his wife Frances, the businessman ordered a second portrait from Philip Richard Morris. Whistler felt betrayed, not by Leyland but by Morris. "The flaw in the friendship like the crack in the china," Whistler chastised Morris, "is useless to explain—the true ring has gone forever. . . . Have you forgotten our old walks & talks in Chelsea? I had taken you into the intimacy of my work and believed in you as a strong sympathizer with whom all the mysteries of the studio might be freely shared." Morris had been a "chosen companion," a "confrere," yet when his "fidelity" was put to the test, he had utterly failed.[27]

More dignified were the largely legal squabbles. The case of John Ruskin became the most important. In combination with his more personal quarrel with Frederick Leyland, it marked a defining moment in Whistler's life and art, as well as in Whistler's readiness to quarrel openly with his "enemies." Yet in testimony at the trial, he was quite restrained, emphasizing that he did not mind criticism. Indeed, he expected it. He only objected to criticism he deemed "unjust," "incompetent," or, as with Ruskin, damaging to his reputation as an artist. So too in his threatened litigation against Sheridan Ford and George du Maurier, done in both instances to halt publication of books. With Ford, it was an unauthorized edition of the *Gentle Art*, which, as a result of the pressure applied by Whistler, appeared in a very limited edition. Du Maurier's sin was to have created an unflattering fictional version of Whistler in the original, serialized magazine version of *Trilby*. Whistler succeeded in forcing him to alter his character in the book.[28]

Whistler was involved in other court cases, usually in suits brought against him by creditors, but the most significant of these legal disputes was with William Eden. Having painted a portrait of Eden's wife on commission, Whistler decided that he liked the picture too much to relinquish it. He returned the money, but Eden wanted the portrait, so sued. Whistler stood firm. Here was a different sort of honor, not to say a legal principle: the right of an artist to control his own work. It was an issue, Whistler said, that "stirred the very depths" of his being. He won on appeal and, as in the Ruskin case, trumpeted his victory by issuing a pamphlet, *The Baronet and the Butterfly*.[29]

In the Eden case, as with his campaigns against Ruskin, the Burlington Fine Arts Club, and the Royal Society of British Artists, Whistler thought it necessary to wage battle over larger issues, but there were numerous, lesser *mano-a-mano* contests, too, when he was simply primed for a fight. Twenty-seven-year-old Irish painter H. Jones Thaddeus first met Whistler at a supper party hosted by Menpes in the mid-1880s. When Whistler asked his opinion of Velázquez, whom Whistler idolized, the younger man expressed similar admiration but qualified it by suggesting that if the Spaniard had a weakness, it was his depictions of horses and dogs, which could not compare to those by Edwin Landseer. Another person might have accepted this opinion as part of the give-and-take of polite conversation, but Whistler would not let it pass. In a cutting, if not belittling, tone, he dismissed the "audacity" of the young "Philistine" in trying to raise a "cheap tea-tray performer" like Landseer above the godlike Velázquez.[30]

It is fair to say that Whistler's most consequential quarrels were the ones that fractured friendships. Even here, not all quarrels were created equal, but they do show that Whistler, in all honesty, knew how to nourish a grudge. As he told fellow artist John Lavery, a devoted friend who had stood by him during his frequently stormy leadership of both the Royal Society of British Artists and the International, "I forgive when I forget." Some of the most bitter and publicized rows had deep roots not to be attributed merely to Whistler's sensitivities. His break with Alphonse Legros, for instance, resulted superficially from Whistler slapping his friend for having called him a liar. What lie remains obscure, but even as a variety of other issues had prepared the ground, Tom Armstrong believed the "real" cause of the incident had been Legros's belief that Whistler had recommended Fantin-Latour, rather than himself, to a potential patron. So, again, the art.[31]

The saddest rupture, and the one Whistler felt most keenly, involved Algernon Swinburne. They had been friends since the early 1860s, when Whistler first fell in with Rossetti's circle. Whistler was so certain of the little poet's loyalty that he asked him, through Theodore Watts-Dunton, to write a review of the "Ten O'Clock" lecture when it was published in 1888. Swinburne complied, but dismissed Whistler's achievement, the most eloquent and profound expression of his artistic theories, as a confused jumble of "truths and semi-truths, admirable propositions and questionable inferences." A devasted Whistler hid his hurt by cavalierly and quite publicly breaking with Swinburne, but there was genuine pain in his questioning, "Why, O brother!" What made this episode especially sad was that Swinburne had been reluctant to write the review, and its ultimately caustic tone had been encouraged by Watts-Dunton, who later confessed as much to William Heinemann. He also begged the publisher not to tell Whistler, almost as though he feared for his life. "He had for years, in fact, shunned all places where Whistler was likely to be," marveled Heinemann.[32]

Nearly as tragic was his discarding of the Thomas Ways, father and son. The father had tutored Whistler in the mysteries of lithography and together with his son had helped Whistler print some part of his etchings and lithographs. The younger Way had idolized Whistler and understood that art, to which "his life was devoted," was the reason for most of his quarrels. "Art was his religion," the son recognized, "and . . . [h]e was as incapable of compromise as Luther." That knowledge and self-awareness protected the Ways from any serious confrontation with Whistler for many years, until the mid-1890s. Then Whistler became unhappy with the design and production of a catalogue of his lithographs compiled by the Ways. He insisted further that some of his paintings owned by the elder Way be returned. When Way resisted, lawyers were brought in to settle the matter. Even then, the friendship might have survived had not Whistler written such an insulting letter to Way that the old bond disintegrated. It was not one of Whistler's finest moments and stands as perhaps the most ill-conceived and least warranted of all his quarrels.[33]

Art aside, points of personal honor served as a second reason for Whistler's pugnacious image. His stand against the Burlington Fine Arts Club, when he insisted that he had not been treated as a gentleman, is perhaps the best example. However, these were also among his most foolish quarrels in that they generally involved actual brawls or physical violence. We know of seven such instances. The most famous and consequential was when, in 1867, Whistler shoved Francis Seymour Haden through the window of a Paris café. This episode, in combination with subsequent events, caused a painful and needless break between the Whistler and Haden families, besides being the root cause of the Burlington affair. Less heralded, though apparently the first instances of violent behavior beyond the rough-and-tumble of boyhood, were a pair of confrontations in Paris in the early 1860s with a cabman and a laborer. In both instances, Whistler fancied that his antagonist had been discourteous. Whistler exchanged blows for similar reasons with two men while returning to England from Chile in 1866. The more notorious of those two incidents had him striking a Haitian passenger, primarily, it seems, because of his race, but ostensibly because he was offended by the man's pretensions. A strained definition of honor, to be sure.[34]

The 1860s marked the most physically combative decade of Whistler's life, but he remained primed when he thought the occasion warranted it. In 1889, he had a celebrated scuffle with William Stott of Oldham at the Hogarth Club. Stott, a former friend, had become an enemy after painting Maud Franklin in the nude, an episode that likely also explains Whistler's subsequent alienation from Maud. However, it was Stott who confronted Whistler by calling him "a liar and a coward." Whistler responded by slapping him and kicking him squarely in the buttocks. When Whistler then demanded that the club "take steps to prevent a recurrence of such an unbearable provocation and monstrous insult," Stott was forced to resign his membership. In 1890, an episode echoing the Stott affair took place in the foyer of the Drury Lane Theatre, although this time Whistler was the aggressor. Augustus Moore, brother of George and editor of a rumormongering weekly newspaper called *The Hawk*, had made some disparaging remarks about Whistler's deceased friend Edward W. Godwin, whose widow had become Whistler's own beloved wife. Whistler flew at his target with cane raised screeching "Hawk! Hawk!" as he thrashed Moore. Again, from the artist's perspective, a point of honor.

In a rare instance of a friend taking Whistler to task, journalist James Runciman admonished the by then fifty-six-year-old artist for the Moore episode: "What the devil are you thinking about? . . . [You], a man of genius who has made a damned fool of himself. . . . You are enough to rile the twelve apostles." While not confronting the artist personally, another journalist friend, Herbert Vivian, mused, "Now one can understand chivalrous indignation about a libel on the dead and the injured feelings of a widow, but one does not often find an ordinary husband burning for bloodshed on behalf of his predecessor." More likely, Vivian concluded, it was Whistler's craving for "advertisement" and notoriety that drove him.[35]

His break with Edward Kennedy resulted from butting heads with an equally proud man. It was a test of wills for Kennedy, a longtime advocate of Whistler's work besides being one of his most intimate companions. A decades-long friendship ended when he tried to dissuade Whistler in 1903, just weeks before the artist's passing, from associating, as mentioned, with Richard Canfield. Kennedy received a rebuke for his efforts, one so sharply worded that he found it impossible at the time to forgive Whistler. Years earlier, William Chase had warned the art dealer, "He will turn on you some day Kennedy, mark my words." A dubious Kennedy had jocularly replied, "Let him turn . . . others can do a formidable turning act too!"[36]

Yet Kennedy would also be among the many people with whom Whistler quarreled who either reconciled with him or regretted, after his death, that they had not. The younger Tom Way, Menpes, Rothenstein, and many other old antagonists attended his funeral or wrote appreciative memorials (fig. 11). Way thought "the Master" worthy of a ceremony at St. Paul's. Rothenstein, in his monumental and important memoir, insisted as late as the 1930s, "My admiration for Whistler never changed. . . . [H]is character was a whole and rounded one, and one accepted it, and still accepts it, as unique and legitimate." Nor did they attempt to hide their sometimes bitter encounters with him. Most of them seemed to take pride in the old battles, as though their run-ins confirmed a certain intimacy with an artist of genius. Wedmore, while describing Whistler as a "strange creature of genius," insisted that all his memories of him were "agreeable." Spielmann, as shown, blamed himself as much as Whistler for their split.[37]

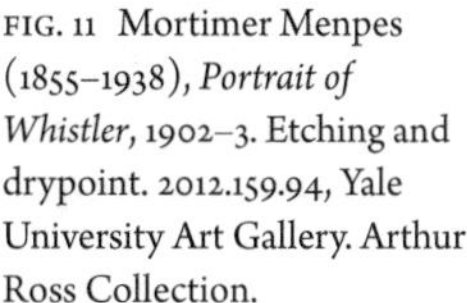

FIG. 11 Mortimer Menpes (1855–1938), *Portrait of Whistler*, 1902–3. Etching and drypoint. 2012.159.94, Yale University Art Gallery. Arthur Ross Collection.

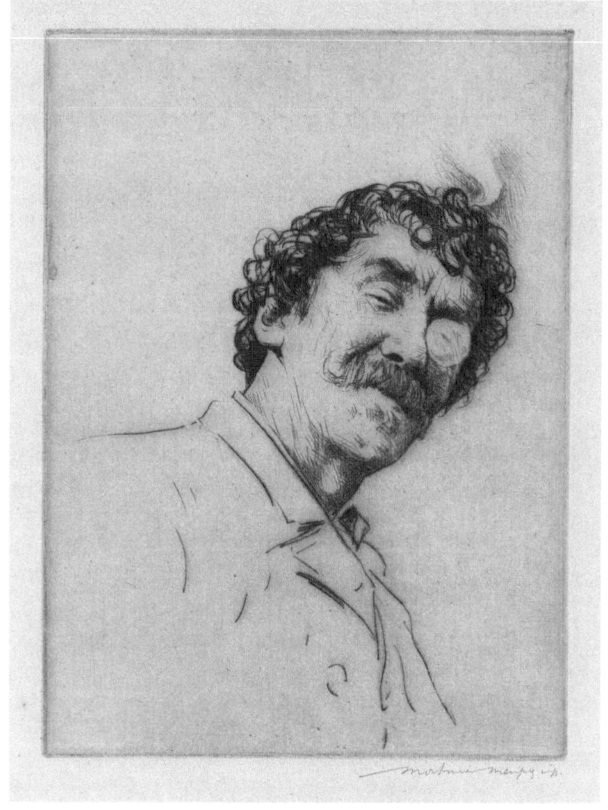

Friends with whom he had never quarreled wondered at how others had drawn his ire. Tom Armstrong and Harper Pennington conceded that the Leyland fiasco had been ill-advised, but neither man ever found personal reason to doubt Whistler's magnanimous nature. The same could be said of Luke Ionides, one of several old friends who believed that most of Whistler's quarrels had been "connected with matters of art." Going still further, Ionides reflected, "I can quite understand that a man who is doing good, honest work, which he knows is right, should feel aggrieved with those who cannot recognize either the sincerity of the artist, or the excellence of the work." Wynford Dewhurst, who had never known a more sincere, kind-hearted, or "generous minded" gentleman, said much the same thing. "To those, who he knew unreservedly, loved him and loved his work," Dewhurst observed, "he was equally loving and kind, and, also serious, very much so, with regard to his methods of work." Edmund W. Gosse, one of the rare art critics to escape Whistler's ire, agreed. "I never suffered once from his tongue or his pen," he declared soon after Whistler's death, "and it always seemed to me that a little tact and a certain quick-witted humour ought to save one from their edge. Well, he was a wonderful and beautiful genius." George Meredith claimed never to have had "a dissension with him, though merry bouts between us were frequent."[38]

Edmund Wuerpel did not know Whistler as well or for as long as these men, but he, too, saw the reason for the artist's regrettable "periods of mental irresponsibility." "It is true," Wuerpel observed, "that he did occasionally worry and fret himself into most unfortunate and uncontrolled outbursts of scorn and sarcasm" when "the injustices of the public or the press aroused within him a very demon of vindictive wit." Even so, he insisted, Whistler "remained the same to those who really knew him."[39]

CHAPTER 6

The Science and Poetry of Whistler's Nocturnes

No set of Whistler paintings has been puzzled over more intensely than the "nocturnes." Other pictures may better express the beauty and delicacy he always sought. Several portraits, his small oils on panels, the Amsterdam etchings, and the wispy lithographs of the 1890s are equally brilliant. Yet the nocturnes remain Whistler's most breathtaking invention, and as his signature group of paintings they have done much to define his legacy.

Not that this was immediately evident. During his lifetime, many people—not just John Ruskin—were perplexed by the new paintings. Though they were more divided in their opinion than one might expect, the negative reactions could be biting. "Eccentric," "strange," "nonsense," and "weird productions—enigmas sometimes so occult that Oedipus might be puzzled to solve them," were among the milder rebukes. What did these daubs of color represent? What story did they tell? More than puzzled, the average viewer regarded them, Theodore Duret ventured, as "incomprehensible and monstrous." Even Henri Fantin-Latour, one of Whistler's most sympathetic friends and oldest admirers, failed to grasp their purpose or meaning.[1]

Whistler took his first significant step toward explaining them himself in May 1878, when interviewed for the *World*'s "Celebrities at Home" series. "He insists that as music is the poetry of sound, so is painting the poetry of sight," explained the journalist, "and that the subject matter has nothing to do with harmony of sound or of colour." Although in this instance he was speaking more specifically of his "harmonies" and "arrangements" rather than the nocturnes, Whistler made his universal intentions clear. The public must understand, he emphasized, that a painting "should have its own merit, and never depend upon dramatic or local interest." The journalist identified this statement as "the corner-stone of Mr. Whistler's art-philosophy."[2]

The artist found a much grander platform six months later, in November 1878, in his lawsuit against John Ruskin. "A nocturne is an arrangement of line, form, and colour first," Whistler declared in an opening statement. "The picture is throughout a problem that I attempt to solve. I make use of any means, any incident or object in nature, that will bring about this symmetrical result." For instance, *Nocturne in Black and Gold: The Falling Rocket,* the painting that had so outraged Ruskin, was merely a representation of fireworks at Cremorne Gardens, not a realistic "view" of the grounds. Of another painting, *Nocturne in Blue and Gold,* done around the same time, he instructed, "It is a scene on the river . . . on the Thames in summertime, by moonlight." *Nocturne in Blue and Silver* was "only a painting of a moonlight scene," he repeated. "As to what the picture represents, that depends upon who looks at it. To some persons it may represent all that I intended, to others, it may represent nothing."[3]

Most historians, having accepted Whistler's explanations of his intent, content themselves with exploring *how* he constructed and executed these masterpieces. They address his "technical choices" and technique, the structure and composition of the pictures. They evaluate his use of paint, his selection of colors, his brushstrokes, the canvases, the application of varnishes. Naturally, they discuss the public's reaction to the paintings, but they seem less curious about *why* he painted them.

He may have been inspired by nothing more than a desire to break free of French realism, which had defined his earlier paintings. In this sense, the nocturnes became part of a natural movement toward Impressionism and Aestheticism, with the Venice etchings and pastels being the next step in that evolution. It began in the mid-1860s with his abandonment of lavish color, thickly applied, as a guiding principle of composition. He focused more on line, arrangement, and pattern, a combination, as it were, of Jean-Auguste-Dominique Ingres and Katsushika Hokusai. He sought beauty in decorative patterns, even if it meant sacrificing a "realistic" depiction of nature.[4]

Whistler was moving toward the belief, stated most forcefully in his "Ten O'Clock" lecture, that an artist's principal challenge must be to correct the deficiencies of nature and "bring about the perfection of harmony worthy [of] a picture." He could not depict the night as it was because the night is, in fact, impenetrable and unremarkable. Rather, he sought to capture a mood. Is it dusk, twilight, midnight? It does not matter. Do his scenes give us a glimpse of Battersea, the streets of Chelsea, Trafalgar Square? Again, that is not his purpose. Time and place are meaningless. Whistler had long since learned from his mother's fondness for Ecclesiastes that "the eye is not satisfied with seeing." As an artist, the inspiration for his nocturnes may have come from nature, but as one devoted follower believed, Whistler's vision was that of "one who has seen something that man has looked at for centuries and never seen before." His nocturnes became Whistler's ultimate vehicle to transform nature through his "painter's eye."[5]

The resulting distillation of nature mutes the landscape and veils physical objects, sometimes dispensing with representational objects altogether. Only setting and subject distinguish the nocturnes from his symphonies, harmonies, and arrangements, and the inspiration for all was artistic experimentation. Yet the nocturnes became his most recognizable pictures, so similar in many instances as to seem formulaic. As one critic declared somewhat unkindly, "All of these pictures strike us alike," but the template allowed him to transfer the idea of a nocturne from painting to etching and lithography. In the 1890s, he laughed to Thomas R. Way as they prepared to print a lithograph, "Now, let us see if we can remember a nocturne." Bernhard Sickert, who insisted that Whistler's nocturnes were the first pictures to arouse his "entire interest and enthusiasm," recognized this ability to move seamlessly between mediums while still maintaining the artistic integrity of each as "the most wonderful characteristic of Whistler's genius."[6]

The sheer number of painted nocturnes is impressive. If we include two pictures from the 1860s that Whistler labeled "crepuscules," he produced forty-nine painted nocturnes, thirty-seven of them in the 1870s. Three (including the crepuscules) were done in the 1860s and five more in the 1880s, the last in 1884. Another four may have been painted in either the 1870s or 1880s, and the total numbers do not include his nocturnes on paper, which would add seven etchings from Venice and Amsterdam, or two nocturnal scenes of Cremorne Gardens not titled "nocturne." Only one lithograph, done in 1878, bears that title, although *The Thames*, done in 1896 from the top floor of the Savoy Hotel, is a nocturne in all but name. In this vein, it has even been suggested that Whistler's etching *Street at Saverne*, published as part of the "French Set" in 1858, should be considered his first "nocturne," given its deep shadows and overcast sky.[7]

Still, the crucial question remains: *Why* did Whistler paint the nocturnes? What sparked the idea? Why did he see the night, and especially a shrouded Thames, as he did? Even a picture of "nothing" must have a source. In art, Whistler was a sponge, soaking up ideas right and left from all manner of people and experiences. Consequently, the work of other artists might explain particular pictures. Utagawa Hiroshige's *Fireworks over Ryōgoku Bridge* (1856), for instance—and as Marion Spielmann proposed—could be a model not only for *Nocturne: Blue and Gold—Old Battersea Bridge* (fig. 12) but also for Whistler's two "fireworks" pictures from Cremorne Gardens: *The Falling Rocket* and *Nocturne: Black and Gold—The Firewheel.* Yet without denying the obvious Asian influence on his art, it is also true that Whistler created these three works years after he had begun painting the night.

I see several other explanations for the invention of the nocturnes. Some of them were proposed by Whistler's contemporaries, others by modern students of his work, but always in isolation. In truth, a labyrinth, rather than a single source of inspiration, helps explain the origins of the nocturnes.

Let's start with nature, particularly the weather, both as God intended it and as humanity altered it. London's mist, fog, and soot-laden atmosphere have often been cited as the inspiration for Whistler's nocturnes. He himself boasted of being the painter of the city's fogs, although in fact only ten of Whistler's nocturnes clearly show atmospheric effects of any kind. That said, fog is endemic to the lower Thames valley, especially in the region of Chelsea, where the river basin is less than ten meters above sea level. Roman legionnaires doubtless complained about the lingering dampness, mist, and murkiness. It grew worse in the seventeenth century when the earliest coal-powered, smoke-producing industries compounded the bleakness. By the early 1800s the gloom, besides being thick and widespread, had also become more prolonged, sometimes lasting for days at a time.[8]

The 1840s, with a growing population and a rapidly expanding number of domestic and industrial coal fires, introduced the "true London fog" of Whistler's day. Their thickness led people to call them "peasoupers," and the coal's sulfurous emissions gave the air a distinctive yellow or brownish color. London's darkened atmosphere shaped the stories of novelists from

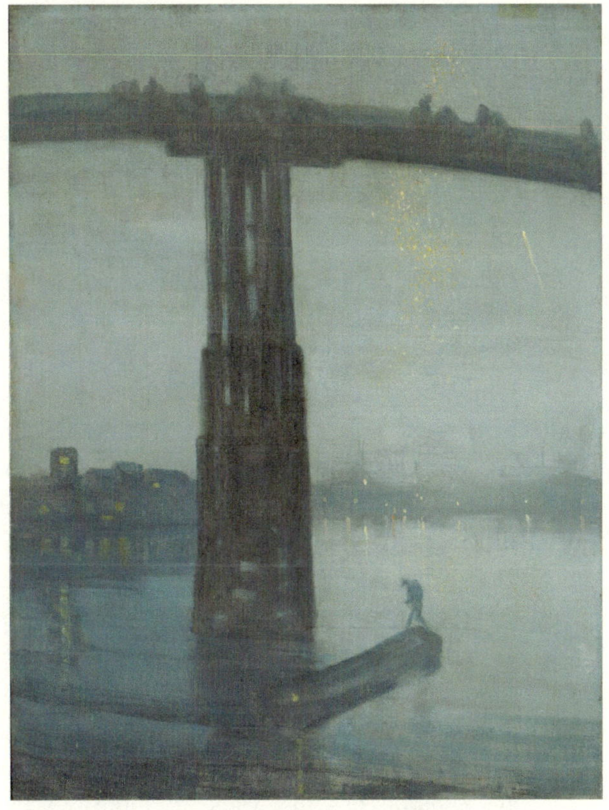

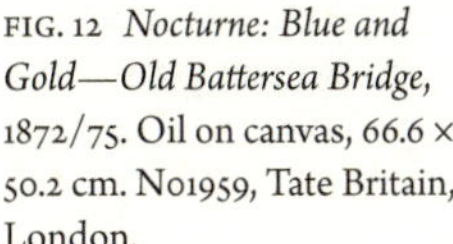

FIG. 12 *Nocturne: Blue and Gold—Old Battersea Bridge*, 1872/75. Oil on canvas, 66.6 × 50.2 cm. N01959, Tate Britain, London.

Charles Dickens to Henry James, sometimes as a character, often as metaphor. Dickens, whose novels Whistler read with delight, coined the term "London ivy" to describe the sooty particles that stung the eyes, clogged the lungs, and coated town and people. "Dickensian gloom" became a byword for the wretchedness and squalor of the city—and many of its people. It also foretold danger, even in the hands of someone like Henry James, who tended to romanticize the threat. The "atmospheric impurities," he wrote in 1877, "become richly suggestive," and the "glutinous London mist . . . in its own somber fashion . . . is extremely picturesque."[9]

As London's atmosphere deteriorated through the 1870s and 1880s, artists coped as best they could with the muted light. Frederic Leighton, speaking as president of the Royal Academy, deplored the "enforced idleness" imposed by the "ubiquitous yellow fog." Some artists tried gallantly to paint the effects of fog and smog while, at the same time, not allowing the atmosphere to obscure the subjects of their pictures. Claude Monet did this remarkably well during his 1870–71 sojourn in London with such paintings as *The Thames Below Westminster* and *Boats in the Pool of London*. Whistler had accepted the challenge even earlier, in the 1860s, with such paintings as *Chelsea in Ice, Grey and Silver: Old Battersea Reach*, and *Grey and Silver: Chelsea Wharf*.[10]

More often, artists settled for landscapes done at twilight or in moonlight, without the complications of atmosphere. Whistler could easily have seen examples by Claude Lorrain, Nicolas Poussin, Aert Van der Neer, Claude Joseph Vernet, Samuel Palmer, or Caspar David Friedrich. A contemporary, Henry Pether, had painted Whistler's own neighborhood in *Cheyne Walk and Battersea Reach by Moonlight*, as did William Holman Hunt in *The Thames at Chelsea, Evening*, in 1853. Augustus Egg, Jean-François Millet, Charles-François Daubigny, and John Jongkind also painted "moonlights" at midcentury, and Whistler's friend George Price Boyce did several watercolors of the lower Thames at evening in the 1860s. Whether depicting rural or urban scenes, these painters sought dramatic effects in the use of shadows, usually cast by the moon, sometimes with an accent of artificial light from lampposts or the glow from a solitary window. Also, like the painters of fog and mist, they tried to capture a moment of clarity, designed to tell a story in an identifiable setting. Whistler wanted none of that—no banal sunsets or glowing moonlights. His renditions of nature would cast more intricate moods.[11]

J. M. W. Turner came closest to capturing London's atmosphere at twilight as Whistler would do. While most of Turner's paintings of the city offer traditional, recognizable views, as in *Moonlight, a Study at Millbank* and *London from Greenwich Park*, other pictures, such as *The Thames above Waterloo Bridge*, are mere swaths of color, with the atmosphere and smoke their subjects. Poet Ezra Pound found an affinity between Turner and Whistler. The pictures of both, he observed, express "beauty in mists, shadows, a hundred places where you never dreamed of seeing it before." As an admirer of Turner early in life, Whistler made an extraordinarily good watercolor copy of one of his atmospheric paintings, *Rockets and Blue Lights*, but it was done in the United States, before he embarked on his student days in Paris. By the time he began his own moonlights, Whistler had rebelled against Turner's use of color and his impressionistic effects. Turner preferred to dissolve his subjects in intense light; Whistler cloaked them in shadow. While acknowledging Turner's genius and admiring some of his work, Whistler eventually dismissed him as "that old amateur." Turner was too angry a painter, a master of chaos and storms who exhibited "no reserve." There was a fierceness even in the bulky, impasto application of his paint, which Whistler, seeking harmony and tranquility, had abandoned by the 1870s.

Turner and Whistler did share an instinct for testing the limits of perception in their use of light and atmosphere. They also used nonnaturalistic colors to achieve a desired effect. However, they often sought very different ends. In his landscapes, Turner wished to create awe-inspiring scenes, most often as a means of conveying the feel and experience of a dawning industrial age through its most notable features: speed and power. In that sense he was very much a painter of modern life, though in ways far different from those later envisioned by Charles Baudelaire. If not telling a story, Turner's landscapes often showcased recognizable current events. Whistler never dreamed of doing such a thing. He painted moods, not scenes.[12]

And dare we think that John Ruskin, Turner's greatest advocate, might have understood Whistler's ends? As it happened, Ruskin was keenly interested in the scientific reasons for London's changing atmosphere, particularly the altered colors and intensity of sunsets. He believed that "old-fashioned" sunsets of "deep scarlet, and the purest rose on purple grey" had become rare by the 1870s, the precise moment Whistler was painting his first nocturnes. This and the diminished clarity of light he attributed to changing weather patterns, which he blamed as early as 1871 on "plague-winds" of carbon emissions drifting southward from the factories of Lancashire. The winds, he decided, intensified the already "poisonous smoke" from hundreds of London chimneys to "*blanch* the sun instead of reddening it." It was as if a "black veil" had descended upon the earth, making "distant objects unintelligible."[13]

As Whistler moved beyond painting daylight scenes to consider the Thames at night, he recognized, if not so astutely, the same phenomenon. Not only did the increased smog alter colors but so, too, the precise moment that twilight could be seen. Twilight comes in three stages as the sun slowly sinks beneath the horizon, and our perception of the colors can be altered at each stage. Consequently, any variety of hues may have suggested themselves to Whistler as appropriate to his river scenes. What is most notable, however, is that none of his Thames nocturnes feature the ubiquitous yellow or brown associated with London's polluted atmosphere. Ruskin's fascination with the pall reflected his growing morbidity of thought. For him, the plague winds seemed "made of dead men's souls." Whistler saw something else: a transcendent beauty.[14]

Monet recognized this variety when he returned to London in the early 1900s. "The fog in London assumes all sorts of colours; there are black, brown, yellow, green, purple fogs, and the interest in painting is to get the objects as seen through all these fogs," he observed. No wonder, with his principal subjects being the Houses of Parliament and Charing Cross Bridge, he had to paint thirty-seven variations to capture the variety. "My practiced eye has found the objects change in appearance in a London fog more and quicker than in any other atmosphere," he explained, "and the difficulty is to get every change down on canvas."[15]

The tints of early morning and evening may also be affected by the temperature, the amount of moisture in the air, or the amount of cloud cover. There are also phenomena known as the "green flash" and "blue flash," when mere glints of those colors appear on the horizon. Look carefully at even a "normal" sunset, and one sees bluish-gray shadows tinged with red. At certain times of the year, usually in late summer, faint bluish crepuscular fingers may radiate across the sky, a result of sunlight being scattered by a hazy atmosphere. After the sun has set, a secondary coloration of pink, red, or purple may linger.[16]

Ten of Whistler's nocturnes are mostly black or brackish, although the ravages of time may have diminished what were once vibrant colors. Five others exhibit no single or dominant tone. Among nine single-color pictures, some shade of blue, be it Prussian blue, ultramarine, cobalt, or cerulean, predominates. Silver or gray define six nocturnes, with green the color of choice in two more. Whether or not these were the shades Whistler saw in nature is impossible to say. He painted the nocturnes from memory, not *en plein air*, and could labor on a picture for weeks, months, or years before realizing the harmony and balance he sought. Not interested in depicting a scene literally, he would have been free to paint sky and water whatever color he wished, or to paint them the same color, as was his usual practice.

When asked how he mixed his colors, Whistler reportedly replied, "With brains." Bernhard Sickert, among the most perceptive commentators on Whistler's paintings, explained that the colors in his nocturnes were more "logical" than "literal," much like the scenes themselves. Whistler believed it more important that colors be harmonious. Thus, a red might become an orange, or purple a warm blue. "A great artist," reasoned Sickert, "has the faculty of convincing his fellows even when he is not telling the truth." Writer and critic Alice Meynell understood this perfectly. The atmospheric "scenery" of London, she observed in the late 1890s, was itself "artificial," the "sky of our manufacture." So who could say what truth lay beneath the "lurid" swirls of "floating smoke"? Whistler's palette reflected his observation of many, many twilight and evening skies.[17]

Scientific and technological advances of the early nineteenth century validated Whistler's unorthodox use of color. Specifically, a new appreciation for the construction of the eye led to a better understanding of vision itself. What the eye perceived became understood as more ambivalent and subjective than certain and rational. The most notable result of this optical revolution would be photography, but it also gave artists more freedom to experiment with color. Coincidentally, a separate development made a wider variety of manufactured synthetic pigments, conveniently packaged in portable tubes, available to artists. Color could be manipulated in ways that made physical existence an "abstraction."[18]

Whistler's source of light also influenced what he saw. Despite their original designation as "moonlights," Whistler never intended to paint the moon, only to convey the atmospheric effects of moonlight as reflected by water or refracted by the elements. In fact, only *Nocturne: Blue and Gold—Southampton Water* shows the moon—a golden, rising moon, as it happens, partially obscured by clouds. At the onset of twilight, the murkiness of the Thames, even without a moon, would have been made visible by the light of stars too faint to be seen, possibly even by the glow of city lights. The effect of these light sources when reflected by passing clouds would have been striking, the result being a constantly shifting scene as first one and then another part of the landscape was cast in shadow or illuminated. Only seven nocturnes, none of the Thames, are illuminated by artificial light(fig. 13). Five are set in Cremorne Gardens, of which two show fireworks displays.[19]

Crucial for judging the influence of natural light is the geographical latitude, time of year, and time of day that Whistler painted, or rather, the times of year and day he wished to represent. Other than scenes obviously set in winter, we have few details about the seasons or the date, much less the time of day. He painted a "crepuscule" at Trouville—*Crepuscule in Opal*—in the autumn of 1865. He began *Crepuscule in Flesh Colour and Green* at Valparaiso somewhere between April and June 1866, although that would have been autumn and early winter in Chile, and he probably did not finish it until returning to England. We also know that *Nocturne: Blue and Silver—Bognor* was done in September 1875; *Nocturne: Grey and Silver—Chelsea Embankment, Winter*, in January 1879.[20] The best documented picture is *Nocturne:*

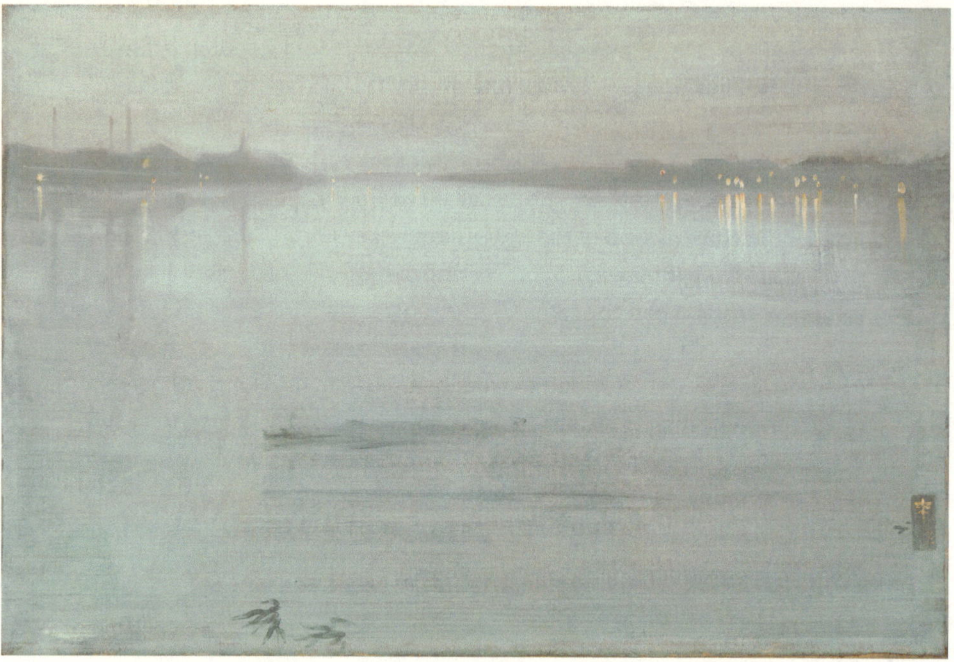

FIG. 13 *Nocturne: Blue and Silver—Cremorne Lights*, 1872. Oil on canvas, 50.2 × 74.9 cm. No. N03420, Tate Britain, London.

Blue and Silver—Chelsea, its creation in the summer of 1871 being described by Anna Whistler in a letter to her sister. [21]

However, the latitudes are near certainties, and this is revealing. The latitude at which we view a sunset or sunrise affects the degree of light and darkness in the sky, and thus the brightness and tones of natural colors. The vast majority of the nocturnes were painted in London, which sits between fifty-two and fifty-one degrees latitude, with one painted at Bognor and three others at Southampton, slightly below fifty-one degrees. As it happens, these latitudes are known for extremes of light and dark, with long evenings and protracted sunsets in spring and summer that allow for the widest variety of colors and twilight effects. Similarly, winters bring gloom and a swift close of daylight.[22]

This is where the two crepuscules are of particular interest. *Crepuscule* means dusk or twilight, and in latitudes below fifty-one degrees, the skies are characteristically streaked with color, or crepuscular rays, as the fading sunlight streams through gaps in the clouds. Valparaiso sits at thirty-three degrees, the lowest that Whistler ever painted. His previous crepuscule, at Trouville, was done at forty-nine degrees. Both were done in autumn, when the crepuscular effect is most striking. The nights at those latitudes, especially at thirty-three degrees, are also clearer and brighter, which gives the skies a unique translucency, despite the more subdued light. Certainly, both pictures are notably lighter in tone than the genuine nocturnes. Interestingly, too, Whistler's original title for the Valparaiso crepuscule was *Twilight at Sea*.

Looking more closely at Chile, it is likely that Whistler's experience there, while operating as a sort of arms dealer for the Chileans in a war against Spain, awakened him to the possibility of darker nocturnes. He commenced at least four other oil paintings in Valparaiso, besides the crepuscule. All of them depict ships in the harbor, and one became an early nocturne, *Nocturne in Blue and Gold: Valparaiso*. As with the crepuscule, Whistler did not complete the picture until returning to London, but he had clearly been inspired while in South America to depict the evening sky in a new way. He began to observe the differences in light and atmosphere while crossing the Isthmus of Panama by train, to be followed by several months witnessing variations of the reflected light on sea and sky at Valparaiso. One of the paintings he apparently finished at Valparaiso was a daylight version of the nocturne. It is often described as a "sketch"; Whistler referred to it vaguely as *Valparaiso Bay*. The sky is relatively brighter than the completed nocturne, but the darkened water and passenger dock suggest that he was already contemplating another "twilight," if not a pure vision of night. He deliberately gives the scene a subdued, shadowed look, rather than trying to illuminate it. From this picture and the crepuscule, Whistler advanced to his authentic nocturnes.[23]

Without being aware of the scientific reasons for all this, Whistler's contemporaries recognized the results. Besides Ruskin, Henry James also noted the "dense darkness" and "thickness of atmosphere" in a London winter, which lasted from November to March. Spring revived the possibility of color, as the reemergence of a "troubled light" created "mysterious tones," James observed. When refracted by London's fog and smoke, this light, as he described it, produced "red gleams and blurs that may or may not be of sunset." The fullness of spring and an approaching summer made the city appear "bright and kind," as the "pall of smoke" turned into a "veil of haze." A more pessimistic Ruskin observed in 1871 that "Grey-Shrouded" morning skies had persisted in London and Oxford "through meagre March, through changelessly sullen April, through despondent May, and darkened June."[24]

The real outliers when considering geography and time of year are the five Venetian nocturnes. At forty-four degrees, they fall between the English and Chilean paintings in latitude. Whistler almost certainly produced them during the summer of 1880, when he acquired a studio in Venice for the express purpose of painting. Unfortunately, only two of these paintings have survived. One is dark blue, the other a combination of light blue and brown (or gold). They contrast starkly with four Venice pastels titled "Nocturne," also probably done in summer but streaked with brilliant colors, much like the atmospheric paintings Turner did in the same city forty years earlier. Still, the darkness of Whistler's two painted nocturnes suggest that the increasingly polluted air of Venice, while far less noxious than in London, may have influenced what he saw on those occasions.[25]

Then we have his final nocturne of the Thames, the 1884 *Nocturne: Silver and Opal—Chelsea*. Despite the title there is no distinct coloration, and it is one of the darkest in the series, nearly impenetrable if looking for landmarks or even a clear delineation between sky and water. It has been described variously as "an evening effect," a study of "mist and smoke," and a picture of "foggy twilight."

Precisely when Whistler began painting it is uncertain, but it so happens that on August 26, 1883, a volcanic eruption on the island of Krakatoa, in Indonesia's Sunda Strait, was so powerful that the drifting ash affected the colors of twilight over Western Europe by late November 1883 and well into the following year. The same phenomenon had occurred in 1815, when another Indonesian volcano, Mount Tambora, created the "sunless summer" of 1816 across Europe. The blackened skies then had mesmerized George Gordon, Lord Byron:

> I had a dream which was not a dream.
> The bright sun was extinguished, and the stars
> Did wander darkling in the eternal space,
> Rayless, and pathless, and the icy earth
> Swung blind and blackening in the moonless air.

One can imagine Whistler reacting similarly to the 1883 eruption. A Royal Society report noted the "peculiar lurid glow" of the sky, "totally unlike our common sunsets," and "the very late hour to which the light was observable—long past the usual hour of the cessation of twilight." The afterglow acquired a haunting, otherworldly quality, the colors sometimes red, purple, or crimson, at other times radiating a soft yellowish-green. The event so unnerved Ruskin that he delivered a pair of public lectures on the subject, published as *The Storm-Cloud of the Nineteenth Century*. No one seems to have associated the bleak skies with the volcanic eruption, and perhaps the timing was only coincidental. However, Walter Sickert was quick to spot the unusual "sense of mystery and [the] infinity of night" in Whistler's painting, "full of space and atmosphere, . . . impressive in its solemnity."[26]

That Whistler then ceased painting London's evening sky confirms Ruskin's fears of the encroaching plague-clouds. Whistler still spoke of London's fogs as "lovely" in 1879, but by the 1890s, he saw them only as "black." They now filled him with "despair" and threatened his health, especially in winter. He complained of not being able to step outside because of the "appalling fog," which seemed to him "a huge coarse brown canvas pulled down over the town—& drawn tight—that we may choke and smother & gasp under it." Alice Meynell agreed. She lamented in 1898 that the city's "climate of smoke" had "painted the surfaces of the town in variants of black."[27]

To think that Whistler may have been responding to meteorological changes in the skies is intriguing when one considers his "scientific" approach to painting. Time and again, starting in 1872, he spoke to friends and followers about the science of painting, from the arrangement of paints on a palette to the precise balance, or "harmony," of the composition. At the Ruskin trial, he called his nocturnes a "problem" to be solved. Later, in the "Ten O'Clock" lecture, he not only spoke of the "science" of painting but also maintained that the artist was "born to pick, and choose, and group with science" what was beautiful in nature and "bring forth from chaos glorious harmony."[28]

In this context, Whistler's symbiotic relationship with Edgar Allen Poe, one of his heroes, is suggestive. Deeply impressed by the scientific advances and debates of his own day, Poe drew on the imaginative power of science for his fiction. His tales and stories are filled with references to scientific phenomena. His fictional detective C. Auguste Dupin preceded Sherlock Holmes in the use of deductive reasoning. Poe even thought of writing as a rational process, and his 1846 essay "The Philosophy of Composition" reflects Whistler's evolving ideas about painting and art in the late 1860s and early 1870s. Poe explains that a poet, like an engineer, must think in precise, deliberate terms. A poem or story has many moving parts—plot, characters, place, situation—but the whole must be calculated to create a single powerful effect based on uniform laws. The ideal goal must be an unblemished beauty, but without this rational appeal the aesthetic object would fail. A poem or story, Poe insists, does not come from a sudden burst of inspiration but from careful construction. It unfolds "step by step, to its completion, with the precision and rigid consequences of a mathematical problem."[29]

As the son of an engineer, Whistler could appreciate Poe's philosophy, as he would have done Poe's struggle to grapple with the consequences of exploding scientific knowledge. He likely knew Poe's "Sonnet—To Science," which begins "Science! True daughter of Old Time thou art! Who altered all things with thy peering eyes." It had been published in an 1830 volume that Poe, dismissed like Whistler from West Point for disciplinary problems, dedicated to the Corps of Cadets. Whistler also shared another aspect of Poe's scientific approach, which was to insist that art be devoid of all political or moral considerations. While not all of this spoke directly to Whistler's nocturnes, the melding of science and art and an appreciation of how one may affect the other significantly shaped his overarching philosophy of art. It is a shame he probably did not know, though it would have delighted him, that Poe preferred the sort of ethereal and atmospheric paintings—"landscapes of an imaginative cast"—he would create two decades after the poet's death.[30]

Another scientific advance that fascinated both Poe and Whistler and could have conceivably inspired the nocturnes was photography. Even though the first publication of Whistler's own image (an 1860 cartoon in *Punch* by George du Maurier) made fun of photographers as "artists," he, unlike many painters, never feared the advent of photography. He grew up with it, having first posed for a camera at age ten. He collected hundreds of photographs during his life. Many were of himself, family, and friends, but he also owned photos of paintings by other artists and photographed his own work extensively. He gave prints of the latter group as gifts and to advertise his work as early as the mid-1860s. He even issued a limited-edition photographic album of his 1892 exhibition *Nocturnes, Marines & Chevalet Pieces*.[31]

More importantly, Whistler was thoroughly conversant with the language of photography. Several friends were avid amateur photographers, and England and France were awash with photographic societies, exhibitions, journals, and manuals by the 1850s and 1860s. The structural photographs of

Parisian bridges, piers, and buildings by Philip Henry Delamotte and Hippolyte Collard in the 1850s may have suggested the artistic possibilities for etching and painting London's bridges in similar fashion. The only known instance of Whistler copying a photograph directly is his 1878 etching *The "Adam and Eve," Old Chelsea*, which relied on a photograph by his friend and neighbor James Hedderly. However, Whistler applied photographic principles of perspective and depth in creating his Thames etchings of 1859. Later experiments with a camera obscura showed him how to reduce the size of a scene and flatten perceptions of depth for the small panel paintings he made at St. Ives in the 1880s. It has been suggested that he may even have consulted photographs or used a camera to assist his work in Venice in 1879–80.[32]

Two possible sources of photographic inspiration for his nocturnes were French photographers Gustave Le Gray and Camille Silvey. Le Gray's reputation rested mainly on his dramatic early evening images of sea and sky, characterized by deeply shadowed or cloudy skies. The subjects and compositions of some of Courbet's seascapes closely match Le Gray's work. Silvey also photographed landscapes, but his most dramatic work showcased city streets, especially in London. His 1859 *Series on the Study of Light* captured brilliantly the effects of sun, fog, and twilight.[33]

Both Le Gray and Silvey exhibited in London and Paris during the 1850s and 1860s. Whistler makes no mention of them during those years, and while appreciating the scientific dimensions of photography and its practical uses, he clearly understood its limitations as an art form. His 1885 watercolor *Blue and Opal: The Photographer* ridicules the hopelessness of photographing a seascape. If photographs by Le Gray, Silvey, and perhaps others did resonate with Whistler, he still would have thought his paintings superior to their "realistic" representations of nature.

Whistler's contemporaries noticed this tension between art and science in his work. Some of them, like J. Comyns Carr, thought Whistler's "theories" restricted him, working against his intuition and the "free and spontaneous enjoyment of the beauty in nature that he intended to convey." However, Whistler's friend and fellow artist Albert Ludovici saw a link to the nocturnes. He vividly recalled a personal half-hour lecture from Whistler "on the envelopment of shadows and cast shadows" and his "mysterious way of dragging one tone into another, by finding the depth and gradations and enveloping one's figure in the general atmosphere, that gave the right effect."[34]

As it happened, many French and British poets, writers, and artists known to Whistler also found romance and wonder in the scientific advances of the late eighteenth and early nineteenth centuries. Just as fireworks displays exploited the fantastical, make-believe elements of chemistry, so did other scientific fields spark the imagination. Ballooning, for instance, which Poe had lampooned but which enchanted Whistler and the crowds at Cremorne Gardens, began as a type of scientific exploration, intended to give people their first panoramic views of the earth. Yet ballooning also revealed the mystical complexity and subtle textures of clouds, feeding both scientific knowledge and romantic visions. William Wordsworth found poetry in the experience of ballooning, while Percy Shelley described clouds as an "airy nest." Turner and John Constable, among others, became absorbed by the challenge of capturing their mystical qualities on canvas. Ruskin, too, long before the plague winds troubled him, found wonder in clouds, partly for religious reasons, but also because he could find no satisfactory scientific explanation for their shape, composition, or color. Some appeared to him as "war-clouds," others as "ghosts" that haunted the skies before slipping away "like a woman's veil." "For my own part," he confessed, "I enjoy the mystery."[35]

This fine line between science and poetry is suggested by Whistler's use of light in the nocturnes. As mentioned, he rarely relied on an obvious source of light for illumination. Consequently, he depended on the placement of artificial light, most often from warehouses, shops, homes, and churches, to fix the eye and relieve what would otherwise be an indistinguishable mass and impenetrable darkness. Other artists had used the same devices to suggest such emotions as isolation or warmth. Henry James, for instance, was impressed by how lamps on London's darkened streets cast a "hue of hospitality" and the delightful way "shop-fronts shine into the fog." Even more to the point, Meynell could write, "Let any lamp or line of lamps come into visible relation with the sky—any sky, whether mysterious night-sky softly embrowned, or a night-sky swept pure by a west wind, or the most ordinary grey of any average evening—and the lamp has indescribable beauties." Whistler could be just as poetic, as when speaking of "palaces in the night," but as an artist, he sought chiefly to place those lights strategically—scientifically—to provide balance or symmetry.[36]

Or would a more important influence than science be poetry itself? Whistler's contemporaries routinely described the nocturnes as "poetic," a reference to their aesthetic appeal and his ability to transform the menace and decay of Dickens's London into something beautiful and mysterious. Poets, novelists, and essayists wondered at how Whistler changed people's perceptions of London and the Thames. Arthur Symons believed the city had been awaiting someone like Whistler to discover its beauty. "The English mist is always at work like a subtle painter," he proposed in 1909, "and London is a vast canvas prepared for the mist to work on." Bernhard Sickert said much the same thing in a single word. The ultimate magic of the nocturnes, he proposed, was that they expressed the "*silence*" of night. "We feel the movement of Even," ventured another enthusiast, "the very steps of the goddess" and the "oncoming of night," in ways that embodied John Keats's ideal of truth in beauty. Whatever his scientific inclinations, Whistler was "essentially a poet-painter," said Ludovici, with the nocturnes expressing "great feeling for the poetry of night." A more youthful friend, Tom Way, also found "mystery and poetry" in the pictures. So sober-minded a critic as Royal Cortissoz agreed that it was not only the "ravishing beauty" of the nocturnes that captivated but also "the poetry of their sentiment." Another critic dubbed Whistler "a pure poet of nature."[37]

Much nineteenth-century poetry was purposefully ambiguous, designed to convey a mood, atmosphere, or sensation. Inspired by these visions, Whistler's "painter's poetry," as he explained in the "Ten O'Clock" lecture, might then "put form and colour into such perfect harmony, that exquisiteness is the result." He would not be duplicating the subjects of the poems, but rather translating the effect their aura and mystery had on his imagination. He would write his unique type of poetry on canvas, the equivalent of songs without words, a transformative conception of the night never before seen.[38]

Whistler enjoyed poetry, so which of his favorite poets might have helped him to reimagine nature, most notably the Thames? His friend Algernon Swinburne was one of them, but no obvious allusions to the night or the mysteries of dusk or twilight appear in his poetry. While often dwelling on death and lost memories, Swinburne was keener on classical and religious metaphors and themes. Even so promising a collection as *Songs Before Sunrise*, published in 1871, is devoted to political revolution. His poetry in the 1860s sometimes spoke of the seasons, wind, and weather but rarely of the hours of day and night. He came closest to a vision of night in "The Last Oracle," which begins, "Years have risen and fallen in darkness or in twilight," before continuing:

For the shades are about us that hover
When darkness is half withdrawn
And the skirts of the dead might cover
The face of the live new dawn.

Later in the same poem, he offers this allusion: "Clothed with clouds and stars and dreams that melt in morning." Still, Whistler would almost have had to be seeking inspiration in Swinburne's poetry to be influenced by such brief and obscure references.

Poe would seem a better bet. English painter Henry Tonks certainly saw a Whistler-Poe connection. Though speaking of Whistler's portraits rather than the nocturnes, he observed, "Just as in the poetry and in some prose of Poe lies an odd power of making us feel we are in a land of mystery and sadness, so Whistler surrounds his figures with a curious atmosphere which makes them somewhat remote from the lives we live, but of singular beauty."[39]

Still, as with Swinburne, Poe's poetry offers few descriptions of the night or twilight. Scattered lines appear here and there, such as "The skies they were ashen and sober" from "Ulalume." Similar images mark "The Sleeper" and "Fairy-Land," but there is nothing sustained or vivid enough to capture the imagination. Of course, an emotional darkness shrouds much of Poe's fictional writing, and with a lyricism that almost equates to poetry. More than likely Whistler knew the line from "Murders in the Rue Morgue": "It was a freak of fancy in my friend . . . to be enamoured of the Night for her own sake." Some such descriptive passages may have resonated with him on evening strolls along the Thames.

We know that Baudelaire's poetry and essays had a substantial influence on Whistler's art and ideas, though with a caveat. A complex thinker who often contradicted himself, Baudelaire remained consistent in at least one respect: He associated beauty with evil. His collection of poems *Flowers of Evil* was aptly named. Whistler seldom thought in terms of good or evil, and he certainly never considered those qualities to have anything to do with art or beauty. That aside, Whistler did embrace some images and metaphors in Baudelaire's poetry. "The Red-Haired Beggar Girl," from *Flowers of Evil*, almost certainly influenced, if not absolutely inspired, Whistler's painting *The White Girl*. He drew on "The Painter of Modern Life" for the section of the "Ten O'Clock" lecture that includes his own most lyrical passage, "And when the evening mist clothes the riverside with poetry. . . ."[40]

As for the nocturnes, numerous Baudelaire poems, including "Misty Sky," "Song of Autumn," "Mists and Rains," and "Morning Twilight" could have sparked Whistler's imagination. One poem, "A Phantom," would have spoken to him directly: "An artist God has set apart / In mockery, I paint the murk." "Parisian Dream" suggests the multicolored possibilities of even a murky river scene:

> Blue sheets of water, left and right,
> Spread between quays of rose and green,
> To the world's end and out of sight,
> And still expanded, though unseen.
> Enchanted rivers, those—with jade
> And jasper were their banks bedecked.
>
> ———————
>
> And every colour, even black,
> Became prismatic, polished bright;
> The liquid gave its glory back
> Mounted in iridescent light.

Such images suggest yet another source of inspiration for the nocturnes in the "other worldly quality of twilight" found in spiritualism. Séances, table-turning, spirit-rapping, and the occult were a Victorian passion by the time Whistler settled in London. Their popularity has been attributed to a revolt against rationalism and traditional Christian morality, but spiritualism, or more properly mesmerism, also had a scientific basis. Offered initially as a form of "animal magnetism" in the writings of eighteenth-century German scientists, it posited an elusive interaction between psychological, physiological, and physical phenomena. Like meteorology, it quickly became a feature of romantic, even "fantastic," poetry and fiction. Leading as well to a fascination with somnambulism (a state of trance) and "second sight," by the 1830s mesmerism was believed to induce chemical changes in the brain and muscles. In the France of Whistler's student days, E. T. A. Hoffman, Théophile Gautier, Alexandre Dumas, and Honoré de Balzac featured scenes in their writings that defied reality. This type of "'spiritualist' aesthetic" led Gautier to believe that the artistic search for "ideal beauty," or *l'art pour l'art,* could best be obtained through the senses and imagination, in a world of the transcendent and infinite.[41]

Exactly when Whistler became intrigued by the prospect of communicating beyond the grave is unknown, but he appears to have attended his first séance at Dante Gabriel Rossetti's home in 1870, on the brink of painting his first London nocturnes. His brother William and Joanna Hiffernan shared his interest. He came to think of Jo as a genuine medium and believed, somewhat enviously, that William was blessed with "the Scotch second-sight." Mortimer Menpes thought Whistler had a "weakness for ghosts," and there were close ties between spiritualism, the afterlife, and Victorian ghost stories. In that vein, one may easily imagine Jo stoking Whistler's curiosity with Irish tales of the supernatural. Whistler appears to have believed in "spirits" rather than "ghosts," but as an artist, he was widely believed, as one critic described him, to be a "mystic" searching for that which "lies just across the border-line of consciousness."[42]

By the 1860s, gothic literature defined Victorian culture as much as the craze over the supernatural, and the fog, mist, and sooty darkness of London made that association inescapable. American novelist Nathaniel Hawthorne insisted that while London's fog might be described as a "distillation of mud," it was also "the ghost of mud, the spiritualized medium of departed mud." Ruskin, as mentioned, imagined his plague wind to be made of dead souls. Several of Whistler's friends, beyond his partners in table-rapping, also thought of this world as but a portal to the next. Architect Edward W. Godwin, for instance, was known to conceal himself in reportedly haunted houses in hopes of seeing or confronting a phantasm.[43]

It was in this realm that Whistler would have felt Poe's influence most directly. Despite—or perhaps because of—his scientific sensibilities, Poe also believed in mesmerism and the occult. Understanding, as he did, the limits of rational thought and empirical science, Poe could readily believe in an otherworldly realm, entered through séances and out-of-body experiences. He questioned the nature of reality most profoundly in his 1844 imaginary dialogue "Mesmeric Revolution," praised (and translated) by Baudelaire as an unprecedented fusion of science and mysticism. A subliminal theme in much of Poe's fiction, with tales of death and resurrection often being central, it also crept into some of his poetry. In "Al Aaraaf" (later retitled "The Messenger Star"), he borrowed a concept from the Koran to describe a netherworld between heaven and hell.[44]

Whistler would have found sympathetic confirmation of a spirit world, perhaps even encouragement to embrace it, in Poe's "Dream-Land":

Where dwells the Ghouls,—
By each spot the most unholy—
In each nook most melancholy,—
There the traveller meets aghast
Sheeted Memories of the Past—
Shrouded forms that start and sigh
As they pass the wanderer by—
White-robed forms of friends long given,
In agony, to the Earth—and Heaven.

Much of Whistler's work prior to 1870, and certainly before 1880, could be said to contain a mystical element, as he moved away from the realism of his early career and began to think and see in more impressionistic terms. His affinity for water, mists, and fireworks, subjects in a natural "state of flux," symbolized the brevity and mutability of life. His *ébauche* technique in painting, characterized by sketchy images, an "unfinished" look, and the fluid consistency of his paint, suggest the same immaterial world. Tom Way found an "indefinable suggestion of mystery" in all of Whistler's work. A later critic suggested that a "cardinal element" of Whistler's painting was its "sense of mystery, of the indefinable, the impalpable."[45]

In fifteen of his nocturnes people fade into their surroundings, most of them mere wisps, unrecognizable as flesh and bone. If not to be appreciated literally as ghosts, their gossamer forms certainly convey a sense of other worldliness. The same was true of most of Whistler's landscapes, and critics found something ethereal even in his formal portraits. "They seem like half-materialized ghosts at a spiritual séance," thought one observer. "I cannot help wondering when they will gain substance and appear more clearly out of their envisioning fog." To paint nature not as it was but as he saw or *envisioned* it fit perfectly with the spiritualist's view that nothing in this world is fixed. All is ephemeral, and so, for Whistler, it was no betrayal of "truth" to rely on his painter's eye to define reality. Whistler's nocturnes, declared Theodore Duret, had reached the very limits of painting, suspended between substance and spirit: "He attained to that extreme region where painting, having become vague, in taking one more step would fall into absolute indefiniteness and could no longer say anything to the eyes." American artist Kenyon Cox proposed, "It is almost as if he painted with thought."[46]

John Ruskin and Thomas Carlyle would have understood, at least theoretically. Both men embraced the difference between perception and sensation. Sight and seeing were more than physiological or corporal, and there were different ways of seeing, as well as expressing what one saw. Carlyle, who became acquainted with Whistler in the early 1870s when sitting for his portrait, explained his views in the essay "Spiritual Optics." Typically, he raged against the "world-devouring armies of illusion and of foul realities," in which the "sensual eye" became an "obstacle" to truth. More sympathetically, Ruskin, in "The Relation to Art of the Science of Light," insisted that while we see *through* the lens of the eye, we see *with* the "soul of the eye." All sight, he concluded, "is an absolutely spiritual phenomenon."[47]

Whistler's contemporaries saw ethereal qualities in the nocturnes that spoke to the era's fashionable view of the hereafter. Even so sober a businessman as Charles Lang Freer, though inclined more toward Buddhism than spiritualism to confirm the existence of a world beyond, found solace in Whistler's art. Symbolist poets and painters, whatever their religious inclinations, were drawn to something ethereal in Whistler. Joris-Karl Huysmans detected "pleasant mesmerizing thoughts" in the nocturnes that carried him by "magical means of transport into unfinished times." For him, Whistler was a "mysterious, slightly ghostly painter," fully entitled to the name "spiritualist." His "glimpses of another world," Huysmans elaborated, evoke "subtle suggestions" that lull "with a sort of incantation whose occult spell escapes us."[48]

Just as Dickens and other writers used fog and shadows as allegory or metaphor, so Whistler employed his vision of London at dusk to suggest its underlying mystical qualities. The "evening mist" he so admired also serves as a "veil," universally understood as a gossamer divide between life and death. More often expressed, as his mother would have known, as a "vale of tears," the religious instruction of his youth and the early deaths of his father and three brothers made Whistler painfully aware of the spiritual element in life. Though not one for traditional religious rituals, he believed in the hereafter. Spiritualism, as for many people in Victorian England, allowed him to maintain some form of Christian faith in an era when ideas about the natural and supernatural were in flux.[49]

This spiritual side of Whistler has also been associated with paintings quite apart from the nocturnes. The dream-like quality of Jo in *The White Girl*, for instance, reminded Whistler's contemporaries of an apparition. If not ghostly or spectral, her fixed and blank gaze suggested a spiritualist or medium in a trancelike state. Similarly, *The Little White Girl* has been credited with "spiritualist implications." Huysmans thought Whistler's women, "those ghost portraits," seemed "to retreat, to sink into the wall, with their enigmatic eyes and glazed, ghoulish red mouths." In a different way, Whistler's "black portraits," which he began at the same time as the nocturnes, have been likened to "embryonic phantoms." One of the artist's contemporaries described the portrait of Pablo de Sarasate as "a sort of apparition called up by some medium in a séance of spiritualism." Indeed, all of Whistler's portraits reminded George du Maurier of ghosts. In conveying this sense of the ambiguous and mysterious, Whistler borrowed devices often used by the Pre-Raphaelites, and did so well before his first séance at Rossetti's Tudor House. It was but a small step, then, for the free play of his imagination to suggest the immaterial quality of nature.[50]

Sorcery aside, there was another type of spiritual consciousness, another way of glimpsing the otherworldly, that may have inspired Whistler. It came not through meditation or mediums, or even prayer, but from a bottle. Some poets and artists in nineteenth-century England and France, especially France, claimed absinthe was essential for opening the doors of perception. For some, the use of drugs generally, including hashish, was another form of mesmerism or spiritual transcendence, the resulting hallucinations and illusions being a means of peering into the infinite and stimulating the imagination, a type of "physiospiritualism." Many of Whistler's friends and acquaintances drank absinthe, some to their regret. Baudelaire, having succumbed to the drink's allure, warned against it. Oscar Wilde would alternately laud and condemn it. Claude Monet, George Moore, Émile Zola, Paul Cézanne, Henri Toulouse-Lautrec, Vincent Van Gogh, and Arthur Symons knew its grip, and Édouard Manet and Edgar Degas turned their experiences with the drink into a pair of their best-known—notorious in some quarters—paintings.[51]

Absinthe was well known in parts of America by the 1830s, when Edgar Allen Poe would mix it with brandy. Whistler probably discovered it during his student days in Paris. He was already addicted to tobacco by then and was no stranger to alcohol. Given the relatively high price of absinthe before the 1870s, Whistler and his impoverished friends undoubtedly settled more often for cheap wine, but it would have been remarkable had his bohemian and revolutionary instincts not led him to the more potent drink as a natural part of a young artist's life.[52]

Whistler's first documented mention of absinthe came in 1866, when in Chile. Whiling away his time as a lookout and spy for his arms-dealing associates, he purchased copious amounts of wine, ale, cognac, sherry, and absinthe to share with the American and British citizens and naval officers with whom he dined and socialized in Valparaiso. By then, the tradition of *a l'heure de l'absinthe,* approximately five o'clock, had become a defining moment of "modern progress and civilization" for Whistler. It could secure friendships, too, as when Whistler first met the critic Dugald S. MacColl. Having toured the Paris Salon and exchanged opinions about this or that artist or painting, the two men went off "arm in arm" to celebrate their new bond with glasses of absinthe. Whistler considered MacColl a "good fellow" ever after. He was likely proud of MacColl, too, when shortly after their first meeting the critic defended the subject matter of Degas's *L'Absinthe.*[53]

Of course, consuming absinthe has its downside, and it was the ruin of more than one artist and poet. As it became cheaper, it was associated with working-class alcoholism and synonymous with depravity and fin de siècle decadence. There is no telling how Whistler responded to absinthe. He does not appear to have overindulged, which would have increased the odds of hallucination, but he surely enjoyed the beverage for some reason other than the ritual of drinking it. And there was a ritual. Because of its naturally bitter taste, few people could enjoy absinthe "straight." Huysmans, while celebrating the decadence with which absinthe was frequently associated, thought it tasted awful, like sucking a copper button, which is why the ancient Greeks named it *apsinthion* ("undrinkable"). It must be diluted, generally by pouring ice water into the glass over a cube of sugar, but that very act of dilution suggested its mystical properties. The naturally emerald hue of absinthe, caused by several herbs and plants, became an opalescent green and yellow. This "louche effect" appeared magical to a person seeking magic. To an artist, it could also suggest how colors might be merged and transformed. Upon drinking it, everything became relative—not only colors but also shapes, sizes, and distances. As Rainer Maria Rilke said of a poet friend, he "gazed silently into his glass of absinthe. . . . He saw his glass of absinthe grow until he felt himself in the center of its opal light, weightless, completely dissolved in the strange atmosphere."[54]

Despite the implications of darkness in their titles, most of Whistler's Thames nocturnes are all about color, perhaps caused by weather patterns and pollutants, but also quite possibly inspired by the dreamlike atmosphere induced by his favored liqueur. Absinthe was not called the "Green Fairy" for nothing, and *a l'heure de l'absinthe* was also known as *l'heure verte,* "the green hour." It stirred the imagination. "A glass of absinthe is as poetical as anything in the world," Oscar Wilde decided. "What difference is there between a glass of absinthe and a sunset?" Perhaps, then, his poetic reference to Whistler in "Symphony in Yellow" resulted from Wilde's own vision of the Thames as seen through the louche prism of absinthe, and it certainly suggests a possibility for how Whistler saw the river.[55]

And Whistler need not have been hallucinating to benefit from absinthe. Indeed, one authority on the subject believes that visual artists have rarely been consciously influenced by drugs of any kind and that alcoholic hallucinations are particularly overrated as sources of inspiration. Yet all that Whistler required was for his imagination—and so, his memory—to be stimulated. In this sense he may have benefited, much like Turner, from a type of hallucination known as synesthesia, in which artists, including musicians, poets, and writers, translate the memory of one type of emotional sensation into another form. A certain sound or atmospheric effect, for example, might suggest a particular color. None of this is to say absolutely, or even to suggest the likelihood, that absinthe inspired the nocturnes. Yet it is certainly possible that the Green Fairy, in combination with other factors, heightened Whistler's already acute observations of nature. Baudelaire would have called it *surnaturalism*, or a "poem that exists on two different planes."[56]

An even more obvious source of synesthesia would be the stimulation of sound, of music. Might this be an underappreciated source of inspiration? Probably not, tempting as the possibility appears. Tom Way saw an obvious connection between music and Whistler's paintings. His nocturnes, Way insisted, aroused "the same feelings as are excited by listening to a nocturne or a Ballade of Chopin—the same mystery and poetry, the same pure sense of beauty." Harper Pennington insisted that Whistler likened his palette to the keyboard of a piano and arranged the paints in "something exactly corresponding to . . . 'absolute pitch' in music." And Whistler's eccentric friend Lady Archibald Campbell wrote a pamphlet titled *Rainbow-Music; the Philosophy of Harmony in Colour-Grouping*, which insisted that all colors have their equivalent in musical notes.[57]

Nonetheless, Whistler never mentioned music as a source of inspiration for his paintings, despite his stated belief in the unity of all the arts. Indeed, at the Ruskin trial, he explained that he called his "night pieces" nocturnes to simplify "the whole set of them." It was "an accident," the artist insisted, that he decided on musical terms for any of his work. They were simply a device. The term *nocturne* had come to him belatedly, from Frederick R.

Leyland, a good pianist and a more serious student of music than Whistler, only after Whistler had already painted his first moonlight.[58]

It seems, though, that science and poetry are crucial for understanding the nocturnes. The influence of science may be seen even in Whistler's technical mastery of the paintings: in his brushstrokes, management of space, and arrangement of compositions. But the science is perfectly balanced by their poetry, which is a painter's poetry, inspired by glimpses of unseen worlds. There is a lightness, one might even say a light-hearted confidence, in the majority, and certainly the best, of the nocturnes, despite their inherent moodiness. It is a quality seen in most of Whistler's paintings, a reflection of his joyous, romantic nature. His waspish, quarrelsome image too often obscures that quality, disguising the playfulness and tongue-in-cheek aspect of both his life and work.

PART 3
Image

CHAPTER 7

Whistler in Popular Culture

Whistler exploited every possibility for self-promotion during his lifetime. With the help of obliging journalists and editors in the popular press, he became one of the world's first "celebrities." Newspapers eagerly printed his letters, interviewed him, and reported his legal disputes. Publication of *The Gentle Art of Making Enemies* ensured the continuing impact of his encounters, to be enjoyed long after the events he documented. Nearly as dramatically, poets like Oscar Wilde and Stéphane Mallarmé paid tribute to him. He was caricatured in *Punch*. Audiences encountered references to him on the London stage. Prominent novelists, including Henry James and George du Maurier, based characters on him. His image—that is, the imagined Whistler—became inseparable from his art, sometimes even obscuring it.

Naturally, it would be foolish to think of Whistler merely as a product of nineteenth-century popular culture. The art eventually triumphed despite his image and flamboyant style. That said, great artists have been routinely embraced by the wider world, a truism even more evident in our twenty-first-century world of electronic media than it was in Whistler's day. Inevitably, for better or worse, popular culture has continued to shape his legacy.

A rush of commemorative poems venerated Whistler within months of his passing. Poets celebrated his image as the Butterfly, "the soul of laughter," whose name would never die. As the emotional fervor waned, these paeans were replaced by tributes to his art, but these were no less admiring. In the mid-1920s Eleanor Jewett, a poet, writer, and longtime art critic for the *Chicago Tribune*, so revered Whistler, and so abhorred modernist painting, that she appended a ten-stanza poem to a review of an exhibition of his etchings. In due course, others would wax eloquent over the enduring beauty of his art, even paying homage to the house where he was born, that "noble shrine," that "home of art and beauty."[1]

All that paled, however, when compared to the most quoted and most meaningful poetical tribute. Ezra Pound so admired Whistler's art and personal style that he imitated him in dress, which Pound, like many others, mistook for a chic dandyism. More profoundly, he believed Whistler to be not just America's "only great artist," but also the greatest American since Abraham Lincoln. Whistler had proved, he submitted, that being born an American did not "eternally damn a man or prevent him from the ultimate and highest achievement in the arts." Pound's epiphany came when viewing a memorial exhibition for Whistler at the Tate in 1912, but he went on to express his admiration in published reviews of other exhibitions and in his private correspondence for the next several years. "I suppose in the long run Jimmy Whistler was not so good a painter as Manet," he admitted, "but he had a damn good run for his money. I don't recall any British painter of his time cropping up in a poem by Mallarmé." In verse, Pound declared: "You and Abe Lincoln from that mass of dolts / Show us there's chance at least of winning through."[2]

Novelists took a less direct approach but remained enthusiastic about Whistler's potential in fiction. The French seemingly led the way. Novelist and poet Henri de Régnier based the character of Cyrille Buttelet in his 1907 work *La Peur de l'Amour* on Whistler, although it was not an entirely flattering characterization. A casual remark by another character suggests that Buttelet shows an unhealthy taste for young girls, perhaps inspired by Whistler's interest in drawing and painting nude or scantily clad prepubescent and teenage girls in the last decade of his life. More enduringly, Marcel Proust drew on Whistler for the painter Elstir in his series of seven novels known collectively as *In Search of Lost Time* (1913–27).

Proust's choice is interesting, for while he was captivated by Whistler's art and personality, he was also a devout follower of John Ruskin. Unfazed by the contradiction, Proust contended that even though the two men "thoroughly despised one another," they were more alike than either would have admitted. "The truth [meaning Beauty] is one," he confided to a friend shortly after Whistler's death, "and they both perceived it." Their "theories" may have been "opposed," Proust admitted, but "at a certain depth they agreed more often than they realized."[3]

Proust proved his reverence for Whistler when he rose from his sickbed—"braving death," he said—to see the painter's 1905 memorial exhibition in Paris. "You know that at the moment there is a terrible reaction against Whistler among the artistic élite in France," Proust told a friend. "He is regarded as a man of exquisite taste who because of that was able to pass himself off as a great painter." That was not at all Proust's opinion; he added that if Whistler did not qualify as a great painter, "there never was one." It may have been this experience that led Proust to model Elstir, presented in the novels as "perhaps the greatest of our age," on Whistler.[4]

The character appears only briefly in the first volume, *Swann's Way*, published in 1913. He is called Biche in that story, but his role (now as Elstir) expands significantly thereafter. How art shapes our lives and memories of the past and the futility of life without art are Proust's central themes. So is the role of morality in art, with Ruskin's ghost and Proust's long-running fascination with the Whistler-Ruskin trial hard to miss. Similarly, he names over one hundred artists and uses specific works of art to introduce aesthetic debates that had shaped his own life.[5]

Intriguingly, Whistler is mentioned in his own right as well as in the guise of Elstir. Using a slightly kaleidoscopic literary device, Proust has both Elstir and other characters speak of Whistler and discuss his paintings, as when describing a "marvellous rose-pink and violet sky . . . reminiscent of so many Whistlers of Venice." More often, Proust uses Elstir to express Whistler's and his own views on art, including an oblique reference to the "Ten O'Clock" lecture. Elstir also meditates on the fate of his own reputation as artistic fashions and styles came and went. Conflating Whistler and Elstir in an especially telling way, Proust, as narrator, considers, "No doubt young men had come along who also loved painting, but painting of another kind; they had not, like Swann, like M. Verdurin, received lessons in taste from Whistler, lessons in truth from Monet, lessons which alone would have qualified them to judge Elstir with justice."[6]

After Proust, Whistler never again appeared in a fictional disguise. He was either presented as himself or served as a point of reference. In the latter case, he might be mentioned only in passing, often as a convenient way to comment on modern art. John Galsworthy used Whistler that way in his Forsyte Chronicles. In *To Let*, published in 1920, young Michael Mont, a once aspiring artist, surveys Soames Forsyte's private picture gallery. Pausing briefly in front of an unidentified Whistler, his only comment is, "D'you think he ever really saw a naked woman, sir?" Whether intended to reflect the views of Mont's generation or Galsworthy's personal opinion is unclear, but Soames himself believes that "art for art's sake and all that . . . was cant." Even in as unlikely a place as Poland, numerous writers, including Irena Krzywicka, Alfred Konar, and Gabriela Zapolska, made use of Whistler, although in their case to express enthusiasm for "modernism" in art.[7]

Fictional attempts to grapple with Whistler's legacy grew scarcer after the 1920s, which seems to confirm one literary scholar's contention that twentieth-century novelists drew inspiration from art and artists less often than in the previous century. What had been an "intimate mingling of the arts" slowly dissolved, at least to the extent that authors seldom turned contemporary artists into fictional characters. Many novelists, including Colm Tóibín, Julian Barnes, and Iain Pears, still draw inspiration from art, but it is usually dead artists that interest them. Quite often, artists do not even appear as characters in their work, but rather as subjects, as in Barnes's *Flaubert's Parrot*. In other instances, they and their art serve mainly as a cause for commentary.[8]

Consider the next fictional tribute to Whistler. In 1946 John Gilmore Wolcott, an American artist, teacher, and writer, published the eccentric and satirical *Fra Angelo Bomberto in the Underworld of Art*. A resident of Lowell, Massachusetts, Whistler's birthplace, Wolcott was rumored at one time to be writing a biography of the artist, and he did impersonate him at local events. His book is not about Whistler, though it does defend Whistler's art. The title character, Fra Angelo, is a modern-day painter who specializes in "Pragmatic Surrealism," which, as he explains it, is a type of "practical supernaturalism." He arrives in Lowell one day because he wants to use the garret of Whistler's birthplace as a studio.

In the course of the story, Fra Angelo, self-proclaimed "spiritual adviser to the world of art, successor to Picasso as primate of modern art," exposes the ways in which corrupt art dealers and short-sighted museum directors stifle creativity and suppress artists of integrity. Whistler had fought the same battle, Wolcott implies, and was still "being maligned" for his theories. Explaining his purpose privately, Wolcott declared, "The book, which has very serious purpose in its satire, I hope will enlighten people concerning this prevalent wide-spread chicanery in the art trade."[9]

Not until 1972 did Whistler play a lead role in fiction. It would be his only star turn, and it came twice in the same year, when both Ted Berkman, a novelist and screenwriter for film and television, and Lawrence Williams, an actor and short-story and television scriptwriter, published fictional accounts of Whistler's life. Berkman's *To Seize the Passing Dream* was the more conventional, but also the more sensational, work. Subtitled *A Novel of Whistler, His Women, and His World,* the book gives readers a lot about the "women." Describing an amorous tussle between Whistler and Joanna Hiffernan, Berkman nearly salivates: "Jimmy fell upon her, onto the statuesque breasts and the warm round thighs, the supple throat and the miraculously long waistline." And so it continues for nearly two full pages. As one reviewer commented, "You can't exactly review a book written like that."[10]

Williams's *I, James McNeill Whistler* is equally implausible. The book purports to be Whistler's autobiography, an approach Williams felt qualified to pursue because his parents had been students at the Académie Carmen. Consequently, as Williams explained, "I kind of grew up on Whistler stories, you know, the jokes and all that." Ever the gentleman, the fictional Whistler betrays no intimate moments with Jo in his own telling of events. In fact, he dispenses with this crucial person in his life in two brief paragraphs, explaining, "For a time Jo was a part of my general scene, but finally not a part of my composition." Similarly, this Whistler never travels to Chile, and he barely mentions his mother, thus sparing readers the Oedipal complex foisted on us by Berkman.[11]

How much a novel can tell us about historical figures is an enduring question, although the odds are against it revealing much more than the public person. Berkman and Williams pile on plenty of biographical facts, but it is hard to believe the Whistler that emerges from either work. Williams in particular, by attempting to maintain Whistler's "voice" over 372 pages, set himself up for failure. That said, at a crucial moment in the shaping of his popular image both authors brought attention to Whistler's life in ways denied to exhibitions of his art and scholarly studies.

As interest in Whistler grew from the 1970s into the 1990s, novelists who set their stories in Chelsea, regardless of the time period, knew at least to mention him. Penelope Fitzgerald, in her 1979 Booker Prize winning *Offshore,* set in the 1960s, not only quotes the most famous passage in the "Ten O'Clock" lecture ("When the evening mist clothes the riverside. . . .") but also has a character declare, "Whistler was a very good painter. You don't want to make any mistake about that. It's only amateurs who think he isn't."

A year later, in 1980, a pair of American fiction writers, Thomas M. Disch and Charles Naylor, launched a surprising trend in fictional portrayals of Whistler. Thomas and Jane Carlyle are the principal characters in their novel *Neighboring Lives,* set in Chelsea between 1834 and 1867, but this is no less the story of their neighbors, including the Rossettis, William Morris, Algernon Swinburne, and Edward Burne-Jones. Whistler, "that young American puppy," also plays a role, as do several of his family members and Walter Greaves. They are poorly portrayed, with an odious Anna, for instance, speaking in an impossible Southern drawl. However—and here is the surprise—the most important person from Whistler's orbit is Jo Hiffernan. Her role is every bit as large as Whistler's. In fact, the novel ends with Jo, believing that Whistler has "abandoned" her by sailing away to Chile, leaving Chelsea for Paris and Gustave Courbet.

Two other novelists subsequently followed suit by making either Jo or Maud Franklin the main character in their accounts of Whistler's life. Cherry Smyth, a London-based Irish writer, poet, curator, and critic, imagines Jo's life with both Whistler and Courbet in *Hold Still* (2014). As the only woman to have written a fictional account of Whistler's life, her perspective on his relationship with Jo rings truer than that of someone like Berkman. Her intimate scenes are less heated and far briefer, and she writes with a twenty-first-century sensibility that emphasizes the struggle of an independent young woman to hold her own in a male-dominated world.

English novelist Matthew Plampin attempts the same with Maud Franklin in *Mrs. Whistler* (2018), while also bringing Frances Leyland into the action. The book is episodic and covers only the years between 1876 and 1880, even though Whistler and Maud lived together long before and after those dates. The action revolves mainly around the painting of the Peacock Room and the Ruskin trial. Yet like Smyth, Plampin allows us to consider Whistler's private life, fictionalized though it may be, from a perspective that does not always place him in a favorable light. Seeing him through the struggles and triumphs of Jo and Maud, Whistler's egotistical and selfish side is laid bare (fig. 14).

Books less focused on Whistler pop up from time to time. He appears in a 2018 novel about James Tissot. *The Hammock,* by American writer Lucy Paquette, weaves Whistler in and out of the story to illustrate something of Tissot's social circle and the London art world. Historical mystery writer

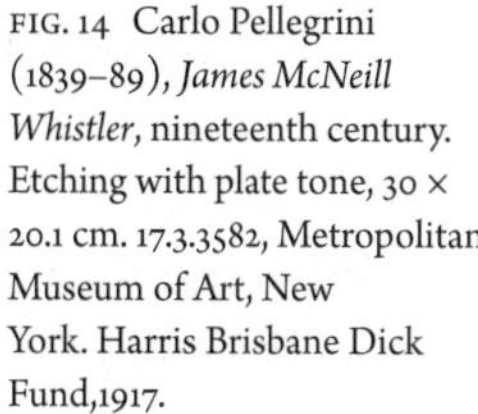

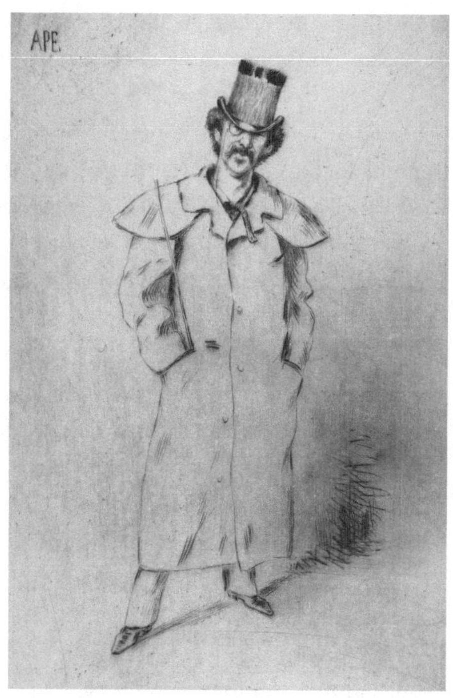

FIG. 14 Carlo Pellegrini (1839–89), *James McNeill Whistler*, nineteenth century. Etching with plate tone, 30 × 20.1 cm. 17.3.3582, Metropolitan Museum of Art, New York. Harris Brisbane Dick Fund,1917.

M. J. Trow gave us a bit of nonsense in 2020 with *Last Nocturne*. The central plot has Whistler hiring a pair of private detectives to dig up dirt on John Ruskin as he prepares for his court battle with the critic. At the same time, the detectives are investigating the murder of several prostitutes in Cremorne Gardens. As the two cases become entwined, the story becomes less and less plausible, but Trow does show that Whistler's quarrel with Ruskin is still well enough known to become fictional fodder. Other books, including Don DeLillo's celebrated *Underworld* (1997) and Mick Herron's *Why We Die* (2006), suggest Whistler's stature through references to his mother's portrait.

Equally imaginative ways of presenting Whistler have come through dramatic performances on stage, radio, film, and television. As with fictional writing, an inkling of what was to come could be seen during his lifetime with an English production of *La Cigale* (*The Grasshopper*) and Gilbert and Sullivan's *Patience*. The former play poked fun at him for his links to Impressionism; the latter, while mocking the Aesthetic movement, had a leading character in the original production displaying Whistler's white forelock and imitating his patented laugh, "Ha ha!" Since then, hundreds of stage plays about famous artists, including musicians, composers, poets, and writers, have been produced. Some productions are more rooted than others in historical reality, but all help to draw their subjects into the realm of popular culture. Visual artists were slower to appear than writers, whose work could be converted to dialogue. El Greco was one of the first, depicted on the London stage in 1936. Vincent Van Gogh, William Hogarth, Pablo Picasso, Mark Rothko, Andy Warhol, and Basquiat have followed more recently, but Whistler arrived on the scene even earlier.[12]

Whistler was first associated with a pair of amateur productions staged as fundraisers during World War I. In December 1916, an "American matinee" at Chelsea's Palace Theatre included tableaux of paintings by Whistler and John Singer Sargent. Next, in March 1917, came "Chelsea on Tiptoe." Ellen Terry appeared as "The Spirit of Chelsea," Augustus John illustrated a printed program, and Edward Elgar wrote and conducted his one-act ballet *The Sanguine Fan* for the event. Described as a "light-hearted tribute" to some of Chelsea's "traditional celebrities," the performance involved a series of skits. One of them, reminiscent of a well-known Max Beerbohm cartoon, had such luminaries as Carlyle, Morris, and Swinburne congregating in Gabriel Rossetti's garden. Whistler appeared through inference in a skit that had the popular actress Julia James portray Connie Gilchrist—subject of a celebrated Whistler painting—and sing the former child star's "Skipping Song."[13]

The first professional presentation to feature Whistler came shortly after the war, but it had a long and tortured history. Highly successful American theatrical producer Oliver Morosco was to stage the play. He had been offered five scripts about Whistler, and at least fourteen others were known to be in circulation. He chose a script written by Sarah Jeffries Curry and Pauline Mackie Cavendish, both experienced writers who had already collaborated on another play. As it happened, Cavendish's mother, when a girl in Stonington, Connecticut, had known Whistler's mother.[14]

However, when Morosco demanded revisions, Cavendish asked the Pennells, whose book she and Curry had already consulted, to "do some collaborative work on the play." Elizabeth Pennell, who enjoyed the "popular art" of comic newspapers and the music hall, agreed to read it. The main plot involved Whistler's portrait of Lady Sybil Eden, but little of the action was related to the controversy that painting inspired. Jo and her father are living with Whistler in Chelsea, a bailiff comes and goes, Lady

Eden becomes infatuated with Whistler as he seems to lead her on, and Jo falls in love with the Edens' son and, in the end, leaves Whistler to marry him. Cavendish, "full of enthusiasm and interest," met several times with the Pennells, who tried to correct some details of the story, but they ultimately found the play so full of "invention . . . that to change it at all would be to change everything." Much would depend on who played Whistler, Elizabeth decided, and "whether he could express what were supposed to be the eccentricities of Whistler and yet retain throughout his dignity and charm."[15]

Noted English actor George Arliss, who had made his mark as Benjamin Disraeli on Broadway, was eager to take on the role of Whistler but ultimately opted to embark on what would become a successful film career. A pity. As a friend of Isabella Stewart Gardner, a noted patron of Whistler, and an acquaintance of John Singer Sargent, Arliss might have brought insight and nuance to the role. Instead, Morosco gave the part to the equally keen Oliver P. Heggie. A veteran of the London and New York stage, the Australian made a "tremendous study" of Whistler's "character." He, too, wished to consult the Pennells, but when revisions to the script delayed production, he signed on to another play. A frustrated Morosco sold his rights to another producer, so that *The Baronet and the Butterfly*, the play's ultimate title, was not performed until the summer of 1924 in New London, Connecticut. It received good reviews, with Heggie, who finally did appear as Whistler, singled out for praise. One critic enthused, "His regal demeanour, his never-failing urbanity, even in crisis, his charm of address, the contemptuous curve of his lips, the mystery of his smile, the superficial condescension and inward imperiousness of the man—it was all beautifully, distinctly, incisively depicted." Sadly, success in the provinces was not enough. The play's Broadway opening was first delayed, then canceled.[16]

American playwright Laurence Eyre brought Whistler to the London stage the following year with *The Wasp*, but it was a short-lived production. Described as episodic, it was only enlivened by including Carlyle, Swinburne, and Oscar Wilde as characters. Eyre's problem may have been that he drew much of his material from the widow of William Merritt Chase, whose husband had not been so enamored of Whistler as the Pennells.[17]

Fast-forward six years, and the unflappable Cavendish and Curry tried again. Further revisions, assisted this time by the established and successful scriptwriter A. E. Thomas, yielded a new title, *Whistler: A Romantic Comedy*, but with the same plot. The new title may have been the doing of a new impresario, Rowland Stebbens. He tried out the play three times in the summer and fall of 1931, in Denver, Baltimore, and Washington, DC, in anticipation of hitting Broadway in early 1932. Richard Hale played Whistler. With his Irish baritone voice, Hale was better known at the time as an opera and concert singer than as an actor, but like Heggie, his performance was singled out as the best part of the play. He was praised for being "uncannily" like Whistler in his "outward appearance, his mannerisms, his precise movements, his quicksilver moods, his periods of sincerity and his rapid-fire method of speech."[18]

It was not enough. The play lost $4,831.23 during its one week in Baltimore and another $5,068.55 after a week in Washington, where it closed on December 12. The New York production, due to open nine days later, was canceled. Hopkins and Curry tried three more times to resurrect the play, in 1934, 1936, and 1939. Having eliminated all of the contributions made by Thomas, they retitled it *Mr. Whistler of Cheyne Walk*, although the plot again remained unchanged. Its last known performance came in 1936, in Pasadena, California.[19]

The Cavendish-Curry saga may only mean that they were not very good playwrights, even though they did have other theatrical successes, and Curry became a prolific novelist. However, it also suggests two difficulties in bringing Whistler's life to the stage. First, despite the successes of Heggie and Hale, is the challenge of communicating his complex personality. Second is the conundrum of fashioning a focused, representative segment of his life.

W. Graham Robertson, who had published his entertaining reminiscences seven years earlier, recognized both problems when he became involved with a benefit performance to honor Sir Henry Irving, who had sat for one of Whistler's most famous portraits. Performed at London's Lyceum Theatre and attended by Queen Mary in May 1938, the program consisted of fifteen scenes, most but not all related to Irving's life. Robertson had a cameo role in a segment depicting the renowned Beefsteak Club, to which both Irving and Whistler belonged. He was appalled at how little effort was made to have the actors look, sound, or behave like the men they were playing. Case in point, Whistler was represented by "a large, heavy man, well over six feet, with a head of long, untidy grey hair, a stoop, and a shy deprecating manner."

A few weeks later Robertson met Richard Whorf, an American artist/actor and younger brother of the watercolorist John Whorf. Richard would become best known as an actor and television director, but in 1938 his chief ambition was to write a play about Whistler and perform the title role. He never did, but his hope led Robertson to reflect, "I can't see any play in Whistler's life-story."[20]

The challenge has largely stymied dramatists ever since. In 1952, Leo Kerz staged the oddly titled *Whistler's Grandmother* as a comedy in London. More substantially, Robert A. Bachmann brought Whistler to the stage in *Whistler's Mother*, also in 1952. The play does not appear to have been seen in the United States, but it had a brief run in London. Its title is misleading, in that Anna Whistler, played by stage and film actress Louise Hampton, has a secondary role. Her main assignment is to steer Whistler into marrying Beatrice, even though that marriage occurred several years after Anna's death. She does sit for her portrait midway through the action, but the rest of this "flat and uninspired drama" consisted mostly of witty conversations between Whistler (played by Robert Beaumont), Wilde, and Swinburne.[21]

A lull in stage productions followed during the 1960s and 1970s, which is curious given that Whistler's reputation, as will be shown, was energized in those decades. Meantime, film and stage actor Vincent Price did his best to keep Whistler in the public eye. A noted collector and connoisseur of art, Price claimed to be on a "self-appointed mission to interest the American people in American culture," and Whistler was one of his passions. He never portrayed the artist as such but did give dramatic readings from *The Gentle Art of Making Enemies*. Appreciating the public's woeful knowledge of the fine arts, he always introduced his hero by saying, "You may not know him offhand, but surely you remember his mother."[22]

The 1980s saw a burst of minor plays about Whistler staged in regional theaters. Lawrence Williams turned his 1972 novel into a one-man show in 1981 for performances in Connecticut and Massachusetts. In the later instance, veteran stage, film, and television actor John Cullum tackled the role. *Whistler's Play*, a unique take on the Ruskin trial written by Howard Burman, was staged in Detroit in 1987–88. American actor Hurd Hatfield, who had first come to fame as a film star with his splendid 1945 performance in the title role of *The Picture of Dorian Gray*, took on the role of Whistler for a more expansive audience. By then in his sixties, Hatfield toured with his one-man play, called *The Son of Whistler's Mother*, in Northern Ireland, Germany, Latvia, and Russia.[23]

Two other plays deserve more detailed comment. Sam Dowling's 1985 *The Riverman* was set in the art world of 1910, but the story explores the friendship of Whistler and Walter Greaves. It was moderately successful, with performances given at least as late as 2011 at some of England's regional theaters, and while Whistler does not appear as a character, he is ever present in the dialogue.

The essence of the plot involves Greaves's ultimately futile effort to be recognized as an artist in his own right. The Pennells loom as the villains who, in their determination to protect Whistler's legacy, try to quash his pretensions. "A genius? Walter Greaves a genius?" an amused Joseph Pennell laughs. "Ha ha ha! He was a boatman on the Battersea ferry!" That was not quite correct, but then many of the details of the play leave the wrong impression. The most preposterous suggestion—yet one central to the plot—is that Whistler had broken a promise to marry Greaves's sister Alice, or "Tinnie," whom he had sketched and sometimes escorted around the grounds of Cremorne Gardens. The details of their supposed romance are revealed in a fictional packet of letters held by Greaves, which Tinnie urges him to publish, at least partly to show up the Pennells. "Silver tongue . . . whisperin' . . . whisperin,'" Tinnie recalls of Whistler's words, "my dearest Tinnie . . . my life my dream my jewel my love . . . Touch . . . let me touch you again my sweet my naughty Tinnie." Walter, as protective as the Pennells of Whistler's memory, agonizes over the decision, but ultimately, in the climactic end of the play, destroys the letters as he cries out in agony, "Jimmy!"[24]

Whistler is more of a living presence in Tamas MacDonald's lauded 1983 play about John Ruskin, *The Plague Wind*. While the Whistler-Ruskin trial serves as a focal point for the story, most of the drama is a psychological study of Ruskin. The title, which comes from the lecture Ruskin gave on the environmental changes wrought by an industrializing world, stands as a metaphor for Ruskin's generally pessimistic view of the modern world. Whistler, who represents this creeping decay in the art world, serves as a convenient foil. Sixty-year-old John Bott, a familiar face in television dramas, played the aging Ruskin. Forty-four-year-old Ian Thompson, better known at the time for his theatrical work, played Whistler at that same age. Reviews of this "impressionistic muddle" were mixed, but Bott was applauded for his sensitive portrayal. One reviewer thought Thompson, in his "arch" performance, came across as "a would-be Oscar Wilde but one who had nothing to declare but feeble jokes." More generous assessments called his performance "splendidly alert," filled with "wit and vivacity," and "colourfully arrogant as the wild and witty Whistler."[25]

Each, in its way, was a fair assessment. Thompson, with feathery forelock, monocle, "natty, white suit," patent-leather shoes, and a nearly four-foot-long cane, looked the stereotypical Whistler. The trial, at his insistence, takes place in a private club, rather than (as was the case) in the courts of law, but the dialogue accurately reflects Whistler's views on artistic criticism. "Never mind that what he says damages my commercial reputation," Whistler explains of his reason for suing the critic. "Ruskin's rantings touch the broader question of artistic conscience." Whistler celebrates his legal victory by clowning and sarcastically mocking Ruskin in a shrill voice as his friends shout, "Art is liberated!" and "Vindicated!" But the play ends with Ruskin, who had earlier shown signs of mental agitation and instability, exuding calm, the plague cloud having passed.[26]

Difficult as it has been to mount a successful theatrical production about Whistler, musicals would seem an even less likely vehicle. In contrast to the numerous plays that have allowed artists to take center stage, the only notable musical tribute to a painter has been Stephen Sondheim's *Sunday in the Park with George*, about Georges Seurat. The experience of composer Frank Tabbita and librettist Stuart Greenman suggest why. They began work on *Peacock* around 2012, but despite completing a significant part of the production, including a dozen songs, they gave up a few years later. Greenman's ill health slowed them for a time, but Whistler himself became the main drag. Both men thought him a fascinating figure and "underrated genius," but they could not present his less appealing qualities—the occasional pettiness, jealousies, and litigiousness—in a way that would make him likable to audiences. Whistler, Tabbita discovered, was "a hard sell" to the "so-called 'Literati'" of the theater world. No theater offered to sponsor the workshops necessary to develop the play. Trusted friends told the duo, "The music is great, the lyrics are clever, the text is excellent—but your central character is a jerk!"[27]

Their experience is confirmed by the circumstances of one of Whistler's rare appearances on the musical stage. *Oscar*, by James Clutton and Damien Landi, is based on the life of Oscar Wilde, and was first staged in 1992, with occasional revivals since. Whistler has a small but important role early in the play when the famous verbal sparring between the erstwhile friends turns into a romantic rivalry for the attentions of Lillie Langtry. As a trio, they sing "The Gentle Art," which ends with Lillie yielding to Oscar's "wit" and the "music" of his voice. The rejected Whistler responds by singing "Whistler's Song." It is a bitter rejoinder, as seen in its opening line, "Do you know what it's like to really hate a man?" as the artist reveals his deep-seated jealousy of the poet. It is a bit over the top, as Clutton freely acknowledges, but it serves the purpose of making Whistler a foil for the play's hero. Whistler provides the "dramatic counterpoint," Clutton explains, to "Oscar's brilliance," much as Salieri does for Mozart in *Amadeus*.[28]

Or as he did for Ruskin in *Plague Wind*. In other words, Whistler is seen popularly as a colorful, buoyant character, but not one to be taken seriously or treated sympathetically. He occupies the same position, if indirectly, in an opera about Ruskin. First produced in 1995, *Modern Painters* by David Lang and Manuela Hoelterhoff does not put Whistler on stage, but the brooding art critic does lament the humiliation of the famous court case.[29]

If not suited for full-fledged musical treatment, Whistler has occasionally made it into the lyrics of individual songs, though virtually all of them date from the 1930s–50s. Most, too, are more about his mother than himself. Cole Porter, for instance, had a hit song in 1934 with "You're the Top," which jauntily decreed: "You're an O'Neill drama, /You're Whistler's mama." A character in Richard Rodgers and Lorenz Hart's 1940 musical *Pal Joey* sings more negatively:

> Zip! I am just a mystic.
> I don't care for Whistler's mother,
> Charlie's aunt and Schubert's brother.
> Zip! I'm misogynistic.

Again showcasing Anna, bluegrass artists the Osborne Brothers recorded "There's a Woman Behind Every Man" in 1959. In addition to mentioning Queen Isabella and, somewhat incongruously, the Statue of Liberty, they extolled Whistler's mother, who "Put her son on the road to fame, / And we don't even know her name."[30]

The medium of radio treated Whistler more reverently. The United States led the way with a pair of radio dramas in 1932 and 1937, the latter being part of the Works Progress Administration project for unemployed writers called "Portraits in Oil." Set in 1876, the half-hour episode featured the Peacock Room and the Ruskin trial, although Oscar Wilde, who did not enter Whistler's life until the 1880s, also puts in an appearance. The program concluded with a narrator describing the trial as a "moral triumph for Whistler," who had gone to court "not for damages but to vindicate *his position*, and therefore, that of *all artists*."[31]

Since then, the British Broadcasting Company has taken the lead. Their first "wireless" Whistler program, "Nocturne at Chelsea," was broadcast in 1939 and featured, intriguingly enough, Romney Brent (born Romulo Larralde in Mexico) as the artist. Written by Whistler biographer James Laver, it included a measure of speculation and fiction but concluded with an old man explaining to a young friend, "My boy, if Whistler taught us anything, he taught us that Beauty is in the eye of the Artist . . . and helps us to see it in the contemporary scene." One week after the program aired, the *Observer* announced a competition for the best "perfectly authenticated story" about Whistler, the winner to receive a prize of three guineas.[32]

The Whistler-Ruskin trial provided the staple plot for BBC radio dramas about the artist into the 1970s. The only surviving script from those decades is for "The Verdict of the Court," broadcast in 1960. Written by Richard Du Cann, the play concludes with its narrator summarizing what had become the modern consensus on the trial. "In my view the result of the case of *Whistler v. Ruskin* was a travesty of justice," he intones. "Then, of course, Whistler was a terribly bad witness. . . . [H]e ought to have given the appearance of a dedicated and sincere artist—which, of course, he was. But it was not in his character to do it."[33]

The one exception to this steady diet of *Whistler v. Ruskin* came with a 1950 BBC production, "The Baronet and the Butterfly." Revisiting the dramatic possibilities hinted at by Cavendish and Curry, the play featured the formidably multitalented Felix Felton as Whistler. Subsequent actors to portray him on radio included Bernard Braden, Al Mancini, John Franklyn-Robbins, and James Jordan. However, as radio audiences declined in numbers, Whistler disappeared from the British airwaves, not to reappear until 2001.[34]

That left cinema and television as potentially important media for telling Whistler's story. American poet Vachel Lindsay saw a natural connection between Whistler's work, if not his life, and cinema as early as 1922. The artist's paintings, he submitted, provided a perfect model for "photoplays." Whistler had been fastidious in his choice of subjects, the poet explained, and kept the picture "well within the frame, low relief, a Velasquez study of tones and a Japanese study of spaces." Most importantly, Whistler understood that a painting should not be "a mere illustration for a story," a vital lesson, Lindsay insisted, at a time when so many movies simply tried to transfer stage plays to film. A perceptive screenwriter who studied Whistler's *Gentle Art*, Lindsay concluded, would be "equipped to welcome the distinction between the old-fashioned stage, where the word rules, and the photoplay, where splendor and ritual are all."[35]

Even so, not until 1934 and the age of "talkies" did well-connected American film producer Julius Klein recognize the possibilities of a movie based on Whistler's life. Whistler was very much in the news that year, the centenary of his birth. Thanks to his mother's portrait having recently toured the country, the artist had suddenly become "an international figure." Ignoring the potential drama of the Ruskin trial, Klein wanted to develop the love story between Whistler and Jo Hiffernan, arranging some of the most important scenes around "The White Girl." Unfortunately, the project came to nothing, even more of a disappointment than the Cavendish-Curry play.[36]

As it turns out, Whistler has never appeared on the silver screen. This is hard to fathom, given the large number of artists whose lives have made successful films. Charles Laughton made a forceful Rembrandt just two years after Klein thought of doing Whistler. Since then, Michelangelo, Vermeer, Goya, Turner, Renoir, Van Gogh, Toulouse-Lautrec, Klimt, Munch, Picasso, Modigliani, Kahlo, Pollack, and others have entered popular culture through cinema.

Yet Whistler has frequently been mentioned in films, which in some ways is at least as impressive. The assumption is that Whistler and his work are so well known that audiences will understand the references and allusions. So, when a mob boss in Guy Ritchie's 2008 crime-comedy *RocknRolla* says, "You know a man's cultured when he's got a Whistler on the wall," everyone can smile. In the 1999 film version of Oscar Wilde's *An Ideal Husband* (though not in Wilde's original play), Miss Mabel attends a private view at the Grosvenor Gallery. She thinks it "exceedingly forgettable," except for a pair of "Studies in Grey" by Whistler. She and Whistler are also upset that Lord Goring did not attend, as he had promised to do, and are undecided as to whether they should forgive him.

Some directors and set designers showcase Whistler's art without commentary. The 2023 version of *Willie Wonka and the Chocolate Factory* provides a remarkably grand example, with some scenes played out against a backdrop that amounts to a version of the Peacock Room. An enormous golden peacock set against a green wall dominates the screen. Whether or not the director intended to feature Whistler's masterpiece is unclear, but he certainly reproduced a shutter from Leyland's celebrated dining room.

As might be expected, Whistler's portrait of his mother often serves as the visual or verbal cue on film. The earliest instance came in 1940, with the film version of Thornton Wilder's Pulitzer-Prize-winning play *Our Town*. Adhering closely to the original script, and in a film adaptation that would have pleased Vachel Lindsay, one character describes the limited cultural opportunities in Grover's Corners. "No, there ain't much culture," he admits. "*Robinson Crusoe* and the Bible; and 'Handel's Largo,' we all know that; and Whistler's Mother. That's about as far as we go." In 1947, *The Spirit of West Point* combined the painting with a reference to Whistler's ill-fated career at the school. The mother of a cadet who is to be expelled comforts him with the reminder that both Whistler and Edgar Allen Poe had been dismissed from West Point, and in the case of Whistler, "Look what he did for *his* mother." The list of other films that either mention Anna or pay homage to her portrait is a long one and includes all genres, from the creepy thriller *Kind Lady* (1951) to the Oscar-winning *Babette's Feast* (1987), the outrageous comedy *Mr. Bean* (1997), and the sci-fi thriller *I Am Legend* (2007).

Since the 1950s, television, the ultimate source of popular recognition, has also shaped Whistler's image through drama, comedy, and documentaries. The earliest shows were American productions. An episode of the series *West Point*, airing in 1956, opened by showing a watercolor painted by Whistler while a cadet. The plot involved a talented modern cadet who had to decide between the army and a career as an artist. When reminded, as he struggles with his decision, that former cadet Whistler became one of the country's "greatest artists," he responds despondently, "He also flunked out of West Point." Sometimes, the reference is a mere throwaway line, as in a 1960 episode of *Alfred Hitchcock Presents* when a woman warmed by her son's devotion comments, "You make me feel like Whistler's mother." There is no other context for the remark, which demonstrates how recognizable Whistler's name had become.

The 1960s smash BBC adaptation of Galsworthy's *Forsyte Saga* mentions Whistler in the same context as the published novel *To Let* but not in the same words. The screenplay demonstrates a deeper understanding of Whistler's work by having Michael Mont tell Soames, "Ah, here's old Whistler. They say his stuff won't last, you know. . . . He painted on black you see, and sooner or later it will all come through. I should sell him off, sir, quick."

Among other British productions, most of which also aired in the United States, the plot of a 1991 episode of *Morse* involves a badly done forgery of Whistler's painting *The Golden Screen*. While not speaking directly about the painting or Whistler, the detective does comment obliquely and disparagingly on Whistler's philosophy of art by saying, "Painters have an annoying habit of painting what they see rather than what's actually there." In a Sherlock Holmes made-for-TV film, *The Master Blackmailer* (1993), starring Jeremy Brett, a young man speaks disapprovingly to his fiancée at the unveiling of a stylish lady's portrait. "I think she's gentler and more beautiful than that," he opines. "I shall insist on Whistler painting you."

However, Whistler's finest on-screen hour came in the 1978 series *Lillie*, about Lillie Langtry. American actor Don Fellows played Whistler in five of the thirteen episodes, the only filmed portrayal of the artist in a speaking role. Of course, the star of the series is Francesca Annis as Langtry, and Peter Egan as Oscar Wilde has a larger part than Fellows, but the latter's performance is admirable. His Whistler is not as assertive or egotistical as he might have been portrayed. There is, for instance, nary a peacock screech, but only a gentle and knowing chuckle. Fellows also captures Whistler's amiable side, showing him as light-hearted, witty, perceptive, gentlemanly, and impeccably dressed. The voice, an American monotone reminiscent of Fellows's own midwestern roots, is about right, although Whistler was known to use a number of accents, depending on circumstances.

The screenwriter, David Butler, takes liberties with the chronology and facts of Whistler's life, but he successfully presents Whistler in a variety of circumstances. We see him working in his studio, attending splendid soirees, and hosting a "Sunday breakfast," where a bailiff serves as waiter. He describes Whistler's Chilean adventure, rejoices in his victory at the Ruskin trial, laughs at the pretensions of the English upper classes, and ridicules the Royal Academy. His relationship with Lillie is also realistically portrayed. In her memoirs, Langtry described Whistler as one of the most fascinating men she had ever met, and the series does convey something of their closeness, although this, too, may have been understated. We do see the two of them redecorating her parlor, doors closed, late at night. Whistler also educates her in aesthetics by explaining the difference between "illustration" and art, the latter intended not to tell a story, but only to express "pure beauty." Whistler's final scene has him bidding adieu to Lillie as he prepares, now bankrupt, to leave for Venice. He laments that he may never finish her portrait, *Symphony in Yellow*, which he had begun. It is true that he never finished the picture, but then he did not begin it until after his return from Venice. In any event, Wilde subsequently plays a larger role in Lillie's life in the series, as he did in reality—and in the Clutton-Landi musical.

On the lighter side, in 1973 *Monty Python's Flying Circus* offered an improbable six-foot-three Whistler in the person of John Cleese. With monocle in place and a long ribbon flowing from his hat, his Whistler exchanges quips with Wilde before both of them turn on an outgunned and stuttering George Bernard Shaw, all in the presence of Edward VII. Make of that what you will. In 1998, an episode of the American comedy series *Becker* has Reggie, owner and chief waitress of the diner where Dr. John Becker hangs out, telling the curmudgeonly title character that he reminds her of a "Symphony in Brown." Looking ahead, a proposed American television series called "Whistler's Mother & His Mistresses" may be in the offing. Described as a drama/comedy in the vein of *Shakespeare in Love*, the script has been floating around since 2022.

Serious treatment of Whistler's life on television did not come until the mid-1980s, at the beginning of a renewed interest in Whistler. The BBC went first with documentaries about the art in 1984, 1994, and 2000. The 2000 program formed part of a series called *The Great Artists: Romantics and Realists*, in which Whistler was one of six artists to receive his own fifty-minute treatment. Artsworld (now Sky Arts) aired a fourth program for British audiences in 2003.

In 2014, PBS in the United States aired *James McNeill Whistler: The Case for Beauty*, with a simultaneous release on DVD. Admitting that I had a hand in its creation, I still believe this show offers the best balance between Whistler's personal life and his art. It is also the most factually accurate of the Whistler documentaries. The scholarly onscreen commentary is enriched by silent dramatizations of Whistler's life narrated by actress Anjelica Huston. Like the other programs, it focuses mostly on his paintings and etchings at the expense of the pastels and lithography, but it carefully explains the evolution of Whistler's ideas, and we hear Whistler himself, through the voice of American actor Kevin Kline, explain his purpose and goals in letters to friends, not simply the usual quotations from the "Ten O'Clock" lecture. Whistler's wit, eccentricities, and pugnacity are on full display, but they are not allowed to overshadow his serious quest for perfection and beauty in art.

Most recently, a French television program looked at some of the places in London associated with Whistler's life, but he was left out of the three most-watched television documentaries on the history of art: Kenneth Clark's *Civilisation* (1969) and its updated version by Simon Schama (2018), and Robert Hughes's *Shock of the New* (1980). All three series found room for the Impressionists, with whom Whistler is frequently associated, but never mentioned his central role in nineteenth-century art.

Whistler has also long been visible in the world of commercial advertising, which may be the surest way to secure a place in popular culture. He occasionally enjoyed that sort of notoriety during his lifetime. In Britain, his name and image were used to advertise a brand of art supplies. Equally appropriate, given his addiction to smoking, a US tobacco firm, Allen & Ginter, included him in a set of artist trading cards used to promote its line of cigarettes in the 1880s.[37]

His association with tobacco continued after his death. In 1910, a brand of "Whistler Cigars" (even though he smoked only cigarettes) appeared on the US market with his portrait (from an 1880s lithograph by Paul Adolphe Rajon) on the box. More appropriately, in the 1930s, Players cigarettes, in Great Britain, followed the American advertising gimmick of trading cards by including Whistler in a set of "Dandies." This misjudged connection of Whistler to dandyism surfaced in another form in 2003, when William N. P. Nicholson's woodcut portrait of a debonair Whistler was used for the book jacket of Klaas Huizing's novel *Der letzte Dandy* (The last dandy), even though the story had nothing to do with Whistler.[38]

More often, Whistler's art, rather than his image, has been the medium. The earliest example came in 1904, when his etched portrait of Sir Garnet Wolseley was turned into a jigsaw puzzle. Since then, dustjackets or covers of books, vinyl records, and compact discs have made use of his paintings. Recordings of Frédéric Chopin or Claude Debussy are likely to be promoted by one of his nocturnes, but the connections are not always so obvious—witness the portrait of Frances Leyland, rather than of Jo Hiffernan, for a paperback edition of Wilkie Collins's *The Woman in White*, or *The Little White Girl* gracing the CD cover of a recital by soprano Georgine Reswick. In the latter case, Jo's trancelike gaze is apparently meant to illustrate the CD's title, *Visions Intérieures*.[39]

However, when it comes to promotional images, nothing comes close to the use of the portrait of his mother, her association with old age and motherhood being most often exploited. As early as World War I, a recruiting poster for the Irish Canadian Rangers needed only to add the legend "Fight for Her" to assert its message. By the 1920s, Anna was selling all variety of commodities, the logic being, as an American advertising executive put it, that famous paintings, instantly recognizable to millions, serve as "the poor man's picture gallery" in consumer marketing. Elizabeth

Pennell spotted a reproduction of Anna's portrait "in the midst of the candy" in a Philadelphia shop display for Mother's Day. Pennell thought the display "appropriate," but not all of Whistler's old friends approved of such abuse. "I cannot refrain from expressing the great resentment I felt," declared Albert Ludovici, "on seeing his very fine portrait of her being used as a poster and plastered over the Tube stations advertising some commodity."[40]

For Americans, Anna's association with motherhood and Mother's Day became ingrained in the 1930s when her portrait toured the United States. That the tour coincided with the anguish and despair of the Great Depression strengthened the connection. Anna became a reassuring symbol of stability, a nurturing maternal figure in trying times, someone who expressed the "dignity and patience of motherhood." Whistler's painting, according to the *New York Times*, provided "the symbol of mother of all ages and all lands," and as an American mother Anna fueled a sense of national pride. In 1934 a US postage stamp bore her image, an honor not accorded her son for another six years.[41]

Unfortunately, as photographs and cheap reproductions of Anna's portrait joined the advertisements, her image became so pervasive as to be ubiquitous. Like the *Mona Lisa*, she became as much a part of popular culture as of "high culture," a status that assured her and her son's immortality but also made them fair game for parody. Anna's portrait became one of the first modern paintings, and easily the first modern portrait, to be both revered as an icon and abused by iconoclasts.

Cartoonists found multiple uses for her, and advertisements became less respectful over time. In 1948, an advertisement for lingerie had an alarmed Anna all but leaping through her frame to prevent Jemie from painting a picture of a "Whistler white" negligee. In the 1950s, a book suggesting creative captions for famous works of art had Anna muttering as she sat stoically, "When's that no-good son of mine going to send the rent money?" In the 1960s, a tavern near Chicago displayed a reproduction of the portrait with Anna holding a martini glass. Other doctored photographs have her performing multiple tasks, such as working at a computer or blowing her nose as a warning against the dangers of COVID-19. She is often replaced in her chair by the likes of Daffy Duck, Bugs Bunny, cats, dogs, and Darth Vader. Jokes about the picture have been made even without the image. For instance: What did Whistler say when he came home to find his mother scrubbing the floor? "Heavens, mother, you're off your rocker."[42]

Whistler himself has been targeted less often. In the decades immediately after his death, caricaturists had at him, much as they did when he was alive. Max Beerbohm was the chief offender, portraying Whistler several times in mocking fashion. In one instance he had a diminutive Whistler explaining the beauty of "blue and white" Chinese porcelain to a much larger and very doubtful Thomas Carlyle. Fanciful images sometimes illustrate reviews of exhibitions or books about him. In 2020, he was presented as one of "A Few Dandies" in a French graphic novel that also mentioned the Monty Python sketch. In 2023, a series of Oscar Wilde playing cards issued by Prospero Art used Whistler as one of the deck's Jokers (Ellen Terry was the other). Undoubtedly, though, Whistler reached the zenith of fame in popular culture when he became a bobblehead figure, used to promote the Lowell Spinners baseball team in his hometown.

Whistler has thus far escaped the perils of television advertising, although at least one visionary saw the possibilities for Anna's portrait. Imagine the scene, he said in the mid-1960s. As a camera dollies in on the painting, Anna suddenly comes to life and faces the audience. Smiling, she holds up a bottle of some aspirin product and says sweetly, "You know, when headache, neuralgia, or the pain of neuritis gets me down, I just reach for ___________, and I'm well in a jiffy. Ask for it by name at your favorite druggist." In 2018, Anna's portrait did appear in a promotional ad for a short-lived American sitcom called "Fresh Off the Boat."[43]

Despite these comedic possibilities, Whistler has also survived as a staple of popular culture since World War II in more substantial ways. In addition to the continued availability of *The Gentle Art of Making Enemies,* with an illustrated edition entering the lists in 2015, his wit and wisdom appear in numerous publications. Successive editions of *Bartlett's Familiar Quotations* and the *Oxford Dictionary of Quotations* give more space to him than to any other visual artist. Anthologies of literary anecdotes and collections of "invective" and "insults" dare not ignore him. He warranted three pages in the 1981 *Oxford Book of American Literary Anecdotes,* and not all the entries involved the taking of scalps. Most recently, a contestant on the popular BBC quiz program *Mastermind* selected Whistler as her "specialist" subject.

Whistler also pops up in magazines and the daily press, sometimes in the oddest ways. From the 1940s through the 1960s, his name appeared in newspaper quizzes that tested historical or general knowledge. Stray comments about his family or life—sometimes correct, often wrong—also appeared. The fact that he flunked out of West Point was always good for a chuckle. Similarly, an article celebrating the 150th anniversary of the US Coast and Geodetic Survey mentioned his brief tenure there. When Connie Gilchrist, by then the Countess of Orkney, died in 1946, one report of her passing began by mentioning her exquisite portrait. Such routine references grew fewer over time, but a renewed interest in "blue and white" china in the 1990s brought Whistler back into the news. A sidebar accompanying a 2021 article about Johannes Brahms in the *BBC Music Magazine* mentions Anna Whistler's death (with an inset of the portrait) as a notable event during that composer's lifetime.[44]

Whistler's complex personality has also served columnists who wish to make a larger point about human nature. Not surprisingly, they sometimes foreground his negative qualities. One writer insisted in the mid-1960s that Whistler remained a "great artist and a miserable human being." Another observer asked in the late 1990s if the artist had been arrogant or only confident? It was a "fine line but a critical distinction," the writer maintained. More often, these commentators have found something to admire in Whistler. Some of them take heart in his devotion to art and his uncompromising principles. Others admire his perseverance, noting how the portrait of his mother, once nearly rejected by the Royal Academy, eventually found its way to the Musée d'Orsay.[45]

While not necessarily qualifying as expressions of popular culture, public recognition of Whistler's stature as an artist has also contributed to his legacy. The earliest attempt to celebrate him came immediately after his death, when friends sought to erect a large and ornate monument on Cheyne Walk. They commissioned Auguste Rodin, a friend of the artist, to sculpt the work, although some people, including John Singer Sargent, thought Whistler would have hated the idea. When Rodin died in 1917, still not having completed his task, the project also died. More successfully, Charles Lang Freer, whose ultimate tribute to Whistler would be the Freer Gallery of Art, commissioned Augustus Saint-Gaudens to sculpt a classical stele for the US Military Academy. It was completed in 1907. Two years earlier, a student of Saint-Gaudens, as already mentioned, had executed a bust of Whistler for the facade of Frederick Keppel's gallery in New York City.[46]

The 1930s and 1940s brought further honors. First, he was inducted into the Hall of Fame for Great Americans, then located on the campus of New York University. His election came in 1930, the same year as Walt Whitman,

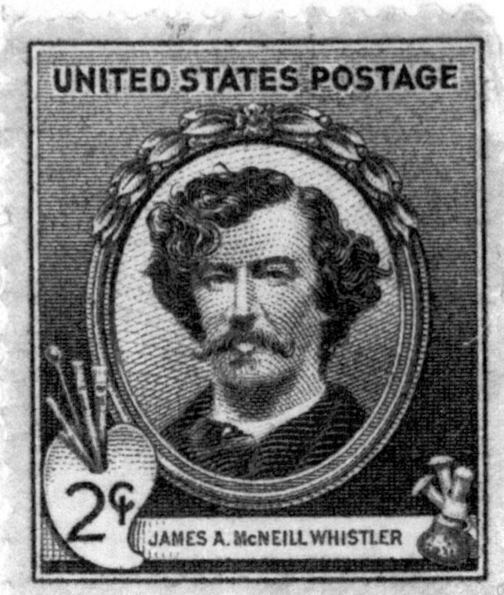

FIG. 15 US two-cent postage stamp with head and shoulders portrait of James McNeill Whistler, 1940. LC-USZC4–2503, Prints and Photographs Division, Library of Congress, Washington, DC.

Matthew Fontaine Maury, and James Monroe. A total of 105 people were nominated that year, and Whistler received the highest number of votes. He was only the fourth artist to be so recognized, after John James Audubon, Gilbert Stuart, and Saint-Gaudens. Inductees were recognized with a bust placed in the open-air colonnade that formed the memorial. His friend Frederick MacMonnies sculpted Whistler's likeness.[47]

In 1940, Whistler's face appeared on a US postage stamp (fig. 15). He was one of five artists selected for recognition that year, the others being Daniel Chester French, Frederick Remington, Saint-Gaudens, and Stuart. The stamps ranged in value from one to ten cents, so to avoid controversy and accusations of favoritism, each man was assigned a value in descending order from the date of his birth. That put Whistler on a two-cent stamp, one cent less than the one for his mother six years earlier. Whistler's stamp was released on September 5, 1940, at Lowell. That in itself would have irritated him, but the government also got his birthdate wrong, announcing it as July 10, 1834—seemingly the fault of the Pennells.[48]

It would be over thirty years before Whistler was again publicly recognized, though perhaps commercialized is a better description. The Hall of Fame for Great Americans issued a Whistler commemorative "medal" in 1973 to help finance its operations. They struck both bronze and silver medals (priced at $4 and $17.50, respectively), with the silver medal issued in a limited edition. One side bore a rather disappointing likeness of Whistler's face, the obverse being a split image, "one-half showing the serious artist at work, and the other half symbolic of his public frivolities and numerous exchanges with critics." Two years later, the Franklin Mint issued a sterling silver coin bearing the portrait of his mother as part of its Bicentennial Collection of the Treasures of American Art. Intended to represent the "supreme triumph of the American artistic genius," each of the one hundred limited-edition coins cost $25.[49]

More substantially and respectfully, the promise of Rodin's unfinished statue was finally realized in 2005, when a life-size bronze likeness of Whistler was erected in a small public garden at the northern foot of Battersea Bridge. Sculpted by Nicholas Dimbleby, Whistler stands atop a substantial granite base, sketchbook in hand, gazing out over the Thames as he did countless times in life.

Several buildings connected to his life have also been identified as suitable memorials. First, in 1907, his birthplace in Lowell, Massachusetts, was purchased by the Lowell Art Association with an eye toward preservation. Whistler had famously denied having been born in Lowell, and in fact spent only two years there when an infant, but the house has been a place of pilgrimage for Whistler enthusiasts ever since. In 1925, the London County Council placed a "blue plaque," signifying a historically significant structure, on his home at 96 Cheyne Walk (2 Lindsey Row during his residence). Whistler had lived there twelve years, longer than at any of his other seven London homes, and painted some of his best-loved work there, including the portrait of his mother. Most recently, in 2012, an identifying plaque was affixed to the wall outside his Paris home, 110 rue du Bac. Another plaque distinguishes the house in Hastings where Anna Whistler spent her final years.[50]

Whistler enthusiasts have organized societies from time to time to commemorate and promote him and his art. The Chicago-based James McNeill Whistler Society, "devoted to keeping alive interest," operated in the mid-twentieth century. More recently, The Whistler Society, based in London but including members in the United Kingdom, United States, Europe, Canada, South America, Australia, and Japan, has been active since its founding in 2012.

For the moment, then, Whistler's legacy seems to be alive and well among the public. If not as broadly recognized as before World War II, he certainly has a loyal following. That said, his legacy in popular culture has depended at least partly on how art critics, historians, and museum directors have assessed him since his death. As it happens, their enthusiasm and respect for Whistler has increased in recent years, although, as the next two chapters explain, not without controversy.

CHAPTER 8

Crafting a Legacy

It is anyone's guess how Whistler would have responded to himself as a bobblehead. I rather think it would have amused him, and he certainly would have laughed to see himself depicted on stage and television. If people thought him a dandy, what of it? If they called him combative and quarrelsome, all the better. He savored the image. But how people would remember his art mattered more to Whistler. That is why he asked the Pennells to catalogue his paintings. He had already written his biography and pronounced his artistic theories in *The Gentle Art*. Would that be enough?

His reputation was bound to have its ups and downs. Being a dead artist is tough. You not only continue to compete with your contemporaries and past masters, but every succeeding generation brings a new challenger. You are unable to respond to new ideas, methods, the market, or the critics. The opportunities to exhibit are much diminished. You fall increasingly behind, appear more and more outdated.

Most of Whistler's contemporaries conceded his status as a master immediately after his passing. Art journals and newspapers around the world offered assessments of his life and work, soon to be reinforced by a flood of memoirs and reminiscences. It was hard to overlook his tempestuous nature, but even former adversaries penned appreciative tributes. Editor and critic Marion Spielmann, with whom Whistler had sparred verbally in the 1880s, thought him far too sensitive to criticism, observing that he attacked people it would have been wiser and more dignified to have ignored. Yet Spielmann confessed that Whistler never "sacrifice[d] a principle or prostitute[d] a thought . . . in order to better his position."[1]

The critics continued to harp on two issues. Yes, his work was mostly fine stuff, but what had been Whistler's chief accomplishment? Had it been his oils? If so, did the portraits, nocturnes, or small panels rank highest? Or had his major gift as an artist been as an etcher? Lithographer? And what of those delicate pastels? The variety and different phases of his work made it hard to decide. More nettlesome, and more lingering, despite the balanced views of people like Spielmann, was Whistler's outsized personality. This simply overshadowed the work for some observers, who allowed flaws in the man to taint the art.

Extravagant judgments appeared on all sides. Veteran American critic William Howe Downes, while praising Whistler's work, warned in April 1904 that his "exact rank" would be "much disputed" for some time to come. That the most fervent "Whistlerians," as Downes labeled them, had made a "cult" of the man did his memory more harm than good. Similarly, Ernest F. Fenollosa, the West's foremost authority on Japanese art and an adviser to Charles Lang Freer on that subject, considered Whistler a "great master" and artistic "pioneer" but calmly reminded his enthusiasts that the "truth" about Whistler's art "must perforce be left to the final verdict of posterity."[2]

A flurry of memorial exhibitions between 1903 and 1905 confirmed Whistler's status as a modern master but left open his place in the history of art. The first important show, held in Boston in February-March 1904, startled Downes, who called it "the most interesting art exhibition ever held in America." Even so, it also reinforced calls for a sober assessment of Whistler's work. Royal Cortissoz, art critic for the *New York Herald* and long a Whistler partisan, thought it had reopened the entire "Whistlerian question." American artist and critic Kenyon Cox, in one of the lengthier reviews of the Boston exhibition, conceded, "It is too early for any definite decision as to its [Whistler's art] ultimate value or as to the artist's relative rank in the hierarchy of artists," even though Cox also believed his work "different in kind from any other that has existed in the world."[3]

Large exhibitions in London and Paris and smaller shows in Glasgow, Edinburgh, and New York produced similar judgments (fig. 16). Bernhard Sickert, an acknowledged "lover of Whistler," praised his "unfailing taste," "sense of colour and line," and "power of invention" when reviewing the

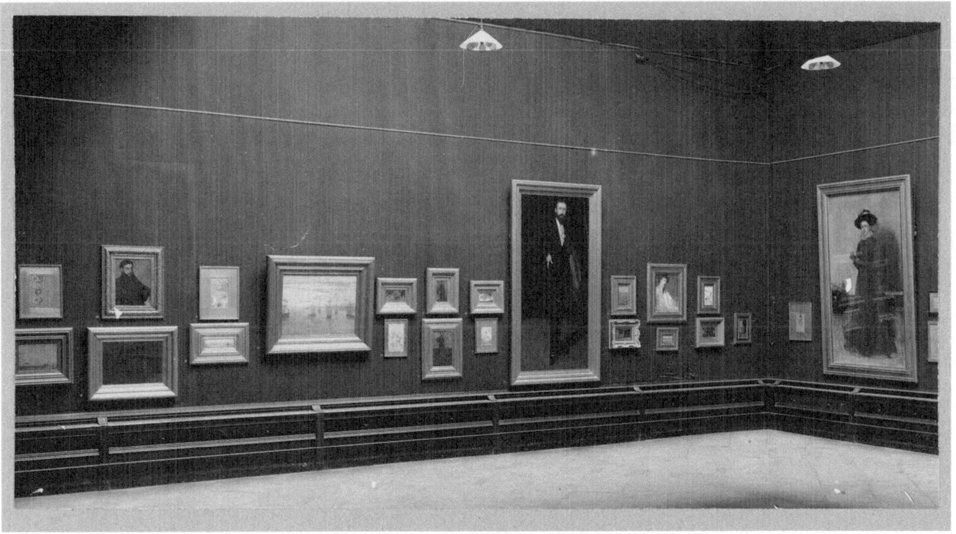

FIG. 16 Whistler paintings on view in the South Room of the New Gallery during the London Memorial Exhibition, 1905. Photograph. LC-DIG-ds-14208, Prints and Photographs Division, Library of Congress, Washington, DC.

London show but conceded that Whistler's "limitations were greater than those of any other great painter." Whistler had influenced the direction of art more than any of his contemporaries, insisted *The Studio*, which believed the "great mass of art criticism" was "now ranged on his side," but that did not stop the magazine from describing his shortcomings. "We must not allow our enthusiasm to run away with us," cautioned the editor; "we must not place him on a pinnacle which his work does not warrant."[4]

Whistler's British friends hoped to promote him by using the Chantrey Bequest to purchase one of his paintings for the nation. Within months of the artist's passing, Dugald S. MacColl, soon to become Keeper of the National Gallery of British Art (now the Tate Britain), was his chief advocate, but he met stiff resistance from the selection committee. The Earl of Carlisle spoke against "excessive modernity," which he associated with the likes of Edgar Degas, Édouard Manet, and Auguste Rodin. Those Frenchmen were bad enough, but he thought even less of Whistler, whom he regarded as "as a sort of early primitive" by comparison. Then, too, few owners of Whistler's major works were willing to part with them. Not until 1905 did Robert H. C. Harrison agree to sell *Nocturne: Blue and Gold—Old Battersea Bridge* to the nation for £2,000. The trustees accepted the painting but insisted that outside funds be used to purchase it. These were supplied by the National Art Collection Fund, established in 1903 by MacColl and others to acquire the work of artists the trustees had ignored. Whistler's painting was exhibited almost immediately, but mistitled and with his name misspelled.[5]

A stalemate ensued until at least the 1920s, as an avalanche of new artistic experiments, trends, and fashions, especially in painting, made Whistler's "daintiness" and restraint seem quaint. His timing was simply unfortunate. The year 1905 may have found Whistler installed at the Tate, but it also marked the start of a momentous, decade-long restructuring in the history of modernism. Fauvism, Expressionism, Cubism, Futurism, Orphism, Rayonism, Vorticism: all took star turns, usually in brief solo acts, often melding into one another or commingling with older traditions, especially Symbolism. Their adherents, though widespread geographically across Europe, represented a minority of artists and generally bewildered the public, but they worked doggedly and with conviction. Often connected to an undercurrent of political anarchy that permeated Europe during the decade, each faction defended its vision as the salvation of art.

Despite divergent theories and techniques, these new schools were united in believing that painting should express strong emotions, even at the expense of what Whistler had most prized: beauty. Avant-garde critics dismissed London's 1905 Whistler exhibition as old-fashioned, with French artist Maurice Denis going so far as to declare, "The influence of Whistler is over." Denis's own 1905 painting *Homage to Cézanne* seemed to foreshadow the future as surely as Henri Fantin-Latour's 1864 *Homage to Delacroix*, featuring Whistler, had done for his generation.[6]

Only one more major exhibition of Whistler's paintings was staged before 1920, at New York's Metropolitan Museum of Art in 1910, although the Tate held a smaller exhibition in 1912. Richard Canfield allowed his considerable collection of paintings to be shown at the Albright Gallery in Buffalo, New York, in 1911, but other shows during the decade in New York, Boston, and Glasgow were limited to etchings, drypoints, and lithographs. The Art Institute of Chicago hosted a more inclusive show in 1917, but the accompanying Walter S. Brewster Collection of Whistleriana proved more extensive than the display of art.

Yet if Whistler seemed to have slipped out of view, the outpouring of memoirs and reminiscences kept him very much in public consciousness. In 1908, the Pennells' book forced some reassessment, as did Bernhard

Sickert's insightful book about Whistler's art. Howard Mansfield, one of the most inveterate collectors of Whistler's printed work, published a descriptive catalogue of his etchings and drypoints in 1909 to accompany an exhibition sponsored by Chicago's Caxton Club. He followed this in the next decade with a series of articles in the *Print Collector's Quarterly*. Edward G. Kennedy issued a more authoritative catalogue in 1910, the same year that Sadakichi Hartmann (Sidney Allen) published *The Whistler Book*. This rambling tribute to Whistler offered a brief biographical sketch but was principally devoted to a critical assessment of his art. In 1913, Elizabeth Luther Cary attempted a catalogue of Whistler's paintings, etchings, and lithographs. That same year, Albert E. Gallatin offered an "iconography" of all known portraits and caricatures of the artist.[7]

A further complication for Whistler's legacy was the question of nationality. As mentioned, Ezra Pound claimed him as an American in 1912, but the National Gallery identified him as British. The problem was that very little in Whistler's nomadic life had ever been "fixed." He had lived longer in Britain than any other country, but had it not been for his wife's failing health in 1894, he might have spent the rest of his life in France, for which he had an abiding affection. He submitted his work to either the British or American sections at international exhibitions, depending on which was most advantageous. Officials at the British Museum admitted that it was "not so easy to decide" where to place Whistler in 1905. "We have hitherto put Whistler's portraits among the Americans, his etchings among those of the British School," they explained. Yet there was nothing distinctly American, British, or French about his art. Naturally not, he would have said, for had he not made clear in his "Ten O'Clock" lecture that art was universal, not to be divided or confined according to geography? He said he was proud to be an American, and never relinquished his US passport, but much of that identity was tied to his affection for West Point. Ultimately, Whistler was a genuine cosmopolitan.[8]

All the while, a vigorous debate was being waged among the people who could significantly influence Whistler's legacy: professional art critics and writers on art. Old supporters, such as MacColl and Cortissoz, continued to wave his banner. Some former skeptics even modified their previously critical attitudes. Christian Brinton, a formidable art critic for several American magazines, had written a terse obituary of Whistler in 1903. By 1906, he was declaring him "a mystic and a martyr," whose art had "unlocked a new and secret chamber of the soul."[9]

However, as younger critics became fixated on "modernism," Whistler seemed likely to get lost in the scuffle. An influential German scholar would not even concede Whistler's place among his contemporaries. Julius Meier-Graefe issued an English translation of his three-volume *Modern Art* in 1908, the same year the Pennells produced their book. Meier-Graefe devoted an entire chapter to Whistler, but his labored and xenophobic appraisal largely dismissed the artist as "an unfrocked Pre-Raphaelite." Whistler had "style" and dressed well, admitted the German, but his "very definite limitations" as a painter placed him beneath Courbet, Manet, and Fantin-Latour. German historian and curator Hans Wolfgang Singer was only somewhat kinder. While acknowledging that Whistler had guided the aesthetics of art onto new paths, he still regarded him as an "excited and angry brawler."[10]

Two British critics, Roger Fry and Clive Bell, also promised trouble. Fry curated two gaudy Post-Impressionist exhibitions in 1910 and 1912. They received a fair amount of critical abuse, and the Chelsea Arts Club, of which Whistler had been a founding member, staged a satirical counter-exhibition in December 1910. Yet the new path was confirmed by a similar 1912 German exhibition in Cologne and one at London's Whitechapel Art Gallery in 1914. Together, Fry and Bell had settled on Henri Matisse and the recently deceased Paul Cézanne as the new champions of modern art, to be joined soon in their estimation by Pablo Picasso and Wassily Kandinsky. An example of the new standard could be seen in a 1908 painting by Matisse, *The Dessert: Harmony in Red*. The title may have reminded people of Whistler, but there was nothing harmonious, in a Whistlerian sense, in Matisse's bold colors and design.[11]

Nonetheless, as they sought to place British art in the wider context of Europe, Whistler's own international credentials, his insistence that geography and nationality played no role in art, appealed to Fry and Bell. After all, Whistler had included Cézanne in exhibitions of the International Society, even though he found his work childish. He had even accepted such artists as Franz von Stuck and Gustav Klimt, whom earlier critics regarded as "weird." Fry and Bell also insisted that abstract qualities of line, form, and arrangement trumped any expression of ideas or sentiment, which had long defined representational art. Bell called it "significant form." Whistler had advocated the same qualities, with the added requirement that art be beautiful. This last issue was clearly a sticking point, for the "decorative," in Fry's estimation, must give way to "formalism." Yet Fry also understood what modern art owed Whistler. He had praised the nocturnes and lamented as much as MacColl the "monstrous injustice" of the Chantrey Bequest's failure to acquire a Whistler painting. In 1909, as an adviser to New York's Metropolitan Museum of Art, Fry persuaded the American museum to purchase Whistler's portrait of Theodore Duret.[12]

Far more appreciative of Whistler's contribution to modern art was British critic and political activist Frank Rutter. He had championed Fry's 1910 exhibition, and was, in fact, the first person to use the term "Post-Impressionist" in print, but Rutter also advocated for Whistler's place in history. He published a translation of Duret's book on Whistler and issued his own tribute in 1911, which rejected the opinions of both Whistler's severest critics and most starry-eyed admirers. Whistler's greatest gift to future generations, Rutter maintained, had been a new way of seeing the world. By noticing things "his predecessors either had not noticed or had not been specially interested in," Whistler "enlarged our minds and widened our sympathies." "By elevating beauty above narrative art," Rutter emphasized, Whistler "paved the way for those who were to prove that art and illustration are not identical."[13]

In America, too, Whistler continued to lurk in the shadows. His work appeared in the landmark Armory Show of 1913, New York's answer to Fry's Post-Impressionist exhibitions. Though the likes of Matisse and Picasso dominated this International Exhibition of Modern Art, many of America's younger artists, including Everett Shinn, Arthur B. Davies, John Sloan, William Glackens, Childe Hassan, Albert Herter, Robert Reid, John Marin, and Edward J. Steichen, continued to admire, even imitate, Whistler. So, too, did older Tonalists such as Thomas Dewing, Dwight W. Tryon, Albert Pinkham Ryder, Granville Redmond, and Leon Dabo.[14]

In this broader context, artists in a country like Poland, which was seeking to "modernize" socially, politically, and culturally at this precise moment, embraced Whistler for his iconoclasm and war against the philistines. Exhibitions of his work in Poland increased in the decade before World War I, and a Polish translation of *The Gentle Art* introduced Poles to his wit and intelligence. Even before 1903, such artists as Anna Bilińska were influenced by Whistler's use of color, his atmospheric Thames scenes of the 1860s, and the nocturnes. Józef Pankiewicz, Olga Boznańska, Stanislaw Wypiański, and others carried that tradition into the twentieth century, not just in landscapes but also in portraiture, and in etching and pastel as well as oils. They also associated his art with Symbolism, which gave fresh meaning and complexity to their work.[15]

Although several Japanese artists admired Whistler's work and ideas during his life, he was not widely known in that country before 1903. Thereafter, as Japanese artists confronted Western modernism, Whistler's association with Aestheticism and his uncompromising character saw his influence spread rapidly. By 1908, there was a Japanese translation of the "Ten O'Clock." In 1909 Yoshida Hiroshi, a "Western-style" (or *yōga*) artist born in 1876, created the Crane Room for the Samurai Trading Company (Samurai Shōkai) in the port city of Yokohama. Clearly influenced by Whistler's Peacock Room, Yoshida worked with the motif of the crane, associated with peace, luck, and longevity in Japan. Hundreds of them covered the four walls of his Crane Room. Not surprisingly, a year earlier he had found in Whistler's work a symbiotic relationship to Japanese art. The American's blending of colors and the harmony of his art, Yoshida insisted, reflected the decorative qualities of *ukiyo-e*, "pictures of the floating world."[16]

We must be careful, though, before saying that artists like Yoshida, let alone Americans and Poles, imitated Whistler. In fact, that was one of Whistler's problems. He could not be imitated successfully, and certainly not duplicated, a fact acknowledged by Yoshida. Whistler had wanted his art to be unique, and it was—to an unfortunate degree. "Other masters, more or less 'great,' may surge out on the scene," observed an artist friend of many years, but Whistler could "never be exactly reproduced; the fraud would be too patent. And his old *mot*, 'imitation is the sincerest insult,' would cover the wretch with confusion." Cortissoz agreed. As a natural rebel, Whistler succeeded in carving out his niche in history, said the critic, but his influence on art was "more a corrective than a constructive force." His art was too personal to inspire more than imitation, and that could not sustain an enduring legacy. "He meant it to exist in and for itself, and so it does," Cortissoz concluded, "like some rare orchid that has no prototype and can have no successor."[17]

It might almost be said that Whistler's magic shone more clearly in the ranks of another breed of artist: photographers. The ways in which Whistler was influenced by photography have already been explained, but equally, he influenced the development of photography in the late nineteenth and early twentieth centuries. His name appeared scores of times—nearly hundreds—in such widely circulated journals as *Camera Work, Camera Notes, Practical Photographer,* the *British Journal of Photography*, and *Photographic News*. From the 1880s to about 1920, photographers who wished to shed their reputations as mere technicians revered Whistler. Launching what has been called an Aesthetic movement in photography, they proclaimed themselves "Pictorialists," in pursuit of "artistic" pictures that looked like paintings.[18]

Two of their number, James Craig Annan and Peter Henry Emerson, paid overt tribute to Whistler's influence in the early 1890s by sending him examples of their work. Annan had already followed in Whistler's footsteps by going to Venice and Holland, where he produced images that echoed the master's etchings in those places. Exactly what work Emerson sent is uncertain, but Whistler did own a copy of *Marsh Leaves*, Emerson's most impressionistic work. Showing the influence of both Whistler and Hokusai, the "misty quality" of its photographs, as one scholar has observed, reminds one of Whistler's nocturnes. Emerson admired much of Whistler's work, especially some portraits, and while he was slower to recognize the nocturnes, he eventually found in them compositional and decorative techniques and subtle tonal effects that could be used to transform photographs into "pictures." Writing privately in 1891, Emerson said, "As for theory I think Whistler is nearer the mark than anyone. . . . I feel that Nature must be there au fond—the Essence of it & resides in Whistler." The following year, he endorsed Whistler's insistence that "the whole aim & subject of a picture is to seek a decorative scheme or pattern either of line or colour."[19]

Annan and Emerson saw in Whistler not some relic of the past, but a "modernist" in every respect, a verdict seconded by a host of avant-garde photographers in the early twentieth century. They praised Whistler's dictum that artists were meant to improve upon Nature, to depict not the landscape but the sensation of the landscape. The limited palette of his nocturnes, with the paint spread smoothly in exquisite bands, each shading imperceptibly into the next, perfectly imitated the parallel bands of sky, sea, and land seen in a photographed landscape or seascape. As Whistler advocate Charles Caffin suggested in 1910, "The tonality of a nocturne is the nearest thing that painting presents to the tonality of a photograph." As if on cue, photographers such as Alfred Stieglitz, Edward Steichen (who excelled as both painter and photographer), and Alvin Langdon Coburn produced a rash of photographic "nocturnes." Photographers also learned from Whistler's technique of manipulating the printing of etchings and lithographs to heighten the soft focus and tonal effects of their negatives in the darkroom.[20]

These devotees admired Whistler's iconoclasm, too, and given their own fight for respectability, they appreciated his war against art critics. "As a pioneer he led the revolt against ignorant criticism by his attack on

Ruskin," Emerson insisted as early as 1899. He described Whistler's life in England as "a long battle for art, and though many do not approve of all his methods, and still less of his brilliant but illogical 'Ten O'Clock,' his work and influence have been for good." Whistler's battles reaffirmed Emerson's own credentials as a rebel.[21]

Coburn, born in Boston, inherited his enthusiasm for Whistler from Steichen. He lived for several years along the Thames, in Hammersmith, and was drawn, as Whistler had been, to the bridges and hidden corners of London. George Bernard Shaw, an admirer, said of him, "Like Whistler, Mr. Coburn has the advantage of looking at London much more imaginatively than any born in London could. What he shews us is there, as the camera testifies; but few of us had seen it until Mr. Coburn shewed it to us." In producing his shadowed photographs of a misty Thames, Coburn tried to capture a single moment, a "fragment of the jumble of nature." "I always think in this connection," he mused, "of Whistler's classic remark that 'nature was creeping up a bit.'" Imagine his delight when, in 1909, Charles Freer commissioned Coburn to take color photographs of his Whistler paintings.[22]

The excitement among photographers waned after the Armory Show, London's Post-Impressionist exhibitions, and World War I. Some observers thought the fullest "flowering of artistic photography" had ended even before then, as early as 1906. Many Pictorialist photographers deserted "impressionistic" images and returned to a sharp focus. They also incorporated a form of abstraction by fracturing their images in accordance with the new modernist fashion. By 1909, Coburn was experimenting with pictures composed entirely of "curves and masses." "I did not see why my own medium should lag behind modern art trends," he explained. His 1917 exhibition of "vortographs" seemed to complete the photographer's journey toward abstraction.[23]

Yet as in painting, many of Whistler's ideas, even if unattributed, held sway. In 1916 Coburn, the most complete and accomplished admirer of the artist, stressed the need for ingenuity in photography in words that echoed Whistler. The duty of all artists, he insisted, was to "express the inexpressible," to "throw off the shackles of conventional representation and attempt something fresh and untried." Coburn advocated "scientific poetry" in photography and encouraged experimentation. "Think of the joy of doing something which it would be impossible to classify," he challenged, "or to tell which was the top and which was the bottom!" Some nineteenth-century critics had said the same about Whistler's paintings, not meaning it as a compliment.[24]

Whistler's ideas might have gained even more credibility had it not been for his contentious writings. Most people delighted in *The Gentle Art,* but once he was removed from the scene and no longer able to defend or explain himself, Whistler's "corrosive wit," as Roger Fry called it—and as Mortimer Menpes had feared—could do as much harm as good. One observer, understanding the danger posed by the so-called "Whistler legend," explained in 1912, "His personality stands out before us as clear cut and vigorous as in the days when he was crushing presumptuous ambition with an epigram. . . . Men who never heard his name during his lifetime have grown up to regard him with warm sympathy or bitter personal dislike." That would remain Whistler's predicament for decades to come. People who objected to the man rather than the art would allow his image to tarnish their view of both, while advocates of the art often found it necessary to defend or excuse the man.[25]

However, judged by the robust sales of his art, Whistler's name remained potent in the decade after his death. Of course, the issue of sales and prices is complex, involving popular taste, critical judgments, and the whole labyrinth that defines the modern art world. It had already been complicated in Whistler's day, but things got even stickier in the twentieth century. Marketing techniques became more innovative and aggressive, and the sheer number of artists and competing voices increased competition for attention. Some people unloaded their Whistlers for fear the work might ultimately depreciate; others bought for precisely the opposite reason. Many potential buyers knew nothing about art, only recognized Whistler's name. The "psychology of the salesroom" took hold as they ruminated about the meaning of "value."[26]

It is impossible to track or enumerate systematically the number, quality, or prices of Whistler's etchings and lithographs that sold, but the print market was robust. His Venice etchings attracted the most attention. The haunting *Nocturne* of 1879–80 went for $1,020 in 1905. In 1915, the same etching brought $2,900, and it sold again in 1917 for $3,900. More spectacularly, J. Pierpont Morgan, the American financier, paid $240,000 for King Edward VI's complete collection of 150 Whistler etchings in 1906, though why Edward, who had known Whistler personally when Prince of Wales, sold them is unclear.[27]

No one followed the market more closely than Charles Freer, who purchased scores of Whistler etchings, drypoints, and lithographs in

1903–4 (fig. 17). He operated mostly through two London dealers, Colnaghi & Obach and William Marchant, but sometimes struck his own deals. He paid 1,240 guineas for twenty-four etchings from the collection of Mortimer Menpes when it was exhibited at the Leicester Galleries in November-December 1903. He also persuaded Morgan to sell him part of the royal collection, specifically the Jubilee Set that Whistler had presented to Queen Victoria in 1887. Other American collectors, Freer said, would also have made almost any sacrifice to get them, and so avenge Edward's "Royal slight." He told a fellow collector in late 1903, "Since the death of Mr. Whistler, great interest has been shown by many people all over the world, who, in earlier years, actually sneered at the things they are now breaking their necks to obtain." He noted that one small drypoint had recently sold for $1,300 in London, adding, "competent experts say that to-day's prices will be still doubled within a year."[28]

Whistler paintings encountered stiffer competition. Charles Holmes thought his work would fit well in a collection of Old Masters, but Rembrandt and Titian easily fetched the higher prices by the end of World War I. That said, the Impressionists were not far behind, and Whistler was more often associated with that group than with earlier generations. Though easier to track than etchings, charting the prices of his paintings is still difficult, even for works sold at public auction, much less private sales through dealers. Based on known statistics, 144 Whistler paintings sold between 1903 and 1914, 88 of them before 1910. It was the largest number of Whistlers ever sold in a similar span of time, although a few caveats are in order. First, in some cases there were multiple sales of the same paintings. That may seem to inflate the numbers, but it also underscores the intense competition among buyers. It should also be acknowledged that Freer alone bought 31 of the pictures. His nearest rival, Richard A. Canfield, sold his own collection of paintings and prints to New York's Knoedler Gallery for $300,000 in 1914, six months before he died.[29]

Rumors abounded about the availability and prices of certain paintings. "All sorts of valuations are already being placed upon Mr. Whistler's paintings," Freer warned Birnie Philip in 1904. William C. Alexander had declined an offer of $50,000 for the portrait of his daughter Cicely. The owner of *The Little White Girl* turned down $30,000. William Burrell, the Glasgow collector, offered the *Fur Jacket* to Freer for £7,000, but the American thought the price too high. Likewise, Freer turned down *The Gold Scab,* Whistler's frightening satirical portrait of Frederick R. Leyland, when it was

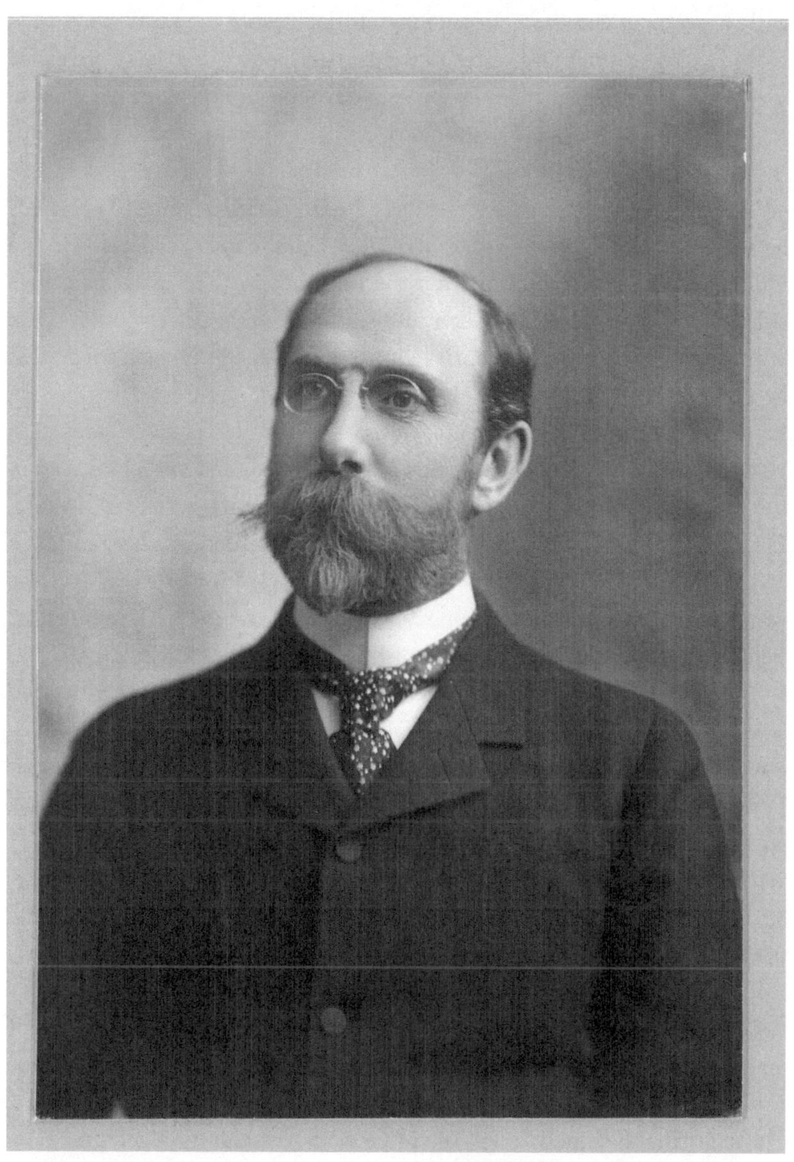

FIG. 17 Charles Lang Freer, ca. 1900. Charles Lang Freer / National Museum of Asian Art Archives, Smithsonian Institution, Washington, DC. Charles Lang Freer Papers, FSA A.01 12.01.8.5-000001.

offered to him for £2,000 in 1910. The picture had been on the market as early as 1904, priced then at only £800. It finally sold in 1912 for an undisclosed amount. Freer did pony up the highest-known purchase prices for a Whistler painting during these years, £5,250 for *La Princesse du Pays de la Porcelaine,* followed closely by £5,040 ($24,545) for the portrait of Henry Irving.[30]

World War I temporarily suspended critical debate about Whistler's legacy, but sales fell off only marginally through the 1920s, especially in the United States, which did not enter the war until 1917. Whistler paintings sold ninety-three times between 1915 and 1928, all at prices competitive with those for his contemporaries, but the market was less frenzied. This could be attributed, in part, to his most sought-after pictures having already found secure homes, either in museums or with collectors who refused to part with them. It was also true that as the European market rebounded in the 1920s, the number of dealers selling "modern" art expanded. In 1921, Duncan Phillips opened America's first museum dedicated to modern art, in Washington, DC. By then, the best of the avant-garde was drawing respectable prices, although even someone like Cézanne or Matisse lagged behind Whistler and the Impressionists.

Old Masters still drew the highest prices, but the decade also witnessed a vogue among the wealthiest collectors for elegant portraits. Rembrandt and Velásquez could easily command six figures, whether in dollars or pounds, and prices for Thomas Gainsborough, George Romney, and Joshua Reynolds soared. John Singer Sargent and Giovanni Boldini, who lived, respectively, until 1925 and 1931, benefited from the trend in portraiture, as did the few Whistler portraits still available. Henry C. Frick reportedly paid £10,000 for *Harmony in Pink and Grey: Portrait of Lady Meux* in 1916. Rumors said that Whistler's portrait of Ellen Sickert, Walter's wife, went for $15,000 in 1920, and that the Cassatt family turned down $60,000 for one of Lois Cassatt, sister-in-law of painter Mary Cassatt. Arthur Studd gave *The Little White Girl,* along with two important nocturnes, to the Tate in 1919. He had earlier declined Freer's offer of $250,000 for all three pictures.[31]

Whistler did even better in the print market, which received a jolt when the lithographs of the eminent British physician Walter Jessop, lately deceased, were auctioned in 1919. Joseph Pennell, who wrote an introduction for the auction catalogue, called it the most important collection of Whistler lithographs ever sold at public auction. Coincidentally, that same year G. Harris Whittemore bought Howard Mansfield's incomparable collection of Whistler etchings and lithographs, described by the *New York Times* as being "without a blemish or flaw," for $350,000. Mansfield, who could not afford simply to donate the collection to some museum, believed this was the only way to keep the collection intact after his death. The print market peaked in the 1920s, with prices inflated by collectors willing to pay more for rarer impressions. Larger numbers of speculators also entered the market as readily as they traded in stocks and real estate. Predictably, prices rose most sharply in the United States, where lithographs, for instance, sold for four to five times what they brought in England.[32]

However, none of this wheeling and dealing seemed to enhance Whistler's reputation. Despite the opening of the Freer Gallery of Art in 1923, with his work, including the Peacock Room, being a featured attraction, Whistler became an afterthought in public consciousness. He retained his status in published histories of art, and there was the occasional exhibition or magazine article, but they yielded no noticeable shift in public perceptions of the man or his work, which some people still found difficult to separate. "His aggressive personality has added to the legend," the *Observer* insisted in 1919, and "thrown a halo about his work which it might not have received attached to a more modest disposition." Whistler, the commentary concluded, was "not so much pioneer as apostle, an apostle of Manet." Two years later, the Pennells were disappointed by the lack of public interest shown in the public dedication of their massive collection of "Whistleriana" at the Library of Congress. "The people don't care a dam [*sic*] about it," Joe fumed; "they care for nothing but the movies and comics."[33]

Walter Sickert best summarized Whistler's uncertain position by the end of the 1920s. As the most successful of the master's followers and the most like him in his wit and charm, Sickert also courted controversy for the pleasure of it, was notoriously fickle, and expressed his opinions unabashedly. His mature work owed as much to Degas and Cézanne as to Whistler, but he continued to cherish his intimacy with Whistler. Whistler had famously quarreled with him in the 1890s, but Sickert laughed about the incident in later years, secure in his own identity as an artist. Contrary to Whistler's public image, Sickert recalled him as "gracious, good-natured, easy-going," with a "heart that was ever lifted up by its courage and genius."[34]

Sickert could be critical of Whistler's work and artistic philosophy but always, he professed, in a "friendly and affectionate way." Unlike his brother Bernhard, he did not think Whistler as an etcher could equal Rembrandt, and he believed many of his paintings, especially the portraits, lacked precision. Only the small oil panels expressed the "essence of his talent." The main problem for Whistler's legacy, as Sickert saw it, was his "egomaniac view of art and life." He refused to be associated with any school or tradition, and he never fully digested or understood the artistic traditions from which he borrowed. He made no lasting contribution to the "language of painting." Whistler's uniqueness became his downfall. None of his students, however much they admired and wished to emulate him, could match his skill and genius. "Fatherless as he came into the world, so he left it childless," Sickert declared.[35]

Whistler's reputation remained in flux over the next fifteen years, from 1930 through the end of World War II, but he at least did not lose ground. The newest phase of "this modern thing," as a New York dealer called the trend toward Abstract Expressionism, looked ominous for Whistler. The founding of New York's Museum of Modern Art (MoMA) in 1929 led more than one observer to predict the triumph of "decadent and degenerate art" in America. At a smaller but eventually more threatening level, Peggy Guggenheim launched her new gallery, Art of This Century, in 1942. Both venues became showcases for the pre–World War I avant-garde, particularly Picasso and Van Gogh.[36]

However, other signs of this "heady artistic period" pointed to a revival of "realism" and "objectivity" in representational art. There had always been a market for this type of "traditional" art, and while that definition fluctuated over time, Whistler's work generally fit its requirements and attributes. In America, the regionalism of Grant Wood and Thomas Hart Benton expressed the nation's cultural roots in representational paintings. Even the grittier realism of the so-called Ashcan School recalled Whistler's early etchings and paintings of the Thames. The geometrical structure of shop fronts and factories inspired Edward Hopper's *Early Sunday Morning* and Charles Sheeler's *Classic Landscape,* much as the architecture of London, Venice, Amsterdam, and Brussels had drawn Whistler. Hopper's "personal brand of perceptual realism," as one critic has called it, further defied the wave of abstraction. His "ambiguous, often crepuscular images about silence and isolation," as in *Night Hawks,* which won first prize ($750) at the Art Institute of Chicago's annual exhibition of American painting in 1942, might well have pleased Whistler. In England, similar impulses guided the New English Art Club and Camden Town Group. The work of such "lowbrow" illustrators as Norman Rockwell, Maxwell Parrish, Ernest H.

Shepard, and Arthur Rackham adorned popular magazine covers and provided the artwork for scores of books on both sides of the Atlantic.[37]

With the very definition of art being more hotly debated than at any time since the turn of the century, nothing better exemplified the confusion than the emergence of Walt Disney. With the release of his animated film *Snow White and the Seven Dwarfs* in 1937, the world had to consider an entirely new art form. It was the most revolutionary development "since the Van Eycks discovered the advantage of oil paint," one critic enthused. *Fantasia*, released in late 1940, and followed by *Bambi* in the summer of 1943, drew similar superlatives. Created by teams of artists, much like the apprentice system of Renaissance workshops, Disney's studio system defined a new "democratic, group-created art which in its use of both machines and personal talent, best symbolizes the 20th century."[38]

The art was regarded as "democratic" in another sense, too. Far from being "highbrow" or concerned with "art for art's sake," Disney's reliance on storytelling and realistic depictions of nature spoke directly to the average person. So, while Picasso, Kandinsky, and Joan Miró worked to define and express new forms and aesthetic philosophies, Disney became "a greater factor leading to popular understanding of these experiments than all the combined efforts of the modern paintings, the museum and gallery directors." And to show that he could cater to the highbrows when it pleased him, there was *Fantasia*.[39]

Beginning in 1940, with Disney being heralded as "a master artist by any definition," museums across the United States staged exhibitions of drawings and watercolors created by his studio, some institutions even purchasing works for their permanent collections. The Museum of Modern Art bestowed its blessing in 1942 with an exhibition of drawing and a three-minute screening from *Bambi*, perhaps the world's first example of conceptual art. The adulation did not last long. When Disney began to combine animation with live actors a few years later, some critics called the films "pathetic compromises." When he released his first nonanimated films in the early 1950s, they called him a "complete sell-out."[40]

But another series of events in the 1930s and 1940s had a more direct impact on Whistler's fortunes. In 1930, James Laver published the first biography of Whistler since the Pennells' book. He acknowledged the challenge. The "dust of controversy" surrounding Whistler had settled only a little since 1903, Laver ventured, and the large number of contradictory writings about him made it difficult to gain "a coherent picture" of his life. The Pennells, he suggested, had not helped matters. Though useful, their "paean" to the artist could be regarded chiefly as "material" for future biographers.[41]

Declaring naively that Whistler had no "private life," Laver provided insights into Whistler's character but offered nothing like a full biography. Rather, he placed the artist's work in historical context. The key to Whistler's art, he decided, was its "simplicity," by which he meant the artist's preference for silhouettes over molded figures, his limited palette, his uncluttered style of exhibition, and his ability to escape the artistic conventions of his day. On this last point, Laver decided that Whistler's greatest achievement had been to liberate painting from storytelling, although this triumph, he predicted, must necessarily diminish the scope and vitality of Whistler's legacy. His reputation would probably "never stand quite as high" as it did in the 1880s.[42]

Events in America in the early 1930s cast doubt on Laver's judgment, and as so often happened in life, Whistler had his mother to thank for a turn in his fortunes. Anna's portrait had been gaining ground as an icon for a decade. When, in 1922, the French government announced it was temporarily moving the picture from the Luxembourg to a small museum in the Tuileries, Americans decried the lack of respect. People who knew little or nothing about Whistler's life, and could not identify any other of his paintings, had taken Anna's portrait to heart as symbolic of motherhood in "all ages and all lands." By the 1930s, with the weight of the Depression weighing heavily on the nation, they embraced this reassuring mother-figure as a symbol of stability and reaffirmation of American values. When the French allowed the painting to be exhibited in the United States for the first time in half a century, more than two million people flocked to see its tour of the country in 1933–34.[43]

The year 1934 also happened to be the centenary of Whistler's birth, and Anna's tour seemed to reawaken Americans to the entirety of his art. Over the next decade, exhibitions large and small popped up around the country, either as solo shows or with Whistler's work adding significantly to thematic exhibitions. Besides his best-known paintings, critics praised his pastels, watercolors, and oils on panels. The most impressive display came in 1934, when the Art Institute of Chicago combined a wide sampling of his art, as in 1917, with the Brewster collection of Whistleriana. Thousands of personal items besides his art filled dozens of galleries. By 1939, despite critics who still regarded him as a "man without a country," Whistler was included in an exhibition of twenty-six American "Old Masters." He was less visible during the war years. As many American galleries hosted shows to benefit the "fighting French," Renoir, Monet, Degas, Cézanne, and Camille Pissarro commanded the spotlight. Even so, Whistler was "prominently displayed" at a 1940 exhibition for British War Relief that featured prewar views of Paris and London.[44]

Two prewar London exhibitions, while more tempered in their praise, joined the parade. As part of the festivities surrounding the coronation of George VI in 1937, the Royal Society of British Artists, which Whistler had once led as president, mounted an exhibition of work by past and present members. His paintings were "among the most observed" in the show, with himself described as an "artistic and emotional rebel." Three years later, on the much larger stage of the National Gallery, he found himself a headliner in "British Painting Since Whistler." It was a somewhat hollow tribute, in that none of his work was displayed. Yet in the words of the usually critical Manchester *Guardian*, "his hostility to stuffiness, his courage in throwing overboard the cliches of his time . . . is everywhere reflected in the exhibition." Whistler, the review continued, "marked the turn of the nineteenth-century tide. He started the host of crosscurrents that can be traced in this exhibition."[45]

And there was more. The Freer Gallery maintained its position as the center of Whistler's art in America with a day-long memorial program in the spring of 1934. The speakers included people who had known Whistler personally. The *Magazine of American Art* published nearly the entirety of the proceedings. In 1936, with the passing of Elizabeth Pennell (Joe had died ten years earlier), the Library of Congress received nearly $400,000 from her estate to maintain the Pennell-Whistler Collection of correspondence, books, pamphlets, clippings, and photographs that the couple had deposited with the library in 1917. The money would also be used to award annual Pennell Prizes in printmaking, with the winning entries added to the library's massive print collection.[46]

Gifts elsewhere confirmed a rejuvenated respect for Whistler. Cornell University received sixty-nine rare Whistler etchings and lithographs from an unnamed benefactor in 1942. The following year, the vast Lessing J. Rosenwald Collection, which included significant Whistler-related correspondence, manuscripts, and prints, went to the Library of Congress. The Havemeyer family donated thirty-eight Whistler etchings to the National Gallery of Art, though their gift was dwarfed when the same institution received *The White Girl* and *L'Andalouse* from the collection of Harris Whittemore.[47]

For people who could not visit the world's museums to enjoy Whistler's work in person, the first "picture book" of his paintings was published in 1938. It included eight full-color photographs, suitable for framing, and an introduction written by James Laver, by that time considered the leading authority on the artist. "James McNeill Whistler has now taken his rightful place among those who have added something of permanent value to the world's heritage," the publishers announced, "with his subtle color values and unerring sense of design."[48]

As the chaos of a world economic depression and global war played havoc with the art market, sales of his work became unpredictable. Events often affected the main markets—in America, Britain, and Europe—differently, but dealers and collectors remained apprehensive. Prices stood up longer in the United States than in Europe once the war began, but values had dipped there too by 1942. The best-selling work continued to come from such past masters as Goya, Romney, and Gainsborough.[49]

Whistler's paintings changed hands frequently in this period—fifty-six times between 1929 and 1945, sometimes under duress. Tulane University had to sacrifice its investment in several Whistler paintings in 1941 to stay afloat. In such a market, not many paintings held their value, although there were exceptions. A nocturne that had sold for 540 guineas (about $3,500) in 1926 brought $9,000 in 1930. When the Untermyer collection went under the hammer in 1940, Whistler's most notorious painting, *Nocturne in Black and Gold: The Falling Rocket*, which Samuel Untermyer had purchased in 1892 for the equivalent of $4,200, sold for $7,500. Another nocturne that sold for $12,000 in 1935 cost three times that sum in 1945. The most money asked for a Whistler painting was $75,000. The dealer, Ferargil Galleries in New York, called it *The White Girl* and described it as "the most beautiful of all Whistler paintings." It was far from that, and certainly not, as one might suppose, the famous *Symphony in White, No. 1*. Rather, it was what would eventually be titled *Harmony in Grey and Peach Colour*, and it remained on the market for a year before being sold for an undisclosed price.[50]

More often, collectors found plenty of bargains. A nocturne that fetched £945 in 1936 brought only £682 three years later. When another Whistler painting sold at auction for $2,700 toward the end of 1945, the head of a Boston gallery declared, "Boy! How values have faded away. I suppose this picture would have brought $15,000 a few years ago, or in the twenty-thousands." Naturally, much depended on the quality and condition of a painting and its perceived importance in Whistler's career. Art was selling, but collectors were less likely to pay premium prices for a mediocre "Old Master" when they could buy contemporary or lesser-known painters for far less. People were astonished, then, when *At the Piano,* the first painting Whistler exhibited at the Royal Academy, sold at a 1940 Christie's auction for 6,100 guineas ($30,500). When donated to the Cincinnati Museum of Art four years later, it provided the cover story for an issue of *Art Digest.*[51]

In the print market, it was a rare sale or exhibition that did not include Whistler's work, but most etchings and lithographs sold at barely a tenth of what they had brought in the 1920s. As with the paintings, condition and circumstances counted. For instance, *Nocturne,* from the ever-popular First Venice Set, brought $1,600 at a New York auction in 1938. Otherwise, with few similar exceptions, the market remained flat, even as Whistler retained his reputation as "master of the etching needle." Even an extremely rare etching, *The Beggars,* also from the First Venice Set, commanded only $550 in 1934 in its ninth and final state.[52]

Meantime, old controversies resurfaced. When a 1942 history of American art declared Whistler and John Singer Sargent the nation's modern "forerunners," one critic asked where that left Albert Pinkham Ryder, Thomas Eakins, and Winslow Homer. When an American commentator suggested that the art world needed another "Ten O'Clock" lecture to "blast" modern complacency, Scottish-born sculptor Alec Miller proposed that, while the lecture was "brilliant and at times suggestive," it must ultimately be remembered as "a curious trifle written in archaic Biblical English." Far superior, Miller insisted (in a comparison that would have enraged Whistler), was Oscar Wilde's essay "The Critic as Artist." When *The Gold Scab,* Whistler's hideous painting of Frederick Leyland as a hybrid man-beast, was publicly exhibited in 1945 for the first time, people were reminded of the artist's vindictive side.[53]

It had been an uneven forty-some years for Whistler's legacy. No one dared predict what might come next.

CHAPTER 9

The Painted Word, and More

As a postwar world tried to right itself, Whistler's legacy looked to be as much up in the air as at any time since 1903. The ferocious debate over the value and status of "modern" art, which abated somewhat in the 1920s, regained momentum among critics and scholars in the late 1930s. A diversity of styles, forms, and subject matter continued, but Abstract Expressionism had sunk deep roots, especially in America. People who did not understand or value it were dismissed as boobs or, at the very least, ill-informed. One critic found it "hard to explain with tolerance" the value and significance of the "Modern Movement" to people unwilling to acknowledge it. MoMA itself drew fire in the early 1950s for exhibiting and purchasing "traditional" works. Before long, even the word "modern" came into question, as "contemporary" or "postmodern" became the preferred terms.[1]

Further complicating matters, the evaluation of art and artists became more complex as professional art critics and art historians developed different interests and priorities. There had been little difference between the two groups in the half century after 1903, with respected critics also producing insightful perspectives on the history of art. However, beginning roughly in the late 1940s, people observed a new division of labor. The discussion centered initially on the role of the critic and the question of who performed this role the best. Some observers, citing Whistler as their prophet, maintained that artists themselves were the "only truly qualified" critics. Most others conceded that the choice lay between old-style criticism and scholarly critiques. In 1954, the College Art Association tried to bridge the gap by awarding annual citations for the best criticism. Their announced purpose was to "encourage the publication of art criticism by qualified writers."[2]

Yet by the 1960s, scholars had pretty much abandoned contemporary criticism in the popular press while, at the same time, scoffing at "dilettantes" who dared attempt to write serious art history. That task, they submitted, should be the strict purview of "historians educated and molded in their own discipline," trained in "documentary research" into specific artistic periods, types of art, and individual works of art. Evolutionary patterns became less important in this "new art history" than studying the "context" of when and where individual works of art were produced. The changes necessarily caused a splintering of art history itself, with many scholars interpreting art socially and culturally, rather than in terms of artistic achievement or formal qualities. Describing, analyzing, and evaluating art and artists from a political, psychoanalytic, feminist, ethnic, economic, or national perspective became ends in themselves.[3]

French Renaissance man André Malraux foresaw the consequences of all this as early as 1949 in *The Psychology of Art*, but American novelist and social commentator Tom Wolfe, reflecting on the situation in 1975, best summarized what had happened. The purpose of art, he declared in *The Painted Word*, had been lost. People had been told they could no longer enjoy a painting simply by *looking* at it. They now required a "persuasive theory" to understand art. "These days," he lamented, "without a theory to go with it, I can't *see* a painting." The theories often came as political statements in the tense atmosphere of the Cold War, or with a commercial message, as corporations exploited art as a commodity. What was more, every new *ism*, be it Fauvism, Cubism, Expressionism, or Vorticism, required a new way of *seeing*. Modern art had regressed, Wolfe concluded, once again being "completely literary," with each work intended to illustrate a text.[4]

He blamed a new style of criticism for the debacle. In the 1940s and 1950s such authorities as Clement Greenberg and Harold Rosenberg had decreed what painting should be. For Greenberg, that meant "flatness" and "the integrity of the picture plane." To this, Rosenberg added the emotional wallop of "Action Painting": Every canvas should present "not a picture but an event." It was only left for Peggy Guggenheim and MoMA to promote artists, such as Jackson Pollock, who best embodied "the Word." Thereafter, Wolfe concluded, "There was no use whatsoever in looking at a picture without knowing about Flatness and associated theorems."[5]

The challenge was to keep up with the latest theorems, as pop art, op art, minimalism, perpetual abstraction, conceptual art, and photo-realism entered the lexicon. Picture frames became relics of the past, as "shaped canvases" grew in popularity. Exhibitions became "installations." Even Greenberg fell behind. To remain relevant, he ditched flatness for Post-Painterly Abstraction. Small wonder the "art historical" community splintered. The variety of artistic expression and its rhetorical-intellectual roots required nimbleness and focused study. Small wonder, too, that this era of the Painted Word caught the attention of social commentators and novelists like Wolfe. Henry James, Oscar Wilde, and George Bernard Shaw had been drawn to art in Whistler's day, but they had entered the critical ranks early in their careers. In the twentieth and twenty-first centuries, established writers including Malraux, John Updike, and Julian Barnes would turn their hands to art criticism.[6]

Whistler surely would have laughed. Like Wolfe, he had disdained the "unattached writer," preachers and priests of art who had "widened the gulf between the people and the painter." He had advocated his own versions of apparently radical innovations, from the flat surfaces of his paintings to the construction of exhibitions as installations. He framed his work but insisted that the frames were part of the composition. Where he diverged, and diverged sharply, from this new world remained his insistence on beauty. Whistler had founded his entire artistic philosophy on that aesthetic principle. Of course, perceptions and definitions of beauty vary over time and from one culture to the next, but in the West, it was being redefined in ways that bewildered the average person, and its significance in evaluating art had been declining since the 1920s. By the 1940s, traditionalists were genuinely alarmed, and by Wolfe's time its value had faded almost completely. American cartoonist Al Capp defined abstract art as "a product of the untalented, sold by the unprincipled to the utterly bewildered."[7]

A popular yearning for the beautiful rejuvenated the popularity of Whistler's work. It began slowly, but between the mid-1940s and 1970s, as measured by the rising prices for his art and the number of exhibitions that featured him, Whistler reclaimed public favor. The exhibitions came first. In 1946, Whistler shared the stage at the Tate with John Singer Sargent, Mary Cassatt, and other American artists who had thrived in Europe and Britain.

The following year he was featured in a loan exhibition at New York's Macbeth Gallery, known for its promotion of American artists. It was Whistler's first one-man show in New York since the Met's 1910 exhibition. Most critics responded with enthusiasm and a willingness to judge his art apart from his controversial personality. "The battles are over, the wounds are healed," proposed the reviewer for *Art Digest*; "it is time to think of Whistler, not in terms of arrogance and eccentricities, but in terms of his individual gifts." To underscore this point, the magazine graced its cover with his best-known self-portrait, done in 1872.[8]

The 1950s saw several exhibitions of Whistler etchings, but the paintings remained a bigger draw. An important show in Los Angeles, "Masters of Art, 1790–1950," presented Whistler's work as an influential predecessor of the Impressionists, Cézanne, Van Gogh, and Gaugin in his use of "color as an artistic rather than a naturalistic element." His mother, as in the past, also played a role in the revival. Her portrait accompanied Whistler's portrait of Thomas Carlyle to star in a 1951 Glasgow exhibition. Both pictures then joined several other of his most distinguished paintings in a 1954 exhibition that opened in Chicago before moving to New York's Metropolitan Museum. Whistler again had to share the stage with Sargent and Cassatt in this "reevaluation" of America's expatriate artists, a popular theme in the decade after the war, but he received the most attention. The Met retained Anna's portrait for three years when its exhibition closed.[9]

As in 1917 and 1934, the Brewster Whistleriana supplemented the Chicago show, but the crowds had clearly come to see The Mother, even if many of them continued to think of the painting more as icon than art. One woman wanted to know, "Where is Whistler's grandmother?" (To which an equally clueless museum employee replied, "In with his mother, I suppose.") With Carlyle's portrait hanging on the opposite wall from Anna, other visitors could be heard saying, "That's Whistler's Father—over there!" Some critics lamented Whistler's technique, and a few, unlike in 1947, puzzled over the contrast between the delicacy of his work and his "singularly complicated personality." Still, the world was again taking notice of him. At the end of the 1950s, he even joined a group of nineteenth-century American artists exhibited in Moscow.[10]

The value of Whistler's work kept pace with this broad exposure. Art prices generally were higher in Paris than in New York and London until the mid-1950s, when in 1957 a series of spectacular auctions in the latter two cities reversed the situation. Impressionist paintings did especially well, with many buyers, alienated by what they regarded as the ugliness and banality of contemporary art, paying record prices for Manet (£113,000) and Cézanne (£200,000). The market remained robust until the global recession of 1973–74. A Velázquez fetched over two million guineas in 1970, the record price for any painting until the 1980s, but both dead and living artists did well. Pop Art led the way among contemporary artists, but auction houses also developed more sophisticated marketing strategies, and everyone benefited from a new appreciation for art as a financial investment.[11]

Whistler did not command the highest prices, but his stock was rising. In 1946, nephew Ross Whistler had found no market for his French Set. "There's a complete lack of interest," he lamented to Joseph Revillon. "I suppose fashions change in art as in everything else." He knew of one Whistler etching, bought for $2,500 in 1926, that would not sell at $50. But by the mid-1960s, both etchings and lithographs were drawing "tremendous interest." The latter lagged a bit, and even an uptick in prices during the 1970s did not match their value of the 1920s. Some observers attributed this to the association of lithographs with sentimentality. Others pointed to the difficulty of determining when they were printed, the rarest impressions having long since been gobbled up. Etchings and lithographs were still available in the 1970s for two-figure sums, whether in dollars or pounds, but the better-quality impressions ran into the many hundreds.[12]

Whistler's paintings overcame an initially sluggish market to sell more briskly than at any time since 1921, thanks partly to his renewed visibility. Shortly after World War II, the curator of the Boston Museum of Art had told the owner of a small (12 × 10 inches) Whistler painting done in Venice, *Sketch of a Girl,* that pictures could languish on the market for a dozen years because of "very high" dealer expenses and "very slow" turnover. This woman was lucky enough to sell her Whistler quickly, but for only $900. The dealer assured her that was a "good deal." Only thirty-two Whistlers are known to have sold between 1946 and 1956, but then the magic of 1957 kicked in. Forty-six pictures went on the market over the next twelve years, followed by forty-four more sales in the 1970s. The most famous was *Nocturne in Black and Gold: The Falling Rocket,* purchased by the Detroit Institute of Art for $12,000 in 1947, $4,500 more than it had commanded in 1940. Yet the most lucrative sale was the $25,000 paid the following year for an 1865 painting, *The Sea* (retitled *Grey and Green. Channel*), probably done at Trouville.[13]

Other notable sales included an unfinished painting, *Harmony in Flesh Colour and Red*, done in the late 1860s, that went for $12,000 in 1960, $10,000 more than its 1946 price. A head-and-shoulders portrait of a young girl brought $7,300 in 1962. A "study" that sold for only £400 shortly after Whistler's death fetched 8,000 guineas at auction in 1970. One of his two portraits of Alice Butt brought 10,000 guineas at auction that same year. An undistinguished painting from the early 1880s increased in value from £105 to £550 between 1947 and 1958. To be sure, these are random examples, but they are in line with prices paid during the same years for such Whistler contemporaries as Degas, Manet, and Renoir. To be considered, as well, is that none of these pictures ranked among Whistler's best.

Exhibition reviews of his work also verify Whistler's revitalized reputation in the 1960s and 1970s. Not counting several etching shows, he either shared headliner status or was the solo star of seven exhibitions in the United States, Britain, and France. These included retrospectives in London and Paris, his first in those cities since 1905, besides an exhibition at the Tate titled *Whistler and His Influence in Britain*. Anna Whistler's portrait made another American tour in 1963–64, including stops in Atlanta, New York, and Detroit. The Art Institute of Chicago, which with its own rich holdings of Whistler's work ranked second only to the Freer Gallery as a favored site for exhibitions of his work in the United States, opened a show in 1968 that rivaled the 1954 extravaganza. One awestruck reviewer described it as "so rich and comprehensive that record keepers find it hard to cite anything comparable." An appreciative assessment in 1978 concluded, "Only now are we getting around to a balanced sense of what Whistler and his art were all about."

Inevitably, Whistler still suffered a few obligatory jabs for his outsized image, but he more often received credit for his artistic "vision." He may have been a "butterfly," acknowledged a reviewer of the 1960 London show, but he was also a "prophet." That sort of praise had rarely been voiced since 1920. Another critic described one of his nocturnes "as original and exciting as the latest Max Ernst." A review of the 1961 Paris exhibition recognized his later oils and etchings as "the ancestors of the pulsating vacua of Rothko." An arts magazine, having used *The Falling Rocket* as its cover illustration, found little difference between that picture and "a contemporary abstract painting." Similar judgments about his influence on the graphic arts followed exhibitions in 1965, 1972, and 1977.[14]

When critics did mention his image and personality, they often did so now to his benefit. In an age of modern self-promotion by such artists as

Rothko, Andy Warhol, and Damien Hurst, Whistler was again recognized as being ahead of his time. Rather than tarnishing his work, his image served as a "hook" to draw in people, precisely as he had used it in life. A review of the 1968 Chicago retrospective began by speaking of Whistler's "intemperate language and bizarre conduct" but went on to marvel at the delicacy of the work and concede that as an artist his "integrity [was] absolute." His ideas had become the foundation of modern art in America and Europe, with "the quiet and timeless poetry" that pervaded his work confirming the "rebirth of interest in Whistler."[15]

This reevaluation was not lost on the publishing world. New editions of the 1905 catalogue raisonné for his lithographs and a reprint of the 1910 catalogue of his etchings appeared in the 1970s. There came, too, an oversized edition of selected etchings with insightful commentary. Improvements in the reproduction of color plates allowed for several picture books of Whistler's paintings and pastels between 1966 and 1979. They also included narratives that amounted to brief biographies of the artist.[16]

More substantially, scholars felt obligated to reexamine Whistler's place in the history of art. The reassessment had begun on a modest scale in the 1940s and 1950s, with the most persuasive statement coming from the esteemed Austrian-born British art historian E. H. Gombrich. His *The Story of Art*, selected by *Art Digest* as the best general history of art in 1951, devoted more attention to Whistler than to Renoir, Monet, Degas, Pissarro, or Matisse. Most scholars followed Gombrich's lead through the 1970s. One author praised Whistler as "a brilliant defender of the artist's right to his own way of seeing," a very modern concept. A history of English art between the 1870s and 1940 credited his "formalist" approach to painting with anticipating the "two-dimensional abstraction of much of twentieth century art." Add to these accounts the journal articles and dissertations devoted to his work, and people were suddenly speaking of "Whistler Studies" as a legitimate field of research.[17]

A series of new biographies was bound to follow. James Laver issued a slightly altered edition of his 1930 book in 1951, but two new books also appeared in the 1950s. Hesketh Pearson, who had met Whistler several times in the 1890s, had already published biographies of Oscar Wilde, Benjamin Disraeli, Bernard Shaw, and Charles Dickens when he tackled the artist in 1952. He had predicted nearly thirty years earlier that Whistler would one day "be the subject of a fascinating biography," a none too subtle jab at the Pennells. Unfortunately, Pearson endorsed a school of biography that discounted the possibility of achieving "truth" in historical writing. Biographers, he believed, could render only an "imaginative portrait" of their subjects, with "accuracy of detail" counting for little. One reviewer spotted another flaw. He thought Pearson's book a competent effort but wearied of his endless recital of the "feuds and quips" of this "quarrelsome, self-centered artist."[18]

Horace Gregory, a writer and lecturer on poetry and critical theory, intended his 1959 *The World of James McNeill Whistler* to be "an interpretation" of the artist's life, rather than a "definitive biography." He did Whistler a service by not allowing the "legend" to overshadow the "serious artist," but he got so many facts wrong—with no indication of his sources—and offered so many odd interpretations that it was hard to take him seriously. He concluded that while the best work of the "paranoid" Whistler would likely endure, it existed "within a penumbra between poetic sensitivity and plastic art." Gregory believed that Whistler's position in art history was "tenuous and uncertain."[19]

Whistler fared better with writers in the 1960s and 1970s, which reflected the positive reaction to the exhibitions of those decades. First came the reflections of art critic and author Denys Sutton, who published two Whistler books in the 1960s. He had already written books on Goya, French drawing, and American painting when, in 1963, he produced *Nocturne: The Art of James McNeill Whistler*. Like Gregory, and as suggested by his title, Sutton declined to call his book a biography. Rather, he aimed to "give some coherence to the development of his art and to place it and his ideas against the contemporary background." The result was the best account of Whistler's art published up to that date. He followed three years later with a richly illustrated sampling of the paintings, etchings, pastels, and watercolors. Yet like Pearson, Sutton was influenced by the formalist New Critics and their insistence on finding "meaning" in a painting. Believing that the work of an artist could be understood apart from the life, he left much unexplained, disconnected, or obscured. As one reviewer put it, he seemed "unable to get Whistler into focus."[20]

The public was reminded of Whistler's own views in 1967 with republication of *The Gentle Art of Making Enemies*. Not that the book had ever entirely disappeared; except for the 1940s, it had been reissued at least once a decade since 1904. However, the 1967 volume, a reproduction of the enlarged 1892 edition, included for the first time a scholarly introduction. As an authority on such modern artists as Amedeo Modigliani, Marc Chagall,

Max Weber, and Edvard Munch, critic, poet, and author Alfred Werner was an unlikely choice to reintroduce Whistler to the world. While providing a useful history of the making of the book, he did not understand its author. Whistler had been a "frustrated, unhappy man," Werner proposed, who had been "hurt deeply, and frequently" since childhood, when "his ego [had] been often and severely lacerated." Nonetheless, Whistler's own words and a clear statement of his aesthetic vision were again in circulation.[21]

In the 1970s, with Whistler a marketable commodity, two more picture books and four biographies hit bookstores. Also telling, and in contrast to previous such ventures, this generation of authors took more care in documenting their work. Three of them—Gordon Fleming, Stanley Weintraub, and Hilary Taylor—were college professors, and all four, including Roy McMullen, had investigated either the Pennell Papers at the Library of Congress or the newly available collection donated by Rosalind Birnie Philip to the University of Glasgow.

Fleming limited the scope of his book to the "young" Whistler, ending the narrative in 1866. Weintraub, who had already written books on Aubrey Beardsley, Bernard Shaw, and the Rossettis, offered the fullest biography, though in casting Whistler as always "the life of the party," he was overly fond of anecdotes and gossip. McMullen focused more on biographical details and "personality" than on an evaluation of the art. His Whistler was an "outsider" and "inauthentic poseur." Comparing the efforts of Weintraub and McMullen, one reviewer characterized the former as a "tale," the latter as "an inquest." Taylor's contribution, a hybrid picture book and narrative based on her doctoral thesis, provided the best summary of the paintings, and some of her observations remain pertinent.[22]

At the same time, critics and commentators committed to modern art resisted any effort to find Whistler a place at the table. Most vociferously opposed was eccentric and opinionated British art historian and collector Douglas Cooper. He welcomed the Weintraub and McMullen books as improvements on the sycophantic Pennells and the "schmoozy, artistically slanted" Laver, Pearson, and Sutton, but he ignored all of them to propose his own evaluation of their man. "Whistler is one of the most insubstantial, perverse, and ultimately pathetic artists . . . to be found in nineteenth-century history," Cooper submitted, and should no longer be "ranked among the 'great' of his time." While acknowledging that Whistler's "pictorial notions" led to Symbolism and the Nabis, this devoted follower of Picasso, Georges Braque, and the Cubists had long since formed his opinion of

Whistler, and no amount of new research or reflection could dissuade him from dismissing Whistler an artist of "no importance."[23]

Despite such intransigence, all the positive work paid off, and the next two decades made it impossible to deny Whistler his rightful place in art history. A significant moment came in 1980, with publication of a comprehensive catalogue raisonné of his paintings. It had been a long time coming. The Pennells had fallen short, and there had been no serious effort to compile one until after World War II. Then, in 1945, Joseph W. Revillon attempted to catalogue the oil paintings. Whistler's great-nephew, a retired civil engineer, threw himself into the project with more enthusiasm than expertise but kept at it until the end of his life in 1955. He called on other Whistler relations, including Ross Whistler, the Hadens, and Birnie Philip, for advice and assistance. Rosalind declined, and other family members lacked the knowledge or ability to help. Denys Sutton joined the project in 1950 by trying to find a publisher for Revillon, but his efforts failed.[24]

Still, Revillon had not labored in vain. In 1975, art historians at the University of Glasgow picked up his work, which he had donated to the university as part of his collected papers. This team of scholars, led by Professor Andrew McLean Young, who had curated the 1960 London retrospective, also benefited from the beneficence of Birnie Philip. Only the Freer Gallery could now match Glasgow as a repository for Whistler's art, and it surpassed the Library of Congress in its collection of Whistler-related correspondence. A reviewer described the completed catalogue as a "treasury" and an "allay of understanding" for scholars and curators. Ironically, the university's administrators nearly undermined this accomplishment when, in the same year of 1980, it proposed selling eleven Whistler pictures, worth an estimated £150,000, to help finance construction of a new art gallery. Thanks to a shrill public protest and subsequent fundraising drive for the gallery, the paintings were retained.[25]

Other major research resources appeared in the 1980s and 1990s. Two came out of the United States. In 1986, Robert H. Getscher, a professor at John Carroll University, teamed with Paul G. Marks, an avid collector of Whistleriana, to produce an exhaustive annotated bibliography of writings by and about Whistler. It totally eclipsed the only similar book, published in 1910. Two years later, Catherine C. Goebel completed her dissertation, an analysis of press reviews of Whistler's work written between 1860 and 1879. Goebel not only evaluated the critical response to Whistler but also made it easier for other researchers to evaluate his work by reproducing all known reviews of his exhibitions during that formative period. In 1995, the Glasgow connection reemerged when Margaret F. MacDonald, a junior member of Young's original research team, completed a catalogue raisonné of Whistler's drawings, pastels, and watercolors.[26]

While most attention was being given, as had always been true, to Whistler's paintings, his etchings and lithographs also drew renewed attention. Much of this exposure came through several publications devoted to those media, including *Print Collector's Newsletter, Tamarind Papers*, and *Print Quarterly*. However, the big breakthrough came with a pair of important books. First, in 1984, came *The Etchings of James McNeill Whistler*. More a narrative history than a genuine catalogue raisonné, it still easily supplanted the reigning work of Thomas R. Way to stand alone as a description of Whistler's etched work. The author was Katherine A. Lochnan, who had begun her research nearly a decade earlier for a thesis at the Courtauld Institute, which was becoming a notable center for graduate work on Whistler. Later, as a curator at the Art Gallery of Ontario, Lochnan went on to stage numerous exhibitions of the artist's work.[27]

Next, in 1998, came a catalogue raisonné of Whistler's lithographs. This stunning two-volume collaborative work, ten years in the making, came out of the Art Institute of Chicago, which had acquired the Mansfield-Whittmore-Crown collection of Whistler's lithographs and etchings as a "long-term loan." Led by project director Martha Tedeschi, it fit the definition of *definitive* as nearly as any published work. One reviewer rightly called it "a staggering achievement."[28]

The historical value of Whistler's work also benefited from new interest in Asian art and its Western interpreters, specifically *japonisme*. The signs had been apparent since at least the 1960s through exhibitions and scholarly publications, and Whistler was associated with the genre from the start. Laver and Sutton had made *japonisme* central to their interpretations of his art. More recent investigations explained how Whistler's fascination with Asian art linked him to the Aesthetic movement and Symbolism. By the 1980s, exhibitions devoted specifically to his association with all those genres were being held in both Japan and the United States.[29]

In fact, it was becoming hard to avoid Whistler. Art magazines, professional journals, and collected essays regularly featured him. Exhibition catalogues and picture biographies reproduced and explained the meaning of his work, his artistic strategies and philosophy, and his working materials and techniques. The catalogues, once mere lists of work being exhibited, had grown in size and become more sophisticated since the 1960s. Now including incisive essays on the art and the artist, and aided, like a new generation of "picture books," by ever more inexpensive methods of color printing, they had become valuable contributions to scholarship as well as means of connecting with a general readership.

And there were exhibitions aplenty. Indeed, the blossoming scholarly interest in Whistler would have been wasted had his work gone unseen by the public. Most gratifying was the sizable number of exhibitions devoted to his printed work. A lithographic show at the Art Institute of Chicago in 1998 to introduce the new catalogue drew the most attention, but there had been opportunities to see both etchings and lithographs all through the 1980s and 1990s. Important shows had opened at Wesleyan University (1983), in Chicago (1984), at Glasgow's Hunterian Gallery (1986), the Art Gallery of Ontario and other Canadian galleries (1986–87), and in Washington, DC (1995). The two-decade span culminated in 1998–99 when the Carnegie Museum of Art organized an exhibition shown in New York, Florida, California, and Canada.

Inevitably, though, artists who work in multiple media are judged first by their paintings, so those exhibitions became crucial tests. Whistler's paintings enjoyed several retrospectives exhibitions in 1984, the 150th anniversary of his birth. Shows in New York, Washington, DC, and Glasgow drew appreciative crowds, while a display of his paintings at the Knoedler Gallery inspired one commentator to say, "There is no excuse for not knowing almost everything there is to know about this artist." Yet that was not entirely true, as demonstrated by the pugnacious Robert Hughes. Commenting on the Freer Gallery's contribution to that year's festivities, he echoed reviewers from the 1960s by contending that, while Whistler had "never faded from view," he was only now "poised for rediscovery." Moreover, Hughes's appreciation of the art was more nuanced than his understanding of the man, whom he dismissed as "a fop and a publicity-crazed liar." Moreover, Hughes added gratuitously, Whistler "hated his father and was fixated on his mother."[30]

Oddly, though, 1994 proved to be a more notable year for Whistler's legacy, highlighted by retrospective exhibitions in London, Paris, and Washington, DC. The Tate hosted the principal show, which subsequently traveled to the Musée d'Orsay and Washington's National Gallery of Art. It also inspired competing exhibitions at the Freer and Washington's National Portrait Gallery. The *Burlington Magazine* promoted the Tate show by devoting an entire issue to Whistler, positing in its lead editorial that his work, "beyond a handful of favourites," remained "curiously unknown and curiously undervalued." Given the increased attention of recent years, that assessment seems doubtful, but the editor was correct when he suggested that one reason for the seeming neglect had been the "inescapable force of his personality." The exhibition, it was hoped, would persuade people to "ignore the trappings" and learn to appreciate Whistler's art.[31]

As it turned out, there was indeed cause for concern. Reviews of the show, ably curated by Margaret MacDonald and writer-critic Richard Dorment, were mostly positive, but some critics, often with expertise that lay outside the nineteenth century and who knew little of Whistler's life, remained unable to separate the art from the man. What one British critic called "an almost apostolic tradition of Whistler-hating" returned with a vengeance. "Remove his words, his sting, and Whistler's art goes limp," pronounced the *Observer*. "He shines only in contrast to the pompous and reverential. Compared with Manet or Degas he's a mere flutterer." While slightly more complimentary, the *Observer*'s companion publication, the *Guardian*, believed Whistler had lost his nerve after the Ruskin trial. He was reduced to cranking out "teeny-weeny pastels and engravings" and making the "same old minimalist points ad nauseum." His art became boring, the review insisted, symptomatic of an artist "just going through the motions."[32]

American critics could be just as obtuse. The *New Yorker*'s Adam Gopnik penned one of the longest but least perceptive reviews. Whistler's personality clearly perturbed him. The artist was a mere "magpie," Gopnik declared, apt at appropriating the "surface traits of other people's style" but unable to "*invent* anything to save his life." Ignoring the printed works, pastels, and watercolors, Gopnik reckoned that among the oil paintings only Whistler's "society portraits" mattered. John Updike was not completely won over either, though he made a pair of telling observations. Whistler's preference for blacks, grays, and "gray's dun brothers," Updike proposed, meant that he would never be as popular as Monet and Cézanne, with their "rainbow" palettes. Then Updike, who himself referred to Whistler as "the butterfly man," leveled an unintended rebuke at critics who failed to see the art for the man. In considering Ruskin's opinion of *The Falling Rocket*, he observed, "The language is snobbish and overwrought. . . . Was Ruskin reviewing the painting or Whistler's insistent, impulsive image?" Good question.[33]

And in truth, the critical reactions did reflect ongoing efforts to deal adequately with Whistler's complex personality, as shown by several books published in the 1990s. These included two new biographies. First, in 1991, Gordon Fleming followed his *Young Whistler* with a full biography, although it was superficial at best. Three years later, to coincide with the Tate retrospective, Ronald Anderson and Anne Koval published *Whistler: Beyond the Myth*. This was a far better researched and more thoughtful book, but it led one reviewer to conclude that, rather than integrating Whistler's personality and his art, the authors had only "put them side by side." They correctly identified vanity, insecurity, and mistrust as keys to understanding Whistler's contradictory and inconsistent public actions, but they did so, as another reviewer observed, without plumbing the emotional depths of his private life. Taking a different approach, Linda Merrill, then a curator at the Freer, tackled two of the most pivotal yet controversial episodes in his life: the Ruskin trial and the Peacock Room's creation. Her meticulously researched, crisply written, definitive accounts of those events burnished our understanding of Whistler by clarifying his ideas and perspectives on art while also touching on some of his less admirable qualities. Similarly, Sarah Burns explored the nuances of Whistler's self-invention as artist and celebrity by showing how he helped to invent the "modern" artist (fig. 18).[34]

Using sales of Whistler's work as an indicator of his reputation at this juncture continued to be complicated by trends in the art market, which, following an international financial downturn between 1979 and 1983, boomed in the remainder of the 1980s before stagnating in the 1990s. Two problems partially dictated the trend. First, the perceived value of art was distorted by a new generation of millionaires who bought art solely as an investment. Second, dealers and promoters became more aggressive than ever in pushing the work on "pliable museums and gullible collectors," as Adam Gopnik characterized the situation. "The old values of art were overturned for the benefit of a new class of the hyper-rich," he elaborated; thus "the market inflated new pictures beyond their intrinsic merit." Or, as Oscar Wilde had summed it up long ago, people knew the price of everything and the value of nothing. Additionally, the market had become more global, as Japanese collectors in particular displayed a passion for Impressionist and Post-Impressionist art.[35]

None of Whistler's paintings went to Japan, but sales of his work did reflect the volatility of the market. Twenty-five Whistler paintings changed hands in the 1980s, although four of them sold a total of ten times. Only eleven paintings were sold in the 1990s, including three that had already been on the market in the 1980s. Notably, Whistler had painted only five

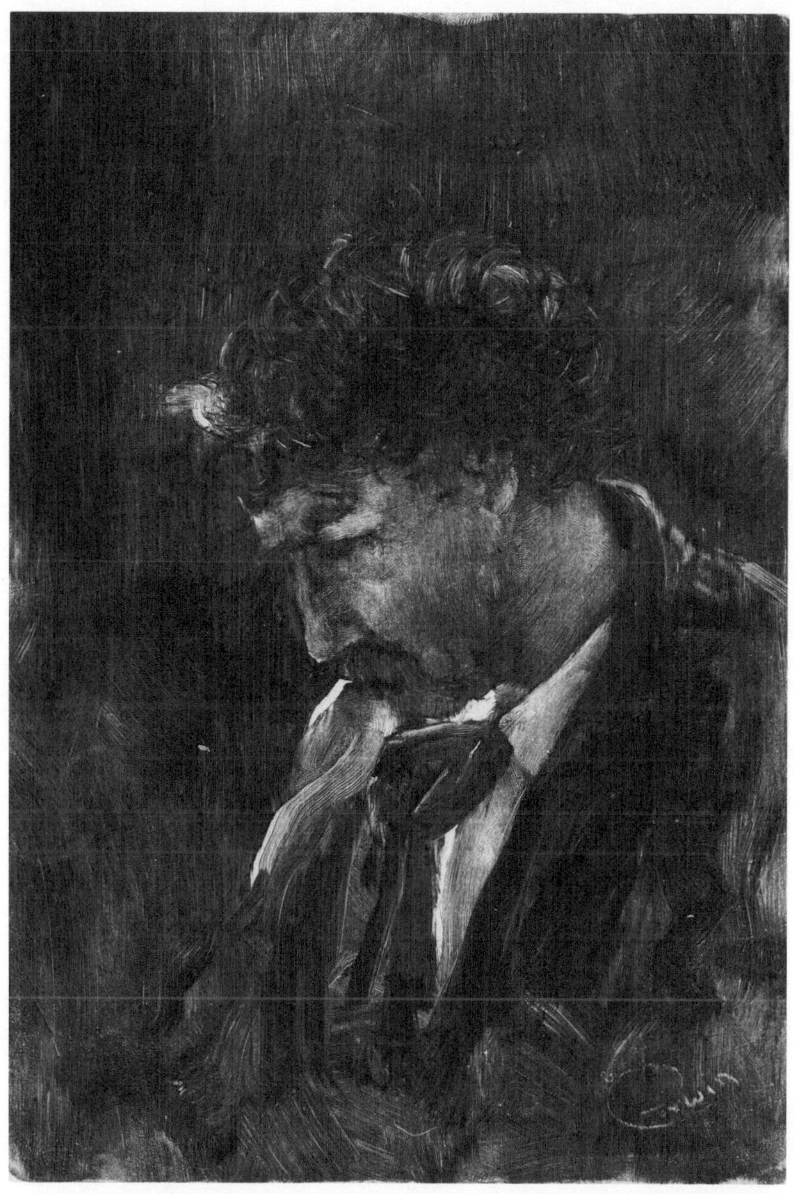

FIG. 18 Charles Abel Corbin (1857–1938), *Portrait of James McNeill Whistler*, 1880. Monotype, 22.4 × 15.4 cm. 60.611.134, Metropolitan Museum of Art, New York, Elisha Whittelsey Collection, Elisha Whittelsey Fund. Photo © The Metropolitan Museum of Art / New York, NY / USA / Art Resource, New York.

of those pictures before 1878, suggesting that most of his early work had already been acquired by museums that intended to keep it. The highest known prices came in the 1990s. *Petie Bonne à la porte d'une auberge,* an 8½ × 5 inch wood panel, went for $85,000 in 1997, but an even smaller panel (5¾ × 9½ inches), *Blue and Glue: Robin Hood's Bay,* fetched $310,000 in 1998. Respectable enough prices, but nothing approaching the multimillions of dollars being doled out for Van Gogh or Picasso.

Beyond fluctuations in the market, Whistler's place in history has remained fixed in the twenty-first century, despite an escalating upheaval among the historical gatekeepers. The division between academic art history and art criticism now seems complete. The term "artwriting" is used to describe the work of critics and "popular historians," with the latter group being distinct from "professional historians of art." The academics too often seem determined to impose modern values and ideologies, particularly political ones, when reinterpreting the intentions and stature of past artists. Within a labyrinth of specializations and "voices," intended to make art and its history more "inclusive," many scholars have jettisoned *art history* for the less restrictive *history of art* (or better yet, *histories* of art). Likewise, national histories have given way to transnational and global histories, the goal being to allow the widest possible "contextualization" of art. The search for "individual identity" has become all important, especially when considering the "social role of identity in the formation of ideology." The very word *artist* is associated with a "geopolitically, socially, and ethnically privileged masculinity." With "reading" a picture or any object in terms of "creative speculation, attention to the psychoanalytic unconscious, and the presentist critical propositions of deconstruction and poststructuralism" now a common goal, the Painted Word reigns supreme.[36]

The cacophony is quite interesting, and certainly not unique to art history. A passion for interdisciplinary studies had touched all the humanities by the late twentieth century, even to the extent of selective integration with the sciences. As a psychologist who saw the value of applying "cognitive psychology . . . to studying the creation and response to art" put it, the study of art is no longer the "exclusive domain of humanists." Economists, sociologists, physicists, neurobiologists, and anthropologists, given the flexible parameters for studying and appreciating art, all have roles to play, as do scholars who study the role of "sensory" perceptions.[37]

Yet Whistler has managed to hold his place, and sometimes improve it, in art history textbooks. The section allotted him in Gombrich had grown by 1995, and few of the newer academy-produced interpretations can deny Whistler's achievements. Some authors, whether writing about American or global art, have reduced their sections on Whistler from what they had been a decade or more ago, but that has happened to many nineteenth-century artists. An ever-increasing span of time must be covered, and the complexity of contemporary art requires more attention. Authors must also contend with numerous "market forces," including the new cultural-social-political framework of diversity and the expectations of a "young readership." Consequently, protests one observer, scholars find themselves rewriting art history "more often and more aggressively than ever before."[38]

Where to place Whistler, and how to define him, is sometimes problematic. Depending on how the contents are organized, textbooks on American art generally place him with the American Impressionists or in a section on expatriates and "cosmopolitanism." That is most often his place in world histories, too; he is no longer in danger of being called a "Victorian" painter, although he is sometimes identified with Aestheticism. Additionally, his name often pops up in separate discussions of Tonalism or the influence of Asian art on the West. The Ruskin case also offers a centerpiece for discussions, and there is generally some mention of Whistler's musical titles. Surprisingly, authors rarely dwell on his flamboyant personality, other than to say that he participated in several controversies.

Popular, or "middlebrow," histories generally give more space to Whistler, even if the commentary tends toward the superficial. Prime examples of authors who understand the art better than the man are Robert Hughes and Paul Johnson. More recently, a survey of British art uses Whistler as a means of attacking the rigidity of Victorian art and society. By bringing the French avant-garde and Parisian modernity to Britain, it contends, this "swashbuckling" American forced a "long overdue reckoning with British morals" by defying "Victorian art's pedantry." Going still further, a "little" history of art by British critic and broadcaster Charlotte Mullins submits that Whistler gave modern artists the "confidence" to "create Western art's first abstract paintings." Similarly, a dual biography of Whistler and John Ruskin describes their confrontation in court as the "battle for modern art."[39]

Museums have further complicated matters amid this fragmentation of art history. Simply put, museum directors and curators often compete with academics in their interpretations of that history, even as they address different audiences. Influenced by an ethos of political correctness and cultural identity, scholars deem it necessary to debunk older portrayals of artists and interpretations of their art in ways that tend to bewilder the public. But museums, for their part, must attract customers, must entertain as well as inform—either that or go out of business. The challenge is not entirely new to the twenty-first century. The role of the "modern" museum was an issue as early as the 1940s. Museums were initially accused of not exhibiting enough contemporary, or "living," art. Very soon, though, it became a question of interpretation, an issue that grew more pressing in the 1960s. The divide with the academy was artificial in many respects but evident enough by the twenty-first century for people to acknowledge that museums and universities represented "two art histories."[40]

That gap is closing, but not always to public satisfaction. When museums feel compelled to explain the "progressive" political value of a work of art and excuse the perceived moral failings of the artist, they risk alienating a public that has grown skeptical of art and artists presented through an "ideological filter." Any hint of subordinating "art to politics" is bound to draw criticism, not just for descriptions of contemporary works, which might be expected, but also for "old masters." When even such an early darling of modernism as Cézanne had to be absolved of colonial intentions at a 2022 Tate Modern exhibition, the eminent defender of modernism Waldemar Januszczak conceded that such "cross-your-fingers and hope scholarship" appeared increasingly strained and artificial.[41]

Small wonder this struggle to "interpret" art compounds public mystification about its meaning. The traditional distinction between "low" and "high" art is indistinct, as is the interplay between modern art and "mass" or "popular" culture. In some quarters, art has become "visual culture" or part of a "history of images." One hears dire warnings about the "end of art," the "death of art," or, slightly less cataclysmic, the "abuse of beauty." At the very least, people recognize a "crisis" in art history. Playwright Tom Stoppard believed in 2001 that with the rise of conceptual art "a fault line in the history of art had been crossed when . . . the thought, the inspiration itself, had come to constitute the achievement." Julian Barnes concurs. "Art changes over time," he concedes; "what *is* art changes, too." So, what *is* art? "The tests are simple," Barnes submits. Art must "interest the eye, excite the brain, spur the mind to reflection and move the heart." Much "fashionable art," he concludes, "bothers only the eye and briefly the brain, but it fails to engage the mind and the heart."[42]

Whistler has survived, sometimes even flourishing, in this atmosphere because he appeals in different ways to all these "post-modern" audiences:

academics, curators, and, most importantly, the public. Anna's portrait, rather than being cast aside as a sentimental relic, has been favorably compared to an abstract painting by Mondrian or a Cubist work by Braque. Meantime, much of the public, which still believes beauty should be a prerequisite for art, finds in him a refuge from what Barnes labels "fashionable art." There is irony in this judgment. Much modern art may be classified as merely decorative, a pejorative word when applied to Whistler's work during his lifetime. Yet to modern eyes, his so-called decoration can be breathtaking, enchanting, so that even people who think him a quarrelsome, conceited, and disagreeable fellow cherish his vision. Some have publicly objected to scholars and curators who question his stature as an artist or his mystique.[43]

A revival of figurative painting since the 1980s has helped. Granted, much of it leans toward photorealism, or "photo-painting," but the style offers some closure between "realism" and modern tastes. Artists working in more traditional veins understand this and have sought a "dialogue" between realism and abstraction. Whistler's painstaking method of painting has led British artist Christian Furr, who is equally at home with representation and abstraction, to meditate on the distinction between "process" and end results in art, the "distillation of effort" as he calls it. Similarly, Shezad Dawood, best known for his multimedia depictions of the natural world, finds himself influenced by both Whistler's art and writings. He most admires Whistler's "facility with styles, influences and forms, from Japanese woodcuts to the tonal and symphonic qualities of his Nocturnes." A confessed "synesthetic," Dawood hears the "musical harmonies" of the paintings. "In some ways Whistler was ahead of his time," Dawood maintains, "in his shifts between figuration and abstraction and in his easy ability to incorporate decorative and patterned surfaces into his painting, something that gave me confidence to do similar." Quick to quote lines from Whistler's writings—his "facility with words"—he appreciates the artist's stand against the philistines of his day.[44]

Indeed, Whistler's methods and aesthetic ideas have proved as enduring as his art. And the influence need not be direct or conscious. Whether or not they have studied his work or read *The Gentle Art*, many artists adhere to Whistler's convictions about color, form, subject, transposition, and integration of the arts. Other contemporary artists, notably painters, continue to be influenced directly by Whistler's ideas and work. Though no longer trying to imitate him in style, as did an earlier generation, tributes abound. Some of them are gentle reflections on the work itself, as with a Jacques Pecnard rendition of *At the Piano*, done, significantly enough, for an illustrated edition of Marcel Proust's *In Search of Lost Time*. In *Whistler vs. Ruskin (Novella in Terre Verte, Yellow and Red)*, from 1992, R. B. Kitaj adapted George Bellows's famous boxing scene of *Dempsey and Firpo* to fashion a metaphysical statement about the trial. So, here we have not only a nod to Whistler's art but also recognition of his role as a champion for artists against critics and the establishment.

Not that any of these artists genuflect before Whistler as the only influence on their work. Frank Auerbach, for instance, sees him as part of a long historical chain, extending back through Whistler, Degas, and Ingres, "all the way to Raphael." The intriguing thing about this lineup is that Degas, Ingres, and Raphael were indeed among the most important influences on Whistler, who learned from and borrowed freely from their ideas and work, underscoring Kenneth Clark's insistence that all great artists are borrowers.[45]

Museums, recognizing Whistler's popularity, often include him in "blockbuster" shows, even when his art is only loosely associated with the exhibition's theme. Since 2000, his work has appeared in dozens of exhibitions, frequently lumped together with the Impressionists, despite his own refusal to be associated with any "school" of art. The centenary of his death in 2003 produced several important shows, most notably in Glasgow and New York, though none was as extensive as the 1995 Tate retrospective. His influence on other artists is another theme, as is his association with particular places—Russia, Venice, Holland, London, Paris—and subjects, such as fashion, nature, and aestheticism. The exposure has been global, too, with exhibitions in France, Australia, Russia, Japan, Chile, Great Britain, and across the United States. Anna's portrait recently hung in the Louvre Abu Dhabi. The Peacock Room even proved adaptable to modernist styles when an "immersive" version was structured as a hologram. More notably, Darren Waterston constructed a grotesquely decadent version of the fabled room. Exhibited in Washington, DC, and London, Waterston intended *Filthy Lucre* (2020) as a "tribute" to Whistler, but the parody also challenged people to reflect on the "subjective nature of beauty." All this was capped most recently by an international conference and significant retrospective exhibition at the Musée des Beaux-Arts in Rouen, France, which emphasized the continuing influence of "Whistlerism."[46]

Even as I write, an equally grand retrospective is scheduled for the Tate Britain and Amsterdam's Van Gogh Museum in 2026–27, although this may be a good place to emphasize a sizable obstacle to mounting a definitive exhibition of Whistler's paintings. Some of the most prominent collections of Whistler's paintings, including those at the Freer Gallery and the University of Glasgow's Hunterian, restrict loans of his works, including a number among his best known. Consequently, the breadth and variety of Whistler paintings may never be fully appreciated through personal experience by many people.

Fortunately, published research during these decades has reinforced the exhibitions, much of it appearing in their catalogues. Whistler has also profited, oddly enough, from the academy's new scholarly agenda. As historians push for an all-encompassing art history, a "diversity of topics and methodologies" has yielded a more "expansive, pluralizing approach" to Whistler and the several "art worlds" in which he operated. The richness, diversity, and originality of Whistler's work and philosophy have saved him from being dismissed as just another dead white male. His self-promotion and celebrity image have become assets in an age of self-promotion and celebrity. He and his work are now interpreted in terms of "aesthetic subjectivities," commodity culture, global networking, and complex transnational cultural contexts. The jargon may not endear him to the public, but it keeps his legacy alive within the scholarly community, as do new directions in scholarly interests, such as his marketing and exhibition strategies. Particular emphasis has been placed on his position within larger artistic movements, despite his attempts to avoid them, as well as his similarities to other artists and his influence on future generations.[47]

The breadth and quality of the new work owes much to the collaboration of a growing number of international scholars who are drawn to Whistler. Whistler Studies, which had been sputtering along since the 1970s, is now a cohesive field of inquiry and research. It appeared most visibly at the University of Glasgow, where by the late 1990s a Centre for Whistler Studies had been created. Its initial goal was to publish an online edition of Whistler's known correspondence, a daunting task that required collecting, transcribing, and annotating ten thousand documents. To this was added the correspondence of Whistler's mother. Launched in 2003, the project changed the scholarly landscape. Of course, something is lost in reading a transcription, rather than holding an actual document and trying to decipher Whistler's handwriting. We are denied, as John Ruskin would have phrased it, the golden stain of time, and a computer screen inevitably puts some distance between us and Whistler. Having begun my own study of Whistler before 2003, I came to understand him through his original letters in ways that would have otherwise eluded me. But the comprehensive nature and ease of access of the online edition has undeniably facilitated far wider and more detailed research on the man and his art.

The Centre for Whistler Studies also served as a gathering place—one might even say rallying point—for enthusiasts. It sponsored conferences and exhibitions, allowed people to exchange ideas, share information, test new interpretations, and create both professional and personal bonds. While some people entered, left, and rejoined the fold as their research interests shifted, Whistler Studies had been validated. Unfortunately the center, which had been funded by the University of Glasgow, was dissolved soon after completing the correspondence project. The void was at least partially filled in 2010 by the Lunder Consortium for Whistler Studies. Headquartered at Colby College in Maine, it has forged a scholarly partnership between Colby's Museum of Art, the Freer Gallery, the University of Glasgow, and the Art Institute of Chicago, to provide a new platform for symposia, exhibitions, and publications. The Lunder Foundation has also been instrumental in providing several online platforms for Whistler's art and writings, including a revised and expanded edition of the 1980 paintings catalogue, a new etchings catalogue, and informative websites for his pastels and publications. Additionally, Catherine Goebel has created a digital archive of all known published reviews of Whistler's work that should soon join the work funded by the Lunders. Taken together, these internet sites make Whistler more accessible than any other artist.[48]

The impact of this scholarly activity on the monetary value of Whistler's work is difficult to judge. Certainly, the catalogues raisonné, on which savvy dealers and auction houses rely when assessing the art, are invaluable resources; the deep dives into scholarly dissection of individual works probably less so. Still, the value of Whistler paintings, etchings, and lithographs has held steady. His paintings lag behind some of his contemporaries, especially the Impressionists and such modernists as Picasso and Matisse. A Monet "haystack," for example, set a record for Impressionists in 2019 by selling for $110,000,000, or £86,000,000.[49] Whistler paintings, nearly all from the mid-1880s on, changed hands or were offered for sale twenty-five times between 2000 and 2024. The most expensive picture, a seascape, cost $1,000,000 in 2006. The only other known prices paid are $361,000 in 2007, $341,000 in 2013, $254,000 in 2014, $106,250 in 2016, $140,000 in 2020, and $190,000 in 2023. A 5 × 8½ inch watercolor, *Chelsea Shopfronts,* sold at auction in 2020 for £60,000 ($75,000), far below the estimated range of £80,000 ($100,000). However, in 2024, *Portrait of Lucas Alexander Ionides,* done in 1860, sold for £428,000 ($544,000), far above the £120,000 estimate.[50]

Whistler's etchings and lithographs have regained some of the luster lost in the 1930s–50s. In 2005, *Art News* described any Whistler lithograph priced under $5,000 as a good deal. One of his most exquisite lithographs, *Little Nude Model, Reading,* was said to be worth $20,000 to $30,000 in 2008. An impression of his haunting etching and drypoint *Nocturne,* done in Venice, sold in 2010 for $282,000, an auction record for any Whistler print. Another Venice etching, *The Beggars,* was estimated to be worth $30,000 to $50,000 when it went under the hammer in 2011.[51]

Yet it could be said that the monetary value of Whistler's work no longer has any bearing on his legacy. In an age of Non-Fungible Tokens, and with "digital art" selling for tens of millions of dollars, the art market is hardly a reliable measure of anything other than current whims. Similarly, what qualifies as "art" for investors is no longer restricted to debates about painting styles or schools of art, but rather, quite literally, how we define *objets d'art.* For so-called millennials, vintage cars, luxury wristwatches, and antiques have more appeal than paintings. As a critic observed in 2020, "To some degree, the market has killed off debate about the qualities of artworks." An influx of nouveaux riche buyers from China, Russia, and the Middle East has further skewed market values, mostly toward contemporary art, although Impressionism and early modernism remain popular. While the art market generally slumped during the COVID-19 pandemic, it was in "overdrive" by 2022, with, as just one example, a Mark Rothko that sold for $35,000 in 1987 going for $82.4 million at the end of 2021.[52]

So, where does that leave Whistler? Precisely where he wished to be left, I suspect, with the world still debating, arguing, speculating, pondering, trying to divine what it all meant (fig. 19). You need only imagine his peacock laugh. Or is it a knowing chuckle? In the concluding entry of *The Gentle Art,* titled "Final Acknowledgments," Whistler addresses the editor of *The World,* Edmund H. Yates ("Atlas"), an avid supporter who had first anointed him a "celebrity":

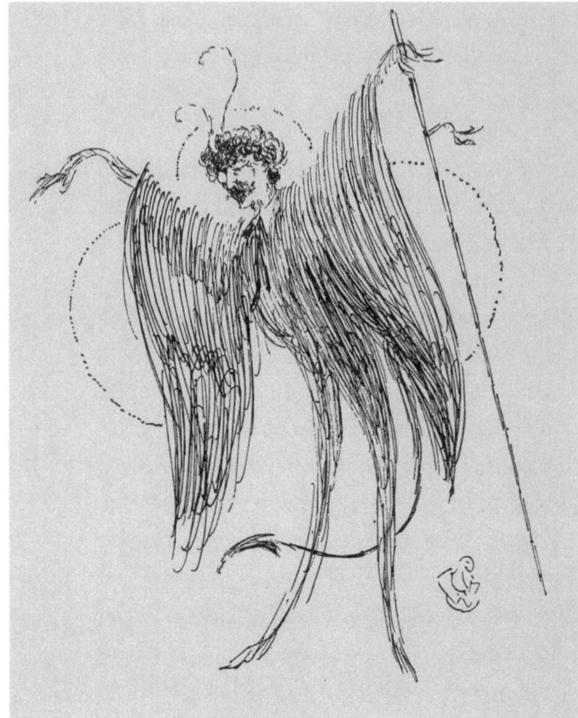

FIG. 19 *Whistler as a Butterfly*, nineteenth–twentieth century. Commercial relief process, 22.9 × 15.1 cm. 1985.1161.37, Metropolitan Museum of Art, New York. Gift of Paul F. Walter, 1985.

These things we like to remember, Atlas, you and I—the bright things, the droll things, the charming things of this pleasant life—and here, too, in this lovely land they are understood—and keenly appreciated.

As to those others—alas! I am afraid we have done with them. It is our amusement to convict—they thought we cared to convince!

Allons! They have served our wicked purpose—Atlas, we "collect" no more.

"*Autres gens, autres moeurs*"

NOTES

CHAPTER 1

1. Anderson and Koval 1994, xv; Burns 1996, 222; K. Jones 2015, 97–99; Sutton 1963, 11; H. Taylor 1978, 58.

2. Fleming 1978, 22 note; McMullen 1973, 11; Merrill 1998, 22–23.

3. K. Jones 2015, 15–44; Young 1970, 81–91; Tinker 1951, 6.

4. Laver 1951, 233; *Observer*, April 25, 1926, p. 11; Hartrick 1939, 106–7.

5. WH to ERP, November 3, 1908, v. 286, PWC; *Nation* 87 (November 26, 1908): 532–33; *Forum* 41 (March 1909): 281.

6. Boughton to Baldry, August 20, 1903, September 11, 1903, BC.

7. Cole copy of *LW* in NAL; Jopling 1925, 297.

8. Stillman to James A. Rose, January 24 [1922], BC.

9. First Canfield quotation from Burns 1996, 244; Canfield to Horace S. Ridings, April 4, 1911, v. 280, PWC; Letter Books XXV: 382–83, FP.

10. M. Sturgis 2005, 240–49; Sickert to WH, n.d., v. 300, PWC; W. Sickert 1908, 1017–28.

11. Sutherland 2014, 343–46.

12. Letter Books XXV: 382–83, FP; W269, WC.

13. Ludovici 1926, 146–47; Hartrick 1939, 106, 114; Tinker 1951, 6; K. Jones 2015, 196–200.

14. Sutherland 2014, 346; Anderson and Koval 1994, xiv–xv; E. Pennell 1929, 2:37–46; E. Pennell 1928, ix, 1, 2, 56. Compare ERP Journal, May 28, July 19, 1900, PP, to *WJ*, 40, 15–46.

15. M27, WC.

16. Addams to WH, n.d., v. 278, Pennington to JP, September 14, 1906, v. 297; Letter Books XXV: 386–91, FP.

17. E. Pennell 1929, 2:37–44; K. Jones 2015, 113–14; *WJ*, 1.

18. Whyte 1929, 207–9; St. John 1990, 97; ERP to WH, January 24, 1908, WH to ERP, January 24, 1908, WH to JP, November 7, 1908, v. 286, J. B. Lippincott Company to JP, May 13, 1921, Box 240, PWC.

19. Hannoosh 2006, 729–31.

20. *LW*, 2:1, 86, 95, 169, 182.

21. Rothenstein 1932, 1:123, 236, 266–67; J. Pennell 1912, 162; McFall to ERP, February 8, 1905, Box 230, PWC; K. Jones 2015, 108–9.

22. P210, WC; JP to Donald McKay Frost, January 17, 1925, HL.

23. *LW*, 2:1.

24. H. Fraser 2014, 136–37; E. Pennell 1906, 1:137.

25. Atkinson 2010, 1–2, 14–23, 46–57; *LW*, 2:1–9, 133–49.

26. Anderson and Koval 1994, xiv–xv; H. Taylor 1978, 53; Sutton 1963, 14; Prideaux 1970, 174.

27. *LW*, 1:155–56, 179, 182–83, 199.

28. *LW*, 1:13–23, 2:32; AWD, July 11, 1844, May 30, 1846 (microfilm copy in AAA); Anderson and Koval 1994, 13; Spencer 1989, 35–36.

29. *LW*, 2:239–41; Pennell Diaries, December 6, 1919, PWC.

30. *LW*, 2:8.

31. Compare *LW*, 1:134–35 and *WJ*, 42–43, to manuscript copy of *LW* in Box 346, f.7, pp. 2–7, PWC, and Pennell Journal, June 3, 1900, PP.

32. *LW*, 1:33; Larned to JP, October 4, 1906, v. 303, PWC.

33. *LW*, 1:7–8; Sutherland and Toutziari 2018, 17–18.

34. *LW*, 1:9, 11–12, 68, 84–85, 112, 124, 184, 187, 193, 250–51, 294.

35. *LW*, 1:30, 47, 133, 185.

36. *LW*, 1:47, 52–53, 76.

37. *LW*, 1:93, 94, 104–5; Edwards to ERP, September 10, 1906, v. 282, PWC.

38. *LW*, 1:94, 104–5.

39. *LW*, 1:142–43; WJ, 83; Rossetti to JP, November 6, 1906; Armstrong to JP, October 8, 1906, v. 278, PWC.

40. *LW*, 1:145, 147, 151.

41. *LW*, 2:216–17, 220; Sutherland 2014, 309, 314–15, 317–18.

42. *LW*, 1:74–75.

43. *LW*, 1:97–98, 102–3, 127–28.

44. *LW*, 1:99–100, 121–22, 126–27.

45. *LW*, 1:161–62, 163, 167.

46. *LW*, 1:168, 215, 298; Stratis and Tedeschi 1998, 1:35–37; Laver 1951, 67.

47. Pennington to WH, November 16, 1908, v. 285, PWC; *LW*, 1:125, 145, 146.

48. K. Jones 2015, 54, 80–85; 112–13; H. Fraser 2014, 165–67; Clarke 2005, 130–44; Hartrick 1939, 117–18.

49. E. Pennell 1929, 2:299–302; Hellman 1927, 168–72; Margaret F. MacDonald to Daniel E. Sutherland, May 3, 2018; K. Jones 2015, 115–22.

50. Pocock 1970, 171–79; *WJ*, 134–35; Robins 2003, 298; CLF to Thomas R. Dewing, June 19, 1911, FP.

51. Stillman to James A. Rose, January 24 [1922], BC; P210, WC; Pennell 1929, 2:216; WH to ERP, February 18, 1913, February 19, 1913, v. 288, PWC; Sutherland 2014, 224–25.

52. Pennell Diaries, October 22, 1919, January 7, 22, February 3, October 18, 21, 1921; J. B. Lippincott Company to JP, July 30, 1921, August 2, 1921, August 17, 1921, September 28, 1921, October 18, 1921; J. Bertram Lippincott to JP, August 22, 1921, Box 240, PWC; E. Pennell 1929, 2:216, 239; W282, P570–72, WC.

53. *WJ*, vi, 1; M26–27, WC.

54. Pennell and Pennell 1921, 293–300; K. Jones 2015, 98.

CHAPTER 2

1. James to JP, September 19, 1903, November 26, 1906, v. 289, Van Dyke to JP, January 2, 1904, Box 270, PWC.

2. *CT*, July 19, 1903, p. 2; Hadley 1903, 334–59; Davies 1936, 75.

3. Way and Dennis 1903, vii.

4. Way and Dennis 1903, 3, 34, 59, 98.

5. Way 1912, 2.

6. Way 1912, 1, 145; Way to ERP, September 27, 1906, v. 301, PWC. Way also published a pair of valuable articles on JW and lithography to coincide with the publication of each book: Way 1903, 10–21; Way 1913, 277–309.

7. Bacher 1908, xiii, 26. Bacher had earlier published a pair of articles on the same subject, but much of that material was repeated in the book.

8. Bacher 1908, 103.

9. Duret 1904; CLF to Canfield, August 1, 1904, FP.

10. Mauclair 1905, 319.

11. Duret 1917, 79, 88–100. This is the English translation by Frank Rutter.

12. Menpes 1904, xix, 65. Menpes first published his reminiscences in a pair of journal articles, but most of that material reappeared in the book.

13. CLF to Duret, December 14, 1903, FP.

14. Eddy 1903; Janey Sevilla Archibald to ERP, February 29, 1908, v. 280, PWC; *CT*, December 4, 1903, p. 7.

15. *GUW* 5419; B. Sickert 1908, 6, 55, 58, 69.

16. Short to WH, September 9, 1906, v. 299, PWC.

17. T. Armstrong 1912, 198.

18. Ionides 1996 [1925], 70.

19. T. Armstrong 1912, 112–13; Du Maurier 1952.

20. *CT*, March 20, 1931, p. 31; Rothenstein 1932, 1:267, 2:51.

21. Ludovici 1906a, 193–95; Ludovici 1906b, 237–39; Ludovici 1926.

22. Jacomb-Hood 1925.

23. J. Carr 1908, 138–39.

24. J. Carr 1914, 89, 91.

25. Robertson 1931, 193–94, 201.

26. Moore 1926, 163–65; Balderston 1916, 171.

27. Rodd 1922, 274–75.

28. Simmons 1922, 130, 223–24.

29. Sherard 1937, 94; Harris 1920, 66, 70, 86–87.

30. Warren 1920, 164.

31. Smalley 1912, 276, 277; Smalley 1903, 239.

32. Cowan 1933, 168–73; Benson 1930; MacColl 1931; Colvin 1922; C. Holmes 1936; Furniss 1919, 71; Leslie Ward 1915, 298–99; Graves 1903, 340–45.

33. Vivian 1923, 75–86.

34. Hallé 1909, 135.

35. J. Lavery 1940; Gay 1930, 46.

36. E. Ward 1923, 253, 268.

37. Redesdale 1916, 1:645–49; Langtry 1925, 62–68; Jopling 1925, 71.

38. Morris 1930; Hartrick 1939, 4.

39. Atherton 1932, 174–79; Havemeyer 1961, 204–14.

40. Bassan 1970, 102–13; Mrs. J. Hawthorne 1881, 658–59; J. Hawthorne 1899, 2956–60; *GUW* 8587.

41. J. Hawthorne 1928, 159, 245; J. Hawthorne 1934, 7, 14.

42. Thaddeus 1912, 16–52; Smith 1939, 205–10.

43. Wedmore 1912, 181–84; Wedmore 1904, 675.

44. Prinsep 1903, 577–80.

45. Spielmann 1903a, 583–84.

46. Spielmann 1903b, 9–10.

47. Pennington 1902, 835–42; *GUW* 4620.

48. Pennington 1904, 156, 160–61, 163–64.

49. Pennington 1910, 773.

50. Thomson 1903, 267.

51. Van Dyke 1904, 10; Van Dyke 1913, 143–44, 153, 160–62, 173; Van Dyke 1920, 149–83.

52. Boughton 1903, 212, 216, 218.

53. Baldry 1903, 237–45.

54. Starr 1908, 528.

55. Wuerpel 1904, 132; Wuerpel 1934, 248–53; Wuerpel 1934a, 316, 321.

56. Bénédite 1905. ERP used the Fantin-Latour correspondence as the centerpiece for E. Pennell 1930.

57. Cortissoz 1913, 181–216.

58. Quilter 1909, 145, 149–50.

59. Keppel 1904a; Keppel 1904b, 145–51.

60. Denker 1995, 152–53; Keppel 1907, 968, 977.

61. Symons 1906, 121–22, 124, 147.

62. Chase 1910, 218–26.

63. Chase 1910, 223, 226.

64. Wilson 1898, 113–15; Lazelle 1915, 710.

65. Key 1908, 928–32; Kobbé 1898, 479–80; Fairman 1904, 306–8.

66. Jackson 1900, 141–43; Crawford 1903, 387–90; Cuneo 1906, 19–28; Glenn 1923, 193–204.

67. Shaw 1968, 198–201.

68. Buel 1913, 694–96.

69. Wray 1915, xl–xlii.

70. RBP to CLF, October 19, 1908, FP.

CHAPTER 3

1. JW to T. Waldo Story [April 3/10, 1887], *GUW* 10035.

2. Fine 1987, 13–26.

3. Randall 1979, 2:665; Mazaroff 2018, 72; Preston 1953, 367; Havemeyer 1961, 15, 211; *WJ*, 165–66.

4. Randall 1979, 2:671–77; Mazaroff 2018, 69.

5. Randall 1979, 2:682–722.

6. Randall 1979, 2:682, 690, 697, 703, 705, 706, 716, 757, 778, 787, 797, 798, 844, 850, 852; Mathews 1994, 265; Havemeyer 1961, 211; *WJ*, 167; Mazaroff 2018, 72–73, 108, 260n21.

7. Sutherland 2014, 195–96; *GUW* 11332, 622, 9265, 9269; Mazaroff 2018, 72–74, 133; Randall 1979, 2:685.

8. Havemeyer 1961, 211; *WJ*, 166–67.

9. Havemeyer 1961, 213; Sutherland 2014, 338; Randall 1979, 2:907, 922, 923; *WJ*, 167; *GUW* 11330.

10. *GUW* 12883, 12876, 12874, 12877, 12873, 12878.

11. *GUW* 12871, 12876, 12879; F45, FC; Havemeyer 1961, 211.

12. *GUW* 12906.

13. *GUW* 12877; F49, F55–57, F61, FC.

14. F47, Mss:5078; F575, WC.

15. F61, F65–67, F71, F73, FC.

16. *Sausalito [California] News*, August 10, 1944.

17. F46, F75, F77, FC.

18. F46, F68, F77, F79–83, FC.

19. F85, F87–88, FC.

20. F577, WC.

21. F577, WC.

22. F69, F83, F85, F88, FC.

23. F91–92, F577, T24, FC.

24. A2, T25–26, FC; Fine 1987, 26n37. Curiously, Ione gave her maiden name as Forbes on the identity card and passport required to visit France. Her marriage certificate says Franklin.

25. T26, FC.

26. T26, FC; Report of death of Mary Maud Franklin Abbott, December 20, 1939, https://www.findagrave.com.

27. T27–28, T30, FC; *Sausalito [California] News*, August 10, 1944, January 15, 1948; *NYT: Books*, January 12, 1948, p. 19.

28. A3, T29–30, FC; https://www.findagrave.com for Ione Tyler; Fine 1987, 25n38 and 25n48.

29. Sutherland 2014, 116, 239–40, 265–66.

30. Sutherland 2014, 265–66; H343–50, WC.

31. July 20, 27, August 3, 10, 1887, H63, WC; *GUW* 2246.

32. May 19, 28, June 6, August 27, 29, 1889, H63, WC.

33. *GUW* 8017.

34. Sutherland 2014, 342; *GUW* 2018, 2020, 12812.

35. Sutherland 2014, 297, 342; *GUW* 2022–23.

36. See https://www.myheritage.com for patents.

37. *London Gazette*, June 3, 1947.

38. *LW*, 2:302; *Times*, November 27, 1923, p. 17; *WJ*, 68, 103–4, 118, 163, 165; *CT*, December 3, 1965, p. C14; MacDonald 1995, M896, 1061, 1123–24, 1127–28, 1146–47, 1149–50, 1152–58.

39. H125, WC.

40. Sutherland 2014, 295, 297, 302–3, 324, 326, 330–32, 337–38.

41. P488, WC; Sutherland 2014, 343–45.

42. RBP to CLF, August 5, 1903, FP.

43. P492, P497, S261–62, G252, WC; Letter Books XI: 470–75, XV: 342–45, XVI: 441–45, 472–76, XVI: 441–45, and CLF to RBP, March 1, 1904, RBP to CLF, January 18 [1905], FP.

44. RBP to CLF, November 22, 1912, FP; *Observer*, June 6, 1915, p. 5; ERP Diaries, June 1, 1915, Box 351, PWC.

45. T. Armstrong 1912, 200; Letter Books XX: 410–17, XIV:373–77 and RBP to CLF, February 1, 1904, FP; P561, P449, WC.

46. Letter Books XXIII: 190–92, 204, 236–37, 280–82, XXIV: 20–22, FP; P561, P559, WC.

47. W266–67, 269, P487, W270, P237, WC; RBP to CLF, October 24, 1903, November 6, 1903, November 13, 1903, CLF to RBP, November 30, 1903, FP.

48. RBP to CLF, August 5, 1903, November 17, 1903, CLF to RBP, September 14, 1903, FP; P487, WC.

49. RBP to CLF, November 6, 1903, March 23, 1905, February 5, 1907, July 10, 1907, FP; W329, W334, WC; *WJ*, 40, 51, 77, 148–49, 191, 194–95, 234, 237, 255–56, 258–60, 263–64, 266, 269–70, 272, 276–77, 281.

50. RBP to CLF, October 29, 1908, November 6, 1908, FP.

51. P540, P542, P544, P547, P569, P571–72, P616, WC.

52. RBP to CLF, November 6, 1903, February 11, 1904, FP.

53. F326, F328, F330–35, WC.

54. Stratis and Tedeschi 1998, 1:20–21; RBP to CLF, August 19, 1903, CLF to RBP, August 20, 1903, September 4, 1903, FP.

55. RBP to CLF, October 17, 1903, January 18, 1904, FP.

56. Stratis and Tedeschi 1998, 1:21, 2:127, 135, 258, 275–77, 281, 296, 434–47; MacDonald 1988, 34–36; *GUW* 13042.

57. P521, P523, P525, WC; RBP to CLF, January 18, 1904, CLF to RBP, February 1, 1904, FP.

58. RBP to CLF, January 18, 1904, CLF to RBP, February 1, 1904, FP; Tedeschi 1997, 15–41; P556, P577, WC.

59. P506, C154–77, H205–17a, WC.

60. CLF to RBP, August [1903], January 28, 1904, RBP to CLF, August 30, 1903, November 6, 1903, December 1, 1903, January 24, 1905, FP; Merrill 1998, 322–41.

61. RBP to CLF, January 8, 1913, FP.

62. Letter Books XXV: 117–18, 132–33, XXIX:376, and RBP to CLF, April 15, June 21, 1913, July 25, 1913, FP; Helen Whistler to ERP, December 15, 1906, Box 292, PWC.

63. J. D. Hobson to RBP, November 7, 1922, November 20, 1922, RBP to Hobson, November 11, 1922, November 18, 1922, all in LB3, S160–61, WC.

64. F341, 343–44, P510, P513, P500–501, P504, P546, WC; RBP to CLF, May 24, 1909, November 22, 1912, FP.

65. P587, P590, P709, P591, P710, WC.

66. X34, and "Notes on Conversation with Rosalind Birnie Philip," n.d., LP.

67. RBP to DS, June 16, 1952, SP; DS to JR, April 14, 1952, May 30, 1952, [March 9, 1954], March 24, 1954, RC.

68. P726, WC; JR to WC, October 11, 1945, December 6, 1945, RC.

69. RBP to CLF, October 1, 1903, FP.

70. CLF to RBP, September 16, 1903, FP.

71. G61–66, 68, WC. A. Hughes 2023, 9–44, provides a detailed account of RBP's bequests to the university in their legal framework.

72. G69–74, G76, P585, WC.

73. G76, G78–80, W27, WC.

74. JR to WC, October 3, 1945, RC.

75. P711, WC; Laurence Ward 2015, 28, 138; Fitzgibbon 1958, 222–30.

76. D. Cox 2015, 248–44.

77. G92, G95, P592, W29–30, P711, WC.

78. X35, LP; YMSM 396, 448, 463; P713, WC.

79. P598, P601, WC.

80. P601, WC; "Notes on a Conversation," LP. Laver (1951, 7–8) suspected that RBP intended to burn all the letters.

81. P718, P726, G254, P720, WC.

82. G254–55, WC.

83. G254–56, P729, WC.

84. P716, P717–18, P720, P729–30, P604, WC.

85. G256, G258, P731, WC.

86. P730, WC; YMSM 520, 521, 538.

87. Death Certificate for RBP, February 7, 1958, Kensington and Chelsea Register Office, Chelsea Old Town Hall, London; Brompton Cemetery Records, Register No. 202309.

CHAPTER 4

1. Mauclair 1905, 318.

2. McMullen 1973, 20; Chaleyssin 1995, 10; McCann 2015, 40–41; Spalding 1994, 6.

3. Shirland 2007, 17; Stephenson 2007, 76; Corbett and Perry 2000, 137; Janes 2016, 172.

4. Prideaux 1970, 11; Fillin-Yeh 2001, 107–8.

5. Feldman 1993, 1–5; Shannon 2006, 121–29; Ribeiro 2017, 273; Janes 2022, 1–11; Hine 2018, 94–99; Larman 2019, 136.

6. Baudelaire 1995, 26–31. For Baudelaire and dandyism, see Feldman 1993, 11–37; Moers 1978, 271–83; Rodgers 2012, 125–39.

7. Baudelaire 1995, 12.

8. Robertson 1931, 188–89; Boughton 1903, 211–12; Rideing 1912, 206; Langtry 1925, 63, 65; Brownell 1879, 637.

9. Redesdale 1916, 2:648; Harris 1920, 67; A. Carr 1926, 106.

10. Denker 1995, 16, 122–24; Eddy 1903, 225.

11. Sutherland 2014, 30, 38, 84; Denker 1995, 22–24.

12. Sutherland 2014, 30–31, 36–37, 40–41; *LW*, 1:36, 2:310.

13. Key 1908, 928; Boughton 1903, 211–12; T. Armstrong 1912, 192–93.

14. A. Sturgis 2006, 7, 23, 130; Kirkham 1996, 112–20; Cruise 2015, 140–41; Calvert 2015, 227–29; Berry 2015, 193–94; Cottom 2013, 241–42.

15. Shirland 2007, 16–19.

16. Bradbury 2019, II:1035, 1064; *GUW* 3432, 12986, 13132; Sutherland 2014, 49, 61; T. Armstrong 1912, 174–75; Denker 1995, 39–40.

17. *LW*, 1:184.

18. February 20, 1867, April 12, 1869, MD.

19. Alsdorf 2012, 35–39, 47–51; Druick and Hoog 1983, 173–80; Laver 1951, 92; MacDonald 2015, 204.

20. J. Roberts 2012, 37, 40, 41, 42; Blanche 1937, 71–79; Blanche 1919, 52–53.

21. Rodgers 2012, 104–8; Adams 1995, 21–25; 53–55; Sussman 1995, 16–31; Singletary 2017, 26–28; Carlyle 1987, 207, 215.

22. Sutherland 2014, 125; Harris 1920, 2; Redesdale 1916, 2:649–51; T. Armstrong 1912, 205–6.

23. Denker 1995, 62, 69–70; Goebel 1988, 1:342–43; Bacher 1908, 81–82; Leslie Ward 1915, 298.

24. *Punch* 1878, 134; *GAME*, 126–28.

25. Bacher 1908, 4, 7, 19, 26; Pennington 1910, 771; McCauley 2004, 88; *WJ*, 195.

26. Quotation from Conway 1912, 190–91.

27. Curry 2004, 49–50; Eddy 1903, 226.

28. *Pall Mall Gazette* 1883, 4; Sutherland 2014, 191–93; MacDonald 2003, 10.

29. Shannon 2006, 122–23, 140–41, 145–49; Tosh 2005, 83–98; Sussman 1995, 166–71.

30. Sutton 1963, 14; Sutherland 2014, 189–90; Laver 1968, 87–92. Having labeled JW a dandy, Sutton describes him on the next page as a "controversial Bohemian."

31. Curry 2004, 38–44; Chase 1910, 222–23, 226; Sutherland 2014, 212.

32. Sutherland 2014, 206–8; *GAME*, 152, 154.

33. Ludovici 1926, 78; Duret 1917, 69.

34. A. Carr 1926, 57–58, 103–4.

35. A. Carr 1926, 303; McMullen 1973, 268.

36. Cecil 1970, 188; Ribeiro 2017, 351–52.

37. Wuerpel 1934, 319; Conway 1912, 189–91; J. Armstrong 1966, 250; H. B. 1887, 18; A. Carr 1926, 106; Morris 1930, 50; Ludovici 1906b, 239; Price 1913, 96; *Studio* 4 (January 1895): 116; Van Dyke 1920, 170; *LW*, 2:6; Robertson 1931, 196; Eddy 1903, 227.

38. Menpes 1904, 10–11.

39. Janes 2022, 1–3, 84–85; J. Carr 1914, 89; Chase 1910, 222; *WJ*, 197; A. Carr 1926, 106.

40. Eddy 1903, 149; Bowdoin 1901, 37–38; Rideing 1912, 202; Duret 1917, 73–74.

41. Burns 1996, 228, 236; Smalley and Escott 1885, 316; Rothenstein 1932, 1:84; Sutherland 2014, 135.

42. McCann 2015, 162–65.

43. Curry 2004, 49–50; Pennington 1910, 771; *LW*, 2:6; J. Carr 1914, 95, 98–99; Van Dyke 1904, 10.

44. Martin 1908, 11; Prinsep 1903, 578; Hallé 1909, 111.

45. Campbell 2004, 15, 35, 44, 46, 126; Buel 1913, 696.

46. A. Sturgis 2006, 7, 23, 130; Burns 1996, 244.

47. Baudelaire 1956, 152–53.

48. B. Sickert 1908, 65–69.

CHAPTER 5

1. Kirsch 2022, 16; comment by Joyce Hill Stoner in *James McNeill Whistler: The Case for Beauty* (Film Odyssey, produced by Karen Thomas, 2014).

2. B. Sickert 1908, 57–58, 61; James to JP, November 26, 1906, December 1, 1906, v. 289, PWC; Van Dyke 1904, 10.

3. Menpes 1904, xxi–xxii.

4. Quote from *LW*, 2:306.

5. Cline 1970, 3:1579; Vivian 1923, 76.

6. Hadley 1903, 334, 351.

7. J. Carr 1908, 137, 139, 142–43, and 1914, 95–96; Harrison to ERP, September 15 [1906], v. 284, PWC.

8. Robertson 1931, 188–89.

9. Spielmann 1903b, 16; Spielmann 1934, 17; Way 1912, 81; T. Armstrong 1912, 205.

10. *Current Literature* 1909, 49; Spielmann 1903b, 10; Chase 1910, 222–24.

11. Prinsep 1903, 582.

12. Smalley 1903, 239; *Guardian*, July 18, 1903, p. 7, November 3, 1908, p. 5.

13. Ionides 1925, 18; Sutherland 2014, 315.

14. *Edinburgh Review* 1905, 457.

15. Sutherland 2014, 72.

16. Sutherland 2014, 71, 86–87; *GUW* 8036.

17. *GUW* 8056.

18. A. Carr 1926, 106; Spielmann 1903b, 16; Hartmann 1910, 196–97; Thomson 1903, 265, 267; Havemeyer 1961, 206, 209–10.

19. *Guardian* 1903, 7.

20. Quoted in Hartmann 1910, 189–91.

21. Wynford Dewhurst to JP, February 9, 1907, Box 221, PWC; Jacomb-Hood 1925, 48.

22. Sutherland 2014, 298; Keppel 1904, 7, 9, 15.

23. *GUW* 1380, 8559; Sutherland 2014, 154, 215; Rothenstein 1932, 1:267.

24. Wedmore 1912, 182–84; E. Ward 1923, 258, 262; Menpes 1904, 23, 25; Housman 1936, 109–10; Houseman 1908, 5.

25. *GUW* 4166, 11494; Menpes 1904, 45; Frederick Keppel to JP, November 6, 1907, v. 290, PWC. Other instances of JW's supposedly faulty memory are provided by Thaddeus 1912, 147, 151, and Wray 1915, xlii.

26. Blathwayt 1917, 208–9; Spielmann 1934, 18; Bradford 1921, 513, 515–17.

27. *GUW* 12825.

28. Merrill 1992, 148; Sutherland 2014, 160–62, 242–45, 276–79.

29. Sutherland 2014, 284–85, 305, 310–11.

30. Thaddeus 1912, 146–48.

31. J. Lavery 1940, 116; T. Armstrong 1912, 13.

32. Sutherland 2014, 225–27; Whistler Notes from WH Journal, entry for April 26, 1903, v. 288, PWC.

33. Way and Dennis 1903, 107–8; Way 1912, 119, 131–41.

34. Sutherland 2014, 98, 100.

35. Sutherland 2014, 235–36, 247–48; Vivian 1923, 76.

36. Sutherland 2014, 336.

37. Way to CLF, July 18, 1903, August 27, 1903, FP; Rothenstein 1932, 1:269; Wray 1915, xlii; Wedmore 1912, 183; Spielmann 1903b, 14.

38. T. Armstrong 1912, 206–7, 213–14; Pennington 1904, 162; Ionides 1925, 15, 17–18; Dewhurst to JP, August 16, 1903, v. 282, Gosse to JP and ERP, July 20, 1903, v. 283, PWC; Cline 1970, 3:1579.

39. Wuerpel 1934, 321.

CHAPTER 6

1. Goebel 1988, 324–34; Duret 1917, 46; Sutherland 2014, 127–28.

2. *GAME*, 126–28.

3. Merrill 1992, 144–46, 150–51.

4. Casteras and Denny 1996, 101.

5. Robertson 1931, 48–49.

6. A. Robinson 1985, 31; Prettejohn 2007, 169–75, 181–85; Merrill 2003, 70–71; B. Sickert 1908, 31, 55.

7. McCann 2015, 96.

8. *GUW* 6686; Corton 2015, 1–16; Brimblecombe 1987, 11–14, 59–60, 71–73, 108–16.

9. Corton 2015, 14–30, 36–37, 135–42; Warner 1987, 15–16, 28, 86; James 1877, 608.

10. Corton 2015, 171–78; Lochnan 2004, 52–53, 126–29; Barringer and Fairclough 2014, 34, 164; A. Robinson 2004, 157–59; YMSM 32, 46, 54, 55.

11. Valance 2018, 2–4; Davidson 2015, 73–77; Lochnan 2004, 16; Hartmann 1910, 75.

12. Lochnan 2004, 24, 27, 33–34, 51, 67–81, 106–7; Flint 2000, 300–305; Robertson 1931, 1:114; Menpes 1904, 80; Zinnes 1980, 287; Kauffman 1975, 13–14; Warrell 2013, 45–47.

13. Warrell 2013, 102–3, 218–19; Brown 2014, 13–14, 21–22, 144–47; Brown 2021, 14, 169–71, 196, 201–3; Nisbet 2017, 114–16.

14. Davidson 2015, 77–80.

15. Corbeau-Parsons 2017, 230 ; Warner 1987, 76–77, 86–87.

16. Davidson 2015, 16–25; Hilton 2000, 210, 281.

17. Meinel and Meinel 1983, 19–20, 26–27, 29–30, 36.

18. Townsend 1994, 690–91; *AD* 28 (October 1, 1953): 22; B. Sickert 1905, 438; Meynell 1898, 9–10, 12.

19. Valance 2018, 33–37; Kalba 2017, 123–25, 136–41, 144–45; YMSM 163, 165–66, 169–70, 174, 204.

20. YMSM 67, 71, 73,100, 205; Hartmann 1910, 20–21.

21. Barnes and Best 2006, 24; *GUW* 10071.

22. Meinel and Meinel 1983, 36–38, 115–20; YMSM 71, 117, 179.

23. Sutherland 2008, 61–73; Sutherland 2014, 97; Sotomayor 2024, 76–85; *GUW* 4335; Meinel and Meinel 1983, 33–34; Davidson 2015, 16–17. For JW's artwork at Valparaiso, see also Manthorne 1989; Dorment and MacDonald 1995, 115–19; Fattal and Salus 2004, 11–22; Gantes and Sotomayor 2019, 29–38.

24. James 1888, 223, 228, 233, 234, 238; Brimblecombe 1987, 116–18; Hilton 2000, 209.

25. MacDonald 2001, 30–33, 59, 62; Grieve 2000, 124, 169–73, 220–21, 162–64; Lochnan 2004, 60–63, 203–29.

26. Davidson 2015, 80–83; R. Holmes 2008, 383; Meinel and Meinel 1983, 39–50; Hilton 2000, 281, 446, 481, 483–84; Hunt 1998, 390–91. YMSM 309 says the painting may have been done in the "early 1880s," but the circumstances as related here suggest a more precise year.

27. *GUW* 6686, 3182, 4826, but see also *GUW* 9723, 4683, 7860, 4747, 3045, 11059, 9976, 7741, 4823, 10656; Meynell 1898, 9–10, 12.

28. Merrill 1992, 144, 148; *GAME*, 142–43.

29. Tresch 2021, 7–11, 47–49, 274–77.

30. Sutherland 2014, 109; Tresch 2021, 47–48, 54–57, 61, 136–40; Cantalupo 2014, 62.

31. Fine 1987, 85–100.

32. Sutherland 2014, 57–58, 94, 150, 129, 198, 259, 261; Alan S. Cole Diary, May 13, 1877, *GUW* 13132; Robins 2007, 17; Grieve 2000, 44.

33. Scharf 1974, 114, 136; Jacobi and Kingsley 2016, 40; Haworth-Booth 1984, 79–81; Haworth-Booth 2010, 48–59.

34. J. Carr 1914, 91; Ludovici 1926, 79, 103.

35. Tresch 2012, 1–12, 125–26, 148; R. Holmes 2008, 159–62, 383; Ruskin 1884a, v. 4, pt. 5, chap. 6, pp. 82–83, and pt. 7, chap. 1, pp. 101–2, 107.

36. Lochnan 2004, 145–47; James 1888, 233; Meynell 1898, 14.

37. Corton 2015, 178–89; Freeman 2007, 91–95, 103–13, 118–29; J. Taylor 2016, 167–85; Symons 1909, 2–3; B. Sickert 1908, 55; *Edinburgh Review* 1905, 456, 461; Ludovici 1926, 79; Way and Dennis 1903, 54; Cortissoz 1913, 203; De Kay 1904, 5.

38. Empson 1966 [1930], 16–17; *GAME*, 147.

39. Tonks 1934, 18.

40. Carrier 1996, 110–12; Cadwallader 2016, 110–12; Sutherland 2014, 69; R. Johnson 1981, 71–75.

41. Barnes and Best 2006, 10, 27; Pearsall 1972, 29–33; Braudy 2016, 61–62; Cadwallader 2016, 11–12; Tresch 2012, 36–37, 46–47, 125–31.

42. Sutherland 2014, 75–76, 117, 119, 141, 144, 150; Bradbury 2019, 2:1084; Menpes 1904, 64–65; *WJ*, 156–58, 272–73; Brinton 1906, 5, 20.

43. Hilton 2000, 209–11; Ruskin 1884b, 47–48; Jacomb-Hood 1925, 114; Killeen 2009, 4, 124–59.

44. Silverman 1991, 56–59, 230–31, 267, 528–29; Tresch 2021, 227–33, 252–54, 289–90, 338.

45. Merrill 2003, 71; Way and Dennis 1903, 3; Bradford 1921, 522.

46. Montfort and Willsdon 2018, 64–71; Valance 2018, 74–79; Duret 1917, 45; Merrill 2003, 71.

47. Smajić 2010, 4–5, 34–38, 40, 42–43.

48. Pyne 1996a, 99, 121, 126–27; Pyne 1996b, 75–97; Merrill 2003, 66; Spencer 1989, 258–68.

49. Sutherland 2014, 88; Cadwallader 2016, 1–13; Meacock 2007, 24–30.

50. Tsui 2006, 460–64, 468–69; Pyne 1996a, 94–99; Spencer 1989, 267; Merrill 2003, 67–68; Shirland 2011, 80–101; Tonks 1934, 18; Sutherland 2014, 68–69, 89–90; Moffa 1991, 34–35, 90–133, 105–6, 199.

51. Carrier 1996, 105–13; Tresch 2012, 129–31, 146–47; Rose 2006, 271–78.

52. Conrad 1988, 96–98.

53. Sutherland 2014, 96–97, 267; Pickvance 1963, 395–96.

54. Rose 2006, 271–78; Arnold 1989, 114; Conrad 1988, 151.

55. Conrad 1988, 40; Baker 2001, 30–31, 36–37; Kalba 2017, 123–41.

56. Critchley 1987, 109–10, 124–25, 137–38; Carrier 1996, 109–10, 117; Hook 2021, 158–62. For a variety of potential sensory influences on JW, see Howes 2024, section 6.

57. Way and Dennis 1903, 54; Pennington 1910, 774; Sutherland 2014, 190–91.

58. Merrill 1992, 144. The best study of the musical influences on JW is Teniswood-Harvey 2006, although she does not consider music as a source of inspiration for the nocturnes.

CHAPTER 7

1. *Boston Evening Transcript*, July 18,1903; *Westminster Gazette*, July 23, 1903; *Daily Telegraph*, February 2, 1904; *CT*, July 31, 1927, p. G6; Marks 1986.

2. Zinnes 1980, 1–2, 32–33, 40–41, 86–89, 260, 271–72; Pound 1912.

3. Sutherland 2014, 228–29; Kolb 1989, 17–19, 137.

4. Kolb 1989, 197–98 and n. 8; Tadié 2000, 455; Carter 2000, 362.

5. R. Fraser 1994, 114–15, 118–19, 137–39, 259–60; Meyers 1975, 96–98; Kilmartin 1983, 26–27, 74; Karpeles 2008, 10, 14.

6. Kilmartin 1983, 130; Karpeles 2008, 107, 146–47, 198–99, 274–75, 304–5; R. Fraser 1994, 133, 139.

7. Paper presented by Aleksandra Budrewicz at Conference on New Research Development in Whistlerism, Musée des Beaux-Arts de Rouen, France, June 21–22, 2024.

8. Muhlstein 2017, 206–8.

9. Wolcott to JWR, June 12, 1946, FC to JWR, April 214, 1947, RC; Wolcott, *Fra Angelo Bomberto*, 3–5.

10. Kavanagh 1973, 18.

11. Daniels 1972, E5; Thwaite 1973, 34.

12. Sutherland 2014, 60, 139, 153, 188; Meyer-Dinkgräfe 2005, vii–viii, 98–115.

13. Hindson 2016, 199–200; Leask 2012, 139; *Observer*, March 11, 1917, p. 3.

14. *NYT*, March 7, 1920, p. 6, June 20, 1920, p. 64; ERP Diaries, July 13, 1921, Box 351, PWC.

15. Cavendish to ERP, May 30, 1921, July 4, 1921, Box 19, PWC; Buchanan and Jones 2021, 213–35; ERP Diaries, June 1, July 13, July 16, 1921.

16. Arliss 1927, 259–60; ERP Diaries, July 13, 1921; Cavendish to ERP, May 30, 1921, October 31, 1921, April 5, 1922, PWC; *NYT*, January 14, 1923, p. 1, June 8, 1924, p. 1.

17. *NYT*, July 25, 1925, p. 6.

18. Hopkins and Curry to Laurence River, Inc., June 3, 1931, and Contracts for *Mr. Whistler*, Productions Records, Box 10, RSP; *CT*, July 19, 1931, p. C5, November 15, 1931, p. C12; *AD* 5 (August 1, 1931); *NYT*, July 19, 1931, p. 1, July 20, 1931, p. 21, October 4, 1931, p. 107, November 29, 1931, p. 1, December 6, 1931, p. 2.

19. Account Books for *Mr. Whistler*, December 1931, Box 10, RSP; *NYT*, December 13, 1931, p. 1, April 15, 1934, p. 1, July 8, 1934, p. 1, August 5, 1934, p. 1, April 5, 1936, p. 1, October 15, 1939, p. 140.

20. *Otago Daily Times* 1938, 32; Preston 1953, 390–91, 394–95.

21. Sutherland and Toutziari 2018, 197.

22. *CT*, May 5, 1961, p. N2, March 20, 1964, p. C3.

23. *NYT*, June 21, 1981, p. 11:22; *NYT*, December 7, 1981, p. C17; *Hilberry Theatre 25th Anniversary Season, 1987–1988* [Detroit, 1987], 30–31, copy in Department of Theatre and Dance Archives, Wayne State University, Detroit; *Independent*, December 31, 1998.

24. Dowling 2007, 49, 106, 111.

25. Tamas MacDonald, "Plague Wind," PS; *Guardian*, April 28, 1983, p. 12.

26. MacDonald, "Plague Wind," 9–10, 14, 62–67.

27. *CAM* 276 (December 2023):12; Tabbita to Daniel E. Sutherland, May 25, 2014, June 17, 2021.

28. Parry 1992, 6–7; Clutton to Daniel E. Sutherland, June 19, 2021.

29. *CT*, August 1, 1995, p. D14.

30. Sutherland and Toutziari 2018, 189, 197.

31. "Whistler" (1932), T-Mss 2000–005, Ser. II, Box 77, f.5, APC; "James McNeill Whistler" (1937), T-Mss 1966–002, Ser. LXXVIII, Box 50, f.11, WPA.

32. *Guardian*, May 13, 1939, p. 14; "Nocturne in Chelsea," BBC; *Observer*, May 21, 1939, p. 26.

33. "The Verdict of the Court," BBC. For other broadcasts, see *Radio Times*, September 19, 1968, p. 24, November 23, 1978, p. 49; *Guardian*, October 12, 1974, p. 4, October 11, 1975, p. 4.

34. *Radio Times*, May 12, 1950, p. 31, May 17, 2001, pp. 130–31; *Guardian*, May 19, 2001, p. E85.

35. Lindsey 1970 [1922], 134, 187.

36. *Chicago Defender* (National Edition), June 16, 1934, p. 12; *AD* 8 (July 1, 1934), p. 13.

37. Sobel 1974, 165–72.

38. Denker 1995, 154–55.

39. Martin Hopkinson to Daniel E. Sutherland, August 29, 2012.

40. Sutherland and Toutziari 2018, 193; Pennell Diaries, May 7, 1920.

41. Sutherland and Toutziari 2018, 187–89.

42. Sutherland and Toutziari 2018, 186, 192–97; *Guardian*, November 27, 1959, p. 16; *CT*, February 2, 1963, p. A5.

43. *CT*, September 11, 1966, p. L29.

44. *CT*, June 25, 1946, p. 14, November 15, 1951, p. E3, April 4, 1952, p. 18, February 19, 1954, p. A1, June 18, 1955, p. A12, December 17, 1955, p. A8, January 7, 1957, p. C9, June 15, 1964, p. C9, October 15, 1967, p. C30, October 14, 1990, p. C17; *Observer*, March 24, 1963, p. 25; *Guardian*, October 3, 1994, p. A3; *NYT*, November 9, 2006, p. E7; *BBC Music Magazine*, January 2021, p. 15.

45. *CT*, July 5, 1964, p. 14, February 10, 1997, p. B6, November 25, 1951, p. 13, June 22, 1954, p. A4, January 1, 1956, p. F17, July 17, 1966, p. M46, January 7, 1981, p. 4.

46. Newton and MacDonald 1978, 221–32; Sutherland 2014, 343; Denker 1995, 151–53.

47. Dolnick 2009, A17; *AN* 71 (November 1920): 196; *CT* October 26, 1930, p. 25; Denker 1995, 153–54.

48. *CT*, August 6, 1939, p. D4, November 19, 1939, p. F5, October 13, 1940, p. C6; Denker 1995, 154–55.

49. *CT*, March 11, 1973, p. E18, October 12, 175, p. S21.

50. F. Coburn 1988, 85–86.

CHAPTER 8

1. Sutherland 2014, 339–42.

2. Downes 1904, 15–17; Fenollsa 1903, 14.

3. K. Cox 1904a, 467–68; K. Cox 1904b, 638; Letter Books XIII: 237–38, FP. Cortissoz quotation from Merrill 2003, 87, which offers the best analysis of the exhibition.

4. B. Sickert 1905, 437–38; *Studio* 1905.

5. Borland 1995, 136–37, 155–56; *Guardian*, July 20, 1904, p. 9; Thornton 1938, 73–82.

6. Jensen 1994, 264–76; Hook 2021, 1–4, 85, 185.

7. Mansfield 1909; Kennedy 1910; Hartmann 1910; Cary 1913; Gallatin 1913.

8. Campbell Dodgson to JP, December 20, 1905, v. 202, PWC.

9. Brinton 1906, 5, 20.

10. Jensen 1994, 263–76; Meier-Graefe 1908, 2:199, 218, 224; Singer 1905, 7, 18–19, 45.

11. H. Taylor 1978, 175–78; Hook 2021, 114–15, 118–19; *Septule and the Racinistes* (1910), copy in Chelsea Arts Club Archives, London; Ticknor 2000, 1; Watson 1992, 179.

12. Baetens and Lyna 2019, 127–28, 130–31; Sutherland 2014, 308, 315; Prettejohn 2007, 193–99; Reed 1996, 8–9, 25–31, 48–51, 128–29; Bell 1914, viii–ix, 39, 42, 272–73; Sutton 1972, 1:310–13.

13. Rutter 1927, 3; Rutter 1911, 129–34, 149–52.

14. R. Hughes 1997, 353–59; Watson 1992, 182.

15. Ewa Bobrowska and Urszula Kozakowska Zaucha, papers presented at Conference on New Research Developments on Whistlerism, Musée des Beaux-Arts de Rouen, France, June 21–22, 2024.

16. Ono 2023, 9, 12, 15–16, 24–25, 30–31, 34–35; Ono 2024, 97–103.

17. Boughton 1903, 216; Cortissoz 1913, 216.

18. Nordström 2011, 35–39; Prodger 2006, 10–11, 15–16.

19. *GUW* 11121, 8991; MacDonald 2001, 137–39, 140; Heijbroek and MacDonald 2000, 117, 120, 122; McWilliams and Sekules 1986, 30–31, 39, 63; Callard 1897, 104–6; Haworth-Booth 1984, 154–63, 170–73; Kelly 2010, 213–47; Weaver 1989, 181–214.

20. Caffin 1910, 34; Weaver 1989, 133–40.

21. Emerson 1899, 98–99, 176–79; McWilliams and Sekules 1986, 30–31.

22. A. Coburn 1966, 38, 44, 48, 74; Heijbroek and MacDonald 2000, 122–24; P. Roberts 2014, 17, 23, 27–29, 35, 38, 52–53.

23. Goldberg 1981, 281, 370–71, 424; Whelan 1995, 255–56; Harker 1979, 92, 134; P. Roberts 2014, 37; Weaver 1989, 281–96; A. Coburn 1966, 92, 102, 104; Nordström 2010, 12.

24. Nordström 2010, 126–27.

25. Burns 1996, 223–37, 240–45; Reed 1996, 9; *Bookman* 1912.

26. Helmreich 2020, 95–97.

27. Stevens 1972, 42–43; MacColl 1906, 517–19; *CT*, April 28, 1906, p. 4.

28. Letter Books, XII: 150–53, 200–203, 259, XX: 187, FP.

29. C. Holmes 1903, 16; Watson 1992, 168, 173; P. A. 1904, 109; Lawton and Merrill 1993, 183–97; Gardiner 1930, 236. Statistics on sales compiled by the author.

30. Letter Books, XII: 71–72, 150–53, XIII: 304–9, Canfield to Cornelia Bentley Sage [1909], Box 48, William Marchant to CLF, January 20, 1904, FP; YMSM 208.

31. Watson 1992, 197–98, 207–8, 212–13, 227–31; Hook 2021, 296, 322–23, 338, 342, 364–66; YMSM 229; ERP Diaries, February 5, 13, 14, 24, 1920, Box 351, PWC; *Observer*, July 27, 1919, p. 8.

32. Stevens 1972, 42–43; *NYT*, March 2, 1919, p. 16; Reid 2007, 110–11; C171, P575, WC.

33. *Observer*, July 27, 1919, p. 8; ERP 1929, II: 234–36.

34. M. Sturgis 2005, 469–70, 599–600; Reed 1996, 119–20; Robins 2003, 177, 186–87, 189, 193.

35. Robins 2003, 179–86, 193–94, 252–53, 659, 670–71.

36. Goldstein 2000, 189–92, 224–32; Watson 1992, 277–78.

37. Hook 2021, 327–39; J. Davis 2003, 569–70; Barter 2016, 14–25; *AD* 17 (November 1942): 5; McConkey 2006, 160–82.

38. *AD* 12 (April 1, 1938): 25; 16 (July 1, 1942): 23, (August 1, 1942): 15.

39. *AD* 15 (December 1, 1940): 11.

40. *AD* 15 (December 15, 1940): 11; 16 (August 1, 1942): 15; 24 (September 15, 1950): 26.

41. Laver 1951, 9–11.

42. Laver 1951, 11, 116–18, 143–44, 244–46; Glazer 2008, 172–73.

43. Sutherland and Toutziari 2018, 186–89.

44. Neal 1980, 27–30; Bennett 1934, 4; *AD* 11 (August 1, 1937): 6, 9; 12 (October 1, 1937): 17, (October 15, 1937): 20, (January 15, 1938): 24, (February 1, 1938): 6, (May 1, 1938): 5, (June 1, 1938), 16; 13 (March 15, 1939): 26; 16 (October 15, 1941): 5; 17 (December 1, 1942): 5, (February 1, 1943): 6, (March 5, 1943): 12; 15 (November 1, 1940): 11.

45. *CT*, March 1, 1937, p. 2; *Guardian*, March 29, 1940, p. 4.

46. *American Magazine of Art* 1934; *NYT*, April 15, 1936, p. 2.

47. *AD* 16 (May 1, 1942): 19; 17 (April 1, 1943): 20, (March 1, 1943): 19, (August 1, 1943): 14.

48. *AD* 12 (April 15, 1938): back cover.

49. Watson 1992, 236–40, 253–54, 260–64, 268; *AD* 16 (August 1, 1942): 13.

50. YMSM 71, 170, 204; *AD* 12 (January 1, 1938): back cover; 13 (October 1, 1938): 26.

51. Note by FC [November 1945], Robert C. Vose to FC, December 26, 1945, RC.

52. Stevens 1972, 43; *AD* 11 (March 15, 1937): 23–24; 12 (September 1, 1938): 30; 13 (November 1938): 25, (January 1, 1939): 25, (March 15, 1939): 60; 15 (February 1, 1941): 26; *NYT*, January 13, 1934, p. 17.

53. *AD* 17 (October 1, 1942): 3; 14 (December 15, 1939): 18; Miller 1941a, 9–10; Miller 1941b, 6; Avery 1946, F1; *AD* 20 (October 15, 1945): 12.

CHAPTER 9

1. S. Davis 1939, 13; R. Pearson 1945, 22; Sterner 1947, 28; R. Pearson 1947, 28; Baur 1951, 15. Summaries of these developments may be found in Hopkins 2000, Rorimer 2001, and Hopkins and Whyte 2021.

2. Boswell 1949, 5; Genauer 1949, 11; Bird 1951, 7; Faison 1954, 5.

3. Frankfurter 1961, 28–29; Ackerman 1960, 253–63.

4. Malraux 1949–50; Wolfe 1975, 6–9, 28–29, 39–48.

5. Wolfe 1975, 49–67.

6. Wolfe 1975, 98–102.

7. *GAME*, 146; *AD* 16 (January 1, 1942): 33, (May 15, 1942): 33; 20 (May 15, 1946): 15; *Washington Post*, June 25, 1966, p. A1.

8. *NYT*, August 11, 1946, p. 56; Neal 1980, 32–33; Breuning 1947, 14.

9. Neal 1980, 37–41; Weller 1954, 7, 24.

10. Barry 1954, C8; Saarinen 1954, SM13; Jewett 1954, F2; *NYT*, July 8, 1959, p. 31.

11. Watson 1992, 303–4, 311–17, 336–37, 344–49, 469–72.

12. Ross Whistler to JR, December 19, 1946, RC; Stevens 1972, 43–45; McNay 1971.

13. WC to JR, October 13, 1947, Marcia H. Haskell to WC, November 28, 1947, RC; YMSM 69.

14. Neal 1980, 42–46; *Detroit News*, September 24, 1978, p. F8; Newton 1960, 7; Wallis 1960, 24; Sutton 1960b, 460–61; Sutton 1960a, 486–87; Spender 1960, 377–78; *Art News* 60 (Summer 1961): 20.

15. Barry 1968, G33.

16. Naylor 1975; Sutton 1966; Holden 1969; Prideaux 1970; Spalding 1994.

17. Gaunt 1945; Hough 1949, 175–87; *AD* 26 (November 1, 1951): 50, 82; Gombrich 1952, 400–403, 430, 435; Larkin 1966, 263, 301–2; Wilmerding 1976, 146–49, 153–58, 164–65, 169, 174, 177–78; Farr 1984, 3, 20; Sandberg 1968, 59–64.

18. H. Pearson 1952; H. Pearson 1926, 279–80; Glazer 2008, 173–74; *Sunday [Chicago] Tribune Magazine of Books*, March 22, 1953, p. 13.

19. Nicholson 1961, 28; Gregory 1959, 9, 241, 244–45.

20. Sutton 1963, 11, 19; *Burlington Magazine*, 107 (June 1965): 324; *TLS* (February 13, 1964): 120.

21. *GAME* 1967, viii–ix 31; Toynbee 1968, 28.

22. Fleming 1978; Weintraub 1974; McMullen 1973; H. Taylor 1978; *CT*, December 3, 1978, p. E1, February 10, 1974, p. F3; *Observer*, July 7, 1974, p. 28; Glazer 2008, 174–76.

23. Cooper 1974, 12–14.

24. JR to WC, August 3, 1945, December 6, 1945, WC to Ross Whistler, May 18, 1945, JR to Lloyd Goodrich, November 14, 1949, DS to JR, October 9, 1959, [March 9, 1950], RC.

25. Young et al. 1980; *NYT Book Reviews*, September 14, 1980, p. 1; *Guardian*, March 17, 1980, p. 2, June 14, 1980, p. 11, June 24, 1980, p. 10, June 27, 1980, p. 12, June 17, 1982, p. 5.

26. Getscher and Marks 1986; Seitz 1910; Goebel 1988; MacDonald 1995.

27. Lochnan 1984.

28. Stratis and Tedeschi 1988; *CT*, May 24, 1998, p. 16. The catalogue may now be found online at https://www.publications.artic.edu.

29. The most recent work is Ono 2003; Ono 2023, but see also Sandberg 1964, 500–507; Dufwa 1981; Levine 1983; Berger 1992; G. Lavery 2019.

30. Shenker 1984, 56–65; R. Hughes 1991, 111–12.

31. Elam 1994, 663.

32. Dorment and MacDonald 1995; Feaver 1994, C2; Hall 1994, A6; Pearce 1994, 23.

33. Gopnik 1995, 68–73; Updike 2005, 83–96.

34. Fleming 1991; Anderson and Koval 1994; *Observer*, October 23, 1995, p. C24; *Boston Book Review*, October 1, 1995; Prettejohn 1996, 301–7; Merrill 1992; Merrill 1998; Burns 1996. Also worth mentioning from the mid-1990s is Bendix 1995, which explored JW's life and work through the prism of design and decoration.

35. Goldstein 2000, 311; Hopkins 2000, 206–8, 236; *CT*, May 24, 1989, p. CN21; *Time Magazine* 136 (December 3, 1990):

124–25; Watson 1992, 362–68, 384–85, 388–94, 399–401, 405–8, 411, 414–15, 416–32, 447–51, 457–59, 473, 485; Gopnik 2017, 151–52.

36. Carrier 1991, 3–4; Kuspit 1984, xi–xii, 83–93; Pollack 2014, 9–10, 16; J. Davis 2003, 545–46; Sheehan 2022, 33–37.

37. Winner 2004, B10; Howes 2024. For the psychological approach as applied (somewhat dubiously) to JW, see Capps 2013 and Weinberg 2001.

38. Gombrich 1995, 530–33, 554, 570, 573, 577; Mills 2002, 2–15; Peers 2006, 124–27.

39. R. Hughes 1997, 237–42; P. Johnson 2003, 520–21, 561–64; J. Jones 2018, 256–59, 262–64; Mullins 2022, 209–11; Murphy 2023.

40. Boswell 1945, 3, 30; Goodrich 1950, 5–6, 20; Kammen 2006, 254; Haxthausen 2002, ix–xiv.

41. *WSJ*, December 19, 2008, p. A19, February 14, 2019, p. A11, November 5, 2020, p. A17; Gibson 2022, A11; Januszczak 2022, 30.

42. Varnedoe and Gopnik 1990, 19; Kuspit 2004; Lang 1984; Danto 1997; Danto 2003; Preziosi 1989, 1–20; Stoppard 2001, 15; Barnes 2015, 230, 235–36.

43. Hopkins 2000, 197–98, 203–4, 208–9, 213–15, 219–31; *WSJ*, June 21, 2023, p. A13.

44. Furr 2024, 1–3; Shezad Dawood to Daniel E. Sutherland, July 29, 2024.

45. *Guardian*, April 25, 2023.

46. Calloway and Orr 2011; J. Robinson 2020, 7; Valette and Calame-Levert 2024.

47. Quotes are from Glazer and Merrill 2013, vii. It is impossible to cite economically the library of publications since 2000, but some worth noting and not cited elsewhere include Corbett 2004; Curry 2023; Fletcher and Helmreich 2011; Glazer 2019; MacDonald 2020; Merrill 2003; Petri 2011; Simpson 2008.

48. Glazer and Merrill 2013, 15–38; https://www.whistlerpaintings.gla.ac.uk; https://www.etchings.arts,gla.ac.uk; https://www.whistlerpastels.gla.ac.uk; https://www.whistlerwritings.gla.ac.uk; https://centreforwhistlercriticism.omeka.net.

49. *Evening Standard*, May 15, 2019, p. 9.

50. YMSM 267, 272, 321, 413, 521a, 538; https://www.christie.com/pdf/onlineonly, from November 26 to December 10, 2020; *CAM*, 286 (October 2024): 8.

51. *Art News* 104 (November 2005): 156; 110 (April 2011), 22; *NYT*, March 18, 2011, p. F20, (September 12, 2008), p. 60.

52. Greenwold 2019, 5–9; *TLS*, March 27, 2020, p. 7; Kinsella 2006, 136–42; Bown 2020, 7.

BIBLIOGRAPHY

Ackerman, James S. 1960. "Art History and the Problems of Criticism." *Daedalus* 89 (Winter): 253–63.

Adams, James Eli. 1995. *Dandies and Desert Saints: Styles of Victorian Manhood.* Ithaca: Cornell University Press.

Alsdorf, Bridget. 2012. *Fellow Men: Fantin-Latour and the Problem of the Group in Nineteenth-Century French Painting.* Princeton: Princeton University Press.

American Magazine of Art. 1934. "Whistler Memorial Program." Anniversary Supplement. 27 (September): 12–19.

Anderson, Ronald, and Anne Koval. 1994. *James McNeill Whistler: Beyond the Myth.* London: John Murray.

Arliss, George. 1927. *Up the Years from Broadway: An Autobiography.* New York: Blue Ribbon.

Armstrong, John Borden. 1966. "Portrait of a Lady: A Recollection of Whistler." *Art Journal* 25 (Spring): 250.

Armstrong, Thomas. 1912. *Thomas Armstrong, C. B.: A Memoir, 1832–1911.* Edited by L. M. Lamont. London: Martin Secker.

Arnold, Wilfred Niels. 1989. "Absinthe." *Scientific American* 260 (June): 112–17.

Atherton, Gertrude. 1932. *Adventures of a Novelist.* New York: Blue Ribbon.

Atkinson, Juliette. 2010. *Victorian Biography Reconsidered: A Study of Nineteenth-Century "Hidden" Lives.* Oxford: Oxford University Press.

Avery, Delos. 1946. "Whistler: The Man Who Loved to be Hated." *Chicago Tribune,* March 31, p. F1.

Bacher, Otto H. 1908. *With Whistler in Venice.* New York: Century.

Baetens, Jan Dirk, and Dries Lyna, eds. 2019. *Art Crossing Borders: The Internationalisation of the Art Market in the Age of Nation States, 1750–1914.* Leiden: Brill.

Baker, Phil. 2001. *The Dedalus Book of Absinthe.* Sawtry, UK: Dedalus.

Balderston, John Lloyd. 1916. "The Dusk of the Gods: A Conversation with George Moore." *Atlantic* 118 (August): 165–75.

Baldry, A. L. 1903. "James McNeill Whistler. His Art and Influence." *Studio* 20 (October): 237–45.

Barnes, Julian. 2015. *Keeping an Eye Open: Essays on Art.* London: Jonathan Cape.

Barnes, Martin, and Kate Best, eds. 2006. *Twilight: Photography in the Magic Hour.* London: Merrell.

Barringer, Tim, and Oliver Fairclough. 2014. *Pastures Green and Dark Satanic Mills: The British Passion for Landscape.* New York: American Federation of Arts.

Barry, Edward. 1954. "Three Great American Artists Come Home." *Chicago Tribune,* January 31, p. C8.

———. 1968. "The Intemperate Mr. Whistler." *Chicago Tribune,* January 14, p. G33.

Barter, Judith A., ed. 2016. *America After the Fall: Painting in the 1930s.* New Haven: Yale University Press.

Bassan, Maurice. 1970. *Hawthorne's Son: The Life and Literary Career of Julian Hawthorne.* Columbus: Ohio State University Press.

Baudelaire, Charles. 1956. *The Mirror of Art: Critical Studies by Charles Baudelaire.* Edited and translated by Jonathan Mayne. Garden City: Doubleday.

———. 1995. *The Painter of Modern Life and Other Essays.* Edited and translated by Jonathan Mayne. 2nd ed. London: Phaidon.

Baur, John I. H. 1951. "American Art After 25 Years: A Richer Diversity Than Ever Before." *Art Digest* 26 (November 1): 15–16.

Bell, Clive. 1914. *Art.* New York: Frederick A. Stokes.

Bendix, Deanna Marohn. 1995. *Diabolical Designs: Paintings, Interiors, and Exhibitions of James McNeill Whistler.* Washington, DC: Smithsonian Institution.

Bénédite, Léonce. 1905. "Artistes Contemporains: Whistler." *Gazette des Beaux-Arts* 33 (May): 401–10, (June): 496–511; 34 (August): 142–58, (September): 231–46.

Bennett, James O'Donnell. 1934. "Art Institute Has Big Exhibit of Whistleriana." *Chicago Tribune*, July 8, p. 4.

Benson, E. F. 1930. *As We Were: A Victorian Peep Show*. London: Longmans, Green.

Berger, Klaus. 1992. *Japonisme in Western Painting from Whistler to Matisse*. Translated by David Britt [1980]. Cambridge: Cambridge University Press.

Berry, Melissa. 2015. "Alphonse Legros and Masculine Identity Constructions in Victorian London. *Visual Culture in Britain* 16 (July): 187–99.

Bird, Paul. 1951. "The Artist as Reviewer." *Art Digest* 25 (April 15): 7.

Blanche, Jacques Émile. 1919. *Propos de Peintre De David à Degas*. Paris: Emile-Paul.

———. 1937. *Portraits of a Lifetime: The Late Victorian Era; The Edwardian Pageant, 1870–1914*. Translated and edited by Walter Clement. London: J. M. Dent and Sons.

Blathwayt, Raymond. 1917. *Through Life and Round the World: Being the Story of My Life*. London: George Allen & Unwin.

Bookman. 1912. "The Whistler Legend." 36 (October 1912): 109.

Borland, Maureen. 1995. *D. S. MacColl: Painter, Poet, Art Critic*. Harpenden, UK: Lennard.

Boswell, Peyton, Jr. 1945. "Museums of the Future." *Art Digest* 19 (February 15): 3.

———. 1949. "Why the Critic?" *Art Digest* 24 (December 1): 5.

Boughton, G. H. 1903. "A Few of the Various Whistlers I Have Known." *Studio* 30 (December): 208–18.

Bowdoin, W. G. 1901. *James McNeill Whistler: The Man and His Work*. London: M. F. Mansfield.

Bown, Matthew. 2020. "Keeping Up with the Gagosians." *Times Literary Supplement*, March 27, pp. 6–7.

Bradbury, Sue, ed. 2019. *The Boyce Papers: The Letters and Diaries of Joanna Boyce, Henry Wells and George Price Boyce*. 2 vols. Woodbridge, UK: Boydell.

Bradford, Gamaliel. 1921. "James McNeill Whistler." *Atlantic* 127 (April): 513–24.

Braudy, Leo. 2016. *Haunted: Ghosts, Witches, Vampires, Zombies, and Other Monsters of the Natural and Supernatural Worlds*. New Haven: Yale University Press.

Breuning, Margaret. 1947. "New York Evaluates Whistler After 37 Years." *Art Digest* 21 (April 15): 14.

Brimblecombe, Peter. 1987. *The Big Smoke: A History of Air Pollution in London Since Medieval Times*. London: Methuen.

Brinton, Christian. 1906. "Whistler from Within." *Munsey's* 36 (October): 3–20.

Brown, David B., Amy Concannon, James Finch, and Sam Smiles. 2021. *Turner's Modern World*. New York: Rizzoli Electa.

Brown, David B., Sam Smiles, and Amy Concannon, eds. 2014. *J. M. W Turner: Painting Set Free*. Los Angeles: Getty.

Brownell, William C. 1879. "Whistler in Painting and Etching." *Scribner's* 18 (August): 481–95.

Buchanan, David, and Kimberly Morse Jones, eds. 2021. *Elizabeth Robins Pennell: Critical Essays*. Edinburgh: University of Edinburgh Press.

Buel, Maria Torrilhom. 1913. "A Visit to Whistler." *Century* 86 (September): 694–96.

Burns, Sarah. 1996. *Inventing the Modern Artist: Art and Culture in Gilded Age America*. New Haven: Yale University Press.

Cadwallader, Jen. 2016. *Spirits and Spirituality in Victorian Fiction*. Basingstoke, UK: Palgrave.

Caffin, Charles H. 1910. "The Art of Eduard J. Steichen." *Camera Work* 30 (April): 23–49.

Callard, Eustace. 1897. "The Influence of Painters on Photography: Whistler, Monet and Manet." *Practical Photographer* 8 (April): 104–8.

Calloway, Stephen, and Lynn Federle Orr. 2011. *The Cult of Beauty: The Aesthetic Movement, 1860–1900*. London: V&A.

Calvert, Robyne Erica. 2015. "Manly Modes: Artistic Dress and the Styling of Masculine Identity." *Visual Culture in Britain* (July): 223–42.

Campbell, Colin, Merlin James, Patricia Reed, and Sanford Schwartz. 2004. *The Art of William Nicholson*. London: Royal Academy of Arts.

Cantalupo, Barbara. 2014. *Poe and the Visual Arts*. University Park: Penn State University Press.

Capps, Donald. 2013. *At Home in the World: A Study in Psychoanalysis, Religion, and Art*. Eugene, OR: Cascade.

Carlyle, Thomas. 1987. *Sartor Resartus*. Edited by Kerry McSweeny and Peter Sabor [1836]. Oxford: Oxford University Press.

Carr, Alice V. 1926. *Mrs. J. Comyns Carr's Reminiscences*. Edited by Eve Adam. London: Hutchinson.

Carr, Joseph Comyns. 1908. *Some Eminent Victorians: Personal Recollections in the World of Art and Letters*. London: Duckworth.

———. 1914. *Coasting Bohemia*. London: Macmillan.

Carrier, David. 1991. *Principles of Art History Writing*. University Park: Penn State University Press.

———. 1996. *High Art: Charles Baudelaire and the Origins of Modernist Painting*. University Park: Penn State University Press.

Cary, Elizabeth Luther. 1913. *The Works of James McNeill Whistler*. London: Longwood.

Casteras, Susan P., and Colleen Denny, eds. 1996. *The Grosvenor Gallery: A Palace of Art in Victorian England*. New Haven: Yale University Press.

Cecil, David, ed. 1970. *The Bodley Head Max Beerbohm*. London: Bodley Head.

Chaleyssin, Patrick. 1995. *James McNeill Whistler: The Strident Cry of the Butterfly*. Bournemouth, UK: Parkstone.

Chase, William M. 1910. "The Two Whistlers: Recollections of a Summer with the Great Etcher." *Century* 80 (June): 218–26.

Clarke, Meaghan. 2005. *Critical Voices: Women and Art Criticism in Britain, 1880–1905*. Aldershot, UK: Ashgate.

Cline, C. L., ed. 1970. *Letters of George Meredith*. 3 vols. Oxford: Oxford University Press.

Coburn, Alvin Langdon. 1966. *Alvin Langdon Coburn Photographer: An Autobiography*. Edited by Helmut and Alison Gernshiem. New York: Dover.

Coburn, F. W. 1988. *Whistler and His Birthplace*. Edited by Edith Williams Burger and Linda De Girolami Cheney. Tewksbury, MA: P&J Printing.

Colvin, Sidney. 1922. *Memories and Notes of Persons and Places, 1853–1912*. New York: Charles Scribner's Sons.

Conrad, Barnaby, III. 1988. *Absinthe: History in a Bottle*. San Francisco: Chronicle.

Conway, John Joseph. 1912. *Footprints of Famous Americans in Paris*. London: John Lane.

Cooper, Douglas. 1974. "On the Make in Paris and London." *New York Review of Books* 21 (August 8): 12–14.

Corbeau-Parsons, Caroline, ed. 2017. *Impressionists in London: French Artists in Exile, 1870–1914*. London: Tate.

Corbett, David Peters. 2004. *The World in Paint: Modern Art and Visibility in England, 1848–1914*. University Park: Penn State University Press.

Corbett, David Peters, and Lara Perry, eds. 2000. *English Art, 1860–1914: Modern Artists and Identity*. Rutgers: Rutgers University Press.

Cortissoz, Royal. 1913. *Art and Common Sense*. New York: Charles Scribner's Sons.

Corton, Christine L. 2015. *London Fog: The Biography*. Cambridge, MA: Belknap.

Cottom, Daniel. 2013. *International Bohemia: Scenes of Nineteenth-Century Life*. Philadelphia: University of Pennsylvania Press.

Cowan, John James. 1933. *From 1846 to 1932*. Edinburgh: Pillans & Wilson.

Cox, Devon. 2015. *The Street of Wonderful Possibilities: Whistler, Wilde and Sargent in Tite Street*. London: Frances Lincoln.

Cox, Kenyon. 1904a. "The Art of Whistler." *Architectural Record* 15 (May): 467–81.

———. 1904b. "Whistler and Absolute Painting." *Scribner's* 35 (May): 637–38.

Crawford, Earl S. 1903. "The Gentle Side of Mr. Whistler." *Reader* 2 (September): 387–90.

Critchley, E. M. R. 1987. *Hallucinations and Their Impact on Art*. Preston, UK: Carnegie.

Cruise, Colin. 2015. "From the Margins: The Male Bohemian Observer in

Mid-Victorian Culture." *Visual Culture in Britain* 16 (July): 137–53.
Cuneo, Cyrus. 1906. "Whistler's Academy of Painting." *Century* 73 (November): 19–28.
Current Literature. 1909. "The Real Whistler." 46: 49.
Curry, David Park. 2004. *James McNeill Whistler: Uneasy Pieces*. Richmond: Virginia Museum of Fine Arts.
———. 2023. *Whistler: Streetscapes, Urban Change*. Waterville, ME: Colby College Museum of Art.
Danto, Arthur C. 1997. *After the End of Art: Contemporary Art and the Pale of History*. Princeton: Princeton University Press.
———. 2003. *The Abuse of Beauty: Aesthetics and the Concept of Art*. Chicago: Open Court.
Davidson, Peter. 2015. *The Last of the Light: About Twilight*. London: Reaktion.
Davies, Gwen F. 1936. *Anonymous, 1871–1933*. London: John Murray.
Davis, John. 2003. "The End of the American Century: Current Scholarship on the Art of the United States." *Art Bulletin* 85 (September): 544–80.
Davis, Stuart. 1939. "Art and the Masses." *Art Digest* 14 (October 1): 13, 34.
De Kay, Charles. 1904. "In Honor of Whistler." *New York Times*, February 28, p. 5.
Denker, Eric. 1995. *In Pursuit of the Butterfly: Portraits of James McNeill Whistler*. Washington, DC: Smithsonian Institution.
Dolnick, Sam. 2009. "A Hall of Fame, Forgotten and Forlorn." *New York Times*, December 5, p. A17.
Dorment, Richard, and Margaret F. MacDonald. 1995. *James McNeill Whistler*. New York: Harry N. Abrams.
Dowling, Sam. 2007. *The Riverman*. London: Lulu.
Downes, William Howe. 1904. "Whistler and His Work." *National Magazine* 20 (April): 15–17.
Druick, Douglas, and Michael Hoog. 1983. *Fantin-Latour*. Ottawa: National Gallery of Canada.
Dufwa, Jacques. 1981. *Winds from the East: A Study in the Art of Manet, Degas, Monet and Whistler, 1856–86*. Stockholm: Almqvist & Wiksell.
Du Maurier, Daphne, ed. 1952. *The Young George Du Maurier: A Selection of His Letters, 1860–67*. Garden City: Doubleday.
Duret, Theodore. 1904. *Historie de J. McN. Whistler et son oeuvre*. Paris: H. Floury.
———. 1917. *Whistler*. Translated by Frank Rutter. Philadelphia: J. B. Lippincott.
Eddy, Arthur Jerome. 1903. *Recollections and Impressions of James A. McNeill Whistler*. Philadelphia: J. B. Lippincott.
Edinburgh Review. 1905. "Works of James McNeill Whistler." 201 (April): 445–67.
Elam, Caroline. 1994. "Whistler in Retrospect." *Burlington Magazine* 136 (October): 663.
Emerson, Peter Henry. 1899. *Naturalistic Photography for Students of Art*. 3rd ed. London: Dawbarn & Ward.
Empson, William. 1966 [1930]. *Seven Types of Ambiguity*. New York: New Directions.
Fairman, Charles E. 1904. "Whistler in Washington." *The Lamp* 29 (November): 306–8.
Faison, S. Lane. 1954. "Art Criticism Today." *Art Digest* 28 (March 1): 5.
Farr, Dennis. 1984. *English Art, 1870–1940*. Oxford: Oxford University Press.
Fattal, Laura Felleman, and Carlos Salus, eds. 2004. *Out of Context: American Artists Abroad*. New York: Praeger.
Feaver, William. 1994. "Float Like a Butterfly, Sting Like a Bee." *Observer*, October 16, p. C12.
Feldman, Jessica R. 1993. *Gender on the Divide: The Dandy in Modernist Literature*. Ithaca: Cornell University Press.
Fenollsa, Ernest F. 1903. "The Place in History of Mr. Whistler's Art." *Lotus* 1 (December): 14–17.
Fillin-Yeh, Susan, ed. 2001. *Dandies: Fashion and Finesse in Art and Culture*. New York: New York University Press.
Fine, Ruth, ed. 1987. *James McNeill Whistler: A Reexamination*. Washington, DC: National Gallery of Art.
Fitzgibbon, Constantine. 1958. *The Winter of the Bombs: The Story of the Blitz of London*. New York: Norton.

Fleming, Gordon H. 1978. *The Young Whistler, 1834–66*. London: George Allen & Unwin.

———. 1991. *James Abbott McNeill Whistler: A Life*. Adlestrop, UK: Windrush.

Fletcher, Pamela, and Anne Helmreich, eds. 2011. *The Rise of the Modern Art Market in London, 1850–1939*. Manchester: Manchester University Press.

Flint, Kate. 2000. *The Victorians and Visual Imagination*. Cambridge: Cambridge University Press.

Frankfurter, Alfred. 1961. "Clio Before the Easel." *Art News* 60 (November): 29.

Fraser, Hilary. 2014. *Women Writing Art History in the Nineteenth Century*. Cambridge: Cambridge University Press.

Fraser, Robert. 1994. *Proust and the Victorians*. New York: St. Martin's.

Freeman, Nicholas. 2007. *Concerning the City: London, Literature, and Art, 1870–1914*. Oxford: Oxford University Press.

Furniss, Harry. 1919. *My Bohemian Days*. London: Hurst & Blackett.

Furr, Christian. 2024. "An Artist's Perspective on Whistler and Process." *Whistler Society Newsletter* 48 (May): 2–3.

Gallatin, Albert E. 1913. *Portraits and Caricatures of James McNeill Whistler: An Iconography*. London: John Lane.

Gantes, Amalia Cross, and Julieta Ogaz Sotomayor. 2019. "James McNeill Whistler. De Valparaíso a Venecia: Un Viaje de Ida y Vuelta." *Revista 180* 44 (December): 29–38.

Gardiner, Alexander. 1930. *Canfield: The True Story of the Greatest Gambler*. Garden City: Doubleday.

Gaunt, William. 1945. *The Aesthetic Adventure*. New York: Harcourt, Brace.

Gay, Walter. 1930. *Memoirs of Walter Gay*. New York: Privately Printed.

Genauer, Emily. 1949. "Have Critics Flunked the Test of Time?" *Art Digest* 24 (December 1): 11.

Getscher, Robert H., and Paul G. Marks. 1986. *James McNeill Whistler and John Singer Sargent: Two Annotated Bibliographies*. New York: Garland.

Gibson, Eric. 2022. "When Connoisseurs Yield to Commissars." *Wall Street Journal*, September 3–4, p. A11.

Glazer, Lee, Emily Jacobson, Blythe McCarthy, and Katherine Roeder. 2019. *Whistler in Watercolors: Lovely Little Games*. Washington, DC: Freer Gallery.

Glazer, Lee, Margaret F. MacDonald, Linda Merrill, and Nigel Thorp, eds. 2008. *James McNeill Whistler in Context*. Washington, DC: Smithsonian Institution.

Glazer, Lee, and Linda Merrill, eds. 2013. *Palaces of Art: Whistler and the Art Worlds of Aestheticism*. Washington, DC: Smithsonian Institution.

Glenn, Isa Urquhart. 1923. "'Cousin Butterfly': Whistler and a Child." *Century* 106 (June): 193–204.

Goebel, Catherine Carter. 1988. "Arrangement in Black and White: The Making of a Whistler Legend." PhD diss., Northwestern University.

Goldberg, Vicki, ed. 1981. *Photography in Print: Writings from 1816 to the Present*. Albuquerque: University of New Mexico Press.

Goldstein, Malcolm. 2000. *Landscape with Figures: A History of Art Dealing in the United States*. Oxford: Oxford University Press.

Gombrich, E. H. 1952. *The Story of Art*. New York: Phaidon.

———. 1995. *The Story of Art*. New York: Phaidon.

Goodrich, Lloyd. 1950. "The Artist and the Museum." *Art Digest* 24 (September 15): 5–6, 20.

Gopnik, Adam. 1995. "Whistler in the Dark." *New Yorker* 71 (July 19): 68–73.

———. 2017. *At the Strangers' Gate: Arrivals in New York*. New York: Knopf.

Graves, Algernon. 1903. "James Abbott McNeill Whistler." *Printseller* 1 (August): 340–45.

Greenwold, Diane Seave. 2019. "Used Cars and Canvases: Information Economics, Art History, and the Art Market." *American Art* 33 (Fall): 5–9.

Gregory, Horace. 1959. *The World of James McNeill Whistler*. New York: Thomas Nelson & Sons.

Grieve, Alastair. 2000. *Whistler's Venice*. New Haven: Yale University Press.

Guardian. 1903. "James M'Neill Whistler." July 18, p. 7.

Hadley, Frank A. 1903. "Whistler, The Man as Told in Anecdote." *Brush and Pencil* 12 (August): 334–59.

Hall, James. 1994. "Less, Less, and Finally Nothing at All." *Observer*, October 18, A6.

Hallé, C. E. 1909. *Notes from a Painter's Life, Including the Founding of Two Galleries*. London: John Murray.

Hannoosh, Michéle. 2006. "Theophile Silvestre's *Historie des artistis vivants*: Art Criticism and Photography." *Art Bulletin* 88 (December): 729–31.

Harker, Margaret. 1979. *The Linked Ring: The Secession Movement in Photography in Britain, 1892–1910*. London: William Heinemann.

Harris, Frank. 1920. *Contemporary Portraits*. First Series. New York: Brentano.

Hartmann, Sadakichi [Sidney Allen]. 1910. *The Whistler Book*. New York: L. C. Page.

Hartrick, Archibald S. 1939. *A Painter's Pilgrimage Through Fifty Years*. Cambridge: Cambridge University Press.

Havemeyer, Louisine W. 1961. *Sixteen to Sixty: Memoirs of a Collector*. New York: Privately Printed.

Haworth-Booth, Mark, ed. 1984. *The Golden Age of British Photography, 1839–1900*. Millerton, NY: Aperture.

———. 2010. *Photographer of Modern Life: Camille Silvey*. Los Angeles: Getty.

Hawthorne, Julian. 1899. "A Champion of Art." *Independent* 52 (November 2): 2956–60.

———. 1928. *Shapes That Pass: Memories of Old Days*. London: Houghton Mifflin.

———. 1934. "Whistler as a Friend Remembers Him." *New York Times Magazine*, July 15, pp. 7, 14.

Hawthorne, Mrs. Julian. 1881. "Mr. Whistler's New Portraits." *Harper's Bazar* 14 (October 15): 658–59.

Haxthausen, Charles W., ed. 2002. *Two Art Histories: The Museum and the University*. Williamstown, MA: Clark Art Institute.

H. B. 1887. "London Letter." *The Critic* 10 (January 8): 18.

Heijbroek, J. F., and Margaret F. MacDonald. 2000. *Whistler and Holland*. Amsterdam: Rijksmuseum.

Hellman, George S. 1927. *Lanes of Memory*. New York: Knopf.

Helmreich, Anne. 2020. "The Art Market as a System: Florence Levy's Statistics." *American Art* 34 (Fall): 92–111.

Hilton, Tim. 2000. *John Ruskin: The Later Years*. New Haven: Yale University Press.

Hindson, Catherine. 2016. *London's West End Actresses and the Origins of Celebrity Charity, 1880–1920*. Ames: Iowa State University Press.

Hine, Samuel. 2018. "The New Dandies." *GQ* 88 (November): 94–99.

Holden, Donald. 1969. *Whistler Landscapes and Seascapes*. New York: Watson-Guptill.

Holmes, Charles J. 1903. *Pictures and Picture Collecting*. London: Anthony Treherney.

———. 1909. "Whistler and Modern Painting." *Burlington Magazine* 14 (January): 204–6.

———. 1936. *Self and Partners (Mostly Self): Being the Reminiscences of C. J. Holmes*. New York: Macmillan.

Holmes, Richard. 2008. *The Age of Wonder: How the Romantic Generation Discovered the Beauty and Horror of Science*. New York: Pantheon.

Hook, Philip. 2021. *Art of the Extreme, 1905–1914*. London: Profile.

Hopkins, Claudia, and Iain Boyd Whyte, eds. 2021. *Hot Art, Cold War: Western and European Writing on American Art, 1945–1990*. New York: Routledge.

Hopkins, David. 2000. *After Modern Art, 1945–2000*. Oxford: Oxford University Press.

Hough, Graham. 1949. *The Last Romantics*. London: Duckworth.

Housman, Laurence. 1908. "The Whistler Legend." *Guardian*, November 3, p. 5.

———. 1936. *The Unexpected Years*. New York: Bobbs-Merrill.

Howes, David. 2024. *Sensorium: Contextualizing the Sense and Cognition in History and Across Cultures*. Cambridge: Cambridge University Press.

Hughes, Alicia. 2023. "A 'Scheme' of My 'Protection': Rosalind Birnie Philip (1873–1958) and the History of the James McNeill Whistler and Beatrix Whistler Collection at the University of Glasgow." *Art Antiquity and Law* 29 (April): 9–44.

Hughes, Robert. 1980. *Shock of the New*. New York: Knopf.

———. 1991. *Nothing If Not Critical: Selected Essays on Art and Artists*. New York: Knopf.

———. 1997. *American Visions: The Epic History of Art in America*. New York: Knopf.

Hunt, John Dixon. 1998. *The Wider Sea: A Life of John Ruskin*. London: Phoenix.

Ionides, Luke. 1996 [1925]. *Memories*. Edited by Julia Ionides. Paris: Herbert Clarke.

Jackson, Louise W. 1900. "Mr. Whistler as a Teacher." *Brush and Pencil* 6 (June): 141–43.

Jacobi, Carol, and Hope Kingsley. 2016. *Painting with Light: Art and Photography from the Pre-Raphaelites to the Modern Age*. London: Tate.

Jacomb-Hood, George Percy. 1925. *With Brush and Pencil*. London: John Murray.

James, Henry. 1877. "London at Midsummer." *Lippincott's* 20 (November): 603–11.

———. 1888. "London." *Century* 37 (December): 219–39.

Janes, Dominic. 2016. *Oscar Wilde Prefigured: Queer Fashioning and British Caricature, 1750–1900*. Chicago: University of Chicago Press.

———. 2022. *British Dandies: Engendering Scandal and Fashioning a Nation*. Oxford: Oxford University Press.

Januszczak, Waldemar. 2022. "Witness Cezanne's Genius." *Sunday Times: Culture*, October 9, pp. 14–15.

Jensen, Robert. 1994. *Marketing Modernism in Fin-de-Siècle Europe*. Princeton: Princeton University Press.

Jewett, Eleanor. 1954. "Mementos of Whistler Exhibit." *Chicago Tribune*, February 7, p. F2.

Johnson, Paul. 2003. *Art: A New History*. New York: HarperCollins.

Johnson, Ron. 1981. "Whistler's Musical Modes: Numinous Nocturnes." *Arts Magazine* 55 (April): 71–75.

Jones, Jonathan. 2018. *Sensations: The Story of British Art from Hogarth to Banksy*. London: Laurence King.

Jones, Kimberly. 2015. *Elizabeth Robins Pennell: Nineteenth-Century Pioneer of Modern Art Criticism*. Farnham, UK: Ashgate.

Jopling, Louise. 1925. *Twenty Years of My Life, 1867 to 1887*. London: John Lane.

Kalba, Laura Anne. 2017. *Color in the Age of Impressionism: Commerce, Technology, and Art*. University Park: Penn State University Press.

Kammen, Michael G. 2006. *Visual Shock: A History of Art Controversies in American Culture*. New York: Knopf.

Karpeles, Eric. 2008. *Paintings in Proust: A Visual Companion to "In Search of Lost Time."* London: Thames & Hudson.

Kauffman, Nelson Blaine. 1975. "The Aesthetic of the Veil: Conceptual Correspondences in the Nocturnes of Whistler and Debussy." PhD diss., Ohio University.

Kelly, Sarah Elizabeth. 2010. "Camera's Lens and Mind's Eye: Whistler and the Science of Art." PhD diss., Columbia University.

Kennedy, Edward G. 1910. *Catalogue of Etchings by J. McN. Whistler*. London: Wunderlich.

Keppel, Frederick. 1904a. *The Gentle Art of Resenting Injuries*. New York: Keppel.

———. 1904b. "One Day with Whistler." *Reader* 3 (January): 145–51.

———. 1907. "Whistler as an Etcher." *Outlook* 85 (April 27): 962–77.

Key, John Ross. 1908. "Recollections of Whistler." *Century* 75 (April): 928–32.

Killeen, Jarlath. 2009. *History of the Gothic: Gothic Literature, 1825–1914*. Cardiff: University of Wales Press.

Kilmartin, Terence, compl. 1983. *A Reader's Guide to "Remembrance of Things Past."* New York: Random House.

Kinsella, Eileen. 2006. "Global Warming." *Art News* 105 (May): 136–42.

Kirkham, Pat, ed. 1996. *The Gendered Object*. Manchester: University of Manchester Press.

Kobbé, Gustav. 1898. "Whistler in the U.S. Coast Survey." *Chap Book* 8 (May): 479–80.

Kolb, Philip, ed. 1989. *Marcel Proust: Selected Letters*. Vol. 2, *1904–1909*. Translated by Terence Kilmartin. Oxford: Oxford University Press.

Kuspit, Donald. 1984. *The Critic as Artist: The Internationality of Art*. Ann Arbor: University of Michigan Press.

———. 2004. *The End of Art*. Cambridge: Cambridge University Press.

Lang, Berel, ed. 1984. *The Death of Art*. New York: Haven Publications.

Langtry, Lillie. 1925. *The Days I Knew*. London: Hutchinson.

Larkin, Oliver. 1966. *Art and Life in America*. Rev. ed. New York: Holt, Rinehart and Winston.

Larman, Alexander. 2019. "Against Nature: Dandyism, Decadence and Debauchery." *Chap* 101 (Autumn): 134–39.

Laver, James. 1951. *Whistler*. 2nd ed. London: White Lion.

———. 1968. *Dandies*. London: Weidenfeld and Nicolson.

Lavery, Grace. 2019. *Quaint, Exquisite: Victorian Aesthetics and the Idea of Japan*. Princeton: Princeton University Press.

Lavery, John. 1940. *The Life of a Painter*. London: Cassell.

Lawton, Thomas, and Linda Merrill. 1993. *Freer: A Legacy of Art*. Washington, DC: Freer Gallery.

Lazelle, H. H. 1915. "Whistler at West Point." *Century* 90 (September): 710.

Leask, Margaret. 2012. *Lena Ashwell*. Hertfordshire: University of Hertfordshire Press.

Levine, Gary, Robert R. Preato, and Francine Tyler. 1983. *La Femme: The Influence of Whistler and Japanese Print Masters on American Art, 1880–1917*. New York: Grand Central Art Galleries.

Lindsey, Vachel. 1970 [1922]. *The Art of the Moving Pictures*. New York: Liveright.

Lochnan, Katherine A. 1984. *The Etchings of James McNeill Whistler*. New Haven: Yale University Press.

———, ed. 2004. *Turner, Whistler, Monet: Impressionist Visions*. London: Tate.

Ludovici, Albert. 1906a. "The Whistlerian Dynasty at Suffolk Street." *Art Journal* 68 (July): 193–95.

———. 1906b. "The Whistlerian Dynasty at Suffolk Street—II." *Art Journal* 68 (August): 237–39.

———. 1926. *An Artist's Life in London and Paris, 1870–1925*. London: Fisher Unwin.

MacColl, D. S. 1906. "The Windsor Whistlers." *Saturday Review* 101 (April 28): 517–19.

———. 1931. *Confessions of a Keeper and Other Papers*. London: Alexander Machose.

MacDonald, Margaret F. 1988. "Whistler's Lithographs." *Print Quarterly* 5 (March): 20–55.

———. 1995. *James McNeill Whistler: Drawings, Pastels and Watercolours: A Catalogue Raisonné*. New Haven: Yale University Press.

———. 2001. *Palaces in the Night: Whistler in Venice*. Berkeley: University of California Press.

———. 2015. "James McNeill Whistler: An Artist on Artists." *Visual Culture in Britain* 16 (July): 200–22.

MacDonald, Margaret F., Charles Brock, Patricia de Montfort, Joanna Dunn, Grischka Petri, Aileen Ribeiro, and Joyce H. Townsend. 2020. *The Woman in White: Joanna Hiffernan and James McNeill Whistler*. New Haven: Yale University Press.

MacDonald, Margaret F., Susan Grace Galassi, Aileen Ribeiro, and Patricia de Montfort. 2003. *Whistler, Women, and Fashion*. New Haven: Yale University Press.

Malraux, André. 1949–50. *The Psychology of Art*. 3 vols. New York: Doubleday.

Mansfield, Howard. 1909. *A Descriptive Catalogue of the Etchings and Dry-Points of James Abbott McNeill Whistler*. Chicago: Caxton Club.

Manthorne, Katherine Emma. 1989. *Tropical Renaissance: North American Artists Exploring Latin America, 1839–1879*. Washington, DC: Smithsonian Institution.

Marks, Paul G., ed. 1986. *The Elusive Butterfly: An Anthology of Poetic Impressions of James A. McNeill Whistler and His Works*. Somerville, MA: Firefly.

Martin, T. Wood. 1908. *Whistler*. New York: F. A. Stokes.

Mathews, Nancy Mowell. 1994. *Mary Cassatt: A Life*. New Haven: Yale University Press.

Mauclair, Camille [Séverin Faust]. 1905. *De Watteau á Whistler*. Paris: Bibliothéque-Charpentier.

Mazaroff, Stanley. 2018. *A Paris Life, A Baltimore Treasure: The Remarkable Lives of George A. Lucas and His Art Collection*. Baltimore: Johns Hopkins University Press.

McCann, Justin, ed. 2015. *Whistler and the World*. Waterville, ME: Colby College Museum of Art.

McCauley, Elizabeth Anne, Alan Chong, Rosella Mamoli Zorzi, and Richard Lingner. 2004. *Gondola Days: Isabella Stewart Gardner and the Palazzo Barbaro Circle*. Boston: Gardner Museum.

McConkey, Kenneth. 2006. *The New English: A History of the New English Art Club*. London: Royal Academy of Arts.

McMullen, Roy. 1973. *Victorian Outsider: A Biography of J. A. M. Whistler*. New York: Dutton.

McNay, Michel. 1971. "Art to Invest In." *Guardian*, December 15, p. 16.

McWilliams, Neil, and Veronica Sekules, eds. 1986. *Life and Landscape: P. H. Emerson, Art and Photography in East Anglia, 1885–1900*. Norwich: University of East Anglia.

Meacock, Joanna. 2007. "Whistler and Scriptural Persuasion." *British Art Journal* 8 (Winter): 24–30.

Meier-Graefe, Julius. 1908. *Modern Art, Being a Contribution to a New System of Aesthetics*. 2 vols. Translated by Florence Simmonds and George W. Chrystal. London: William Heinemann.

Meinel, Aden, and Marjorie Meinel. 1983. *Sunsets, Twilights, and Evening Skies*. Cambridge: Cambridge University Press.

Menpes, Mortimer. 1904. *Whistler As I Knew Him*. London: Adam and Charles Black.

Merrill, Linda. 1992. *A Pot of Paint: Aesthetics on Trial in Whistler v Ruskin*. Washington, DC: Smithsonian Institution.

———. 1998. *The Peacock Room: A Cultural Biography*. New Haven: Yale University Press.

Merrill, Linda, ed. 2003. *After Whistler: The Artist and His Influence on American Painting*. New Haven: Yale University Press.

Meyer-Dinkgräfe, Daniel. 2005. *Biographical Plays about Famous Artists*. Cambridge: Cambridge University Press.

Meyers, Jeffrey. 1975. *Painting and the Novel*. Manchester: University of Manchester Press.

Meynell, Alice. 1898. *London Impressions*. London: Archibald Constable.

Miller, Alex. 1941a and 1941b. "Art Criticism from Plato to Whistler." *Art and Reason* 7 (May): 9–10, (June): 6.

Mills, Cynthia. 2002. "Textbooks for a New Generation." *American Art* 16 (Summer): 2–15.

Moers, Ellen. 1978. *The Dandy: Brummell to Beerbohm*. Reprint. Lincoln: University of Nebraska Press.

Moffa, Lenora R. 1991. "The Paintings of James McNeill Whistler, 1859–1777: A Technique of Mutability." PhD diss., Emory University.

Montfort, Patricia de, and Clare A. P. Willsdon. 2018. *Whistler and Nature*. London: Mellon Centre.

Moore, George. 1926. *Confessions of a Young Man*. Rev. ed. London: William Heinemann.

Morris, Harrison S. 1930. *Confessions in Art*. New York: Sears.

Muhlstein, Anka. 2017. *The Pen and the Brush: How Passion for Art Shaped Nineteenth-Century French Novels*. Translated by Adriana Hunter. New York. Other Press.

Mullins, Charlotte. 2022. *A Little History of Art*. New Haven: Yale University Press.

Murphy, Paul Thomas. 2023. *Falling Rocket: James Whistler, John Ruskin, and the Battle for Modern Art*. New York: Pegasus.

Naylor, Maria. 1975. *Selected Etchings of James McNeill Whistler*. New York: Dover.

Neal, Molly Keith. 1980. "James McNeill Whistler: The Changing Image of the Artist in Periodical Literature—1903 to 1979." MA thesis, University of Louisville.

Newton, Eric. 1960."Butterfly and Prophet." *Guardian*, September 1, p. 7.

Newton, Joy, and Margaret F. MacDonald. 1978. "Rodin: The Whistler Monument." *Gazette de Beaux-Arts*, ser. 6, v. 92 (December): 221–32.

Nicholson, Harold. 1961. "The Butterfly on the Wheel." *Observer*, December 3, p. 28.

Nisbet, James. 2017. "Environmental Abstraction and the Polluted Image." *American Art* (Spring): 114–31.

Nordström, Alison, Luca Ackerman, Ryuchi Kaneko, Gail Newton, and David Wooters. 2011. *Truth Beauty: Pictorialism and Photography as Art, 1845–1945*. Vancouver: Douglas & McIntyre.

Ono, Ayako. 2003. *Japonisme in Britain: Whistler, Menpes, Henry Hornel and Nineteenth-Century Japan*. London: Routledge.

———. 2023. *Whistler and Artistic Exchange between Japan and the West: After Japonisme in Britain*. London: Routledge.

———. 2024. "The Crane Room Inspired by the Peacock Room." *Ten O'Clock* 5 (December): 97–103.

Otago Daily Times [New Zealand]. 1938. "Henry Irving Centenary." June 18, p. 32.

P. A. 1904. "What Modern Pictures are Worth Collecting?" *Burlington Magazine* 6 (November): 109.

Pall Mall Gazette. 1883. "Mr. Whistler's Latest Arrangement." February 19, p. 4.

Parry, James. 1992. "'Oscar'—The Musical." *The Wildean* 1 (July): 6–7.

Pearce, Edward. 1994. "Critical Faculties and Artistic Impulses." *Guardian*, December 24, p. 23.

Pearsall, Ronald. 1972. *The Table-Rappers: The Victorians and the Occult*. Thrupp-Stroud, UK: Sutton.

Pearson, Hesketh. 1926. *The Whispering Gallery*. New York: Boni & Liveright.

———. 1952. *The Man Whistler*. London: Methuen.

Pearson, Ralph M. 1945. "What Is Modern Art?" *Art Digest* 19 (February 15): 22.

———. 1947. "Name Calling in Art." *Art Digest* 21 (August 1): 28.

Peers, Alexandra. 2006. "Canon Fodder." *Art News* 105 (February): 124–27.

Pennell, Elizabeth R. 1906. *Charles Godfrey Leland: A Biography*. 2 vols. New York: Houghton, Mifflin.

———. 1928. *The Art of Whistler*. New York: Modern Library.

———. 1929. *Life and Letters of Joseph Pennell*. 2 vols. Boston: Little, Brown.

———. 1930. *Whistler the Friend*. Philadelphia: J. B. Lippincott.

Pennell, Joseph. 1912. "The Triumph of Whistler." *Bookman* 36 (October): 158–64.

Pennell, Joseph, and Elizabeth R. 1921. "The Pennell Whistleriana in the Library of Congress." *American Magazine of Art* 12 (September): 293–300.

Pennington, Harper. 1902. "Artist Life in Venice." *Century* 64 (October): 835–42.

———. 1904. "James A. McNeill Whistler." *International Quarterly* 10 (October): 156–64.

———. 1910. "The Whistler I Knew." *Metropolitan Magazine* 31 (March): 769–76.

Petri, Grischka. 2011. *Arrangement in Business: The Art Markets and the Career of James McNeill Whistler*. Hildesheim: Geog Olms Verlag.

Pickvance, Ronald. 1963. "*L'Absinthe* in England." *Apollo* 77 (May): 395–98.

Pocock, Tom. 1970. *Chelsea Reach: The Brutal Friendship of Whistler and Walter Greaves*. London: Hodder and Stoughton.

Pollack, Griselda. 2014. "Whither Art History?" *Art Bulletin* 96 (March): 9–23.

Pound, Ezra. 1912. "To Whistler, American." *Poetry Magazine* 1 (October): 7.

Preston, Kerrison, ed. 1953. *Letters from Graham Robertson*. London: Hamish Hamilton.

Prettejohn, Elizabeth. 1996. "Locked in the Myth." *Art History* 19 (June): 301–7.

———. 2007. *Art for Art's Sake: Aestheticism in Victorian Painting*. New Haven: Yale University Press.

Preziosi, Donald. 1989. *Rethinking Art History: Meditations on a Coy Science*. New Haven: Yale University Press.

Price, Julius M. 1913. *My Bohemian Days in Paris*. London: T. Werner Laurie.

Prideaux, Tom. 1970. *The World of Whistler, 1843–1903*. New York: Time-Life.

Prinsep, Val. 1903. "James A. McNeill Whistler: 1834–1903. Personal

Recollections." *Magazine of Art*, 1 n.s. (October): 577–80.
Prodger, Phillip, Patrick Daum, and Francis Ribemont. 2006. *Impressionist Camera: Pictorial Photography in Europe, 1888–1918*. London: Merrell.
Punch. 1878. "Music at Home." 74 (March 30): 134.
Pyne, Kathleen. 1996a. *Art and the Higher Life: Painting and Evolutionary Thought in Late Nineteenth-Century America*. Austin: University of Texas Press.
———. 1996b. "Portrait of a Collector as an Agnostic: Charles Lang Freer and Connoisseurship." *Art Bulletin* 78 (March): 75–97.
Quilter, Mary, ed. 1909. *Opinions on Men, Women, and Things*. London: Swan Sonnenschein.
Randall, Lillian M. C., ed. 1979. *Diary of George A. Lucas: An American Art Agent in Paris, 1857–1909*. 2 vols. Princeton: Princeton University Press.
Redesdale, Lord [Algernon Bertram Freeman-Mitford]. 1916. *Memories*. 2 vols. New York: Dutton.
Reed, Christopher, ed. 1996. *A Roger Fry Reader*. Chicago: University of Chicago Press.
Régnier, Henri. 1907. *La Peur de l'Amour*. Paris: Société du Mercure de France.
Reid, Natalie Sarah. 2007. "Purchasing, Praising and Promoting Whistler's Etchings: The American Collector Howard Mansfield (1849–1938)." MA thesis, University of Glasgow.
Ribeiro, Aileen. 2017. *Clothing Art: The Visual Culture of Fashion, 1600–1914*. New Haven: Yale University Press.
Rideing, William H. 1912. *Many Celebrities and a Few Others: A Bundle of Reminiscences*. London: Eveleigh Nash.
Roberts, Jane. 2012. *Jacques-Émile Blanche*. Paris: Gourcuff Gradenigo.
Roberts, Pamela Glasson. 2014. *Alvin Langdon Coburn*. Madrid: Fundación Mapfre.
Robertson, Walford Graham. 1931. *Life Was Worth Living: The Reminiscences of W. Graham Robertson*. New York: Harper Brothers.
Robins, Anna Gruetzner, ed. 2003. *Walter Sickert: The Complete Writings on Art*. Oxford: Oxford University Press.
———. 2007. *A Fragile Modernism: Whistler and his Impressionist Followers*. New Haven: Yale University Press.
Robinson, Alan. 1985. *Symbol to Vortex: Poetry, Painting, and Ideas, 1885–1914*. New York: St. Martin's.
———. 2004. *Imagining London, 1770–1900*. Basingstoke, UK: Palgrave.
Robinson, James, Florence Tyler, and Darren Waterston. 2020. *Darren Waterston's Filthy Lucre: Whistler's Peacock Room Reimagined*. London: V&A.
Rodd, James Rennell. 1922. *Social and Diplomatic Memories, 1884–1893*. London: Edward Arnold.
Rodgers, Nigel. 2012. *The Dandy: Peacock or Enigma?* London: Bene Factum.
Rorimer, Anne. 2001. *New Art in the 60s and 70s: Redefining Reality*. London: Thames and Hudson.
Rose, F. Clifford, ed. 2006. *The Neurobiology of Painting*. San Diego: Academic Press.
Rothenstein, William. 1932. *Men and Memories: A History of the Arts, 1872–1922*. 2 vols. New York: Tudor.
Ruskin, John. 1884a. *Modern Painters*. 5 vols. New York: John Wiley.
———. 1884b. *The Storm-Cloud of the Nineteenth Century*. New York: John Wiley.
Rutter, Frank. 1911. *James McNeill Whistler: An Estimate and a Biography*. New York: Mitchell Kennerley.
———. 1927. *Since I Was Twenty-Five*. London: Constable.
Saarinen, Aline B. 1954. "Profile of Whistler's Mother." *New York Times*, February 14, p. SM 13.
Sandberg, John. 1964. "Japonisme and Whistler." *Burlington Magazine* 106 (November): 500–7.
———. 1968. "Whistler Studies." *Art Bulletin* 50 (March): 59–64.
Scharf, Aaron. 1974. *Art and Photography*. Rev. ed. Harmondsworth, UK: Penguin.
Seitz, Don C. 1910. *Writings By and About James Abbott McNeill Whistler: A Bibliography*. Edinburgh: Otto Schulze.
Shannon, Brent. 2006. *The Cut of His Coat: Men, Dress, and Consumer Culture in Britain, 1860–1914*. Athens: Ohio University Press.
Shaw, Edith. 1968. "Four Years with Whistler." *Apollo* 87 (March): 198–201.

Sheehan, Tanya. 2022. "Where to Begin: Marking Race in Surveys of American Art." *American Art* 36 (Fall): 33–37.

Shenker, Israel. 1984. "Whistler's Art Came First; Enemies Were the Next in Line." *Smithsonian* 15 (April): 56–65.

Sherard, Robert Harborough. 1937. *Bernard Shaw, Frank Harris and Oscar Wilde.* New York: Greystone.

Shirland, Jonathan. 2007. "'A Singularity of Appearance Counts Doubly in a Democracy of Clothes': Whistler, Fancy Dress and the Camping of Artists' Dress in the Late Nineteenth Century." *Visual Culture in Britain* 8 (June): 15–35.

———. 2011. "'Embryonic Phantoms': Materiality, Marginality and Modernity in Whistler's Black Portraits." *Art History* 34 (February): 80–101.

Sickert, Bernhard. 1905. "The Whistler Exhibition." *Burlington Magazine* 6 (March): 430–39.

———. 1908. *Whistler.* London: Duckworth.

Sickert, Walter. 1908. "The New Life of Whistler." *Fortnightly Review,* 84 n.s. (December): 1017–28.

Silverman, Kenneth. 1991. *Edgar A. Poe: Mournful and Never-Ending Remembrance.* New York: HarperCollins.

Simmons, Edward. 1922. *From Seven to Seventy: Memories of a Painter and a Yankee.* New York: Harper Brothers.

Simpson, Marc, Wanda M. Corn, Cody Hartley, Michael J. Lewis, Leo G. Mazow, and Joyce Hill Stoner. 2008. *Like Breath on Glass: Whistler, Inness, and the Art of Painting Softly.* Williamstown, MA: Clark Art Institute.

Singer, Hans Wolfgang. 1905. *James McNeill Whistler.* New York: Charles Scribner's Sons.

Singletary, Suzanne M. 2017. *James McNeill Whistler and France: A Dialogue in Paint, Poetry, and Music.* London: Routledge.

Smajić, Srdjan. 2010. *Ghost Seers, Detectives, and Spiritualism: Theories of Vision in Victorian Literature and Science.* Cambridge: Cambridge University Press.

Smalley, George M. 1903. "James McNeill Whistler." *Times Literary Supplement,* August 7, p. 239.

———. 1912. *Anglo-American Memories.* New York: Putnam's Sons.

Smalley, George W., and Thomas Hay Sweet Escott. 1885. *Society in London by a Foreign Resident.* 3rd ed. London: Chatto & Windus.

Smith, Logan Pearsall. 1939. *Unforgotten Years.* Boston: Little, Brown.

Sobel, Robert. 1974. *The Entrepreneurs: Explorations within the American Business Tradition.* New York: Houghton Mifflin Harcourt.

Sotomayor, Julieta Ogaz. 2024. "Whistler in Valparaíso." *Ten O'Clock* 5 (December): 76–85.

Spalding, Frances. 1994. *Whistler.* Rev. ed. London: Phaidon.

Spencer, Robin, ed. 1989. *Whistler: A Retrospective.* New York: Wing Books.

Spender, Stephen. 1960. "Three Painters Haunted by Greatness." *Listener* 64 (September 8): 77–78.

Spielmann, Marion H. A. 1934. "Whistler's Wit." *The Times,* July 14, p. 17.

———. 1903a. "James A. McNeill Whistler: 1834–1903. The Man and the Artist." *Magazine of Art,* 1 n.s. (October): 582–84.

———. 1903b. "James A. McNeill Whistler: 1834–1903. The Man and the Artist." *Magazine of Art,* 2 n.s. (November): 8–16.

Starr, Sidney. 1908. "Personal Recollections of Whistler." *Atlantic* 101 (August): 528–37.

Stephenson, Andrew. 2007. "Precarious Poses: The Problem of Artistic Visibility and its Homosocial Performances in Late-Nineteenth-Century London." *Visual Culture in Britain* 8 (June): 73–103.

Sterner, Albert. 1947. "On Modern Art." *Art Digest* 21 (January 15): 22.

Stevens, Elisabeth. 1972. "The Rise, Fall and Rise of the Whistler Print Market." *Art News* 71 (November): 42–45.

St. John, John. 1990. *William Heinemann: A Century of Publishing, 1890–1990.* London: William Heinemann.

Stoppard, Tom. 2001. "Making It." *Times Literary Supplement,* June 15, p. 15.

Stratis, Harriet K., and Martha Tedeschi, eds. 1998. *The Lithographs of James McNeill*

Whistler. 2 vols. Chicago: Art Institute of Chicago.

Studio. 1905. "The International Society's Whistler Exhibition." 34 (April): 224–32.

Sturgis, Alexander, Rupert Christiansen, Lois Oliver, and Michael Wilson. 2006. *Rebels and Martyrs: The Image of the Artist in the Nineteenth-Century*. London: National Gallery.

Sturgis, Matthew. 2005. *Walter Sickert: A Life*. New York: Harper.

Sussman, Herbert. 1995. *Victorian Masculinities: Manhood and Masculine Poetics in Early Victorian Literature and Art*. Cambridge: Cambridge University Press.

Sutherland, Daniel E. 2008. "Portrait of the Artist as Arms Dealer." *American Nineteenth-Century* 9 (March): 61–73.

———. 2014. *Whistler: A Life for Art's Sake*. New Haven: Yale University Press.

Sutherland, Daniel E., and Georgia Toutziari. 2018. *Whistler's Mother: Portrait of an Extraordinary Life*. New Haven: Yale University Press.

Sutton, Denys. 1960a. "New Light on Whistler's Art." *Country Life* 122 (September 8): 486–87.

———. 1960b. "A Whistler Exhibition." *Burlington Magazine* 102 (October): 460–61.

———. 1963. *Nocturne: The Art of James McNeill Whistler*. London: Country Life.

———. 1966. *James McNeill Whistler: Paintings, Etchings, Pastels and Watercolours*. London: Phaidon.

———, ed. 1972. *Letters of Roger Fry*. 2 vols. London: Chatto & Windus.

Symons, Arthur. 1906. *Studies in Seven Arts*. New York: Dutton.

———. 1909. *London: A Book of Aspects*. London: Privately Printed.

Tadié, Jean-Yzes. 2000. *Marcel Proust*. Translated by Euan Cameron. New York: Viking.

Taylor, Hilary. 1978. *James McNeill Whistler*. New York: Putnam.

Taylor, Jesse Oak. 2016. *The Sky of Our Manufacture: The London Fog in British Fiction from Dickens to Woolf*. Charlottesville: University of Virginia Press.

Tedeschi, Martha. 1997. "Whistler and the English Print Market." *Print Quarterly* 14 (March): 15–41.

Teniswood-Harvey, Arabella. 2006. "Colour-Music: Musical Modelling in James McNeill Whistler's Art." PhD diss., University of Tasmania.

Thaddeus, H. Jones. 1912. *Recollections of a Court Painter*. London: John Lane.

Thomson, D. Croal. 1903. "James Abbott McNeill Whistler." *Art Journal* 55 n.s. (September): 265–68.

Thornton, Alfred. 1938. *The Diary of an Art Student of the Nineties*. London: Pitman & Sons.

Ticknor, Lisa. 2000. *Modern Life and Modern Subjects: British Art in the Early Twentieth Century*. New Haven: Yale University Press.

Tinker, Edward Larocque. 1951. *The Pennells*. New York: Privately Printed.

Tonks, Henry. 1934. "Whistler." *The Times*, July 10, p. 18.

Tosh, John. 2005. *Manliness and Masculinities in Nineteenth-Century Britain: Essays on Gender, Family, and Empire*. Harlow, UK: Pearson.

Townsend, Joyce H. 1994. "Whistler's Oil Painting Materials." *Burlington Magazine* 136 (October): 690–95.

Toynbee, Philip. 1968. "Aesthete with a Rapier." *Observer*, May 19, p. 28.

Tresch, John. 2012. *The Romantic Machine: Utopian Science and Technology after Napoleon*. Chicago: University of Chicago Press.

———. 2021. *The Reason for the Darkness: Edgar Allen Poe and the Forging of American Science*. New York: Farrar, Straus and Giroux.

Tsui, Aileen. 2006. "The Phantasm of Aesthetic Anatomy in Whistler's Work: Titling *The White Girl*." *Art History* 29 (June): 444–75.

Updike, John. 2005. *Still Looking: Essays on American Art*. New York: Knopf.

Valance, Hélène. 2018. *Nocturne: Night in American Art, 1890–1917*. Translated by Jane Marie Todd. New Haven: Yale University Press.

Valette, Laura, and Florence Calame-Levert, eds. 2024. *James Abbott McNeill*

Whistler: L'effet papillon. Paris: Silvan Editoriale.

Van Dyke, John C. 1904. "What Is All This Talk About Whistler?" *Ladies' Home Journal* 21 (March): 10.

———. 1913. *Art for Art's Sake: Seven University Lectures on the Technical Beauties of Painting*. New York: Charles Scribner's Sons.

———. 1920. *American Painting and Its Tradition*. New York: Charles Scribner's Sons.

Varnedoe, Kirk, and Adam Gopnik. 1990. *High and Low: Modern Art and Popular Culture*. New York: Harry N. Abrams.

Vivian, Herbert. 1923. *Myself Not Least, Being the Personal Reminiscences of "X."* New York: Henry Holt.

Wallis, Neville. 1960. "Rediscovering Whistler." *Observer*, September 1, p. 24.

Ward, Edwin A. 1923. *Recollections of a Savage*. London: Herbert Jenkins.

Ward, Laurence. 2015. *The London County Council Bomb Damage Maps, 1939–1945*. London: Thames and Hudson.

Ward, Leslie. 1915. *Forty Years of "Spy."* London: Chatto & Windus.

Warner, Malcolm, ed. 1987. *The Image of London: Views by Travellers and Emigrés, 1550–1920*. London: Trefoil.

Warrell, Ian, ed. 2013. *J. M. W. Turner: The Making of a Master*. London: Tate.

Warren, Arthur. 1920. *London Days: A Book of Reminiscences*. Boston: Little, Brown.

Watson, Peter. 1992. *From Manet to Manhattan: The Rise of the Modern Art Market*. New York: Random House.

Way, Thomas R. 1903. "Mr. Whistler as a Lithographer." *Studio* 30 (October): 10–21.

———. 1912. *Memories of James McNeill Whistler, The Artist*. London: John Lane.

———. 1913. "Whistler's Lithographs." *Print Collector's Quarterly* 3 (October): 277–309.

Way, Thomas R., and G. R. Dennis. 1903. *The Art of James McNeill Whistler: An Appreciation*. London: George Bell and Sons.

Weaver, Mike, ed. 1989. *British Photography in the Nineteenth Century: The Fine Art Tradition*. Cambridge: Cambridge University Press.

Wedmore, Frederick. 1904. "The Place of Whistler." *Nineteenth Century* 55 (April): 665–75.

———. 1912. *Memories*. London: Methuen.

Weinberg, Jonathan. 2001. *Ambition and Love in Modern American Art*. New Haven: Yale University Press.

Weintraub, Stanley. 1974. *Whistler: A Biography*. New York: Weybright and Talley.

Weller, Allen S. 1950. "Expatriates' Return." *Art Digest* 24 (September 15): 7, 24–25.

Whelan, Richard. 1995. *Alfred Stieglitz: A Biography*. Boston: Little, Brown.

Whyte, Frederic. 1929. *William Heinemann: A Memoir*. New York: Doubleday.

Wilmerding, John. 1976. *American Art*. New Haven: Yale University Press.

Wilson, Thomas. 1898. "Whistler at West Point." *Book Buyer* 17 n.s. (September): 113–15.

Winner, Ellen. 2004. "Art History Can Trade Insights with the Sciences." *Chronicle of Higher Education*, July 2, p. B10.

Wolfe, Tom. 1975. *The Painted Word*. New York: Farrar, Straus and Giroux.

Wray, Henry Russell. 1915. "An Afternoon with James McNeill Whistler." *International Studio* 56 (August): xl–xlii.

Wuerpel, Edmund H. 1904. "My Friend Whistler." *Independent* 56 (January 21): 131–36.

———. 1934. "Whistler—The Man [Pt.2]." *American Magazine of Art* 27 (June): 312–21.

Young, Andrew McLaren, Margaret MacDonald, Robin Spencer, and Hamish Miles. 1980. *The Paintings of James McNeill Whistler*. 2 vols. New Haven: Yale University Press.

Young, Mahonri Sharp. 1970. "The Remarkable Joseph Pennell." *American Art Journal* 2 (Spring): 81–91.

Zinnes, Harriet, ed. 1980. *Ezra Pound and the Visual Arts*. New York: New Directions.

INDEX

Artworks by Whistler are indexed under entries beginning "Whistler, James Abbott McNeill," followed by the medium (e.g., etchings, lithographs).